Thomas Paine

The Works of Thomas Paine, Secretary for Foreign Affairs

To the Congress of the United States in the late war. Vol. 1

Thomas Paine

The Works of Thomas Paine, Secretary for Foreign Affairs
To the Congress of the United States in the late war. Vol. 1

ISBN/EAN: 9783337235130

Printed in Europe, USA, Canada, Australia, Japan

Cover: Foto ©Thomas Meinert / pixelio.de

More available books at **www.hansebooks.com**

THE

W O R K S

OF

T H O M A S   P A I N E,

SECRETARY FOR FOREIGN AFFAIRS,
TO THE
CONGRESS OF THE UNITED STATES,
IN THE LATE WAR.

————————

IN TWO VOLUMES.

————————

VOL. I.

————————

PHILADELPHIA:
PRINTED BY JAMES CAREY,
No. 83, NORTH SECOND-STREET.

————

1797.

ADVERTISEMENT.

THIS firſt volume of T. PAINE's WORKS contains that author's publications during his reſidence in America.—Of theſe, ſome have never appeared in any former edition of his Works; particularly Diſſertations on Government, on the Affairs of the Bank, and on Paper Money, two numbers of The Criſis, and the Miſcellaneous Pieces at the cloſe of the volume.—The editor thinks it incumbent on him to account for the introduction and arrangement of ſome of theſe productions.

Having ſeen but one edition of Mr. Paine's Works in which it was attempted to give THE CRISIS, and that one being imperfect, as it wanted No. X. and No. XII. exertions were made to ſupply the deficiency, by a recurrence to contemporary newſpapers and other publications :—In this reſearch, the piece which is here introduced as No. X. was found in the Pennſylvania Gazette. It appears to have been written in a hurry, or, at leaſt, for inſtant publication ; for although it was publiſhed in three parts, viz. in the papers of the 20th and 27th of February, and 6th of March, 1782, it bears date not from the appearance of the firſt part, but from that of the laſt.—This hurry may ſerve to account for the omiſſion of the title and number, without which it was originally publiſhed.

The letter to the Earl of Shelburne, which has hitherto been detached from The Criſis, is, evidently, No. XII of that work, which can no otherwiſe be ſupplied.—Its date, ſignature, and mode of publication (in the newſpapers), leave no doubt of this on the editor's mind.

The numbers of The Criſis being thus completed, the editor had ſtill left two pieces ſigned Common Senſe, which, appearing to be of the ſame family, he has claſſed under the general head, as ſupernumeraries, according to their dates.—The latter of thefe never appeared but in the newfpapers of the day.

At a time when confiderable progrefs had been made in printing this volume, the editor was informed that Mr. Paine had fent fome contributions to the Pennfylvania Magazine.—On which applica-cation was made to Mr. R. Aitken, the publifher of that work, who very obligingly pointed out the pieces written by Mr. P. It was then too late to give them their chronological precedence, and they were neceffarily placed at the end of the volume, under the head Mifcellaneous Pieces. It is neceffary to add, that two of thofe ef-fays, namely, a defcription of a new electrical machine, then not known in America, and a method of building frame houfes in Eng-land, are omitted ; the former being ufelefs at prefent, when electricity is fo much better underflood—and the latter inapplicable in this country.

A few other articles, which (Mr. Aitken fays) were merely *banded* by Mr. P. for publication, have not, on fo doubtful a claim, obtained a place here. Thefe were hiftoric facts, and he could therefore, at moft, have only furnifhed the language with which they are clothed.

Philadelphia, December 24, 1796.

CONTENTS

OF THE

FIRST VOLUME.

———————

	Page.
COMMON SENSE,	1
Epiſtle to Quakers,	48
The Criſis, No. I.	53
No. II.	60
No. III.	74
No. IV.	102
No. V.	105
No. VI.	127
No. VII.	135
No. VIII.	153
No. IX.	159
The Criſis Extraordinary,	164
The Criſis, No. X.	178
No. XI.	197
A Supernumerary Criſis,	205
The Criſis, No. XII.	209
No. XIII.	217
A Supernumerary Criſis,	223
Public Good,	227
Letter to Abbe Raynal,	261
Diſſertations on Government, the Affairs of the Bank, and Paper-Money,	319
Miſcellaneous Pieces, in Proſe and Verſe,	371

ADDRESSED TO THE

INHABITANTS OF AMERICA,

ON THE FOLLOWING

INTERESTING SUBJECTS,

viz.

I. Of the Origin and Defign of Government in general: with concife Remarks on the Englifh Conflitution.

II. Of Monarchy and Hereditary Succeffion.

III. Thoughts on the prefent State of American Affairs.

IV. Of the prefent Ability of America: with fome mifcellaneous Reflections.

To which is added,

AN APPENDIX.

MAN KNOWS NO MASTER SAVE CREATING HEAVEN,
OR THOSE WHOM CHOICE AND COMMON GOOD ORDAIN.
THOMSON.

PHILADELPHIA:
PRINTED BY JAMES CAREY,
No. 83, *North Second-Street.*

1796.

INTRODUCTION.

PERHAPS the fentiments contained in the following pages, are not *yet* fufficiently fafhionable to procure them general favour; a long habit of not thinking a thing *wrong*, gives it a fuperficial appearance of being *right*, and raifes at firft a formidable outcry in defence of cuftom. But the tumult foon fubfides. Time makes more converts than reafon.

As a long and violent abufe of power, is generally the means of calling the right of it in queftion (and in matters too which might never have been thought of, had not the fufferers been aggravated into the inquiry) and as the King of England hath undertaken in his *own right*, to fupport the Parliament in what he calls *theirs*, and as the good people of this country are grievoufly oppreffed by the combination, they have an undoubted privilege to enquire into the pretenfions of both, and equally to reject the ufurpation of either.

In the following fheets, the author hath ftudioufly avoided every thing which is perfonal among ourfelves. Compliments as well as cenfure to individuals make no part thereof. The wife, and the worthy, need not the triumph of a pamphlet; and thofe whofe fentiments are injudicious, or unfriendly, will ceafe of themfelves unlefs too much pains are beftowed upon their converfion.

The caufe of America is in a great meafure the caufe of all mankind. Many circumftances have, and will arife, which are not local, but univerfal, and through which the principles of all lovers of mankind are affected, and in the event of which, their affections are interefted. The laying a country defolate with fire and fword, declaring war againft the natural rights of all mankind, and extirpating the defenders thereof from the face of the earth, is the concern of every man to whom nature hath given the power of feeling; of which clafs, regardlefs of party cenfure, is

THE.AUTHOR.

Philadelphia, February 14, 1776.

A 2

COMMON SENSE.

*Of the origin and defign of government in general: with concife re-
marks on the Englifh conftitution.*

SOME writers have fo confounded fociety with government, as
to leave little or no diftinction between them; whereas they are not
only different, but have different origins. Society is produced by
our wants, and government by our wickednefs; the former promotes
our happinefs *pofitively* by uniting our affections, the latter *negatively*
by reftraining our vices. The one encourages intercourfe, the other
creates diftinctions. The firft is a patron, the laft is a punifher.

Society in every ftate is a bleffing, but government even in its beft
ftate is but a neceffary evil; in its worft ftate an intolerable one; for
when we fuffer, or are expofed to the fame miferies by *a government*,
which we might expect in a country *without government*, our calamity
is heightened by reflecting that we furnifh the means by which we
fuffer. Government, like drefs, is the badge of loft innocence; the
palaces of kings are built on the ruins of the bowers of paradife. For
were the impulfes of confcience clear, uniform and irrefiftibly obeyed,
man would need no other lawgiver; but that not being the cafe, he
finds it neceffary to furrender up a part of his property to furnifh
means for the protection of the reft; and this he is induced to do by
the fame prudence which in every other cafe advifes him out of two
evils to choofe the leaft. *Wherefore,* fecurity being the true defign
and end of government, it unanfwerably follows, that whatever *form*
thereof appears moft likely to enfure it to us, with the leaft expence
and greateft benefit, is preferable to all others.

In order to gain a clear and juft idea of the defign and end of government, let us fuppofe a fmall number of perfons fettled in fome
fequeftered part of the earth, unconnected with the reft, they will
then reprefent the firft peopling of any country, or of the world.

In this state of natural liberty, society will be their first thought.
A thousand motives will excite them thereto ; the strength of one
man is so unequal to his wants, and his mind so unfitted for perpetual
solitude, that he is soon obliged to seek assistance and relief of another,
who in his turn requires the same. Four or five united would be able
to raise a tolerable dwelling in the midst of a wildernefs, but *one* man
might labour out the common period of life without accomplishing
any thing; when he had felled his timber he could not remove it, nor
erect it after it was removed ; hunger in the mean time would urge
him from his work, and every different want call him a different way.
Disease, nay even misfortune, would be death, for though neither
might be mortal, yet either would disable him from living, and reduce
him to a state in which he might rather be said to perish than to die.

Thus necessity, like a gravitating power, would soon form our
newly arrived emigrants into society, the reciprocal blessings of which
would supersede, and render the obligations of law and government
unnecessary while they remained perfectly just to each other; but as
nothing but heaven is impregnable to vice, it will unavoidably happen,
that in proportion as they surmount the first difficulties of emigration,
which bound them together in a common cause, they will begin to
relax in their duty and attachment to each other; and this remissnefs
will point out the necessity of establishing some form of government
to supply the defect of moral virtue.

Some convenient tree will afford them a state-house, under the
branches of which the whole colony may assemble to deliberate on
public matters. It is more than probable that their first laws will
have the title only of *Regulations*, and be enforced by no other
penalty than public disesteem. In this first parliament every man, by
natural right, will have a seat.

But as the colony increases, the public concerns will increase likewise, and the distance at which the members may be separated, will
render it too inconvenient for all of them to meet on every occasion as
at first, when their number was small, their habitations near, and
the public concerns few and trifling. This will point out the convenience of their consenting to leave the legislative part to be managed
by a select number chosen from the whole body, who are supposed
to have the same concerns at stake which those have who appointed
them, and who will act in the same manner as the whole body would
act were they present. If the colony continue encreasing, it will
become necessary to augment the number of the representatives, and

that the interest of every part of the colony may be attended to, it will be found best to divide the whole into convenient parts, each part sending its proper number; and that the *elected* might never form to themselves an interest separate from the *electors*, prudence will point out the propriety of having elections often ; because as the *elected* might by that means return and mix again with the general body of the *electors*, in a few months their fidelity to the public will be secured by the prudent reflection of not making a rod for themselves. And as this frequent interchange will establish a common interest with every part of the community, they will mutually and naturally support each other, and on this (not on the unmeaning name of King) depends the *strength of government, and the happiness of the governed.*

Here then is the origin and rise of government ; namely, a mode rendered necessary by the inability of moral virtue to govern the world ; here too is the design and end of government, viz. freedom and security. And however our eyes may be dazzled with show, or our ears deceived by sound ; however prejudice may warp our wills, or interest darken our understanding, the simple voice of nature and reason will say, it is right.

I draw my idea of the form of government from a principle in nature, which no art can overturn, viz. that the more simple any thing is, the less liable it is to be disordered, and the easier repaired when disordered; and with this maxim in view, I offer a few remarks on the so-much-boasted constitution of England. That it was noble for the dark and slavish times in which it was erected, is granted. When the world was over-run with tyranny, the least remove therefrom was a glorious rescue. But that it is imperfect, subject to convulsions, and incapable of producing what it seems to promise, is easily demonstrated.

Absolute governments (though the disgrace of human nature) have this advantage with them, that they are simple ; if the people suffer, they know the head from which their suffering springs, know likewise the remedy, and are not bewildered by a variety of causes and cures. But the constitution of England is so exceedingly complex, that the nation may suffer for years together without being able to discover in which part the fault lies; some will say in one and some in another, and every political physician will advise a different medicine.

I know it is difficult to get over local or long standing prejudices, yet if we will suffer ourselves to examine the component parts of the English constitution, we shall find them to be the base remains of two ancient tyrannies, compounded with some new republican materials.

Firſt.—The remains of monarchical tyranny in the perſon of the king.

Secondly —The remains of ariſtocratical tyranny in the perſons of the peers.

Thirdly.—The new republican materials, in the perſons of the commons, on whoſe virtue depends the freedom of England.

The two firſt, by being hereditary, are independent of the people; wherefore in a *conſtitutional ſenſe* they contribute nothing towards the freedom of the ſtate.

To ſay that the conſtitution of England is a union of three powers, reciprocally checking each other, is farcical; either the words have no meaning, or they are flat contradictions.

To ſay that the commons is a check upon the king, preſuppoſes two things :

Firſt.—That the king is not to be truſted without being looked after; or in other words, that a thirſt for abſolute power is the natural diſeaſe of monarchy.

Secondly.—That the commons, by being appointed for that purpoſe, are either wiſer or more worthy of confidence than the crown.

But as the ſame conſtitution which gives the commons a power to check the king by withholding the ſupplies, gives afterwards the king a power to check the commons, by empowering him to reject their other bills ; it again ſuppoſes that the king is wiſer than thoſe whom it has already ſuppoſed to be wiſer than him. A mere abſurdity!

There is ſomething exceedingly ridiculous in the compoſition of monarchy; it firſt excludes a man from the means of information, yet empowers him to act in caſes where the higheſt judgment is required. The ſtate of a king ſhuts him from the world, yet the buſineſs of a king requires him to know it thoroughly; wherefore the different parts, by unnaturally oppoſing and deſtroying each other, prove the whole character to be abſurd and uſeleſs.

Some writers have explained the Engliſh conſtitution thus; the king, ſay they, is one, the people another; the peers are an houſe in behalf of the king; the commons in behalf of the people; but this hath all the diſtinctions of an houſe divided againſt itſelf; and though the expreſſions be pleaſantly arranged, yet when examined they appear idle and ambiguous; and it will always happen, that the niceſt conſtruction that words are capable of, when applied to the deſcription of ſomething which either cannot exiſt, or is too incomprehenſible to be

COMMON SENSE. 9

within the compafs of defcription, will be words of found only, and
though they may amufe the ear, they cannot inform the mind, for
this explanation includes a previous queftion, viz. *How came the king
by a power which the people are afraid to truft, and always obliged to
check?* Such a power could not be the gift of a wife people, neither
can any power, *which needs checking,* be from God; yet the provifion,
which the conftitution makes, fuppofes fuch a power to exift.

But the provifion is unequal to the tafk; the means either cannot or
will not accomplifh the end, and the whole affair is a *felo de fe;* for
as the greater weight will always carry up the lefs, and as all the wheels
of a machine are put in motion by one, it only remains to know
which power in the conftitution has the moft weight, for that will
govern; and though the others, or a part of them, may clog, or, as
the phrafe is, check the rapidity of its motion, yet fo long as they
cannot ftop it, their endeavours will be ineffectual; the firft moving
power will at laft have its way, and what it wants in fpeed is fupplied
by time.

That the crown is this overbearing part in the Englifh conftitution
needs not be mentioned, and that it derives its whole confequence
merely from being the giver of places and penfions is felf-evident,
wherefore, though we have been wife enough to fhut and lock a door
againft abfolute monarchy, we at the fame time have been foolifh
enough to put the crown in poffeffion of the key.

The prejudice of Englifhmen, in favour of their own government
by king, lords and commons, arifes as much or more from national
pride than reafon. Individuals are undoubtedly fafer in England than
in fome other countries, but the *will* of the king is as much the *law*
of the land in Britain as in France, with this difference, that inftead
of proceeding directly from his mouth, it is handed to the people
under the more formidable fhape of an act of parliament. For the
fate of Charles the Firft, hath only made kings more fubtle—not more
juft.

Wherefore, laying afide all national pride and prejudice in favour of
modes and forms, the plain truth is, that *it is wholly owing to the
conftitution of the people, and not the conftitution of the government,* that
the crown is not as oppreffive in England as in Turkey.

An enquiry into the *conftitutional errors* in the Englifh form of government is at this time highly neceffary; for as we are never in a pro
per condition of doing juftice to others, while we continue under the
influence of fome leading partiality, fo neither are we capable of do

VOL. I. B

it to ourfelves while we remain fettered by an obftinate prejudice. And
as a man who is attached to a proftitute is unfitted to choofe or judge
of a wife, fo any prepoffeffion in favour of a rotten conftitution of government will difable us from difcerning a good one.

Of monarchy and hereditary fucceffion.

MANKIND being originally equals in the order of creation, the
equality could only be deftroyed by fome fubfequent circumftance;
the diftinctions of rich and poor, may in a great meafure be accounted
for, and that without having recourfe to the harfh ill-founding names
of oppreffion and avarice. Oppreffion is often the *confequence*, but feldom or never the *means* of riches; and though avarice will preferve a
man from being neceffitoufly poor, it generally makes him too timo-
rous to be wealthy.

But there is another and greater diftinction for which no truly natural or religious reafon can be affigned, and that is, the diftinction of
men into KINGS and SUBJECTS. Male and female are the diftinctions of nature; good and bad the diftinctions of heaven: but how a
race of men came into the world fo exalted above the reft, and diftinguifhed like fome new fpecies, is worth enquiring into, and whether
they are the means of happinefs or of mifery to mankind.

In the early ages of the world, according to the fcripture chrono-
logy, there were no kings; the confequence of which was there were no
wars; it is the pride of kings which throws mankind into confufion.
Holland without a king hath enjoyed more peace for this laft century
than any of the monarchical governments in Europe. Antiquity favours the fame remark; for the quiet and rural lives of the firft patriarchs hath a happy fomething in them, which vanifhes away when we
come to the hiftory of Jewifh royalty.

Government by kings was firft introduced into the world by the
Heathens, from whom the children of Ifrael copied the cuftom. It
was the moft profperous invention the devil ever fet on foot for the
promotion of idolatry. The Heathens paid divine honours to their
deceafed kings, and the Chriftian world hath improved on the plan by
doing the fame to their living ones. How impious is the title of *facred
majefty*, applied to a worm, who in the midft of his fplendour is crum-
bling into duft!

As the exalting one man fo greatly above the reft, cannot be juftified on the equal rights of nature, fo neither can it be defended on the authority of Scripture; for the will of the Almighty, as declared by Gideon and the prophet Samuel, exprefsly difapproves of government by kings. All anti-monarchical parts of Scripture, have been very fmoothly gloffed over in monarchical governments, but they undoubtedly merit the attention of countries, which have their governments yet to form. " *Render unto Cæfar the things which are Cæfar's,*" is the Scripture doctrine of courts, yet it is no fupport of monarchical government, for the Jews at that time were without a king, and in a ftate of vaffalage to the Romans.

Near three thoufand years paffed away from the Mofaic account of the creation, till the Jews under a national delufion requefted a king. Till then their form of government (except in extraordinary cafes, where the Almighty interpofed) was a kind of republic, adminftered by a judge and the elders of the tribes. Kings they had none, and it was held finful to acknowledge any being under that title but the Lord of Hofts. And when a man ferioufly reflects on the idolatrous homage which is paid to the perfons of kings, he need not wonder, that the Almighty, ever jealous of his honour, fhould difapprove of a form of government which fo impioufly invades the prerogative of heaven.

Monarchy is ranked in fcripture as one of the fins of the Jews, for which a curfe in referve is denounced againft them. The hiftory of that tranfaction is worth attending to.

The children of Ifrael being oppreffed by the Midianites, Gideon marched againft them with a fmall army, and victory, through the divine interpofition, decided in his favour. The Jews elate with fuccefs, and attributing it to the generalfhip of Gideon, propofed making him a king, faying, *Rule thou over us, thou and thy fon, and thy fon's fon.* Here was temptation in its fulleft extent; not a kingdom only, but an hereditary one; but Gideon in the piety of his foul replied, *I will not rule over you, neither fhall my fon rule over you.* THE LORD SHALL RULE OVER YOU. Words need not be more explicit; Gideon doth not *decline* the honour, but denieth their right to give it; neither doth he compliment them with invented declarations of his thanks, but in the pofitive ftyle of a Prophet charges them with difaffection to their proper Sovereign, the King of Heaven.

About one hundred and thirty years after this, they fell again into the fame error. The hankering which the Jews had for the idolatrous cuſtoms of the Heathens, is ſomething exceedingly unaccountable; but ſo it was, that laying hold of the miſconduct of Samuel's two ſons, who were entruſted with ſome ſecular concerns, they came in an abrupt and clamorous manner to Samuel, ſaying, *Behold thou art old, and thy ſons walk not in thy ways, now make us a king to judge us like all the other nations.* And here we cannot but obſerve that their motives were bad, viz. that they might be *like* unto other nations, *i. e.* the Heathens, whereas their true glory lay in being as much *unlike* them as poſſible. *But the thing diſpleaſed Samuel when they ſaid, Give us a king to judge us ; and Samuel prayed unto the Lord, and the Lord ſaid unto Samuel, Hearken unto the voice of the people in all that they ſay unto thee, for they have not rejected thee, but they have rejected me,* THAT I SHOULD NOT REIGN OVER THEM. *According to all the works which they have done ſince the day that I brought them out of Egypt, even unto this day ; wherewith they have forſaken me and ſerved other Gods; ſo do they alſo unto thee. Now therefore hearken unto their voice, howbeit, proteſt ſolemnly unto them and ſhew them the manner of the king that ſhall reign over them,* i. e. not of any particular king, but the general manner of the kings of the earth, whom Iſrael was ſo eagerly copying after. And notwithſtanding the great diſtance of time and difference of manners, the character is ſtill in faſhion. *And Samuel told all the words of the Lord unto the people, that aſked of him a king. And he ſaid, this ſhall be the manner of the king that ſhall reign over you ; he will take your ſons and appoint them for himſelf, for his chariots, and to be his horſemen, and ſome ſhall run before his chariots* (this deſcription agrees with the preſent mode of impreſſing men) *and he will appoint him captains over thouſands, and captains over fiſties, and will ſet them to ear his ground and to reap his harveſt, and to make his inſtruments of war, and inſtruments of his chariots ; and he will take your daughters to be confectionaries, and to be cooks and to be bakers* (this deſcribes the expence and luxury as well as the oppreſſion of kings) *and he will take your fields and your olive yards, even the beſt of them, and give them to his ſervants ; and he will take the tenth of your ſeed, and of your vineyards, and give them to his officers and to his ſervants* (by which we ſee that bribery, corruption and favouritiſm are the ſtanding vices of kings) *and he will take the tenth of your men ſervants, and your maid ſervants, and your goodlieſt young men, and your aſſes, and put them to his work ; and he will take the tenth of your ſheep, and ye ſhall be his ſervants, and ye ſhall cry out in that day becauſe of your king which ye ſhall have choſen,* AND THE LORD WILL NOT HEAR YOU IN THAT DAY. This accounts for the continuation of monarchy ; neither do the characters of the few good kings which have lived fince, either fanctify the title, or blot out the finfulnefs of the origin ; the high encomium given of David takes no notice of him *officially as a king*, but only as a *man* after God's own heart. *Neverthelefs the people refufed to obey the voice of Samuel, and they faid, Nay, but we will have a king over us, that we may be like all the nations, and that our king may judge us, and go out before us, and fight our battles.* Samuel continued to reafon with them, but to no purpofe ; he fet before them their ingratitude, but all would not avail ; and feeing them fully bent on their folly, he cried out, *I will call unto the Lord, and he fhall fend thunder and rain* (which then was a punifhment, being in the time of wheat harveft) *that ye may perceive and fee that your wickednefs is great which ye have done in the fight of the Lord,* IN ASKING YOU A KING. *So Samuel called unto the Lord, and the Lord fent thunder and rain that day, and all the people greatly feared the Lord and Samuel. And all the people faid unto Samuel, Pray for thy fervants unto the Lord thy God that we die not, for* WE HAVE ADDED UNTO OUR SINS THIS EVIL, TO ASK A KING. Thefe portions of fcripture are direct and pofitive. They admit of no equivocal conftruction. That the Almighty hath here entered his proteft againft monarchical government is true, or the fcripture is falfe. And a man hath good reafon to believe, that there is as much of king-craft, as prieft-craft, in withholding the fcripture from the public in Popifh countries. For monarchy in every inftance is the Popery of government.

To the evil of monarchy we have added, that of hereditary fucceffion ; and as the firft is a degradation and leffening of ourfelves, fo the fecond, claimed as a matter of right, is an infult and impofition on pofterity. For all men being originally equals, no *one* by *birth,* could have a right to fet up his own family, in perpetual preference to all others for ever, and though himfelf might deferve *fome* decent degree of honours of his contemporaries, yet his defcendants might be far too unworthy to inherit them. One of the ftrongeft *natural* proofs of the folly of hereditary right in Kings, is, that nature difapproves it, otherwife fhe would not fo frequently turn it into ridicule, by giving mankind an *Afs for a Lion.*

Secondly, as no man at firft could poffefs any other public honours than were beftowed upon him, fo the givers of thofe honours could have no power to give away the right of pofterity, and though they might fay, " We choofe you for *our* head," they could not, without manifeft injuftice to their children, fay " that your children and your children's children fhall reign over *ours* for ever." Becaufe fuch an unwife, unjuft, unnatural compact might (perhaps) in the next fucceffion put them under the government of a rogue, or a fool. Moft wife men in their private fentiments, have ever treated hereditary right with contempt ; yet it is one of thofe evils, which when once eftablifhed is not eafily removed ; many fubmit from fear, others from fuperflition, and the more powerful part fhares with the king, the plunder of the reft.

This is fuppofing the prefent race of kings in the world to have had an honourable origin; whereas it is more than probable, that, could we take off the dark covering of antiquity, and trace them to their firft rife, we fhould find the firft of them nothing better than the principal ruffian of fome reftlefs gang, whofe favage manners, or pre-eminence in fubtilty obtained him the title of chief among plunderers ; and who by increafing in power, and extending his de-predations, over-awed the quiet and defencelefs to purchafe their fafety by frequent contributions. Yet his electors could have no idea of giving hereditary right to his defcendants, becaufe fuch a perpetual exclufion of themfelves was incompatible with the free and unreftrained principles they profeffed to live by. Wherefore, here-ditary fucceffion in the early ages of monarchy could not take place as a matter of claim, but as fomething cafual or complimental ; but as few or no records were extant in thofe days, and traditionary hiftory ftuffed with fables, it was very eafy, after the lapfe of a few generations, to tramp up fome fuperflitious tale, conveniently timed, Mahomet like, to cram hereditary right down the throats of the vulgar. Perhaps the diforders which threatened, or feemed to threaten, on the deceafe of a leader and the choice of a new one (for elections among ruffians could not be very orderly) induced many at firft to favour hereditary pretenfions; by which means it happened, as it hath happened fince, that what at firft was fubmitted to as a convenience, was afterwards claimed as a right.

England, fince the conqueft, hath known fome few good monarchs, but groaned beneath a much larger number of bad ones; yet no man in his fenfes can fay that their claim under William the Conqueror is a very honourable one. A French baftard, landing with an armed banditti, and eftablifhing himfelf king of England againft the confent of the natives, is in plain terms a very paltry, rafcally original.—

It certainly hath no divinity in it. However, it is needless to spend much time in expoſing the folly of hereditary right ; if there are any ſo weak as to believe it, let them promiſcuouſly worſhip the aſs and lion, and welcome. I ſhall neither copy their humility, nor diſturb their devotion.

Yet I ſhould be glad to aſk, how they ſuppoſe kings came at firſt ? The queſtion admits but of three anſwers, viz. either by lot, by election, or by uſurpation If the firſt king was taken by lot, it eſtabliſhes a precedent for the next, which excludes hereditary ſucceſſion. Saul was by lot, yet the ſucceſſion wa not hereditary, neither does it appear from that tranſaction there was any intention it ever ſhould. If the firſt king of any country was by election, that likewiſe eſtabliſhes a precedent for the next; for to ſay, that the right of all future generations is taken away, by the act of the firſt electors, in their choice not only of a king, but of a family of kings for ever, hath no parallel in or out of ſcripture but the doctrine of original ſin, which ſuppoſes the free will of all men loſt in Adam; and from ſuch compariſon, and it will admit of no other, hereditary ſucceſſion can derive no glory. For as in Adam all ſinned, and as in the firſt electors all men obeyed ; as in the one all mankind were ſubjected to ſatan, and in the other to ſovereignty; as our innocence was loſt in the firſt, and our authority in the laſt; and as both diſable us from re-aſſuming ſome former ſtate and privilege, it unanſwerably follows that original ſin and hereditary ſucceſſion are parallels. Diſhonourable rank ! Inglorious connexion ! Yet the moſt ſubtile ſophiſt cannot produce a juſter ſimile.

As to uſurpation, no man will be ſo hardy as to defend it; and that William the Conqueror was an uſurper is a fact not to be contradicted. The plain truth is, that the antiquity of Engliſh monarchy will not bear looking into.

But it is not ſo much the abſurdity as the evil of hereditary ſucceſſion which concerns mankind. Did it enſure a race of good and wiſe men, it would have the ſeal of divine authority, but as it opens a door to the *fooliſh*, the *wicked*, and the *improper*, it hath in it the nature of oppreſſion. Men who look upon themſelves born to reign, and others to obey, ſoon grow inſolent; ſelected from the reſt of mankind, their minds are early poiſoned by importance ; and the world they act in differs ſo materially from the world at large, that they have but little opportunity of knowing its true intereſts, and when they ſucceed to the government, are frequently the moſt ignorant and unfit of any throughout the dominions.

Another evil which attends hereditary fucceffion is, that the throne is fubject to be poffeffed by a minor at any age ; all which time the regency, acting under the cover of a king, have every opportunity and inducement to betray their truft. The fame national misfortune happens, when a king, worn out with age and infirmity, enters the laft ftage of human weaknefs. In both thefe cafes the public becomes a prey to every mifcreant, who can tamper fuccefsfully with the follies either of age or infancy.

The moft plaufible plea, which hath ever been offered in favour of hereditary fucceffion, is, that it preferves a nation from civil wars; and were this true, it would be weighty ; whereas, it is the moft barefaced falfity ever impofed upon mankind. The whole hiftory of England difowns the fact. Thirty kings and two minors have reigned in that diftracted kingdom fince the conqueft, in which time there have been (including the revolution) no lefs than eight civil wars and nineteen rebellions. Wherefore inftead of making for peace, it makes againft it, and deftroys the very foundation it feems to ftand on.

The conteft for monarchy and fucceffion, between the houfes of York and Lancafter, laid England in a fcene of blood for many years. Twelve pitched battles, befides fkirmifhes and fieges, were fought between Henry and Edward, twice was Henry prifoner to Edward, who in his turn was prifoner to Henry. And fo uncertain is the fate of war and the temper of a nation, when nothing but perfonal matters are the ground of a quarrel, that Henry was taken in triumph from a prifon to a palace, and Edward obliged to fly from a palace to a foreign land ; yet, as fudden tranfitions of temper are feldom lafting, Henry in his turn was driven from the throne, and Edward re-called to fucceed him. The parliament always following the ftrongeft fide.

This conteft began in the reign of Henry the Sixth, and was not entirely extinguifhed till Henry the Seventh, in whom the families were united. Including a period of 67 years, viz. from 1422 to 1489.

In fhort, monarchy and fucceffion have laid (not this or that kingdom only, but) the world in blood and afhes. 'Tis a form of government which the word of God bears teftimony againft, and blood will attend it.

If we enquire into the bufinefs of a king, we fhall find (and in ome countries they have none) that after fauntering away their lives without pleasure to themselves or advantage to the nation, they withdraw from the scene, and leave their successors to tread the same idle round. In absolute monarchies the whole weight of business, civil and military, lies on the king; the children of Israel in their request for a king urged this plea, "that he may judge us, and go out before us and fight our battles." But in countries where he is neither a judge nor a general, as in England, a man would be puzzled to know what is his business.

The nearer any government approaches to a republic, the less business there is for a king. It is somewhat difficult to find a proper name for the government of England. Sir William Meredith calls it a republic; but in its present state it is unworthy of the name, because the corrupt influence of the crown, by having all the places in its disposal, hath so effectually swallowed up the power, and eaten out the virtue of the house of commons (the republican part in the constitution) that the government of England is nearly as monarchical as that of France or Spain. Men fall out with names without understanding them. For it is the republican and not the monarchical part of the constitution of England which Englishmen glory in, viz. the liberty of choosing an house of commons from out of their own body—and it is easy to see that when republican virtue fails, slavery ensues. Why is the constitution of England sickly, but because monarchy hath poisoned the republic, the crown hath engrossed the commons?

In England a king hath little more to do than to make war and give away places; which, in plain terms, is to impoverish the nation and set it together by the ears. A pretty business indeed for a man to be allowed eight hundred thousand sterling a-year for, and worshipped into the bargain! Of more worth is one honest man to society, and in the sight of God, than all the crowned ruffians that ever lived.

Thoughts on the present state of American affairs.

IN the following pages I offer nothing more than simple facts, plain arguments, and common sense; and have no other preliminaries to settle with the reader, than that he will divest himself of prejudice and prepossession, and suffer his reason and his feelings to determine for themselves; that he will put *on*, or rather that he will not put *off*, the true character of a man, and generoufly enlarge his views beyond the prefent day.

Volumes have been written on the fubject of the ftruggle between England and America. Men of all ranks have embarked in the controverfy, from different motives, and with various defigns ; but all have been ineffectual, and the period of debate is clofed. Arms, as the laft refource, decide the conteft ; the appeal was the choice of the king, and the continent hath accepted the challenge.

It has been reported of the late Mr. Pelham (who though an able minifter was not without his faults) that on his being attacked in the houfe of commons, on the fcore, that his meafures were only of a temporary kind, replied, *" they will laft my time."* Should a thought fo fatal and unmanly poffefs the colonies in the prefent conteft, the name of anceftors will be remembered by future generations with deteftation.

The fun never fhined on a caufe of greater worth. 'Tis not the affair of a city, a county, a province, or a kingdom, but of a continent—of at leaft one eighth part of the habitable globe. 'Tis not the concern of a day, a year, or an age ; pofterity are virtually involved in the conteft, and will be more or lefs affected, even to the end of time, by the proceedings now. Now is the feed-time of continental union, faith, and honour. The leaft fracture now will be like a name engraved with the point of a pin on the tender rind of a young oak; the wound will enlarge with the tree, and pofterity read it in full grown characters.

By referring the matter from argument to arms, a new era for politics is ftruck; a new method of thinking hath arifen. All plans, propofals, &c. prior to the nineteenth of April, *i. e.* to the commencement of hoftilities, are like the almanacks of the laft year ; which, though proper then, are fuperfeded and ufelefs now. Whatever was advanced by the advocates on either fide of the queftion then, terminated in one and the fame point, viz. a union with Great-Britain; the only difference between the parties was the method of effecting it ; the one propofing force, the other friendfhip; but it hath fo far happened that the firft hath failed, and the fecond hath withdrawn her influence.

As much hath been faid of the advantages of reconciliation, which, like an agreeable dream, hath paffed away and left us as we were, it is but right, that we fhould examine the contrary fide of the argument, and enquire into fome of the many material injuries which thefe colonies fuftain, and always will fuftain, by being connected with and dependant on Great-Britain. To examine that connexion and dependance, on the principles of nature and common sense; to see what we have to trust to, if separated, and what we are to expect, if dependant.

I have heard it afferted by some, that as America hath flourished under her former connexion with Great-Britain, that the same connexion is neceffary towards her future happinefs, and will always have the same effect. Nothing can be more fallacious than this kind of argument. We may as well affert that becaufe a child has thrived upon milk, that it is never to have meat, or that the firft twenty years of our lives is to become a precedent for the next twenty. But even this is admitting more than is true, for I answer roundly, that America would have flourished as much, and probably much more, had no European power had any thing to do with her. The commerce, by which she hath enriched herself are the neceffaries of life, and will always have a market while eating is the custom of Europe.

But she has protected us, say some. That she hath engroffed us is true, and defended the continent at our expence as well as her own, is admitted, and she would have defended Turkey from the same motive, viz. the sake of trade and dominion.

Alas! we have been long led away by ancient prejudices, and made large sacrifices to superstition. We have boasted the protection of Great-Britain, without considering, that her motive was *interest* not *attachment*; that she did not protect us from *our enemies* on *our account*, but from *her enemies* on *her own account*, from those who had no quarrel with us on *any other account*, and who will always be our enemies on the *same account*. Let Britain wave her pretensions to the continent, or the continent throw off the dependance, and we should be at peace with France and Spain were they at war with Britain. The miseries of Hanover last war ought to warn us against connexions.

It hath lately been afferted in parliament, that the colonies have no relation to each other but through the parent country, *i. e.* that Pennfylvania and the Jerfeys, and so on for the reft, are fifter colonies by the way of England; this is certainly a very round about way of proving relationship, but it is the nearest and only true way of proving enemyship, if I may so call it. France and Spain never were, nor perhaps ever will be our enemies as *Americans*, but as our being the *subjects of Great-Britain*.

But Britain is the parent country, say some. Then the more shame upon her conduct. Even brutes do not devour their young, nor favages make' war upon their families ; wherefore the affertion, if true, turns to her reproach ; but it happens not to be true, or only partly 'o, and the phrafe *parent* or *mother country* hath been jefuitically adopted by the king and his parafites, with a low papiftical defign of gaining an unfair bias on the credulous weaknefs of our minds. Europe, and not England, is the parent country of America. This new world hath been the afylum for the perfecuted lovers of civil and religious liberty from *every part* of Europe. Hither have they fled, not from the tender embraces of the mother, but from the cruelty of the monfter ; and it is fo far true of England, that the fame tyranny which drove the firft emigrants from home, purfues their defcendants ftill.

In this extenfive quarter of the globe, we forget the narrow limits of three hundred and fixty miles (the extent of England) and carry our friendfhip on a larger fcale ; we claim brotherhood with every European Chriftian, and triumph in the generofity of the fentiment.

It is pleafant to obferve by what regular gradations we furmount the force of local prejudice, as we enlarge our acquaintance with the world. A man born in any town in England divided into parifhes, will naturally affociate moft with his fellow parifhioners (becaufe their interefts in many cafes will be common) and diftinguifh him by the name of *neighbour* ; if he meet him but a few miles from home, he drops the narrow idea of a ftreet, and falutes him, by the name of *townfmen* ; if he travel out of the county, and meets him in any other, he forgets the minor divifions of ftreet and town, and calls him *countryman*, i. e. *county-man* ; but if in their foreign excurfions they fhould affociate in France or any other part of *Europe*, their local remembrance would be enlarged into that of *Englifhmen*. And by a juft parity of reafoning, all Europeans meeting in America, or any other quarter of the globe, are *countrymen* ; for England, Holland, Germany, or Sweden, when compared with the whole, ftand in the fame places on the larger fcale, which the divifions of ftreet, town, and county do on the fmaller ones ; diftinctions too limited for continental minds. Not one third of the inhabitants, even of this province, are of Englifh defcent. Wherefore I reprobate the phrafe of parent or mother country applied to England only, as being falfe, felfifh, narrow and ungenerous.

But admitting, that we were all of Englifh defcent, what does it amount to? Nothing. Britain, being now an open enemy, extinguifhes every other name and title : And to fay that reconciliation is our duty, is truly farcical. The firft king of England, of the prefent line (William the Conqueror) was a Frenchman, and half the Peers of England are defcendants from the fame country; wherefore, by the fame method of reafoning, England ought to be governed by France.

Much hath been faid of the united ftrength of Britain and the colonies, that in conjunction they might bid defiance to the world. But this is mere prefumption ; the fate of war is uncertain, neither do the expreffions mean any thing ; for this continent would never fuffer itfelf to be drained of inhabitants, to fupport the Britifh arms in either Afia, Africa, or Europe.

Befides, what have we to do with fetting the world at defiance ? Our plan is commerce, and that, well attended to, will fecure us the peace and friendfhip of all Europe ; becaufe, it is the intereft of all Europe to have America a *free port*. Her trade will always be a protection, and her barrennefs of gold and filver fecure her from invaders.

I challenge the warmeft advocate for reconciliation, to fhew a fingle advantage that this continent can reap, by being connected with Great-Britain. I repeat the challenge ; not a fingle advantage is derived. Our corn will fetch its price in any market in Europe, and our imported goods muft be paid for, buy them where we will.

But the injuries and difadvantages we fuftain by that connexion, are without number ; and our duty to mankind at large, as well as to ourfelves, inftruct us to renounce the alliance : Becaufe, any fubmiffion to or dependance on Great-Britain, tends directly to involve this continent in European wars and quarrels ; and fets us at variance with nations, who would otherwife feek our friendfhip, and againft whom, we have neither anger nor complaint. As Europe is our market for trade, we ought to form no partial connexion with any part of it. It is the true intereft of America to fteer clear of European contentions, which fhe never can do, while, by her dependance on Britain, fhe is made the make-weight in the fcale of Britifh politics.

Europe is too thickly planted with kingdoms to be long at peace, and whenever a war breaks out between England and any foreign power, the trade of America goes to ruin, *becaufe of her connexion with Britain*. The next war may not turn out like the laft, and fhould it not, the advocates for reconciliation now will be wifhing for feparation then, becaufe, neutrality in that cafe, would be a fafer convoy than a man of war. Every thing that is right or natural pleads for feparation.   The blood of the flain, the weeping voice of nature cries, 'TIS TIME TO PART.   Even the diftance at which the Almighty hath placed England and America, is a ftrong and natural proof, that the authority of the one, over the other, was never the defign of Heaven.   The time likewife at which the conti- nent was difcovered, adds weight to the argument, and the manner in which it was peopled encreafes the force of it.   The reforma- tion was preceded by the difcovery of America, as if the Almighty gracioufly meant to open a fanctuary to the perfecuted in future years, when home fhould afford neither friendfhip nor fafety.

The authority of Great-Britain over this continent, is a form of government, which fooner or later muft have an end: And a ferious mind can draw no true pleafure by looking forward, under the pain- ful and pofitive conviction, that what he calls " the prefent conftitu- tion" is merely temporary.   As parents, we can have no joy, know- ing that *this government* is not fufficiently lafting to enfure any thing which we may bequeath to pofterity: And by a plain method of argu- ment, as we are running the next generation into debt, we ought to do the work of it, otherwife we ufe them meanly and pitifully.   In order to difcover the line of our duty rightly, we fhould take our children in our hand, and fix our ftation a few years farther into life; that eminence will prefent a profpect, which a few prefent fears and prejudices conceal from our fight.

Though 1 would carefully avoid giving unneceffary offence, yet I am inclined to believe, that all thofe who efpoufe the doctrine of reconciliation, may be included within the following defcriptions.

Interefted men, who are not to be trufted; weak men, who *cannot* fee; prejudiced men, who *will not* fee; and a certain fet of moderate men, who think better of the European world than it deferves: and this laft clafs, by an ill-judged deliberation, will be the caufe of more calamities to this continent than all the other three.

It is the good fortune of many to live diftant from the fcene of forrow ; the evil is not fufficiently brought to *their* doors to make *them* feel the precarioufnefs with which all American property is pof- feffed.   But let our imaginations tranfport us for a few moments to Bofton, that feat of wretchednefs will teach us wifdom, and inftruct us for ever to renounce a power in whom we can have no truft.   The inhabitants of that unfortunate city, who but a few months ago were in eafe and affluence, have now no other alternative than to ftay and ftarve, or turn out to beg.   Endangered by the fire of their friends if they continue within the city, and plundered by the foldiery if they leave it. In their prefent fituation they are prifoners without the hope of redemption, and in a general attack for their relief, they would be expofed to the fury of both armies

Men of paffive tempers look fomewhat lightly over the offences of Britain, and, ftill hoping for the beft, are apt to call out, *" Come, come, we fhall be friends again, for all this."* But examine the paffions and feelings of mankind—Bring the doctrine of reconciliation to the touchftone of nature, and then tell me, whether you can hereafter love, honour, and faithfully ferve the power that hath carried fire and fword into your land? If you cannot do all thefe, then are you only deceiving yourfelves, and by your delay bringing ruin upon your pofterity. Your future connexion with Britain, whom you can neither love nor honour, will be forced and unnatural, and being formed only on the plan of prefent convenience, will in a little time .fall into a relapfe more wretched than the firft. But if you fay, you can ftill pafs the violations over, then I afk, Hath your houfe been burnt? Hath your property been deftroyed before your face? Are your wife and children deftitute of a bed to lie on, or bread to live on? Have you loft a parent or a child by their hands, and yourfelf the ruined and wretched furvivor? If you have not, then are you not a judge of thofe who have. But if you have, and can ftill fhake hands with the murderers, then are you unworthy the name of hufband, father, friend, or lover, and whatever may be your rank or title in life, you have the heart of a coward, and the fpirit of a fycophant.

This is not inflaming or exaggerating matters, but trying them by thofe feelings and affections which nature juftifies, and without which, we fhould be incapable of difcharging the focial duties of life, or enjoying the felicities of it. I mean not to exhibit horror for the purpofe of provoking revenge, but to awaken us from fatal and unmanly flumbers, that we may purfue determinately fome fixed object. It is not in the power of Britain or of Europe to conquer America, if fhe does not conquer herfelf by *delay* and *timidity.* The prefent winter is worth an age if rightly employed, but if loft or neglected, the whole continent will partake of the misfortune; and there is no punifhment which that man will not deferve, be he who, or what, or where he will, that may be the means of facrificing a feafon fo precious and ufeful.

It is repugnant to reafon, to the univerfal order of things, to all

examples from former ages, to suppose, that this continent can
longer remain subject to any external power. The most sanguine
in Britain does not think so. The utmost stretch of human wisdom
cannot, at this time, compass a plan short of separation, which
can promise the continent even a year's security. Reconciliation is
now a fallacious dream. Nature hath deserted the connexion, and
art cannot supply her place. For, as Milton wisely expresses, " never can true reconcilement grow, where wounds of deadly hate have
pierced so deep."

Every quiet method for peace hath been ineffectual. Our prayers
have been rejected with disdain; and only tended to convince us, that
nothing flatters vanity, or confirms obstinacy in kings more than
repeated petitioning—and nothing hath contributed more than that
very measure to make the kings of Europe absolute : Witness Den-
mark and Sweden. Wherefore, since nothing but blows will do,
for God's sake, let us come to a final separation, and not leave the
next generation to be cutting throats, under the violated unmeaning
names of parent and child.

To say, they will never attempt it again, is idle and visionary ; we
thought so at the repeal of the stamp-act, yet a year or two unde-
ceived us : As well may we suppose that nations, which have been
once defeated, will never renew the quarrel.

As to government matters, it is not in the power of Britain to do
this continent justice : The business of it will soon be too weighty,
and intricate, to be managed with any tolerable degree of convenience, by a power, so distant from us, and so very ignorant of us ;
for if they cannot conquer us, they cannot govern us. To be always
running three or four thousand miles with a tale or a petition, waiting
four or five months for an answer, which when obtained requires five
or six more to explain it in, will in a few years be looked upon as
folly and childishness—There was a time when it was proper, and
there is a proper time for it to cease.

Small islands not capable of protecting themselves, are the proper
objects for kingdoms to take under their care; but there is something
very absurd, in supposing a continent to be perpetually governed by
an island. In no instance hath nature made the satellite larger than
its primary planet ; and as England and America, with respect to
each other, reverses the common order of nature, it is evident they
belong to different systems : England to Europe, America to
itself

I am not induced by motives of pride, party or refentment, to efpoufe the doctrine of feparation and independence; I am clearly, pofitively, and confcientioufly perfuaded that it is the true intereſt of this continent to be fo; that every thing fhort of *that* is mere patchwork, that it can afford no lafting felicity,—that it is leaving the fword to our children, and fhrinking back at a time, when, a little more, a little farther, would have rendered this continent the glory of the earth.

As Britain hath not manifefted the leaſt inclination towards a compromife, we may be affured that no terms can be obtained worthy the acceptance of the continent, or any ways equal to the expence of blood and treafure we have been already put to.

The object contended for, ought always to bear fome juſt proportion to the expence. The removal of North, or the whole deteftable junto, is a matter unworthy the millions we have expended. A temporary ftoppage of trade, was an inconvenience, which would have fufficiently balanced the repeal of all the acts complained of, had fuch repeals been obtained; but if the whole continent muſt take up arms, if every man muſt be a foldier, it is fcarcely worth our while to fight againſt a contemptible miniftry only. Dearly, dearly, do we pay for the repeal of the acts, if that is all we fight for; for in a juſt eftimation, it is as great a folly to pay a Bunker-hill price for law, as for land. As I have always confidered the independency of this continent, as an event which, fooner or later, muſt arrive, fo, from the late rapid progrefs of the continent to maturity, the event could not be far off. Wherefore, on the breaking out of hoftilities, it was not worth the while to have difputed a matter, which time would have finally redreffed, unlefs we meant to be in earneſt; otherwife, it is like wafting an eftate on a fuit at law, to regulate the trefpaffes of a tenant, whofe leafe is juſt expiring. No man was a warmer wifher for reconciliation than myfelf, before the fatal nineteenth of April 1775,* but the moment the event of that day was made known, I rejected the hardened, fullen-tempered Pharaoh of England for ever; and difdain the wretch, that with the pretended title of FATHER OF HIS PEOPLE can unfeelingly hear of their flaughter, and compofedly fleep with their blood upon his foul.

But admitting that matters were now made up, what would be the event? I anfwer, the ruin of the continent. And that for feveral reafons.

Firſt. The powers of governing ftill remaining in the hands of

* *Maffacre at Lexington.*

the king, he will have a negative over the whole legiflation of this continent. And as he hath fhewn himfelf fuch an inveterate enemy to liberty, and difcovered fuch a thirft for arbitrary power; is he, or is he not, a proper man to fay to thefe colonies, " *You fhall make no laws but what I pleafe?*" And is there any inhabitant in America fo ignorant, as not to know, that according to what is called the *prefent conftitution,* that this continent can make no laws but what the king gives leave to? and is there any man fo unwife, as not to fee, that (confidering what has happened) he will fuffer no law to be made here, but fuch as fuit *his* purpofe? We may be as effectually enflaved by the want of laws in America, as by fubmitting to laws made for us in England. After matters are made up (as it is called) can there be any doubt, but the whole power of the crown will be exerted, to keep this continent as low and humble as poffible? Inftead of going forward we fhall go backward, or be perpetually quarrelling or ridiculoufly petitioning.—We are already greater than the king wifhes us to be, and will he not hereafter endeavour to make us lefs? To bring the matter to one point, Is the power who is jealous of our profperity, a proper power to govern us? Whoever fays *No* to this queftion is *an independent,* for independency means no more, than whether we fhall make our own laws, or, whether the king, the greateft enemy this continent hath, or can have, fhall tell us " *there fhall be no laws but fuch as I like.*"

But the king you will fay has a negative in England; the people there can make no laws without his confent. In point of right and good order, there is fomething very ridiculous, that a youth of twenty-one (which hath often happened) fhall fay to feveral millions of people, older and wifer than himfelf, I forbid this or that act of yours to be law. But in this place I decline this fort of reply, though I will never ceafe to expofe the abfurdity of it; and only anfwer, that England being the king's refidence, and America not fo, makes quite another cafe. The king's negative *here* is ten times more dangerous and fatal than it can be in England; for *there* he will fcarcely refufe his confent to a bill for putting England into as ftrong a ftate of defence as poffible, and in America he would never fuffer fuch a bill to be paffed.

America is only a fecondary object in the fyftem of Britifh politics —England confults the good of *this* country, no farther than it anfwers her *own* purpofe. Wherefore, her own intereft leads her to fupprefs the growth of *ours* in every cafe which doth not promote her advantage, or in the leaft interferes with it. A pretty ftate we should soon be in under such a second-hand government, confidering what has happened! Men do not change from enemies to friends by the alteration of a name: And in order to shew that reconciliation *now* is a dangerous doctrine, I affirm, *that it would be policy in the king at this time, to repeal the acts, for the sake of re-instating himself in the government of the provinces;* in order, that HE MAY ACCOMPLISH BY CRAFT AND SUBTILTY, IN THE LONG RUN, WHAT HE CANNOT DO BY FORCE AND VIOLENCE IN THE SHORT ONE. Reconciliation and ruin are nearly related.

Secondly, That as even the best terms, which we can expect to obtain, can amount to no more than a temporary expedient, or a kind of government by guardianship, which can last no longer than till the colonies come of age, so the general face and state of things, in the interim, will be unsettled and unpromising. Emigrants of property will not choose to come to a country whose form of government hangs but by a thread, and which is every day tottering on the brink of commotion and disturbance; and numbers of the present inhabitants would lay hold of the interval, to dispose of their effects, and quit the continent.

But the most powerful of all arguments, is, that nothing but independence, *i. e.* a continental form of government, can keep the peace of the continent and preserve it inviolate from civil wars. I dread the event of a reconciliation with Britain now, as it is more than probable, that it will be followed by a revolt some where or other, the consequences of which may be far more fatal than all the malice of Britain.

Thousands are already ruined by British barbarity. (Thousands more will probably suffer the same fate.) Those men have other feelings than us who have nothing suffered. All they *now* possess is liberty, what they before enjoyed is sacrificed to its service, and having nothing more to lose, they disdain submission. Besides, the general temper of the colonies, towards a British government, will be like that of a youth, who is nearly out of his time; they will care very little about her. And a government which cannot preserve the peace, is no government at all, and in that case we pay our money for nothing; and pray what is it that Britain can do, whose power will be wholly on paper, should a civil tumult break out the very day after reconciliation? I have heard some men say, many of whom I believe spoke without thinking, that they dreaded an independence, fearing that it would produce civil wars. It is but seldom that our

firſt thoughts are truly correct, and that is the caſe here ; for there
are ten times more to dread from a patched-up connexion than from
independence. I make the ſufferers' caſe my own, and I proteſt,
that were I driven from houſe and home, my property deſtroyed,
and my circumſtances ruined, that as a man, ſenſible of injuries, I
could never reliſh the doctrine of reconciliation, or conſider myſelf
bound thereby.

The colonies have manifeſted ſuch a ſpirit of good order and
obedience to continental government, as is ſufficient to make every
reaſonable perſon eaſy and happy on that head. No man can aſſign
the leaſt pretence for his fears, on any other grounds, than ſuch as
are truly childiſh and ridiculous, viz. that one colony will be ſtriving
for ſuperiority over another.

Where there are no diſtinctions there can be no ſuperiority ; perfect
equality affords no temptation. The republics of Europe are all
(and we may ſay always) in peace. Holland and Swiſſerland are
without wars, foreign or domeſtic : Monarchical governments, it is
true, are never long at reſt : the crown itſelf is a temptation to enter-
priſing ruffians at home ; and that degree of pride and inſolence ever
attendant on regal authority, ſwells into a rupture with foreign
powers, in inſtances where a republican government, by being
formed on more natural principles, would negociate the miſtake.

If there is any true cauſe of fear reſpecting independence, it is
becauſe no plan is yet laid down. Men do not ſee their way out—
Wherefore, as an opening into that buſineſs, I offer the following
hints ; at the ſame time modeſtly affirming, that I have no other
opinion of them myſelf, than that they may be the means of giving
riſe to ſomething better. Could the ſtraggling thoughts of individuals be collected, they would frequently form materials for wiſe and
able men to improve into uſeful matter.

Let the aſſemblies be annual, with a preſident only. The repre-
ſentation more equal. Their buſineſs wholly domeſtic, and ſubject
to the authority of a continental congreſs.

Let each colony be divided into ſix, eight, or ten, convenient
diſtricts, each diſtrict to ſend a proper number of delegates to congreſs, ſo that each colony ſend at leaſt thirty. The whole number
in congreſs will be at leaſt 390. Each congreſs to ſit ....
and to chooſe a preſident by the following method. When the
delegates are met, let a colony be taken from the whole thirteen colonies by lot, after which, let the whole congreſs chooſe (by ballot)
a preſident from out of the delegates of that province. In the next

congrefs, let a colony be taken by lot from twelve only, omitting that colony from which the prefident was taken in the former congrefs, and fo proceeding on till the whole thirteen fhall have had their proper rotation. And in order that nothing may pafs into a law but what is fatisfactorily juft, not lefs than three-fifths of the congrefs to be called a majority. He that will promote difcord, under, a government fo equally formed as this, would have joined Lucifer in his revolt.

But as there is a peculiar delicacy, from whom, or in what manner, this bufinefs muft firft arife, and as it feems moft agreeable and confiftent, that it fhould come from fome intermediate body between the governed and the governors, that is, between the congrefs and the people, let a CONTINENTAL CONFERENCE be held, in the. following manner, and for the following purpofe.

A committee of twenty-fix members of congrefs, viz. two for each colony. Two members from each houfe of affembly, or provincial convention; and five reprefentatives of the people at large, to be chofen in the capital city or town of each province, for, and in behalf of the whole province, by as many qualified voters as fhall think proper to attend from all parts of the province for that purpofe; or, if more convenient, the reprefentatives may be chofen in two or three of the moft populous parts thereof. In this conference, thus affembled, will be united, the two grand principles of bufinefs, *knowledge* and *power*. The members of congrefs, affemblies, or convention, by having had experience in national concerns, will be able and ufeful counfellors, and the whole, being empowered by the people, will have a truly legal authority.

The conferring members being met, let their bufinefs be to frame a CONTINENTAL CHARTER, or Charter of the United Colonies (anfwering to what is called the Magna Charter of England); fixing the number and manner of choofing members of congrefs, members of affembly, with their date of fitting, and drawing the line of bufinefs and jurifdiction between them: (Always remembering, that our ftrength is continental, not provincial:) Securing freedom and property to all men, and above all things, the free exercife of religion, according to the dictates of confcience; with fuch other matter as is neceffary for a charter to contain. Immediately after which, the faid conference to diffolve, and the bodies which fhall be chofen conformable to the faid charter, to be the legiflators and governors of this continent for the time being: Whofe peace and happinefs, may God preferve, Amen.

Should any body of men be hereafter delegated for this or some similar purpose, I offer them the following extracts from that wise observer on governments, *Dragonetti*. " The science" says he " of " the politician confists in fixing the true point of happinefs and " freedom. Thofe men would deferve the gratitude of ages, who " should difcover a mode of government that contained the greatest " fum of individual happinefs, with the leaft national expence."

Dragonetti on Virtue and Rewards.

But where, fays fome, is the king of America? I'll tell you, friend, he reigns above, and doth not make havoc of mankind like the royal brute of Britain. Yet that we may not appear to be defcctive even in earthly honours, let a day be folemnly fet apart for proclaiming the charter; let it be brought forth placed on the divine law, the word of God; let a crown be placed thereon, by which the world may know, that fo far as we approve of monarchy, that in America THE LAW IS KING. For as in abfolute governments the king is law, fo in free countries the law ought to be king; and there ought to be no other. But left any ill ufe should afterwards arife, let the crown at the conclufion of the ceremony be demolished, and fcattered among the people whofe right it is.

A government of our own is our natural right: And when a man ferioufly reflects on the precarioufnefs of human affairs, he will become convinced, that it is infinitely wifer and fafer, to form a conftitution of our own in a cool deliberate manner, while we have it in our power, than to truft fuch an interefting event to time and chance. If we omit it now, fome Maffanello * may hereafter arife, who laying hold of popular difquietudes, may collect together the defperate and the dif-contented, and by affuming to themfelves the powers of government, may fweep away the liberties of the continent like a deluge. Should the government of America return again into the hands of Britain, the tottering fituation of things, will be a temptation for fome defperate adventurer to try his fortune; and in fuch a cafe, what relief can Britain give! Ere she could hear the news, the fatal bufinefs might be done; and ourfelves fuffering like the wretched Britons under the oppreffion of the Conqueror. Ye that oppofe independence now, ye know not what ye do; ye are opening a door to eternal tyranny, by keeping vacant the feat of government. There are thoufands and tens

---

* *Thomas Anello, otherwife Maffanello, a fisherman of Naples, who after fpiriting up his countrymen in the public market place, againft the oppreffion of the Spaniards, to whom the place was then fubject, prompted them to revolt, and in the fpace of a day became king.*

of thoufands, who would think it glorious to expel from the continent, that barbarous and hellifh power, which hath ftirred up the Indians and Negroes to deftroy us—the cruelty hath a double guilt, it is dealing brutally by us, and treacheroufly by them.

To talk of friendfhip with thofe in whom our reafon forbids us to have faith, and our affections, wounded through a thoufand pores, inftruct us to deteft, is madnefs and folly. Every day wears out the little remains of kindred between us and them; and can there be any reafon to hope, that as the relationfhip expires, the affection will encreafe, or that we fhall agree better, when we have ten times more and greater concerns to quarrel over than ever?

Ye that tell us of harmony and reconciliation, can ye reftore to us the time that is paft? Can ye give to proftitution its former innocence? Neither can ye reconcile Britain and America. The laft cord now is broken, the people of England are prefenting addreffes againft us. There are injuries which nature cannot forgive; fhe would ceafe to be nature if fhe did. As well can the lover forgive the ravifher of his miftrefs, as the continent forgive the murders of Britain. The Almighty hath implanted in us thefe unextinguifhable feelings, for good and wife purpofes. They are the guardians of his image in our hearts. They diftinguifh us from the herd of common animals. The focial compact would diffolve, and juftice be extirpated the earth, or have only a cafual exiftence were we callous to the touches of affection. The robber, and the murderer, would often efcape unpunifhed, did not the injuries which our tempers fuftain, provoke us into juftice.

O ye that love mankind! Ye that dare oppofe, not only the tyranny, but the tyrant, ftand forth! Every fpot of the old world is over run with oppreffion. Freedom hath been haunted round the globe. Afia, and Africa, have long expelled her.—Europe regards her like a ftranger, and England hath given her warning to depart. O! receive the fugitive, and prepare in time an afylum for mankind.

Of the prefent ability of America: with fome mifcellaneous reflections.

I HAVE never met with a man, either in England or America, who hath not confeffed his opinion, that a feparation between the countries, would take place one time or other: and there is no inftance, in which we have fhewn lefs judgment, than in endeavouring to defcribe, what we call, the ripenefs or fitnefs of the continent for independence.

As all men allow the meafure, and vary only in their opinion of the time, let us, in order to remove miftakes, take a general furvey of things, and endeavour, if poffible, to find out the *very* time. But we need not go far, the inquiry ceafes at once, for, the *time hath found us.* The general concurrence, the glorious union of all things prove the fact.

It is not in numbers, but in unity, that our great ftrength lies; yet our prefent numbers are fufficient to repel the force of all the world. The continent hath, at this time, the largeft body of armed and difciplined men of any power under heaven; and is juft arrived at that pitch of ftrength, in which, no fingle colony is able to fupport, itfelf, and the whole, when united, can accomplifh the matter, and either more, or lefs than this, might be fatal in its effects. Our land force is already fufficient, and as to naval affairs, we cannot be infenfible, that Britain would never fuffer an American man of war to be built, while the continent remained in her hands. Wherefore, we fhould be no forwarder an hundred years hence in that branch, than we are now; but the truth is, we fhould be lefs fo, becaufe the timber of the country is every day diminifhing, and that which will remain at laft, will be far off or difficult to procure.

Were the continent crowded with inhabitants, her fufferings under the prefent circumftances would be intolerable. The more fea-port towns we had, the more fhould we have both to defend and to lofe. Our prefent numbers are fo happily proportioned to our wants, that no man need be idle. The diminution of trade affords an army, and the neceffities of an army create a new trade.

Debts we have none; and whatever we may contract on this account will ferve as a glorious memento of our virtue. Can we but leave pofterity with a fettled form of government, an independent conftitution of its own, the purchafe at any price will be cheap. But to expend millions for the fake of getting a few vile acts repealed, and routing the prefent miniftry only, is unworthy the charge, and is ufing pofterity with the utmoft cruelty; becaufe it is leaving them the great work to do, and a debt upon their backs, from which they derive no advantage. Such a thought is unworthy a man of honour, and is the true characteriftic of a narrow heart and a pedling politician.

The debt we may contract doth not deferve our regard, if the work be but accomplifhed. No nation ought to be without a debt. A national debt is a national bond; and when it bears no intereft, is in no cafe a grievance. Britain is oppreffed with a debt of upwards of one hundred and forty millions fterling, for which fhe pays upwards of four millions intereft. And as a compenfation for her debt, fhe has a large navy ; America is without a debt, and without a navy ; yet for the twentieth part of the Englifh national debt, could have a navy as large again. The navy of England is not worth, at this time, more than three millions and a half fterling.

The following calculations are given as a proof that the above eftimation of the navy is a juft one. [See *Entick's Naval Hiftory, Intro.* page 56.]

The charge of building a fhip of each rate, and furnifhing her with mafts, yards, fails and rigging, together with a proportion of eight months boatfwain's and carpenter's fea-ftores, as calculated by Mr. Eurchett, Secretary to the navy.

For a fhip of 100 guns	—	—	£.35,553
90	—	—	— 29,886
80	—	—	23,638
70	—	—	— 17,785
60	—	—	14,197
50	—	—	— 10,606
40	—	—	7,558
30	—	—	— 5,846
20	—	—	3,710

And from hence it is eafy to fum up the value, or coft rather, of the whole Britifh navy, which in the year 1757, when it was at its greateft glory confifted of the following fhips and guns.

Ships.	Guns.	Coft of one.	Coft of all.
6 —	100 —	£.55,553 —	£.213,318
12 —	90 —	29,886 —	358,632
12 —	80 —	23,638 —	283,656
43 —	70 —	17,785 —	764,755
35 —	60 —	14,197 —	496,895
40 —	50 —	10,605 —	424,240
45 —	40 —	7,558 —	340,110
58 —	20 —	3,710 —	215,180
85 Sloops, bombs, and fire-fhips, one with another, at		} 2,000 —	170,000
		Coft,	£.3,266,786
Remains for guns,	—	—	233,214
		Total,	£.3,500,000

No country on the globe is so happily situated, or so internally
capable of raising a fleet as America: Tar, timber, iron, and cordage are her natural produce. We need go abroad for nothing.
Whereas the Dutch, who make large profits by hiring out their ships
of war to the Spaniards and Portuguese, are obliged to import most
of the materials they use. We ought to view the building a fleet as
an article of commerce, it being the natural manufacture of this country. It is the best money we can lay out. A navy when finished is
worth more than it cost. And is that nice point in national policy,
in which commerce and protection are united. Let us build; if we
want them not, we can sell; and by that means replace our paper currency with ready gold and silver.

In point of manning a fleet, people in general run into great errors;
it is not necessary that one fourth part should be sailors. The Terrible
privateer, captain Death, stood the hottest engagement of any ship last
war, yet had not twenty sailors on board, though her complement of
men was upwards of two hundred. A few able and social sailors will
soon instruct a sufficient number of active landmen in the common
work of a ship. Wherefore, we never can be more capable to begin
on maritime matters than now, while our timber is standing, our fish-
eries blocked up, and our sailors and shipwrights out of employ. Men
of war, of seventy and eighty guns were built forty years ago in
New-England, and why not the same now ? Ship-building is America's greatest pride, and in which, she will in time excel the whole
world. The great empires of the east are mostly inland, and consequently excluded from the possibility of rivalling her. Africa is in
a state of barbarism; and no power in Europe, hath either such an extent of coast, or such an internal supply of materials. Where nature
hath given the one, she has withheld the other; to America only hath
she been liberal of both. The vast empire of Russia is almost shut
out from the sea; wherefore, her boundless forests, her tar, iron, and
cordage are only articles of commerce.

In point of safety, ought we to be without a fleet? We are not the
little people now, which we were sixty years ago; at that time we might
have trusted our property in the streets, or fields rather ; and slept
securely without locks or bolts to our doors or windows. The case
is now altered, and our methods of defence, ought to improve, with
our increase of property. A common pirate, twelve months ago,
might have come up the Delaware, and laid the city of Philadelphia
under instant contribution, for what sum he pleased ; and the same

might have happened to other places. Nay, any daring fellow, in a brig of fourteen or sixteen guns, might have robbed the whole continent, and carried off half a million of money. These are circumstances which demand our attention, and point out the neceſſity of naval protection.

Some, perhaps, will ſay, that after we have made it up with Britain, ſhe will protect us. Can we be ſo unwiſe as to mean, that ſhe ſhall keep a navy in our harbours for that purpoſe? Common ſenſe will tell us, that the power which hath endeavoured to ſubdue us, is of all others, the moſt improper to defend us. Conqueſt may be effected under the pretence of friendſhip; and ourſelves, after a long and brave reſiſtance, be at laſt cheated into ſlavery. And if her ſhips are not to be admitted into our harbours, I would aſk, how is ſhe to protect us? A navy three or four thouſand miles off can be of little uſe, and on ſudden emergencies, none at all. Wherefore, if we muſt hereafter protect ourſelves, why not do it for ourſelves? Why do it for another?

The Engliſh liſt of ſhips of war, is long and formidable, but not a tenth part of them are at any one time fit for ſervice, numbers of them not in being; yet their names are pompouſly continued in the liſt, if only a plank be left of the ſhip: and not a fifth part of ſuch as are fit for ſervice, can be ſpared on any one ſtation at one time. The Eaſt and Weſt Indies, Mediterranean, Africa, and other parts over which Britain extends her claim, make large demands upon her navy. From a mixture of prejudice and inattention, we have contracted a falſe notion reſpecting the navy of England, and have talked as if we ſhould have the whole of it to encounter at once, and for that reaſon, ſuppoſed, that we muſt have one as large; which not being inſtantly practicable, has been made uſe of by a ſet of diſguiſed tories to diſcourage our beginning thereon. Nothing can be further from truth than this; for if America had only a twentieth part of the naval force of Britain, ſhe would be by far an over match for her; becauſe, as we neither have, nor claim any foreign dominion, our whole force would be employed on our own coaſt, where we ſhould, in the long run, have two to one the advantage of thoſe who had three or four thouſand miles to ſail over, before they could attack us, and the ſame diſtance to return in order to refit and recruit. And although Britain, by her fleet, hath a check over our trade to Europe, we have as large a one over her trade to the Weſt Indies, which, by laying in the neighbourhood of the continent, is entirely at its mercy.

Some method might be fallen on to keep up a naval force in time

of peace, if we should not judge it neceffary to fupport a conftant
navy. If premiums were to be given to merchants, to build and
employ in their fervice, fhips mounted with twenty, thirty, forty, or
fifty guns (the premiums to be in proportion to the lofs of bulk to
the merchants), fifty or fixty of thofe fhips, with a few guard-fhips
on conftant duty, would keep up a fufficient navy, and that without
burdening ourfelves with the evil fo loudly complained of in England,
of fuffering their fleet, in time of peace, to lie rotting in the docks.
To unite the finews of commerce and defence is found policy; for
when our ftrength and our riches play into each other's hand, we need
fear no external enemy.

In almoft every article of defence we abound. Hemp flourifhes
even to ranknefs, fo that we need not want cordage. Our iron is
fuperior to that of other countries. Our fmall arms equal to any in
the world. Cannon we can caft at pleafure. Saltpetre and gunpowder
we are every day producing. Our knowledge is hourly improving.
Refolution is our inherent character, and courage hath never yet
forfaken us. Wherefore, what is it that we want? Why is it that
we hefitate? From Britain we can expect nothing but ruin. If fhe
is once admitted to the government of America again, this continent
will not be worth living in. Jealoufies will be always arifing; infurrections will be conftantly happening; and who will go forth to quell
them? Who will venture his life to reduce his own countrymen to
a foreign obedience? The difference between Pennfylvania and
Connecticut, refpecting fome unlocated lands, fhews the infignificance
of a Britifh government, and fully proves, that nothing but continental
authority can regulate continental matters.

Another reafon why the prefent time is preferable to all others, is,
that the fewer our numbers are, the more land there is yet unoccupied,
which inftead of being lavifhed by the king on his worthlefs dependants, may be hereafter applied, not only to the difcharge of the
prefent debt, but to the conftant fupport of government. No nation
under heaven hath fuch an advantage as this.

The infant ftate of the colonies, as it is called, fo far from being
againft, is an argument in favour of, independence. We are fufficiently numerous, and were we more fo, we might be lefs united. It
is a matter worthy of obfervation, that the more a country is peopled,
the fmaller their armies are. In military numbers, the ancients far
exceeded the moderns: And the reafon is evident, for trade being
the confequence of population, men become too much abforbed

thereby to attend to any thing elfe. Commerce diminifhes the fpirit, both of patriotifm and military defence. And hiftory fufficiently informs us, that the braveft atchievements were always accomplifhed in the non-age of a nation. With the increafe of commerce, England hath loft its fpirit. The city of London, notwithftanding its numbers, fubmits to continued infults with the patience of a coward. The more men have to lofe, the lefs willing are they to venture. The rich are in general flaves to fear, and fubmit to courtly power with the trembling duplicity of a fpaniel.

Youth is the feed-time of good habits, as well in nations as in individuals. It might be difficult, if not impoffible, to form the continent into one government half a century hence. The vaft variety of interefts, occafioned by an increafe of trade and population, would create confufion. Colony would be againft colony. Each being able, might fcorn each other's affiftance : And while the proud and foolifh gloried in their little diftinctions, the wife would lament, that the union had not been formed before. Wherefore, the *prefent time* is the *true time* for eftablifhing it. The intimacy which is contracted in infancy, and the friendfhip which is formed in misfortune, are, of all others, the moft lafting and unalterable. Our prefent union is marked with both thefe characters : we are young, and we have been diftreffed ; but our concord hath withftood our troubles, and fixes a memorable era for pofterity to glory in.

The prefent time, likewife, is that peculiar time, which never happens to a nation but once, viz. the time of forming itfelf into a government. Moft nations have let flip the opportunity, and by that means have been compelled to receive laws from their conquerors, inftead of making laws for themfelves. Firft, they had a king, and then a form of government ; whereas the articles or charter of government, fhould be formed firft, and men delegated to execute them afterward : but from the errors of other nations, let us learn wifdom, and lay hold of the prefent opportunity—*To begin government at the right end.*

When William the Conqueror fubdued England, he gave them law at the point of the fword ; and until we confent that the feat of government, in America, be legally and authoritatively occupied, we fhall be in danger of having it filled by fome fortunate ruffian, who may treat us in the fame manner, and then, where will be our freedom ? where our property ?

As to religion, I hold it to be the indifpenfible duty of all go-

vernments, to protect all confcientious profeffors thereof, and I know
of no other bufinefs which government hath to do therewith. Let
a man throw afide that narrownefs of foul, that felfifhnefs of principle,
which the niggards of all profeffions are fo unwilling to part with,
and he will be at once delivered of his fears on that head. Sufpicion
is the companion of mean fouls, and the bane of all good fociety.
For myfelf, I fully and confcientiously believe, that it is the will of
the Almighty, that there fhould be a diverfity of religious opinions
among us : It affords a larger field for our Chriftian kindnefs. Were
we all of one way of thinking, our religious difpofitions would want
matter for probation ; and on this liberal principle, I look on the
various denominations among us, to be like children of the fame
family, differing only, in what is called, their Chriftian names.

In a former page, I threw out a few thoughts on the propriety
of a Continental Charter (for I only prefume to offer hints, not plans)
and in this place, I take the liberty of re-mentioning the fubject, by
obferving, that a charter is to be underftood as a bond of folemn obligation, which the whole enters into, to fupport the right of every
feparate part, whether of religion, perfonal freedom, or property.
A firm bargain and a right reckoning make long friends.

I have heretofore likewife mentioned the neceffity of a large and
equal reprefentation ; and there is no political matter which more
deferves our attention. A fmall number of electors, or a fmall number of reprefentatives, are equally dangerous. But if the number of
the reprefentatives be not only fmall, but unequal, the danger is increafed. As an inftance of this, I mention the following ; when
the affociators' petition was before the houfe of affembly of Pennfylvania, twenty-eight members only were prefent, all the Bucks County
members, being eight, voted againft it, and had feven of the Chefter
members done the fame, this whole province had been governed by
two counties only ; and this danger it is always expofed to. The
unwarrantable ftretch likewife, which that houfe made in their laft
fitting, to gain an undue authority over the delegates of that province, ought to warn the people at large, how they truft power out of
their own hands. A fet of inftructions for their delegates were put
together, which in point of fenfe and bufinefs would have difhonoured
a fchool-boy, and after being approved by a *few*, a *very few* without
doors, were carried into the houfe, and there paffed *in behalf of the
whole colony ;* whereas, did the whole colony know, with what ill-
will that houfe had entered on fome neceffary public meafures, they

would not hefitate a moment to think them unworthy of fuch a truft.

Immediate neceffity makes many things convenient, which if continued would grow into oppreffions. Expedience and right are different things. When the calamities of America required a confultation, there was no method fo ready, or at that time fo proper, as to appoint perfons from the feveral houfes of affembly for that purpofe ; and the wifdom with which they have proceeded hath preferved this continent from ruin. But as it is more than probable that we fhall never be without a CONGRESS, every well-wifher to good order, muft own, that the mode for choofing members of that body, deferves confideration. And I put it as a queftion to thofe, who make a ftudy of mankind, whether *reprefentation and election* is not too great a power for one and the fame body of men to poffefs? Whenever we are planning for pofterity, we ought to remember, that virtue is not hereditary.

It is from our enemies that we often gain excellent maxims, and are frequently furprifed into reafon by their miftakes. Mr. Cornwall (one of the lords of the treafury) treated the petition of the New-York affembly with contempt, becaufe *that* houfe, he faid, confifted but of twenty-fix members, which trifling number, he argued, could not with decency be put for the whole. We thank him for his involuntary honefty.*

To CONCLUDE, however ftrange it may appear to fome, or however unwilling they may be to think fo, matters not, but many ftrong and ftriking reafons may be given, to fhew, that nothing can fettle our affairs fo expeditioufly as an open and determined declaration for independence. Some of which are,

Firft.—It is the cuftom of nations, when any two are at war, for fome other powers, not engaged in the quarrel, to ftep in as mediators, and bring about the preliminaries of a peace: but while America calls herfelf the fubject of Britain, no power, however well difpofed fhe may be, can offer her mediation. Wherefore, in our prefent ftate we may quarrel on for ever.

Secondly.—It is unreafonable to fuppofe, that France or Spain will give as any kind of affiftance, if we mean only, to make ufe of that affiftance for the purpofe of repairing the breach, and ftrengthening

* *Thofe who would fully underftand of what great confequence a large and equal reprefentation is to a ftate, fhould read Burgh's Political Difquifitions.*

the connection between Britain and America; becaufe, thofe powers would be fufferers by the confequences.

Thirdly.—While we profefs ourfelves the fubjects of Britain, we mult, in the eye of foreign nations, be confidered as rebels. The precedent is fomewhat dangerous to *their peace,* for men to be in arms under the name of fubjects; we, on the fpot, can folve the paradox : but to unite refiftance and fubjection, requires an idea much too refined for common underftanding.

Fourthly.—Were a manifeflo to be publifhed, and difpatched to foreign courts, fetting forth the miferies we have endured, and the peaceable methods we have ineffectually ufed for redrefs ; declaring, at the fame time, that not being able, any longer, to live happily or fafely under the cruel difpofition of the Britifh court, we had been driven to the neceffity of breaking off all connexions with her; at the fame time, affuring all fuch courts of our peaceable difpofition towards them, and of our defire of entering into trade with them. Such a memorial would produce more good effects to this continent, than if a fhip were freighted with petitions to Britain.

Under our prefent denomination of Britifh fubjects, we can neither be received nor heard abroad : The cuftom of all courts is againft us, and will be fo, until, by an independence, we take rank with other nations.

Thefe proceedings may at firft appear ftrange and difficult ; but, like all other fteps, which we have already paffed over, will in a little time become familiar and agreable ; and, until an independence is declared, the continent will feel itfelf like a man who continues putting off fome unpleafant bufinefs from day to day, yet knows it muft be done, hates to fet about it, wifhes it over, and is continually haunted with the thoughts of its neceffity

---

A P P E N D I X.

SINCE the publication of the firft edition of this pamphlet, or rather, on the fame day on which it came out, the king's fpeech made its appearance in this city. Had the fpirit of prophecy directed the birth of this production, it could not have brought it forth at a more feafonable juncture, or a more neceffary time.—The bloody mindednefs of the one, fhews the neceffity of purfuing the doctrine of the other. Men read by way of revenge :—And the fpeech, inftead of terrifying, prepared a way for the manly principles of independence.

Ceremony, and even filence, from whatever motives they may arife, have a hurtful tendency, when they give the leaft degree of countenance to bafe and wicked performances; wherefore, if this maxim be admitted, it naturally follows, that the king's fpeech, as being a piece of finifhed villany, deferved, and ftill deferves, a general execration, both by the congrefs and the people. Yet, as the domeftic tranquility of a nation, depends greatly, on the *chaftity* of what may properly be called NATIONAL MANNERS, it is often better, to pafs fome things over in filent difdain, than to make ufe of fuch new methods of diflike, as might introduce the leaft innovation, on that guardian of our peace and fafety. And, perhaps, it is chiefly owing to this prudent delicacy, that the king's fpeech, hath not, before now, fuffered a public execution. The fpeech, if it may be called one, is nothing better than a wilful, audacious libel againft the truth, the common good, and the exiftence of mankind; and is a formal and pompous method of offering up human facrifices to the pride of tyrants. But this general maffacre of mankind, is one of the privileges, and the certain confequences of kings; for as nature knows them *not*, they know *not* her, and although they are beings of our *own* creating, they know not *us*, and are become the gods of their creators. The fpeech hath one good quality, which is, that it is not calculated to deceive, neither can we, if we would, be deceived by it. Brutality and tyranny appear on the face of it. It leaves us at no lofs : and every line convinces, even in the moment of reading, that he, who hunts the woods for prey, the naked and untutored Indian, is lefs favage than the king of Britain.

Sir John Dalrymple, the putative father of a whining jefuitical piece, fallacioufly called, " *The address of the people of* England *to the inhabitants of* America," hath, perhaps, from a vain fuppofition, that the people *here* were to be frightened at the pomp and defcription of a king, given (though very unwifely on his part) the real character of the prefent one : " But," fays this writer, " if you are inclined to pay compliments to an adminiftration, which we do not complain of" (meaning the Marquis of Rockingham's at the repeal of the Stamp Act), " it is very unfair in you to withhold them from that prince, *by whofe* NOD ALONE *they were permitted to do any thing.*" This is toryifm with a witnefs ! Here is idolatry even without a mafk : And he who can calmly hear, and digeft fuch doctrine, hath forfeited his claim to rationality ; is an apostate from the order of manhood ; and ought to be considered—as one, who hath not only given up the proper dignity of man, but funk himself beneath the rank of animals, and contemptibly crawls through the world like a worm.

However, it matters very little now, what the king of England either fays or does; he hath wickedly broken through every moral and human obligation, trampled nature and confcience beneath his feet ; and by a fteady and conftitutional fpirit of infolence and cruelty, procured for himfelf an univerfal hatred. It is *now* the intereft of America to provide for herfelf. She hath already a large and young family, whom it is more her duty to take care of, than to be granting away her property, to fupport a power who is become a reproach to the names of men and Chriftians—YE, whofe office is to watch over the morals of a nation, of whatfoever fect or denomination ye are of, as well as ye, who are more immediately the guardians of the public liberty, if you wifh to preferve your native country uncontaminated by European corruption, ye muft in fecret wifh a feparation—But leaving the moral part to private reflection, I fhall chiefly confine my further remarks to the following heads :

Firft, That it is the intereft of America to be feparated from Britain.

Secondly, Which is the eafieft and moft practicable plan, RECONCILIATION or INDEPENDENCE ? with fome occafional remarks.

In fupport of the firft, I could, if I judged it proper, produce the opinion of fome of the ableft and moft experienced men on this continent ; and whofe fentiments, on that head, are not yet publicly known. It is in reality a felf-evident pofition : For no nation in a ftate of foreign dependence, limited in its commerce, and cramped and fettered in its legiflative powers, can ever arrive at any material eminence. America doth not yet know what opulence is ; and although the progrefs which fhe hath made ftands unparalleled in the hiftory of other nations, it is but childhood, compared with what fhe would be capable of arriving at, had fhe, as fhe ought to have, the legiflative powers in her own hands. England is, at this time, proudly coveting what would do her no good, were fhe to accomplifh it ; and the continent hefitating on a matter which will be her final ruin if neglected. It is the commerce and not the conqueft of America by which England is to be benefited, and that would in a great meafure continue, were the countries as independent of each other as France and Spain ; becaufe in many articles, neither can go to a better market. But it is the independence of this country on Britain or any other, which is now the main and only object worthy of contention, and which, like all other truths difcovered by neceffity, will appear clearer and ftronger every day.

Firft, Becaufe it will come to that one time or other.

Secondly, Becaufe the longer it is delayed, the harder it will be to accomplifh.

I have frequently amufed myfelf both in public and private companies, with filently remarking the fpecious errors, of thofe who fpeak without reflecting. And among the many which I have heard, the following feems the moft general, viz. that had this rupture happened forty or fifty years hence, inftead of *now*, the continent would have been more able to have fhaken off the dependence. To which I reply, that our military ability, *at this time*, arifes from the experience gained in the laft war, and which in forty or fifty years time, would have been totally extinct. The continent, would not, by that time, have had a general, or even a military officer left ; and we, or thofe who may fucceed us, would have been as ignorant of martial matters as the ancient Indians : And this fingle pofition, clofely attended to, will unanfwerably prove that the prefent time is preferable to all others. The argument turns thus—at the conclufion of the laft war, we had experience, but wanted numbers ; and forty or fifty years hence, we fhould have numbers, without experience ; wherefore, the proper point of time, muft be fome particular point between the two extremes, in which a fufficiency of the former remains, and a proper increafe of the latter is obtained : And that point of time is the prefent time.

The reader will pardon this digreffion, as it does not properly come under the head I firft fet out with, and to which I again return by the following pofition, viz.

Should affairs be patched up with Britain, and fhe remain the governing and fovereign power of America (which, as matters are now circumftanced, is giving up the point entirely), we fhall deprive ourfelves of the very means of finking the debt we have, or may contract. The value of the back lands which fome of the provinces are clandeftinely deprived of, by the unjuft extenfion of the limits of Canada, valued only at five pounds fterling per hundred acres, amount to upwards of twenty-five millions, Pennfylvania currency ; and the quit-rents at one penny fterling per acre, to two millions yearly.

It is by the sale of those lands that the debt may be sunk, without burden to any, and the quit-rent reserved thereon, will always lessen, and in time, will wholly support the yearly expence of government. It matters not how long the debt is in paying, so that the lands when sold be applied to the discharge of it, and for the execution of which, the congress for the time being, will be the continental trustees.

I proceed now to the second head, viz. Which is the easiest and most practicable plan, RECONCILIATION or INDEPENDENCE? with some occasional remarks.

He who takes nature for his guide is not easily beaten out of his argument, and on that ground, I answer generally—That INDEPENDENCE being a SINGLE SIMPLE LINE, contained within ourselves; and reconciliation, a matter exceedingly perplexed and complicated, and in which, a treacherous, capricious court is to interfere, gives the answer without a doubt.

The present state of America is truly alarming to every man who is capable of reflection. Without law, without government, without any other mode of power than what is founded on, and granted by courtesy. Held together by an unexampled concurrence of sentiment, which, is nevertheless subject to change, and which, every secret enemy is endeavouring to dissolve. Our present condition, is, Legislation without law; wisdom without a plan; a constitution without a name; and, what is strangely astonishing, perfect independence contending for dependence. The instance is without a precedent; the case never existed before; and who can tell what may be the event? The property of no man is secure in the present unbraced system of things. The mind of the multitude is left at random, and seeing no fixed object before them, they pursue such as fancy or opinion starts. Nothing is criminal; there is no such thing as treason; wherefore, every one thinks himself at liberty to act as he pleases. The tories dared not have assembled offensively, had they known that their lives, by that act, were forfeited to the laws of the state. A line of distinction should be drawn, between English soldiers taken in battle, and inhabitants of America taken in arms. The first are prisoners, but the latter traitors. The one forfeits his liberty, the other his head.

Notwithstanding our wisdom, there is a visible feebleness in some of our proceedings which gives encouragement to dissentions. The Continental Belt is too loosely buckled. And if something is not done in time, it will be too late to do any thing, and we shall fall into a state, in which, neither *Reconciliation* nor *Independence* will be practicable. The king and his worthlefs adherents are got at their old game of dividing the continent, and there are not wanting among us, printers, who will be bufy in fpreading fpecious falfehoods. The artful and hypocritical letter which appeared a few months ago in two of the New-York papers, and likewife in others, is an evidence that there are men who want either judgment or honefty.

It is eafy getting into holes and corners and talking of reconciliation: But do fuch men ferioufly confider, how difficult the tafk is, and how dangerous it may prove, fhould the continent divide thereon. Do they take within their view, all the various orders of men whofe fituation and circumftances, as well as their own, are to be confidered therein. Do they put themfelves in the place of the fufferer whofe *all* is *already* gone, and of the foldier, who hath quitted *all* for the defence of his country? If their ill-judged moderation be fuited to their own pri- vate fituations *only*, regardlefs of others, the event will convince them, that " they are reckoning without their hoft."

Put us, fay fome, on the footing we were on in fixty-three: To which I anfwer, the requeft is not *now* in the power of Britain to comply with, neither will fhe propofe it ; but if it were, and even fhould be granted, I afk, as a reafonable queftion, By what means is fuch a corrupt and faithlefs court to be kept to its engagements? Another parliament, nay, even the prefent, may hereafter repeal the obligation, on the pretence, of its being violently obtained, or un- wifely granted ; and in that cafe, Where is our redrefs?—No going to law with nations ; cannon are the barrifters of crowns ; and the fword, not of juftice, but of war, decides the fuit. To be on the footing of fixty-three, it is not fufficient, that the laws only be put on the fame ftate, but, that our circumftances, likewife, be put on the fame ftate ; our burnt and deftroyed towns repaired or built up, our private loffes made good, our public debts (contracted for defence) difcharged ; otherwife, we fhall be millions worfe than we were at that enviable period. Such a requeft, had it been complied with a year ago, would have won the heart and foul of the continent— but now it is too late " The Rubicon is paffed."

Befides, the taking up arms, merely to enforce the repeal of a pe- cuniary law, feems as unwarrantable by the divine law, and as repug- nant to human feelings, as the taking up arms to enforce obedience thereto. The object, on either fide, doth not juftify the means ; for the lives of men are too valuable to be caft away on fuch trifles. It is the violence which is done and threatened to our perfons ; the de-

ſtruction of our property by an armed force; the invaſion of our
country by fire and ſword, which conſcientiouſly qualifies the uſe of
arms: And the inſtant, in which ſuch a mode of defence became neceſſary, all ſubjection to Britain ought to have ceaſed; and the independency of America, ſhould have been conſidered, as dating its era
from, and publiſhed by, *the firſt muſket that was fired againſt her.*
This line is a line of conſiſtency; neither drawn by caprice, nor extended by ambition; but produced by a chain of events, of which
the colonies were not the authors.

I ſhall conclude theſe remarks, with the following timely and well-
intended hints. We ought to reflect, that there are three different
ways, by which an independency may hereafter be effected; and that
one of thoſe *three*, will, one day or other, be the fate of America,
viz. By the legal voice of the people in congreſs; by a military
power; or by a mob: It may not always happen that our ſoldiers
are citizens, and the multitude a body of reaſonable men; virtue, as
I have already remarked, is not hereditary, neither is it perpetual.
Should an independency be brought about by the firſt of thoſe
means, we have every opportunity and every encouragement before
us, to form the nobleſt, pureſt conſtitution on the face of the earth.
We have it in our power to begin the world over again. A ſituation,
ſimilar to the preſent, hath not happened ſince the days of Noah
until now. The birth-day of a new world is at hand, and a race of
men, perhaps as numerous as all Europe contains, are to receive their
portion of freedom from the events of a few months. The reflection
is awful—and in this point of view, How trifling, how ridiculous, do
the little, paltry cavillings, of a few weak or intereſted men appear,
when weighed againſt the buſineſs of a world.

Should we neglect the preſent favourable and inviting period, and
an independence be hereafter effected by any other means, we muſt
charge the conſequence to ourſelves, or to thoſe rather, whoſe narrow and prejudiced ſouls, are habitually oppoſing the meaſure, without either enquiring or reflecting. There are reaſons to be given in
ſupport of independence, which men ſhould rather privately think of,
than be publicly told of. We ought not now to be debating whether we ſhall be independent or not, but, anxious to accompliſh it on
a firm, ſecure, and honourable baſis, and uneaſy rather that it is not
yet began upon. Every day convinces us of its neceſſity. Even the
tories (if ſuch beings yet remain among us) ſhould, of all men, be the
moſt ſolicitous to promote it; for, as the appointment of committees

at firft, protected them from popular rage, fo, a wife and well-eftab-
lifhed form of government, will be the only certain means of continuing it fecurely to them. *Wherefore*, if they have not virtue enough
to be WHIGS, they ought to have prudence enough to wifh for
independence.

In fhort, independence is the only BOND that can tie and keep
us together. We fhall then fee our object, and our ears will be legally fhut againft the fchemes of an intriguing, as well as a cruel,
enemy. We fhall then too, be on a proper footing to treat with
Britain ; for there is reafon to conclude, that the pride of that court,
will be lefs hurt by treating with the American ftates for terms of
peace, than with thofe, whom fhe denominates, " rebellious fubjects," for terms of accommodation. It is our delaying it that encourages her to hope for conqueft, and our backwardnefs tends only
to prolong the war. As we have, without any good effect therefrom,
withheld our trade to obtain a redrefs of our grievances, let us *now*
try the alternative, by *independently* redreffing them ourfelves, and
then offering to open the trade. The mercantile and reafonable part
of England, will be ftill with us ; becaufe, peace *with* trade, is preferable to war *without* it. And if this offer be not accepted, other
courts may be applied to.

On thefe grounds I reft the matter. And as no offer hath yet
been made to refute the doctrine contained in the former editions of
this pamphlet, it is a negative proof, that either the doctrine cannot
be refuted, or, that the party in favour of it are too numerous to be
oppofed. WHEREFORE, inftead of gazing at each other, with
fufpicious or doubtful curiofity, let each of us, hold out to his neighbour the hearty hand of friendfhip, and unite in drawing a line,
which, like an act of oblivion, fhall bury in forgetfulnefs every former
diffention. Let the names of whig and tory be extinct ; and let
none other be heard among us, than thofe of *a good citizen, an open
and refolute friend, and a virtuous fupporter of the* rights *of* mankind
and of the FREE AND INDEPENDENT STATES OF
AMERICA.

END OF COMMON SENSE.

To the Reprefentatives of the Religious Society of the People called Quakers, or to fo many of them as were concerned in publifhing a late piece, entitled " THE ANCIENT TESTIMONY *and* PRINCIPLES *of the People called* QUAKERS *renewed, with refpect to the* KING *and* GOVERNMENT, *and touching the* COMMOTIONS *now prevailing in thefe and other parts of* AMERICA, *addreffed to the* PEOPLE IN GENERAL."

THE Writer of this is one of thofe few, who never difhonours religion either by ridiculing, or cavilling at any denomination whatfoever. To God, and not to man, are all men accountable on the fcore of religion. Wherefore, this epiftle is not fo properly addreffed to you as a religious, but as a political body, dabbling in matters, which the profeffed Quietude of your Principles inftruct you not to meddle with.

As you have, without a proper authority for fo doing, put yourfelves in the place of the whole body of the Quakers, fo the writer of this, in order to be on an equal rank with yourfelves, is under the neceffity of putting himfelf in the place of all thofe who approve the very writings and principles, againft which your teftimony is directed : And he hath chofen their fingular fituation, in order that you might difcover in him, that prefumption of character which you cannot fee in yourfelves. For neither he nor you have any claim or title to *Political Reprefentation.*

When men have departed from the right way, it is no wonder that they ftumble and fall. And it is evident from the manner in which ye have managed your teftimony, that politics (as a religious body of men) is not your proper walk ; for however well adapted it might appear to you, it is, neverthelefs, a jumble of good and bad put unwifely together, and the conclufion drawn therefrom, both unnatural and unjuft.

The two firft pages (and the whole doth not make four) we give you credit for, and expect the fame civility from you, becaufe the love and defire of peace is not confined to Quakerifm, it is the *natural*, as well as the religious wifh of all denominations of men. And on this ground, as men labouring to eftablifh an Independent Conftitution of our own, do we exceed all others in our hope, end, and

-sim. *Our plan is peace for ever.* We are tired of contention with Britain, and can fee no real end to it but in a final feparation. We act confiftently, becaufe for the fake of introducing an endlefs and uninterrupted peace, do we bear the evils and burdens of the prefent day. We are endeavouring, and will fteadily continue to endeavour, to feparate and diffolve a connexion which has already filled our land with blood ; and which, while the name of it remains, will be the fatal caufe of future mifchiefs to both countries.

We fight neither for revenge nor conqueft ; neither from pride nor paffion ; we are not infulting the world with our fleets and armies, nor ravaging the globe for plunder. Beneath the fhade of our own vines are we attacked ; in our own houfes, and on our own lands, is the violence committed againft us. We view our enemies in the characters of Highwaymen and Houfebreakers, and having no defence for ourfelves in the civil law, are obliged to punifh them by the military one, and apply the fword, in the very cafe where you have before now applied the halter.——Perhaps we feel for the ruined and infulted fufferers in all and every part of the continent, with a degree of tendernefs which hath not yet made its way into fome of your bofoms. But be ye fure that ye miftake not the caufe and ground of your Teftimony. Call not coldnefs of foul, religion ; nor put the *Bigot* in the place of the *Chriftian.*

O ye partial minifters of your own acknowledged principles ! If the bearing arms be finful, the firft going to war muft be more fo, by all the difference between wilful attack and unavoidable defence.

Wherefore if ye really preach from confcience, and mean not to make a political hobby-horfe of your religion, convince the world thereof, by proclaiming your doctrine to our enemies, *for they likewife bear* ARMS. Give us proof of your fincerity by publifhing it at St. James's, to the commanders in chief at Bofton, to the Admirals and Captains who are piratically ravaging our coafts, and to all the murdering mifcreants who are acting in authority under HIM whom ye profefs to ferve. Had ye the honeft foul of *Barclay*[*] ye would

---

[*] " *Thou haft tafted of profperity and adverfity ; thou knoweft what* " *it is to be banifhed thy native country, to be over-ruled as well as to rule,* " *and fet upon the throne ; and being* oppreffed *thou haft reafon to know* " *how* hateful *the* oppreffer *is both to God and man : If after all thefe* " *warnings and advertifements, thou doft not turn unto the Lord with all* " *thy heart, but forget him who remembered thee in thy diftrefs, and give*

preach repentance to *your* king ; Ye would tell the Royal tyrant his fins, and warn him of eternal ruin. Ye would not fpend your partial invectives againft the injured and infulted only, but like faithful minifters, would cry.aloud and *fpare none.* Say not that ye are perfecuted, neither endeavour to make us the authors of that reproach, which ye are bringing upon yourfelves ; for we teftify unto all men, that we do not complain againft you becaufe ye are *Quakers,* but becaufe ye pretend to.*be* and are ɴoᴛ Quakers.

Alas ! it feems by the particular tendency of fome part of your teftimony, and other parts of your conduct, as if all fin was reduced to, and comprehended in *the act of bearing arms,* and that by the *people only.* Ye appear to us, to have miftaken party for confcience ; becaufe the general tenor of your actions wants uniformity : and it is exceedingly difficult to us to give credit to many of your pretended fcruples ; becaufe we fee them made by the fame men, who, in the very inftant that they are exclaiming againft the mammon of this world, are, neverthelefs, hunting after it with a ftep as fteady as Time, and an appetite as keen as Death.

The quotation which ye have made from Proverbs, in the third page of your teftimony, that, " when a man's ways pleafe the Lord, he maketh even his enemies to be at peace with him ;" is very unwifely chofen on your part ; becaufe it amounts to a proof, that the king's ways (whom ye are fo defirous of fupporting) do *not* pleafe the Lord, otherwife his reign would be in peace.

I now proceed to the latter part of your teftimony, and that, for which all the foregoing feems only an introduction, viz.

" It hath ever been our judgment and principle, fince we were " called to profefs the light of Chrift Jefus, manifefted in our confci- " ences unto this day, that the fetting up and putting down kings " and governments, is God's peculiar perogative ; for caufes beft " known to himfelf: And that it is not our bufinefs to have any hand " or contrivance therein ; nor to be bufy bodies above our ftation,

" up *thyfelf to follow luft and vanity, furely great will be thy condemna-* " *tion.—Againft which fnare, as well as the temptation of thofe who* " *may or do feed thee, and prompt thee to evil, the moft excellent and pre-* " *valent remedy will be, to apply thyfelf to that light of Chrift which* " *fhineth in thy confcience, and which neither can, nor will flatter thee,* " *nor fuffer thee to be at eafe in thy fins."*

Barclay's Addrefs to Charles II.

" much lefs to plot and contrive the ruin, or overturn any of them,
" but to pray for the king, and fafety of our nation, and good of all
" men : That we may live a peaceable and quiet life, in all goodli-
" nefs and honefty ; *under the government which God is pleafed to fet*
" *over us.*"——If thefe are *really* your principles why do ye not
abide by them ? Why do ye not leave that, which ye call God's
Work, to be managed by himfelf ? Thefe very principles inftruct
you to wait with patience and humility, for the event of all public
meafures, and to receive *that event* as the divine will towards you.
Wherefore, what occafion is there for your *political teftimony* if you
fully believe what it contains ? And the very publifhing it proves,
that either ye do not believe what ye profefs, or have not virtue
enough to practife what ye believe.

The principles of Quakerifm have a direct tendency to make a man
the quiet and inoffenfive fubject of any, and every government *which
is fet over him.* And if the fetting up and putting down of kings
and governments is God's peculiar perogative, he moft certainly will
not be robbed thereof by us ; wherefore, the principle itfelf leads you
to approve of every thing; which ever happened, or may happen to
kings as being his work. OLIVER CROMWELL thanks you.——
CHARLES, then, died not by the hands of man ; and fhould the prefent
Proud Imitator of him come to the fame untimely end, the writers
and publifhers of the teftimony, are bound by the doctrine it contains,
to applaud the fact. Kings are not taken away by miracles, neither
are changes in governments brought about by any other means than
fuch as are common and human ; and fuch as we are now ufing. Even
the difperfing of the Jews, though foretold by our Saviour, was effected by arms. Wherefore, as ye refufe to be the means on one fide,
ye ought not to be meddlers on the other ; but to wait the iffue in
filence ; and unlefs you can produce divine authority, to prove, that
the Almighty who hath created and placed this *new* world, at the
greateft diftance it could poffibly ftand, eaft and weft, from every part
of the old, doth, neverthelefs, difapprove of its being independent
of the corrupt and abandoned court of Britain ; unlefs, I fay, ye can
fhew this, how can ye, on the ground of your principles, juftify the
exciting and ftirring up the people " firmly to unite in the *abhorrence*
" of all fuch *writings*, and *meafures*, as evince a defire and defign to
" break off the *happy* connexion we have hitherto enjoyed, with the
" kingdom of Great Britain, and our juft and neceffary fubordination
" to the king, and thofe who are lawfully placed in authority under

" him." What a flap in the face is here! the men, who, in the very paragraph before, have quietly and passively resigned up the ordering, altering and disposal of kings and governments, into the hands of God, are now recalling their principles, and putting in for a share of the business. Is it possible, that the conclusion, which is here justly quoted, can any ways follow from the doctrine laid down ! The inconsistency is too glaring not to be seen; the absurdity too great not to be laughed at ; and such as could only have been made by those, whose understandings were darkened by the narrow and crabby spirit of a despairing political party ; for ye are not to be considered as the whole body of the Quakers, but only as a factional and fractional part thereof.

Here ends the examination of your testimony (which I call upon no man to abhor, as ye have done, but only to read and judge of fairly) ; to which I subjoin the following remark; " That the setting up " and putting down of kings," must certainly mean, the making him a king, who is yet not so, and the making him no king who is already one. And pray what hath this to do in the present case? We neither may to set up nor to put down, neither to make nor to unmake, but to have nothing to do with them. Wherefore your testimony, in whatever light it is viewed, serves only to dishonour your judgment, and for many other reasons had better have been let alone than published.

First. Because it tends to the decrease and reproach of all religion whatever, and is of the utmost danger to society, to make it a party in political disputes.

Secondly. Because it exhibits a body of men, numbers of whom disavow the publishing political testimonies, as being concerned therein and approvers thereof.

Thirdly. Because it hath a tendency to undo that continental harmony and friendship which yourselves by your late liberal and charitable donations hath lent a hand to establish ; and the preservation of which, is of the utmost consequence to us all.

And here without anger, or resentment I bid you farewel. Sincerely wishing, that as men and Christians, ye may always fully and uninterruptedly enjoy every civil and religious right; and he, in your turn, the means of securing it to others ; but that the example which ye have unwisely set, of mingling religion with politics, *may be disavowed and reprobated by every inhabitant of* AMERICA.

THE CRISIS.

NUMBER I.

December 23, 1776.

THESE are the times that try men's souls. The summer soldier and the sublime patriot will, in this crisis, shrink from the service of his country; but he that stands it NOW, deserves the love and thanks of man and woman. Tyranny, like hell, is not easily conquered; yet we have this consolation with us, that the harder the conflict, the more glorious the triumph. What we obtain too cheap, we esteem too lightly: 'Tis dearness only that gives every thing its value. Heaven knows how to put a proper price upon its goods; and it would be strange indeed, if so celestial an article as FREEDOM should not be highly rated. Britain, with an army to enforce her tyranny, has declared that she has a right *(not only to* TAX) but "*to* BIND *us in* ALL CASES WHATSOEVER," and if being *bound in that manner,* is not slavery, then is there not such a thing as slavery upon earth. Even the expression is impious, for so unlimited a power can belong only to GOD.

Whether the independence of the continent was declared too soon, or delayed too long, I will not now enter into as an argument; my own simple opinion is, that had it been eight months earlier, it would have been much better. We did not make a proper use of last winter, neither could we, while we were in a dependant state. However, the fault, if it were one, was all our own; we have none to blame but ourselves. But no great deal is lost yet; all that Howe has been doing for this month past is rather a ravage than a conquest, which the spirit of the Jerseys a-year ago would have quickly repulsed, and which time and a little resolution will soon recover.

I have as little superstition in me as any man living, but my secret opinion has ever been, and still is, that God Almighty will not give up a people to military destruction, or leave them unsupportedly to perish, who had so earnestly and so repeatedly sought to avoid the calamities of war, by every decent method which wifdom could invent. Neither have I fo much of the infidel in me, as to fuppofe that HE has relinquifhed the government of the world, and given us up to the care of devils ; and as I do not, I cannot fee on what grounds the king of Britain can look up to Heaven for help againft us : A common murderer, a highwayman, or a houfe-breaker, has as good a pretence as he.

'Tis furprifing to fee how rapidly a panic will fometimes run through a country. All nations and ages have been fubject to them : Britain has trembled like an ague at the report of a French fleet of flat bottomed boats; and in the fourteenth century the whole Englifh army, after ravaging the kingdom of France, was driven back like men petrified with fear ; and this brave exploit was performed by a few broken forces collected and headed by a woman, Joan of Arc. Would, that Heaven might infpire fome Jerfey maid to fpirit up her countrymen, and fave her fair fellow fufferers from ravage and ravifh-ment ! Yet panics, in fome cafes, have their ufes, they produce as much good as hurt. Their duration is always fhort ; the mind foon grows through them, and acquires a firmer habit than before. But their peculiar advantage is, that they are the touchftones of fincerity and hypocrify, and bring things and men to light, which might otherwife have lain for ever undifcovered. In fact, they have the fame effect on fecret traitors, which an imaginary apparition would have upon a private murderer. They fift out the hidden thoughts of man, and hold them up in public to the world. Many a difguifed tory has lately fhewn his head, that fhall penitentially fo-lemnize with curfes the day on which Howe arrived upon the Delaware.

As I was with the troops at Fort-Lee, and marched with them to the edge of Pennfylvania, I am well acquainted with many circum-ftances, which thofe who lived at a diftance know but little or no-thing of. Our fituation there was exceedingly cramped, the place being on a narrow neck of land between the North River and the Hackenfack. Our force was inconfiderable, being not one fourth fo great as Howe could bring againft us. We had no army at hand to have relieved the garrifon, had we fhut ourfelves up and ftood on the defence. Our ammunition, light artillery, and the beft part of our ftores, had been removed upon the apprehenfion that Howe would endeavour to penetrate the Jerfeys, in which cafe Fort-Lee could be of no ufe to us ; for it muft occur to every thinking man, whether in

the army or not, that thefe kind of field forts are only for temporary
purpofes, and laft in ufe no longer than the enemy directs his force
againft the particular object, which fuch forts are raifed to defend.
Such was our fituation and condition at Fort-Lee on the morning of
the 20th of November, when an officer arrived with information that
the enemy with 200 boats had landed about feven or eight miles above:
Major General Greene, who commanded the garrifon, immediately
ordered them under arms, and fent exprefs to his Excellency General
Wafhington at the town of Hackenfack, diftant by the way of the
ferry fix miles.   Our firft object was to fecure the bridge over the
Hackenfack, which laid up the river between the enemy and us,
about fix miles from us, and three from them.   General Wafhington
arrived in about three quarters of an hour, and marched at the head
of the troops towards the bridge, which place I expected we fhould
have a brufh for; however they did not choofe to difpute it with us, and
the greateft part of our troops went over the bridge, the reft over the
ferry, except fome which paffed at a mill on a fmall creek, between
the bridge and the ferry, and made their way through fome marfhy
grounds up to the town of Hackenfack, and there paffed the river.
We brought off as much baggage as the waggons could contain, the
reft was loft.   The fimple object was to bring off the garrifon, and
to march them on till they could be ftrengthened by the Jerfey or
Pennfylvania militia, fo as to be enabled to make a ftand.   We ftaid
four days at Newark, collected in our out-pofts with fome of the Jerfey
militia, and marched out twice to meet the enemy on information of
their being advancing, though our numbers were greatly inferior to
theirs.   Howe, in my little opinion, committed a great error in generalfhip in not throwing a body of forces off from Staten-Ifland
through Amboy, by which means he might have feized all our ftores
at Brunfwick, and intercepted our march into Pennfylvania: But if
we believe the power of hell to be limited, we muft likewife believe
that their agents are under fome providential control.

    I fhall not now attempt to give all the particulars of our retreat to
the Delaware; fuffice it for the prefent to fay, that both officers and
men, though greatly haraffed and fatigued, frequently without reft,
covering, or provifion, the inevitable confequences of a long retreat,
bore it with a manly and martial fpirit.   All their wifhes were one,
which was, that the country would turn out and help them to drive
the enemy back.   Voltaire has remarked that King William never
appeared to full advantage but in difficulties and in action; the fame

remark may be made on General Washington, for the character fits him. There is a natural firmness in some minds which cannot be unlocked by trifles, but which, when unlocked, discovers a cabinet of fortitude; and I reckon it among those kind of public blessings, which we do not immediately see, that GOD hath blest him with uninterrupted health, and given him a mind that can even flourish upon care.

I shall conclude this paper with some miscellaneous remarks on the state of our affairs ; and shall begin with asking the following question. Why is it that the enemy have left the New-England provinces, and made these middle ones the seat of war? The answer is easy : New-England is not infested with tories, and we are. I have been tender in raising the cry against these men, and used numberless arguments to shew them their danger, but it will not do to sacrifice a world to either their folly or their baseness. The period is now arrived, in which either they or we must change our sentiments, or one or both must fail. And what is a tory? Good GOD! what is he? I should not be afraid to go with an hundred whigs against a thousand tories, were they to attempt to get into arms. Every tory is a coward, for a servile, slavish, self-interested fear is the foundation of toryism ; and a man under such influence, though he may be cruel, never can be brave.

But, before the line of irrecoverable separation be drawn between us, let us reason the matter together : Your conduct is an invitation to the enemy, yet not one in a thousand of you has heart enough to join him. Howe is as much deceived by you as the American cause is injured by you. He expects you will all take up arms, and flock to his standard with muskets on your shoulders. Your opinions are of no use to him, unless you support him personally, for 'tis soldiers, and not tories, that he wants.

I once felt all that kind of anger, which a man ought to feel, against the mean principles that are held by the tories : A noted one, who kept a tavern at Amboy, was standing at his door, with as pretty a child in his hand, about eight or nine years old, as most I ever saw, and after speaking his mind as freely as he thought was prudent, finished with this unfatherly expression, " *Well ! give me peace in my day.*" Not a man lives on the continent but fully believes that a separation must some time or other finally take place, and a generous parent should have said, " *If there must be trouble, let it be in my day, that my child may have peace ;*" and this single reflection, well applied, is fufficient to awaken every man to duty. Not a place upon earth might be fo happy as America. Her fituation is remote from all the wrangling world, and fhe has nothing to do but to trade with them. A man may eafily diftinguifh in himfelf between temper and principle, and I am as confident, as I am that GOD governs the world, that America will never be happy till fhe gets clear of foreign dominion. Wars, without ceafing, will break out till that period arrives, and the continent muft in the end be conqueror ; for though the flame of liberty may fometimes ceafe to fhine, the coal can never expire.

America did not, nor does not want force ; but fhe wanted a proper application of that force. Wifdom is not the purchafe of a day, and it is no wonder that we fhould err at the firft fetting off. From an excefs of tendernefs, we were unwilling to raife an army, and trufted our caufe to the temporary defence of a well-meaning militia. A fummer's experience has now taught us better ; yet with thofe troops, while they were collected, we were able to fet bounds to the progrefs of the enemy, and, thank GOD ! they are again affembling. I always confidered a militia as the beft troops in the world for a fudden exertion, but they will not do for a long campaign. Howe, it is probable, will make an attempt on this city ; fhould he fail on this fide the Delaware, he is ruined : If he fucceeds, our caufe is not ruined. He ftakes all on his fide againft a part on ours; admitting he fucceeds, the confequence will be, that armies from both ends of the continent will march to affift their fuffering friends in the middle ftates ; for he cannot go every where, it is impoffible. I confider Howe as the greateft enemy the tories have ; he is bringing a war into their country, which, had it not been for him and partly for themfelves, they had been clear of. Should he now be expelled, I wifh with all the devotion of a Chriftian, that the names of whig and tory may never more be mentioned ; but fhould the tories give him encouragement to come, or affiftance if he come, I as fincerely wifh that our next year's arms may expel them from the continent, and the congrefs appropriate their poffeffions to the relief of thofe who have fuffered in well-doing. A fingle fuccefsful battle next year will fettle the whole. America could carry on a two years war by the confifcation of the property of difaffected perfons, and be made happy by their expulfion. Say not that this is revenge, call it rather the foft refentment of a fuffering people, who, having no object in view but the GOOD of ALL, have ftaked their OWN ALL upon a feemingly doubtful event. Yet it is folly to argue against determined hardnefs ; eloquence may ftrike the ear, and the language of forrow draw forth the tear of compaffion, but nothing can reach the heart that is fteeled with prejudice.

Quitting this clafs of men, I turn with the warm ardour of a friend to thofe who have nobly ftood, and are yet determined to ftand the matter out : I call not upon a few, but upon all : not on THIS ftate or THAT ftate, but on EVERY ftate ; up and help us ; lay your fhoulders to the wheel ; better have too much force than too little, when fo great an object is at ftake. Let it be told to the future world, that in the depth of winter, when nothing but hope and virtue could furvive, that the city and the country, alarmed at one common danger, came forth to meet and to repulfe it. Say not, that thoufands are gone, turn out your tens of thoufands ; throw not the burden of the day upon Providence, but *" fhew your faith by your works,"* that God may blefs you. It matters not where you live, or what rank of life you hold, the evil or the bleffing will reach you all. The far and the near, the home counties and the back, the rich and the poor, will fuffer or rejoice alike. The heart that feels not now, is dead : The blood of his children will curfe his cowardice, who fhrinks back at a time when a little might have faved the whole, and made *them* happy. I love the man that can fmile in trouble, that can gather ftrength from diftrefs, and grow brave by reflection. 'Tis the bufinefs of little minds to fhrink ; but he whofe heart is firm, and whofe confcience approves his conduct, will purfue his principles unto death. My own line of reafoning is to myfelf as ftrait and clear as a ray of light. Not all the treafures of the world, fo far as I believe, could have induced me to fupport an offenfive war, for I think it murder ; but if a thief break into my houfe, burn and deftroy my property, and kill or threaten to kill me, or thofe that are in it, and to *" bind me in all cafes whatfoever,"* to his abfolute will, am I to fuffer it ? What fignifies it to me, whether he who does it, is a king or a common man ; my countryman or not my countryman ? whether it is done by an individual villain, or an army of them ? If we reafon to the root of things we fhall find no difference ; neither can any juft caufe be affigned why we fhould punifh in the one cafe and pardon in the other. Let them call me rebel, and welcome, I feel no concern from it ; but I fhould fuffer the mifery of devils, were I to make a whore of my foul by fwearing allegiance to one whofe character is that of a fottifh, ftupid, ftubborn worthlefs, brutifh man. I conceive likewife a horrid idea in receiving

mercy from a being, who at the laft day fhall be fhrieking to the
rocks and mountains to cover him, and fleeing with terror from the
orphan, the widow, and the flain of America.

There are cafes which cannot be overdone by language, and this is
one. There are perfons too who fee not the full extent of the evil which
threatens them, they folace themfelves with hopes that the enemy, if
they fucceed, will be merciful. It is the madnefs of folly to expect
mercy from thofe who have refufed to do juftice ; and even mercy,
where conqueft is the object, is only a trick of war : The cunning of
the fox is as murderous as the violence of the wolf; and we ought to
guard equally againft both. Howe's firft object is partly by threats
and partly by promife, to terrify or feduce the people to deliver up
their arms, and receive mercy. The miniftry recommended the fame
plan to Gage, and this is what the tories call making their peace ;
" *a peace which paffeth all underftanding*" indeed! A peace which would
be the immediate forerunner of a worfe ruin than any we have yet
thought of. Ye men of Pennfylvania, do reafon upon thefe things!
Were the back countries to give up their arms, they would fall an
eafy prey to the Indians, who are all alarmed : This perhaps is what
fome tories would not be forry for. Were the home counties to deliver
up their arms, they would be expofed to the refentment of the back
counties, who would then have it in their power to chaftife their defection at pleafure. And were any one ftate to give up its arms,
THAT ftate muft be garrifoned by all Howe's army of Britons and
Heffians to preferve it from the anger of the reft. Mutual fear is a
principal link in the chain of mutual love, and woe be to that ftate
that breaks the compact. Howe is mercifully inviting you to barbarous deftruction, and men muft be either rogues or fools that will
not fee it. I dwell not upon the powers of imagination; I bring reafon to your ears; and in language as plain as A, B, C, hold up truth
to your eyes.

I thank GOD that I fear not. I fee no real caufe for fear. I know
our fituation well, and can fee the way out of it. While our army
was collected, Howe, dared not rifk a battle, and it is no credit to him
that he decamped from the White Plains, and waited a mean opportunity to ravage the defencelefs Jerfeys ; but it is great credit to us,
that, with a handful of men, we fuftained an orderly retreat for near
an hundred miles, brought off our ammunition, all our field pieces, the
greateft part of our ftores, and had four rivers to pafs. None can fay
that our retreat was precipitate, for we were near three weeks in per-

forming it, that the country might have time to come in. Twice we marched back to meet the enemy and remained out till dark. The sign of fear was not seen in our camp, and had not some of the cowardly and disaffected inhabitants spread false alarms through the country, the Jerseys had never been ravaged. Once more we are again collected and collecting, our new army at both ends of the continent is recruiting fast, and we shall be able to open the next campaign with sixty thousand men, well armed and cloathed. This is our situation, and who will may know it. By perseverance and fortitude we have the prospect of a glorious issue; by cowardice and submission, the sad choice of a variety of evils—a ravaged country—a depopulated city —habitations without safety, and slavery without hope—our homes turned into barracks and bawdy-houses for Hessians, and a future race to provide for whose fathers we shall doubt of. Look on this picture and weep over it! and if there yet remains one thoughtless wretch who believes it not, let him suffer it unlamented.

COMMON SENSE.

THE CRISIS.—NUMBER II.

Philadelphia, January 13, 1777.

TO LORD HOWE.

" *What's in the name of* LORD *that I should fear,*
" *To bring my grievance to the public ear ?*"

CHURCHILL.

UNIVERSAL empire is the prerogative of a writer. His concerns are with all mankind, and though he cannot command their obedience, he can assign them their duty. The Republic of Letters is more ancient than monarchy, and of far higher character in the world, than the vassal court of Britain; he that rebels against reason is a real rebel, but he that in defence of reason, rebels against tyranny, has a better title to " DEFENDER OF THE FAITH," than George the Third.

As a military man your lordship may hold out the sword of war, and call it the " *Ultima Ratio Regum :*" *The last reason of kings ;* we in return can show you the sword of justice, and call it, " The beſt ſcourge of tyrants." The firſt of theſe two may threaten, or even frighten, for a while, and caſt a ſickly langour over an inſulted people, but reaſon will ſoon recover the debauch, and reſtore them again to tranquil fortitude. Your lordſhip, I find, has now commenced author, and publiſhed a Proclamation; 1 have publiſhed a Criſis; as they ſtand, they are the antipodes of each other; both cannot riſe at once, and one of them muſt deſcend:——And ſo quick is the revolution of things, that your lordſhip's performance, I ſee, has already fallen many degrees from its firſt place, and is now juſt viſible on the edge of the political horizon.

It is ſurpriſing to what pitch of infatuation blind folly and obſtinacy will carry mankind, and your lordſhip's drowſy proclamation is a proof that it does not even quit them in their ſleep. Perhaps you thought America too was taking a nap, and therefore choſe, like Satan to Eve, to whiſper the deluſion ſoftly, leſt you ſhould awaken her. This continent, ſir, is too extenſive to ſleep all at once, and too watchful, even in its ſlumbers, not to ſtartle at the unhallowed foot of an invader. You may iſſue your proclamations, and welcome, for we have learned to " reverence ourſelves," and ſcorn the inſulting ruffian that employs you. America, for your deceaſed brother's ſake, would gladly have ſhewn you reſpect, and it is a new aggravation to her feelings, that Howe ſhould be forgetful, and raiſe his ſword againſt thoſe, who at their own charge raiſed a monument to his brother. But your maſter has commanded, and you have not enough of nature left to refuſe. Surely! there muſt be ſomething ſtrangely degenerating in the love of monarchy, that can ſo completely wear a man down to an ingrate, and make him proud to lick the duſt that kings have trod upon. A few more years, ſhould you ſurvive them, will beſtow on you the title of ' an old man :' And in ſome hour of future reflection you may probably find the likeneſs of Wolſey's deſpairing penitence—" had I ſerved my God as faith- " fully as I have ſerved my king, he would not thus have forſaken " me in my old age."

The character you appear to us in is truly ridiculous. Your friends, the tories, announced your coming, with high deſcriptions of your unlimited powers; but your proclamation has given them the lie, by ſhewing you to be a commiſſioner without authority. Had your powers been ever ſo great, they were nothing to us, farther than we pleaſed; becauſe we had the ſame right which other nations had, to do what we thought was beſt. " *The* UNITED STATES *of*

AMERICA" will found as pompoufly in the world or in hiftory, as " The kingdom of Great-Britain ;" the character of *general Wafhington*, will fill a page with as much luftre as that of *lord Howe :* and the *congrefs* have as much right to command the *king and parliament* of London, to defift from legiflation, as *they* or *you* have to command the congrefs. Only fuppofe how laughable fuch an edict would appear from us, and then, in that merry mood, do but turn the tables upon yourfelf, and you will fee how your proclamation is received here. Having thus placed you in a proper pofition in which you may have a full view of folly, and learn to defpife it, I hold up to you, for that purpofe, the following quotation from your own lunarian proclamation.—" And we (lord Howe and general Howe) do command (and in his majefty's name forfooth) all fuch perfons as are affembled together, under the name of general or provincial congreffes, committees, conventions or other affociations, by whatever name or names known and diftinguifhed, to defift and ceafe from all fuch treafonable actings and doings."

You introduce your proclamation by referring to your declarations of the 14th of July and 19th of September. In the laft of thefe, you funk yourfelf below the character of a private gentleman. That I may not feem to accufe you unjuftly, I fhall ftate the circumftance: By a verbal invitation of yours, communicated to congrefs by general Sullivan, then a prifoner on his parole, you fignified your defire of conferring with fome members of that body as private gentlemen. It was beneath the dignity of the American Congrefs to pay any regard to a meffage that at beft was but a genteel affront, and had too much of the minifterial complexion of tampering with private perfons ; and which might probably have been the cafe, had the gentlemen who were deputed on the bufinefs, poffeffed that kind of eafy virtue which an Englifh courtier is fo truly diftinguifhed by. Your requeft however was complied with, for honeft men are naturally more tender of their civil than their political fame. The interview ended as every fenfible man thought it would ; for your lordfhip knows, as well as the writer of the Crifis, that it is impoffible for the king of England to promife the repeal, or even the revifal of any acts of parliament ; wherefore, on your part, you had nothing to fay, more than to requeft, in the room of demanding, the entire furrender of the continent ; and then, if that was complied with, to promife that the inhabitants fhould efcape with their lives. This was the upfhot of the conference. You informed the conferees that you were two months in foliciting thefe powers. We afk, What powers? for as commiffioner you have none. If you mean the power of pardoning, it is an oblique proof that your mafter was determined to facrifice all before him; and that you were two months in diffuading him from his purpofe Another evidence of his favage obftinacy! From your own account of the matter we may juftly draw thefe two conclufions: firft, that you ferve a monfter; and fecondly, that never was a meffenger fent on a more foolifh errand than yourfelf. This plain language may perhaps found uncouthly to an ear vitiated by courtly refinements; but words were made for ufe, and the fault lies in deferving them, or the abufe in applying them unfairly.

Soon after your return to New-York, you publifhed a very illiberal and unmanly hand bill againft the congrefs; for it was certainly ftepping out of the line of common civility, firft to fcreen your national pride by foliciting an interview with them as private gentlemen, and in the conclufion to endeavour to deceive the multitude by making a hand bill attack on the whole body of the congrefs; you got them together under one name, and abufed them under another. But the king you ferve, and the caufe you fupport, afford you fo few inftances of acting the gentleman, that out of pity to your fituation the congrefs pardoned the infult by taking no notice of it.

You fay in that hand bill, " that they, the congrefs, difavowed every purpofe for reconciliation not confonant with their extravagant. and inadmiffible claim of independence." Why, God blefs me! what have you to do with our independence? We afk no leave of yours to fet it up; we afk no money of yours to fupport it; we can do better without your fleets and armies than with them; you may foon have enough to do to protect yourfelves without being burdened with us. We are very willing to be at peace with you, to buy of you and fell to you, and, like young beginners in the world, to work for our own living; therefore, why do you put yourfelves out of cafh, when we know you cannot fpare it, and we do not defire you to run into debt? I am willing, fir, you fhould fee your folly in every view I can place it, and for that reafon defcend fometimes to tell you in jeft what I wifh you to fee in earneft. But to be more ferious with you, why do you fay, " their independence?" To fet you right, fir, we tell you, that the independency is ours, not theirs. The congrefs were authorifed by every ftate on the continent to publifh it to all the world, and in fo doing are not to be confidered as the inventors, but only as

the heralds that proclaimed it, or the office from which the fenfe of
the people received a legal form ; and it was as much as any or all
their heads were worth, to have treated with you on the fubject of
fubmiffion under any name whatever. But we know the men in whom
we have trufted; can England fay the fame of her parliament?

I come now more particularly to your proclamation of the 30th of
November laft. Had you gained an entire conqueft over all the armies of America, and then put forth a proclamation, offering (what
you call) mercy, your conduct would have had fome fpecious fhow of
humanity ; but to creep by furprife into a province, and there endeavour to terrify and feduce the inhabitants from their juft allegiance
to the reft by promifes, which you neither meant, nor were able to
fulfil, is both cruel and unmanly : Cruel in its effects; becaufe, unlefs
you can keep all the ground you have marched over, how are you, in
the words of your proclamation to fecure to your profelytes " the enjoyment of their property?" What are to become either of your new
adopted fubjects, of your old friends the tories, in Burlington, Bor-
dentown, Trenton, Mountholly, and many other places, where you
proudly lorded it for a few days, and then fled with the precipitation
of a purfued thief? What, I fay, are to become of thofe wretches?
What are to become of thofe who went over to you from this city and
ftate? What more can you fay to them than " Shift for yourfelves?"
Or what more can they hope for than to wander like vagabonds over
the face of the earth? You may now tell them to take their leave of
America, and all that once was theirs. Recommend them, for confolation, to your mafter's court; there perhaps they may make a fhift
to live on the fcraps of fome dangling parafite, and choofe companions
among thoufands like themfelves. A traitor is the fouleft fiend on
earth!

In a political fenfe we ought to thank you for thus bequeathing eftates to the continent; we fhall foon, at this rate, be able to carry on a
war without expence, and grow rich by the ill policy of lord Howe,
and the generous defection of the tories. Had you fet your foot into
this city, you would have beftowed eftates upon us which we never
thought of, by bringing forth traitors we were unwilling to fufpect.
But thefe men, you'll fay, " are his majefty's moft faithful fubjects ;"
let that honour then be all their fortune, and let his majefty take them
to himfelf.

I am now thoroughly difgufted with them ; they live in ungrateful
eafe, and bend their whole minds to mifchief. It feems as if God

had given them over to a fpirit of infidelity, and that they are open to conviction in no other line but that of punifhment. It is time to have done with tarring, feathering, carting, and taking fecurities for their future good behaviour; every fenfible man muft feel a confcious fhame at feeing a poor fellow hawked for a fhow about the ftreets, when it is known he is only the tool of fome principal villain, biaffed into his offence by the force of falfe reafoning, or bribed thereto through fad neceffity. We difhonour ourfelves by attacking fuch trifling characters, while greater ones are fuffered to efcape; 'tis our duty to find *them* out, and their proper punifhment would be to exile them from the continent for ever. The circle of them is not fo great as fome imagine ; the influence of a few have tainted many who are not naturally corrupt. A continual circulation of lies among thofe who are not much in the way of hearing them contradicted, will in time pafs for truth; and the crime lies not in the believer but the inventor. I am not for declaring war againft every man that appears not fo warm as myfelf: Difference of conftitution, temper, habit of fpeaking, and many other things will go a great way in fixing the outward character of a man, yet fimple honefty may remain at bottom. Some men have naturally a military turn, and can brave hardfhips and the rifk of life with a cheerful face ; others have not ; no flavery appears to them fo great as the fatigue of arms, and no terror fo powerful as that of perfonal danger : What can we fay ? We cannot alter nature, neither ought we to punifh the fon becaufe the father begot him in a cowardly mood. However, I believe moft men have more courage than they know of, and that a little at firft is enough to begin with. I knew the time when I thought that the whittling of a cannon ball would have frightened me almoft to death: but I have fince tried it, and find I can ftand it with as little difcompofure, and, I believe, with a much eafier confcience than your lordfhip. The fame dread would return to me again were I in your fituation, for my folemn belief of your caufe is, that it is heilifh and damnable, and under that conviction every thinking man's heart *muft* fail him.

From a concern that a good caufe fhould be difhonoured by the leaft difunion among us, I faid in my former paper, No. I. " That fhould the enemy now be expelled, I wifh, with all the fincerity of a Chriftian, that the names of whig and tory might never more be mentioned," but there is a knot of men among us of fuch a venomous caft, that they will not admit even one's good wifhes to act in their favour. Inftead of rejoicing that heaven had, as it were, providentially preferved this city from plunder and deftruction, by delivering fo great a part of the enemy into our hands with fo little effufion of blood, they ftubbornly affected to difbelieve it till within an hour, nay, half an hour, of the prifoners arriving; and the Quakers put forth a teftimony, dated the 20th of December, figned, " John Pemberton," declaring their attachment to the Britifh government.* Thefe men are continually harping on the great fin of *our* bearing arms, but the king of Britain may lay wafte the world in blood and famine, and they, poor fallen fouls, have nothing to fay.

In fome future paper I intend to diftinguifh between the different kind of perfons who have been denominated tories; for this I am clear in, that all are not fo who have been called fo, nor all men whigs who were once thought fo; and as I mean not to conceal the name of any true friend when there fhall be occafion to mention him, neither will I that of an enemy who ought to be known, let his rank, ftation or religion be what it may. Much pains have been taken by fome to fet your lordfhip's private character in an amiable light, but as it has chiefly been done by men who know nothing about you, and who are no ways remarkable for their attachment to us, we have no juft authority for believing it. George the third was impofed upon us by the fame arts, but TIME, at length, has done him juftice, and the fame fate may probably attend your lordfhip. Your avowed purpofe here, is to kill, conquer, plunder, pardon, and enflave; and the ravages of your army through the Jerfeys have been marked with as much barbarifm as if you had openly profeffed yourfelf the prince of ruffians; not even the appearance of humanity has been preferved either on the march or the retreat of your troops; no general order that I could ever learn, has ever been iffued to prevent or even forbid your troops from robbery, wherever they came, and the only inftance of juftice, if it can be called fuch, which has diftinguifhed you for impartiality, is, that you treated

---

* *I have ever been careful of charging offences upon whole focieties of men, but as the paper referred to is put forth by an unknown fet of men, who claim to themfelves the right of reprefenting the whole; and while the whole fociety of Quakers admit its validity by a filent acknowledgment, it is impoffible that any diftinction can be made by the public; and the more fo, becaufe the New-York paper of the 30th of December, printed by permiffion of our enemies, fays that " the Quakers begin to fpeak openly of their attachment to the Britifh conftitution." We are certain that we have many friends among them, and wifh to know them.*

and plundered all alike ; what could not be carried away has been destroyed, and mahogany furniture has been deliberately laid on the fire for fuel, rather than the men should be fatigued with cutting wood.* There was a time when the whigs confided much in your supposed candour, and the tories rested themselves in your favour ; the experiments have now been made, and failed; in every town, nay every cottage, in the Jerseys, where your arms have been, is a testimony against you. How you may rest under this sacrifice of character I know not ; but this I know, that you sleep and rise with the daily curses of thousands upon you ; perhaps the misery which the tories have suffered by your proffered mercy may give them some claim to their country's pity, and be in the end the best favour you could shew them.

In a folio general-order book belonging to colonel Rhol's battalion, taken at Trenton, and now in the possession of the council of safety for this state, the following barbarous order is frequently repeated, " His excellency the COMMANDER IN CHIEF orders, that all " inhabitants who shall be found with arms, not having an officer " with them, shall be immediately taken and hung up." How many you may thus have privately sacrificed we know not, and the account can only be settled in another world. Your treatment of prisoners, in order to distress them to enlist into your infernal service, is not to be equalled by any instance in Europe. Yet this is the humane lord Howe and his brother, whom the tories and their three quarter kindred the Quakers, or some of them at least, have been holding up for patterns of justice and mercy !

A bad cause will ever be supported by bad means, and bad men, and whoever will be at the pains of examining strictly into things, will find that one and the same spirit of oppression and impiety, more or less, governs through your whole party in both countries : Not many days ago I accidentally fell in company with a person of this city, noted for espousing your cause, and on my remarking to him, " that it appeared clear to me, by the late providential turn of affairs, that GOD Almighty was visibly on our side," he replied, " We care

* *As some people may doubt the truth of such wanton destruction, I think it necessary to inform, that one of the people called Quakers, who lives at Trenton, gave me this information at the house of Mr. Michael Hutchinson (one of the same profession) who lives near to Trenton ferry, on the Pennsylvania side, Mr. Hutchinson being present.*

nothing for that, you may have HIM, and welcome; if we have but enough of the devil on our fide we fhall do." However carelefsly this might be fpoken matters not, 'tis ftill the infenfible principle that directs all your conduct, and will at laft moft affuredly deceive and ruin you.

If ever a nation was mad and foolifh, blind to its own intereft and bent on its own deftruction, it is Britain. There are fuch things as national fins, and though the punifhment of individuals may be referved to another world, national punifhment can only be inflicted in this world. Britain, as a nation, is in my inmoft belief the greateft and moft ungrateful offender againft GOD on the face of the whole earth: Bleffed with all the commerce fhe could wifh for, and furnifhed by a vaft extenfion of dominion, with the means of civilizing both the eaftern and weftern world, fhe has made no other ufe of both than proudly to idolize her own " Thunder," and rip up the bowels of whole countries for what fhe could get :—Like Alexander fhe has made war her fport, and inflicted mifery for prodigality fake. The blood of India is not yet repaid, nor the wretchednefs of Africa yet requited. Of late fhe has enlarged her lift of national cruelties, by her butcheriy deftruction of the Caribbs of St. Vincents, and in returning an anfwer by the fword to the meek prayer for " *Peace, liberty and fafety.*" Thefe are ferious things, and whatever a foolifh tyrant, a debauched court, a trafficking legiflature or a blinded people may think, the national account with heaven muft fome day or other be fettled: All countries have fooner or later been called to their reckoning; the proudeft empires have funk when the balance was ftruck; and Britain, like an individual penitent, muft undergo her day of forrow, and the fooner it happens to her the better: As I wifh it over, I wifh it to come, but withal wifh that it may be as light as poffible.

Perhaps your lordfhip has no tafte for ferious things; by your connexions in England I fhould fuppofe not: Therefore I fhall drop this part of the fubject, and take it up in a line in which you will better underftand me.

By what means, may I afk, do you expect to conquer America? If you could not effect it in the fummer, when our army was lefs than yours, nor in the winter, when we had none, how are you to do it? In point of generalfhip you have been outwitted, and in point of fortitude outdone: Your advantages turn out to your lofs, and fhow us that it is in our power to ruin you by gifts: Like a game of drafts, we can move out of *one* ſquare to let you come in, in order that we may afterwards take two or three for one; and as we can always keep a double corner for ourſelves, we can always prevent a total defeat. You cannot be ſo inſenſible, as not to ſee that we have two to one the advantage of you, becauſe we conquer by a drawn game, and you loſe by it. Burgoyne might have taught your lordſhip this knowledge; he has been long a ſtudent in the doctrine of chances.

I have no other idea of conquering countries than by ſubduing the armies which defend them: Have you done this, or can you do this? If you have not, it would be civil in you to let your proclamations alone for the preſent; otherwiſe, you will ruin more tories by your grace and favour than you will whigs by your arms.

Were you to obtain poſſeſſion of this city, you would not know what to do with it more than to plunder it. To hold it in the manner you hold New-York, would be an additional dead weight upon your hands; and if a general conqueſt is your object, you had better be without the city than with it. When you have defeated all our armies, the cities will fall into your hands of themſelves; but to creep into them in the manner you got into Princetown, Trenton, &c. is like robbing an orchard in the night before the fruit be ripe, and running away in the morning. Your experiment in the Jerſeys is ſufficient to teach you that you have ſomething more to do than barely to get into other people's houſes; and your new converts, to whom you promiſed all manner of protection, and ſeduced into new guilt by pardoning them from their former virtues, muſt begin to have a very contemptible opinion both of your power and your policy. Your authority in the Jerſeys is now reduced to the ſmall circle which your army occupies, and your proclamation is no where elſe ſeen unleſs it be to be laughed at. The mighty ſubduers of the continent are retreated into a nut-ſhell, and the proud forgivers of our ſins are fled from thoſe they came to pardon; and all this at a time when they were diſpatching veſſel after veſſel to England with the great news of every day. In ſhort, you have managed your Jerſey expedition ſo very dextrouſly that the dead only are conquerors, becauſe none will diſpute the ground with them.

In all the wars you have formerly been concerned in, you had only armies to contend with; in this caſe you have both an army and a country to combat with. In former wars, the countries followed the fate of their capitals; Canada fell with Quebec, and Minorca with Port Mahon or St. Philips; by ſubduing thoſe, the conquerors

opened a way into, and became mafters of the country : Here it is
otherwife ; if you get poffeffion of a city here, you are obliged to
fhut yourfelves up in it, and can make no other ufe of it, than to
fpend your country's money in.   This is all the advantage you have
drawn from New-York ; and you would draw lefs from Philadelphia,
becaufe it requires more force to keep it, and is much farther from
the fea.   A pretty figure you and the tories would cut in this city,
with a river full of ice, and a town full of fire; for the immediate
confequence of your getting here would be, that you would be can-
nonaded out again, and the tories be obliged to make good the
damage ; and this, fooner or later, will be the fate of New-York.

I wifh to fee the city faved, not fo much from military as from
natural motives.   'Tis the hiding place of women and children, and
lord Howe's proper bufinefs is with our armies.   When I put all
the circumftances together which ought to be taken, I laugh at your
notion of conquering America.   Becaufe you lived in a little country,
where an army might run over the whole in a few days, and where a
fingle company of foldiers might put a multitude to the route, you
expected to find it the fame here.   It is plain that you brought over
with you all the narrow notions you were bred up with, and imagined
that a proclamation in the king's name was to do great things ; but
Englifhmen always travel for knowledge, and your lordfhip, I hope,
will return, if you return at all, much wifer than you came.

We may be furprifed by events we did not expect, and in that
interval of recollection you may gain fome temporary advantage :
Such was the cafe a few weeks ago, but we foon ripen again into
reafon, collect our ftrength, and while you are preparing for a triumph, we come upon you with a defeat.   Such it has been, and fuch
it would be were you to try it an hundred times over.   Were you to
garrifon the places you might march over, in order to fecure their
fubjection (for remember you can do it by no other means), your
army would be like a ftream of water running to nothing.   By the
time you reached from New-York to Virginia, you would be reduced
to a ftring of drops not capable of hanging together ; while we, by
retreating from ftate to ftate, like a river turning back upon itfelf,
would acquire ftrength in the fame proportion as you loft it, and in
the end be capable of overwhelming you.   The country in the mean
time would fuffer, but 'tis a day of fuffering, and we ought to expect
it.   What we contend for is worthy the affliction we may go through.
If we get but bread to eat, and any kind of raiment to put on, we

ought not only to be contented, but thankful. More than *that* we ought not to look for, and lefs than *that* Heaven has not yet fuffered us to want.   He that would fell his birthright for a little *falt*, is as worthlefs as he who fold it for *porridge* without falt.   And he that would part with it for a gay coat, or a *plain* coat, ought forever to be a flave in buff.   What are falt, fugar and finery, to the ineftimable bleffings of " Liberty and fafety !"   Or what are the inconveniencies of a few months to the tributary bondage of ages ?   The meaneft peafant in America, bleft with thefe fentiments, is a happy man compared with a New-York tory ; he can eat his morfel without repining, and when he has done, can fweeten it with a repaft of wholefome air ; he can take his child by the hand and blefs it, without feeling the confcious fhame of neglecting a parent's duty.

In publifhing thefe remarks I have feveral objects in view.

On your part they are, to expofe the folly of your pretended authority as a commiffioner ; the wickednefs of your caufe in general ; and the impoffibility of your conquering us at any rate.   On the part of the public my meaning is, to fhew them their true and folid intereft ; to encourage them to their own good, to remove the fears and falfities which bad men had fpread, and weak men had encouraged ; and to excite in all men a love for union, and a cheerfulnefs for duty.

I fhall fubmit one more cafe to you refpecting your conqueft of this country, and then proceed to new obfervations :

Suppofe our armies in every part of this continent were immediately to difperfe, every man to his home, or where elfe he might be fafe, and engage to re-affemble again on a certain future day ; it is clear that you would then have no army to contend with, yet you would be as much at a lofs in that cafe as you are now ; you would be afraid to fend your troops in parties over the continent, either to difarm, or prevent us from affembling, left they fhould not return ; and while you kept them together, having no army of ours to difpute with, you could not call it a conqueft ; you might furnifh out a pompous page in the London Gazette or the New-York paper, but when we returned at the appointed time, you would have the fame work to do you had' at firft.

It has been the folly of Britain to fuppofe herfelf more powerful than fhe really is, and by that means has arrogated to herfelf a rank in the world fhe is not entitled to : for more than this century paft fhe has not been able to carry on a war without foreign affiftance.   In

Marlborough's campaigns, and from that day to this, the number of
German troops and officers affifting her have been about equal with
her own; ten thoufand Heffians were fent to England laft war to proteft her from a French invafion; and fhe would have cut but a poor
figure in her Canadian and Weft-Indian expeditions, had not America
been lavifh both of her money and men to help her along. The only
inftance in which fhe was engaged fingly, that I can recollect, was
againft the rebellion in Scotland in forty-five and forty-fix, and in that,
out of three battles, fhe was twice beaten, till by thus reducing their
numbers (as we fhall yours) and taking a fupply fhip that was coming
to Scotland with clothes, arms and money (as we have often done) fhe
was at laft enabled to defeat them. England was never famous by
land ; her officers have generally been fufpected of cowardice, have
more of the air of a dancing-mafter than a foldier, and by the
fample we have taken prifoners we give the preference to ourfelves. Her ftrength of late has lain in her extravagance; but as her
finances and her credit are now low, her finews in that line begin to
fail faft. As a nation fhe is the pooreft in Europe ; for were the whole
kingdom, and all that is in it, to be put up to fale like the eftate of
a bankrupt, it would not fetch as much as fhe owes; yet this thought-
lefs wretch muft go to war, and with the avowed defign too of making
us beafts of burden, to fupport her in riot and debauchery, and to affift
her afterwards in diftreffing thofe nations who are now our beft
friends. This ingratitude may fuit a tory, or the unchriftian peev-
ifhnefs of a fallen Quaker, but none elfe.

'Tis the unhappy temper of the Englifh to be pleafed with any
war, right or wrong, be it but fuccefsful ; but they foon grow difcontented with ill fortune, and it is an even chance that they are as
clamorous for peace next fummer, as the king and his minifters were
for war laft winter. In this natural view of things, your lordfhip
ftands in a very ugly critical fituation : Your whole character is ftaked
upon your laurels; if they wither, you wither with them; if
they flourifh, you cannot live long to look at them; and at
any rate, the black account hereafter is not far off. What
lately appeared to us misfortunes, were only bleffings in difguife ; and the feeming advantages on your fide have turned out to
our profit. Even our lofs of this city, as far as we can fee, might
be a principal gain to us : The more furface you fpread over, the
thinner you will be, and the eafier wiped away; and our confolation
under that apparent difafter would be, that the eftates of the tories

would become fecurities for the repairs. In fhort, there is no old ground we can fail upon, but fome new foundation rifes again to fupport us. "We have put, fir, our hands to the plough, and curfed be he that looketh back."

Your king, in his fpeech to parliament laft fpring, declared to them, "That he had no doubt but the great force they had enabled him to fend to America, would effectually reduce the rebellious colonies." It has not, neither can it; but it has done juft enough to lay the foundation of its own next year's ruin. You are fenfible that you left England in a divided diftracted ftate of politics, and, by the command you had here, you became a principal prop in the court party; their fortunes reft on yours; by a fingle exprefs you can fix their value with the public, and the degree to which their fpirits fhall rife or fall; they are in your hands as ftock, and you have the fecret of the alley with you. Thus fituated and connected, you become the unintentional mechanical inftrument of your own and their overthrow. The king and his minifters put conqueft out of doubt, and the credit of both depended on the proof. To fupport them in the interim, it was neceffary you fhould make the moft of every thing; and we can tell by Hugh Gaine's New York paper what the complexion of the London Gazette is. With fuch a lift of victories the nation cannot expect you will afk new fupplies; and to confefs your want of them, would give the lie to your triumphs, and impeach the king and his minifters of treafonable deception. If you make the neceffary demand at home, your party finks; if you make it not you fink yourfelf; to afk it now is too late, and to afk it before was too foon, and unlefs it arrive quickly will be of no ufe. In fhort, the part you have to act, cannot be acted; and I am fully perfuaded that all you have to truft to is, to do the beft you can with what force you have got, or little more. Though we have greatly exceeded you in point of generalfhip and bravery of men, yet, as a people, we have not entered into the full foul of enterprize; for I, who know England and the difpofition of the people well, am confident, that it is eafier for us to effect a revolution there, than you a conqueft here; a few thoufand men landed in England with the declared defign of depofing the prefent king, bringing his minifters to trial, and fetting up the duke of Gloucefter in his ftead, would affuredly carry their point, while you were grovelling here ignorant of the matter. As I fend all my papers to England, this, like COMMON SENSE, will find its way there; and though it may put one party on their guard, it will inform the other and the nation in general of our defign to help them.

Thus far, fir, I have endeavoured to give you a picture of prefent affairs : You may draw from it what conclufions you pleafe.   I wifh as well to the true profperity of England as you can, but I confider *Independence as America's natural right and intereft*, and never could fee any real differvice it would be to Britain.   If an Englifh merchant receives an order, and is paid for it, it fignifies nothing to him who governs the country.   This is my creed of politics.   If I have any where expreffed myfelf over warmly, 'tis from a fixt immoveable hatred I have, and ever had, to cruel men and cruel meafures.   I have likewife an averfion to monarchy, as being too debafing to the dignity of man ; but I never troubled others with my notions till very lately, nor ever publifhed a fyllable in England in my life.   What I write is pure nature, and my pen and my foul have ever gone together. My writings I have always given away, referving only the expence of printing and paper, and fometimes not even that.   I never courted either fame or intereft, and my manner of life, to thofe who know it, will juftify what I fay.   My ftudy is to be ufeful, and if your lordfhip loves mankind as well as I do, you would, feeing you cannot conquer us, caft about and lend your hand towards accomplifhing a peace. Our independence, with God's bleffing, we will maintain againft all the world ; but as we wifh to avoid evil ourfelves, we wifh not to inflict it on others.   I am never over inquifitive into the fecrets of the cabinet, but I have fome notion, that if you neglect the prefent opportunity, that it will not be in our power to make a feparate peace with you afterwards ; for whatever treaties or alliances we form, we fhall moft faithfully abide by; wherefore you may be deceived if you think you can make it with us at any time.   A lafting independent peace is my wifh, end and aim ; and to accomplifh that, " *I pray* " *God the* Americans *may never be defeated, and I truft while they have* " *good officers, and are well commanded,*" and willing to be commanded, " *that they* NEVER WILL."

COMMON SENSE.

THE CRISIS.—NUMBER III.

Philadelphia, April 19, 1777.

IN the progrefs of politics, as in the common occurrences of life, we are not only apt to forget the ground we have travelled over, but frequently neglect to gather up experience as we go.   We expend, if I may fo fay, the knowledge of every day on the circumſtances that produce it, and journey on in ſearch of new matter and new refinements : But as it is pleaſant, and ſometimes uſeful, to look back, even to the firſt periods of infancy, and trace the turns and windings through which we have paſſed, ſo we may likewiſe derive many advantages by halting a while in our political career, and taking a review of the wondrous complicated labyrinth of little more than yeſterday.

Truly, may we fay, that never did man grow old in ſo ſhort a time ! We have crowded the buſineſs of an age into the compaſs of a few months, and have been driven through ſuch a rapid ſucceſſion of things, that, for the want of leiſure to think, we unavoidably waſted knowledge as we came, and have left nearly as much behind us as we brought with us : But the road is yet rich with the fragments, and, before we fully loſe ſight of them, will repay us for the trouble of ſtopping to pick them up.

Were a man to be totally deprived of memory, he would be incapable of forming any juſt opinion ; every thing about him would ſeem a chaos ; he would have even his own hiſtory to aſk from every one ; and by not knowing how the world went in his abſence, he would be at a loſs to know how it *ought* to go on when he recovered, or rather, returned to it again. In like manner, though in a leſs degree, a too great inattention to paſt occurrences retards and bewilders our judgment in every thing ; while, on the contrary, by comparing what is paſt with what is preſent, we frequently hit on the true character of both, and become wiſe with very little trouble. It is a kind of counter-march, by which we get into the rear of time, and mark the movements and meaning of things as we make our return. There are certain circumſtances, which, at the time of their happening, are kind of riddles, and as every riddle is to be followed by its anſwer, ſo thoſe kind of circumſtances will be followed by their events, and thoſe events are always the true ſolution. A conſiderable ſpace of time may lapſe between, and unleſs we continue our obſervations from the one to the other, the harmony of them will paſs away unnoticed : But the misfortune is, that partly from the preſſing neceſſity of ſome inſtant things, and partly from the impatience of our own tempers, we are frequently in ſuch a hurry to make out the meaning of every thing as faſt as it happens, that we thereby never truly underſtand it; and not only ſtart new difficulties to ourſelves by ſo doing, but, as it were, embarraſs Providence in her good deſigns.

K 2

I have been civil in ftating this fault on a large fcale, for, as it now ftands, it does not appear to be levelled againft any particular fet of men ; but were it to be refined a little farther, it might afterwards be applied to the tories with a degree of ftriking propriety : Thofe men have been remarkable for drawing fudden conclufions from fingle facts. The leaft apparent mifhap on our fide, or the leaft feeming advantage on the part of the enemy, have determined with them the fate of a whole campaign. By this hafty judgment they have converted a retreat into a defeat ; miftook generalfhip for error ; while every little advantage purpofely given the enemy, either to weaken their ftrength by dividing it, embarrafs their councils by multiplying their objects, or to fecure a greater poft by the furrender of a lefs, has been inftantly magnified into a conqueft. Thus, by quartering ill policy upon ill principles, they have frequently promoted the caufe they defigned to injure, and injured that which they intended to promote.

It is probable the campaign may open before this number comes from the prefs. The enemy have long lain idle and amufed themfelves with carrying on the war by proclamations only. While they continue their delay our ftrength increafes, and were they to move to action now, it is a circumftantial proof they have no reinforcement coming ; wherefore, in either cafe, the comparative advantage will be ours. Like a wounded difabled whale, they want only time and room to die in ; and though in the agony of their exit, it may be unfafe to live within the flapping of their tail, yet every hour fhortens their date and leffens their power of mifchief. If any thing happens while this number is in the prefs, it will afford me a fubject for the laft pages of it. At prefent I am tired of waiting ; and as neither the enemy, nor the ftate of politics, have yet produced any thing new, I am thereby left in the field of general matter undirected by any ftriking or particular object. This Crifis, therefore, will be made up rather of variety than novelty, and confift more of things ufeful than things wonderful.

The fuccefs of the caufe, the union of the people, and the means of fupporting and fecuring both, are points which cannot be too much attended to. He who doubts of the former is a defponding coward, and he who wilfully difturbs the latter is a traitor. Their characters are eafily fixt, and under thefe fhort defcriptions I leave them for the prefent.

One of the greateft degrees of fentimental union which America ever knew, was in denying the right of the British parliament " *to bind the colonies in all cases whatsoever.*" The declaration is in its form an almighty one, and is the loftiest stretch of arbitrary power that ever one set of men, or one country claimed over another. Taxation was nothing more than the putting the declared right into practice ; and this failing, recourse was had to arms, as a means to establish both the right *and* the practice, or to answer a worse purpose, which will be mentioned in the course of this number. And in order to repay themselves the expence of an army, and to profit by their own injustice, the colonies were, by another law, declared to be in a state of actual rebellion, and of consequence all property therein would fall to the conquerors.

The colonies, on their part, FIRST, denied the right ; SE-CONDLY, they suspended the use of taxable articles, and petitioned against the practice of taxation : and these failing, they THIRDLY, defended their property by force, as soon as it was forcibly invaded, and in answer to the declaration of rebellion and non-protection, pub-lished their declaration of independence and right of self-protection.

These, in a few words, are the different stages of the quarrel; and the parts are so intimately and necessarily connected with each other as to admit of no separation. A person, to use a trite phrase, must be a whig or a tory in the lump. His feeling, as a man, may be wounded; his charity, as a Christian, may be moved; but his political principles must go through all the cases on one side or the other. He cannot be a whig in *this* stage, and a tory in *that*. If he says he is against the united independence of the continent, he is to all intents and purposes against her in all the rest; because THIS LAST com-prehends the whole. And he may just as well say, that Britain was right in declaring us rebels; right in taxing us; and right in declaring her " *right to bind the colonies in all cases whatsoever.*" It signifies no-thing what neutral ground, of his own creating, he may skulk upon for shelter, for the quarrel in no stage of it hath afforded any such ground ; and either we or Britain are absolutely right or absolutely wrong through the whole.

Britain, like a gamester nearly ruined, hath now put all her losses into one bet, and is playing a desperate game for the total. If she wins it, she wins from *me* my life; she wins the continent as the for-feited property of rebels ; the right of taxing those that are left as reduced subjects ; and the power of binding them slaves: And the sin-gle die which determines this unparalleled event is, whether we support our independence or she overturn it.   This is coming to the point at once.   Here is the touch-stone to try men by.   *He that is not a supporter of the independent states of America, in the same degree that his religious and political principles would suffer him to support the government of any other country, of which he called himself a subject, is, in the American sense of the word,* A TORY; *and the instant that he endeavours to bring his toryism into practice, he becomes* A TRAITOR. The first can only be detected by a general test, and the law hath already provided for the latter.

It is unnatural and impolitic to admit men who would root up our independence to have any share in our legislation, either as electors or representatives ; because the support of our independence rests in a great measure on the vigour and purity of our public bodies.   Would Britain, even in time of peace, much less in war, suffer an election to be carried by men who professed themselves to be her subjects, or allow such to sit in parliament?   Certainly not.

But there are a certain species of tories with whom conscience or principle hath nothing to do, and who are so from avarice only.   Some of the first fortunes in the continent, on the part of the whigs, are staked on the issue of our present measures.   And shall disaffection only be rewarded with security?   Can any thing be a greater inducement to a miserly man, than the hope of making his mammon safe? And though the scheme be fraught with every character of folly, yet, so long as he supposes, that by doing nothing materially criminal against America on one part, and by expressing his private disapprobation against independence, as palliative with the enemy on the other part, he stands thereby in a safe line between both, while, I say, this ground be suffered to remain, craft and the spirit of avarice will point it out, and men will not be wanting to fill up this most contemptible of all characters.

These men, ashamed to own the sordid cause from whence their disaffection springs, add thereby meanness to meanness, by endeavouring to shelter themselves under the mask of hypocrisy ; that is, they had rather be thought to be tories from *some kind of principle*, than tories by having *no principle at all*.   But till such time as they can show some real reason, natural, political, or conscientious, on which their objections to independence are founded, we are not obliged to give them credit for being tories of the first stamp, but must set them down as tories of the last.

In the second number of the Crisis I endeavoured to shew the impossibility of the enemy making any conquest of America, that nothing was wanting on our part but patience and perfeverance, and that, with thefe virtues, our fuccefs, as far as human fpeculation could difcern, feemed as certain as fate. But as there are many among us, who, influenced by others, have regularly gone back from the principles they once held, in proportion as we have gone forward; and as it is the unfortunate lot of many a good man to live within the neighbourhood of difaffected ones ; I fhall therefore, for the fake of confirming the one and recovering the other, endeavour, in the fpace of a page or two, to go over fome of the leading principles in fupport of independence. It is a much pleafanter tafk to prevent vice than to punifh it; and however our tempers may be gratified by refentment, or our national expences eafed by forfeited eftates, harmony and friendfhip is neverthelefs the happieft condition a country can be bleft with.

The principal arguments in fupport of independence may be comprehended under the four following heads.

Firft,—The natural right of the continent to independence.

Secondly,—Her intereft in being independent.

Thirdly,—the neceffity,—and

Fourthly,—The moral advantages arifing therefrom.

I. The natural right of the continent to independence, is a point which never yet was called in queftion. It will not even admit of a debate. To deny fuch a right, would be a kind of atheifm againft nature : And the beft anfwer to fuch an objection would be, " *The fool hath faid in his heart there is no God.*"

II. The intereft of the continent in being independent is a point as clearly right as the former. America, by her own internal induftry, and unknown to all the powers of Europe, was at the beginning of the difpute, arrived at a pitch of greatnefs, trade and population, beyond which it was the intereft of Britain not to fuffer her to pafs, left fhe fhould grow too powerful to be kept fubordinate. She began to view this country with the fame uneafy malicious eye, with which a covetous guardian would view his ward whofe eftate he had been enriching himfelf by for twenty years, and faw him juft arriving at manhood. And America owes no more to Britain for her prefent maturity, than the ward would to his guardian for being twenty-one years of age. That America hath flourifhed *at the time* fhe was under the government of Britain, is true ; but there is every natural reafon to believe, that had fhe been an independent country from the firft fettlement thereof, uncontrolled by any foreign power, free to make her own laws, regulate and encourage her own commerce, fhe had by this time been of much greater worth than now. The cafe is fimply this, The firft fettlers in the different colonies were left to fhift for themfelves, unnoticed and unfupported by any European government; but as the tyranny and perfecution of the old world daily drove numbers to the new, and as, by the favour of Heaven on their induftry and perfeverence, they grew into importance, fo, in a like degree, they became an object of profit to the greedy eyes of Europe. It was impoffible in this ftate of infancy, however thriving and promifing, that they could refift the power of any armed invader that fhould feek to bring them under his authority. In this fituation Britain thought it worth her while to claim them, and the continent received and acknowledged the claimer. It was, in reality, of no very great importance who was her mafter, feeing, that from the force and ambition of the different powers of Europe fhe muft, till fhe acquired ftrength enough to affert her own right, acknowledge fome one. As well, perhaps, Britain as another; and it might have been as well to have been under the ftates of Holland as any. The fame hopes of engroffing and profiting by her trade, by not oppreffing it too much, would have operated alike with any mafter, and produced to the colonies the fame effects. The clamour of protection, likewife, was all a farce; becaufe, in order to make *that* protection neceffary, fhe muft firft, by her own quarrels create us enemies. Hard terms! indeed!

To know whether it be the intereft of the continent to be independent, we need only afk this eafy, fimple queftion: Is it the intereft of a man to be a boy all his life? The anfwer to one will be the anfwer to both. America hath been one continued fcene of legiflative contention from the firft king's reprefentative to the laft; and this was unavoidably founded in the natural oppofition of intereft between the old country and the new. A governor fent from England, or receiving his authority therefrom, ought never to have been confidered in any other light than that of a genteel commiffioned fpy, whofe private bufinefs was information, and his public bufinefs a kind of civilized oppreffion. In the firft of thefe characters he was to watch the tempers, fentiments and difpofition of the people, the growth of trade, and the increafe of private fortunes; and in the latter, to fupprefs all fuch acts of the affemblies, however beneficial to the people, which did not directly or indirectly throw fome increafe of power or profit into the hands of thofe who fent him.

America, till now, could never be called a *free country*, becaufe

her legiflation depended on the will of a man three thoufand miles
diftant, whofe intereft was in oppofition to ours, and who, by a fingle
" no," could forbid what law he pleafed.

The freedom of trade, likewife, is, to a trading country, an article
of fuch vaft importance, that the principal fource of wealth depends
upon it; and it is impoffible that any country can flourifh, as it
otherwife might do, whofe commerce is engroffed, cramped and fettered by the laws and mandates of another—yet thefe evils, and more
than I can here enumerate, the continent has fuffered by being under
the government of Great-Britain. By an independence we clear the
whole at once—put an end to the bufinefs of unanfwered petitions
and fruitlefs remonftrances—exchange Britain for Europe—fhake
hands with the world—live at peace with mankind—and trade to any
market where we beft can buy and fell.

III. The neceffity, likewife, of being independent, even before
it was declared, became fo evident and important, that the continent
ran the rifk of being ruined every day fhe delayed it.   There were
reafons to believe that Britain would endeavour to make an European
matter of it, and rather than lofe the whole, would difmember it like
Poland, and difpofe of her feveral claims to the higheft bidder. Genoa,
failing in her attempts to reduce Corfica, made a fale of it to the
French, and fuch traffics have been common in the old world. We
had at that time no Ambaffador in any part of Europe, to counteract
her negociations, and by that means fhe had the range of every foreign court uncontradicted on our part. We even knew nothing of
the treaty for the Heffians till it was concluded, and the troops ready
to embark. Had we been independent before, we had probably prevented her obtaining them. We had no credit abroad, becaufe of
our rebellious dependency. Our fhips could claim no protection in
foreign ports, becaufe we afforded them no juftifiable reafon for granting it to us.   The calling ourfelves fubjects, and at the fame time
fighting againft the power we acknowledged, was a dangerous precedent to all Europe. If the grievances juftified our taking up arms,
they juftified our feparation ; if they did not juftify our feparation,
neither could they juftify our taking up arms. All Europe was interefted in reducing us as rebels, and all Europe (or the greateft part
at leaft) is interefted in fupporting us as independent ftates. At home
our condition was ftill worfe: Our currency had no foundation, and
the fall of it would have ruined whig and tory alike. We had no
other law than a kind of moderated paffion ; no other civil power

than an honest mob ; and no other protection than the temporary attachment of one man to another. Had independence been delayed a few months longer, this continent would have been plunged into irrecoverable confusion: Some violent for it, some against it, till in the general cabal the rich would have been ruined, and the poor destroyed. It is to independence that every tory owes the present safety he lives in ; for by *that*, and *that only*, we emerged from a state of dangerous suspense, and became a regular people.

The necessity likewise of being independent, had there been no rupture between Britain and America, would in a little time have brought one on. The increasing importance of commerce, the weight and perplexity of legislation, and the entangled state of European politics, would daily have shewn to the continent the impossibility of continuing subordinate ; for, after the coolest reflections on the matter, *this must* be allowed, that Britain was too jealous of America, to govern it justly ; too ignorant of it, to govern it well ; and too distant from it, to govern it at all.

IV. But, what weigh most with all men of serious reflection are the MORAL ADVANTAGES arising from independence : War and desolation are become the trades of the old world ; and America neither could, nor can be under the government of Britain without becoming a sharer of her guilt, and a partner in all the dismal commerce of death. The spirit of duelling, extended on a national scale, is a proper character for European wars. They have seldom any other motive than pride, or any other object than fame. The conquerors and the conquered are generally ruined alike, and the chief difference at last is, that the one marches home with his honours, and the other without them. 'Tis the natural temper of the English to fight for a feather, if they suppose *that feather* to be an affront ; and America, without the right of asking why, must have abetted in every quarrel and abided by its fate. It is a shocking situation to live in, that one country must be brought into all the wars of another, whether the measure be right or wrong, or whether she will or not ; yet this, in the fullest extent, was, and ever would be, the unavoidable consequence of the connexion. Surely ! the Quakers forgot their own principles, when in their late testimony they called *this connexion* with these military and miserable appendages hanging to it, " *The happy constitution.*"

Britain, for centuries past, has been nearly fifty years out of every hundred at war with some power or other. It certainly ought to be a confcientious as well as political confideration with America, not to dip her hands in the bloody work of Europe. Our fituation affords us a retreat from their cabals, and the prefent happy union of the ftates bids fair for extirpating the future ufe of arms from one quarter of the world ; yet fuch have been the irreligious politics of the prefent leaders of the Quakers, that, for the fake of they fcarce know what, they would cut off every hope of fuch a blefling by tying this continent to Britain, like Hector to the chariot-wheel of Achilles, to be dragged through all the miferies of endlefs European wars.

The connection, viewed from this ground, is diftreffing to every man who has the feelings of humanity. By having Britain for our mafter, we became enemies to the greateft part of Europe, and they to us ; and the confequence was war inevitable. By being our own mafters, independent of any foreign one, we have Europe for our friends, and the profpect of an endlefs peace among ourfelves. Thofe who were advocates for the Britifh government over thefe colonies, were obliged to limit both their arguments and their ideas to the period of an European peace only : The moment Britain became plunged in war, every fuppofed convenience to us vanifhed away, and all we could hope for was *net to be ruined.* Could this be a defirable condition for a young country to be in ?

Had the French purfued their fortune immediately after the defeat of Braddock laft war, this city and province had then experienced the woeful calamities of being a Britifh fubject. A fcene of the fame kind might happen again ; for America, confidered as a fubject to the crown of Britain, would ever have been the feat of war and the bone of contention between the two powers.

On the whole, if the future expulfion of arms from one quarter of the world would be a defirable object to a peaceable man ;—if the freedom of trade to every part of it can engage the attention of a man of bufinefs ;—if the fupport or fall of millions of currency can affect our interefts ;—if the entire poffeffion of eftates, by cutting off the lordly claims of Britain over the foil, deferves the regard of landed property ;—and if the right of making our own laws, uncontrolled by royal or minifterial fpies or mandates, be worthy our care as freemen ;—then are all men interefted in the fupport of independence ; and may he that fupports it not, be driven from the blefling, and live unpitied beneath the fervile fufferings of fcandalous fubjection !

We have been amufed with the tales of ancient wonders ; we have

read, and wept over, the hiftories of other nations; applauded, cen-
fured or pitied, as their cafes affected us.—The fortitude and patience
of the fufferers—the juftnefs of their caufe—the weight of their oppreffions and oppreffors—the object to be faved or loft—with all the
confequences of a defeat or a conqueft—have, in the hour of fympathy,
bewitched our hearts and chained it to their fate : But where is the
power that ever made war upon petitioners ? Or where is the war on
which a would was ftaked till now ?

We may not, perhaps, be wife enough to make all the advantages
we ought of our independence ; but they are, nevertheless, marked
and prefented to us with every character of GREAT and GOOD,
and worthy the hand of him who fent them.   I look through the
prefent trouble to a time of tranquility, when we fhall have it in our
power to fet an example of peace to all the world.   Were the Quakers
really impreffed and influenced by the quiet principles they profefs to
hold, they would, however they might difapprove the means, be the
firft of all men to approve of INDEPENDENCE, becaufe, by
feparating from the cities of Sodom and Gomorrah, it affords an
opportunity, never given to man before, of carrying their favourite
principle of peace into general practice, by eftablifhing governments
that fhall hereafter exift without wars.   Oh ye fallen, cringing prieft
and Pemberton-ridden people ! what more can we fay of ye than that
a religious Quaker is a valuable character, and a political Quaker a
real Jefuit.

Having thus gone over fome of the principal points in fupport of
independence, I muft now requeft the reader to return back with me
to the period when it firft began to be a public doctrine, and to examine the progrefs it has made among the various claffes of men.   The
era I mean to begin at, is the breaking out of hoftilities, April 19th,
1775.   Until this event happened, the continent feemed to view the
difpute as a kind of law-fuit for a matter of right, litigating between
the old country and the new ; and fhe felt the fame kind and degree
of horror, as if fhe had feen an oppreffive plaintiff, at the head of a
band of ruffians, enter the court, while the caufe was before it, and
put the judge, the jury, the defendant and his council, to the fword.
Perhaps a more heart-felt convulfion never reached a country with the
fame degree of power and rapidity before, and never may again.
Pity for the fufferers, mixt with indignation at the violence, and
heightened with apprehenfions of undergoing the fame fate, made
the affair of Lexington the affair of the continent.   Every part of

it felt the fhock, and all vibrated together.   A general promotion of
fentiment took place : Thofe who had drank deeply into whiggifh
principles, that is, the right and neceffity not only of oppofing, but
wholly fetting afide the power of the crown as foon as it became
practically dangerous (for in theory it was always fo) ftept into the
firft ftage of independence ; while another clafs of whigs, equally
found in principle, but not fo fanguine in enterprize, attached
themfelves the ftronger to the caufe, and fell clofe in with the rear of
the former ; their partition was a mere point.   Numbers of the moderate men, whofe chief fault, *at that time*, arofe from their enter-
taining a better opinion of Britain than fhe deferved, convinced now
of their miftake, gave her up and publicly declared themfelves good
whigs.   While the tories, feeing it was no longer a laughing matter,
either funk into filent obfcurity, or contented themfelves with coming
forth and abufing General Gage : Not a fingle advocate appeared
to juftify the action of that day ; it feemed to appear to every one
with the fame magnitude, ftruck every one with the fame force, and
created in every one the fame abhorrence.   From this period we may
date the growth of independence.

If the many circumftances, which happened at this memorable
time, be taken in one view, and compared with each other, they will
juftify a conclufion which feems not to be attended to, I mean a fixt
defign in the king and miniftry of driving America into arms, in order
that they might be furnifhed with a pretence for feizing the whole.
continent, as the immediate property of the crown.   A noble plunder for hungry courtiers !

It ought to be remembered, that the firft petition from the congrefs was at this time unanfwered on the part of the Britifh king.
That the motion, called lord North's motion, of the 20th of February, 1775, arrived in America the latter end of March.   This motion was to be laid by the feveral governers, then in being, before the
affembly of each province ; and the firft affembly before which it was
laid, was the affembly of Pennfylvania in *May* following.   This being a juft ftate of the cafe, I then afk, why were hoftilities commenced between the time of paffing the refolve in the houfe of commons,
of the 20th of February, and the time of the affemblies meeting to
deliberate upon it ? Degrading and infamous as that motion was, there
is, neverthelefs, reafon to believe that the king and his adherents were
afraid the colonies would agree to it, and left they fhould, took effectual care they fhould not, by provoking them with hoftilities in the

interest. They had not the least doubt at that time of conquering America at one blow; and what they expected to get by a conquest being infinitely greater than any thing they could hope to get either by taxation or accommodation, they seemed determined to prevent even the possibility of hearing each other, left America should disappoint their greedy hopes of the whole, by listening even to their own terms. On the one hand they refused to hear the petition of the continent, and on the other hand took effectual care the continent should not hear them.

That the motion of the 20th of February and the orders for commencing hostilities were both concerted by the same person or persons, and not the latter by General Gage, as was falsely imagined at first, is evident from an extract of a letter of his to administration, read among other papers in the house of commons; in which he informs his masters, *That though their idea of his disarming certain counties was a right one, yet it required him to be master of the country, in order to enable him to execute it.* This was prior to the commencement of hostilities, and consequently before the motion of the 20th of February could be deliberated on by the several assemblies.

Perhaps it may be asked, why was the motion past, if there was at the same time a plan to aggravate the Americans not to listen to it? Lord North assigned one reason himself, which was, *a hope of dividing them.* This was publicly tempting them to reject it; that if, in case the injury of arms should fail of provoking them sufficiently, the insult of such a declaration might fill it up. But by passing the motion and getting it afterwards rejected in America, it enabled them, in their wretched idea of politics, among other things, to hold up the colonies to foreign powers with every possible mark of disobedience and rebellion. They had applied to those powers not to supply the continent with arms, ammunition, &c. and it was necessary they should incense them against us, by assigning on their own part some seeming reputable reason why. By dividing, it had a tendency to weaken the states, and likewise to perplex the adherents of America in England. But the principal scheme, and that which has marked their character in every part of their conduct, was a design of precipitating the colonies into a state which they might afterwards deem rebellion, and under that pretence put an end to all future complaints, petitions and remonstrances, by seizing the whole at once. They had ravaged one part of the globe, till it could glut them no longer; their prodigality required new plunder, and through the East-India article TEA they hoped to transfer their rapine from that quarter of the world to this. —Every defigned quarrel had its pretence ; and the fame barbarian avarice accompanied the *plant* to America, which ruined the country which produced it.

That men never turn rogues without turning fools, is a maxim, fooner or later, univerfally true. The commencement of hoftilities, being in the beginning of April, was, of all times the worft chofen : The congrefs were to meet the tenth of May following, and the diftrefs the continent felt at this unparalleled outrage gave a ftability to *that body*, which no other circumftance could have done. It fuppreffed too, all inferior debates, and bound them together by a neceffitous affection, without giving them time to differ upon trifles. The fuffering likewife, foftened the whole body of the people into a degree of pliability, which laid the principal foundation-ftone of union, order and government ; and which, at any other time, might only have fretted and then faded away unnoticed and unimproved : But Providence, who beft knows how to time her misfortunes as well as her immediate favours, chofe this to be the time : And who dares difpute it ?

It did not feem the difpofition of the people at this crifis to heap petition upon petition, while the former remained unanfwered : The meafure, however, was carried in congrefs, and a fecond petition was fent ? of which I fhall only remark, that it was fubmiffive even to a dangerous fault, becaufe the prayer of it appealed folely to, what it called, the prerogative of the crown, while the matter in difpute was confeffed to be conftitutional. But even this petition, flattering as it was, was ftill not fo harmonious as the chink of cafh, and confequently not fufficiently grateful to the tyrant and his miniftry. From every circumftance it is evident, that it was the determination of the Britifh court to have nothing to do with America but to conquer it fully and abfolutely. They were certain of fuccefs, and the field of battle was to be the only place of treaty. I am confident there are thoufands and tens of thoufands in America who wonder *now* they fhould ever think otherwife; but the fin of that day was the fin of civility, yet it operated againft our prefent good in the fame manner that a civil opinion of the devil would againft our future peace.

Independence was a doctrine fcarce and rare even towards the conclufion of the year feventy-five : All our politics had been founded on the hope or expectation of making the matter up—a hope, which, though general on the fide of America, had never entered the head or heart of the Britifh court. Their hope was conqueft and confifcation.

Good Heavens! what volumes of thanks does America owe to Britain? What infinite obligations to the tool, that fills, with paradoxical vacancy, the throne! Nothing but the sharpest essence of villany, compounded with the strongest distillation of folly, could have produced a menstruum that would have effected a separation. The congress in seventy-four administered an abortive medicine to independence, by prohibiting the importation of goods, and the succeeding congress rendered the dose still more dangerous by continuing it. Had independence been a settled system with America (as Britain has advanced), she ought to have *doubled* her importation, and prohibited in some degree her exportation. And this single circumstance is sufficient to acquit America before any jury of nations of having a continental plan of independence in view: A charge, which had it been true, would have been honourable, but is so grossly false, that either the amazing ignorance, or the wilful dishonesty of the British court, is effectually proved by it.

The second petition, like the first, produced no answer; it was scarcely acknowledged to be received; the British court were too determined in their villany even to act it artfully, and in their rage for conquest neglected the necessary subtilties for obtaining it. They might have divided, distracted and played a thousand tricks with us, had they been as cunning as they were cruel.

This last indignity gave a new spring to independence. Those who knew the savage obstinacy of the king and the jobbing gambling spirit of the court, predicted the fate of the petition, as soon as it was sent from America; for the men being known, their measures were easily foreseen. As politicians we ought not so much to ground our hope on the reasonableness of the thing we ask, as on the reasonableness of the person of whom we ask it : Who would expect discretion from a fool, candour from a tyrant, or justice from a villain.

As every prospect of accommodation seemed now to fail fast, men began to think seriously on the matter; and their reason being thus stript of the false hope which had long encompassed it, became approachable by fair debate; yet still the bulk of the people hesitated; they startled at the novelty of independence, without once considering that our getting into arms at first was a more extraordinary novelty, and that all other nations had gone through the work of independence before us. They doubted, likewise, the ability of the continent to support it, without reflecting, that it required the same force to obtain an accommodation by arms as an independence. If the one was acquirable, the other was the fame; becaufe, to accomplifh either, it was neceffary that our ftrength fhould be too great for Britain to fubdue; and it was too unreafonable to fuppofe, that with the power of being mafters, we fhould fubmit to be fervants.* Their caution at this time, was exceedingly mifplaced; for if they were able to defend their property and maintain their rights by arms, they confequently were able to defend and fupport their independence; and in proportion as thefe men faw the neceffity and rightnefs of the meafure, they honeftly and openly declared and adopted it, and the part they have acted fince, has done them honour, and fully eftablifhed their characters. Error in opinion has this peculiar advantage with it, that the foremoft point of the contrary ground may at any time be reached by the fudden exertion of a thought; and it frequently happens in fentimental differences that fome ftriking circumftance, or fome forcible reafon, quickly conceived, will effect in an inftant what neither argument nor example could produce in an age.

I find it impoffible in the fmall compafs I am limited to, to trace out the progrefs which independence has made on the minds of the different claffes of men, and the feveral reafons by which they were moved. With fome, it was a paffionate abhorrence againft the king

---

* *In this ftate of political fufpenfe the pamphlet* Common Senfe *made its appearance, and the fuccefs it met with does not become me to mention. Dr. Franklin, Mr. Samuel and John Adams, were feverally fpoken of as the fuppofed author. I had not, at that time, the pleafure either of perfonally knowing or being known to the two laft gentlemen. The favour of Dr. Franklin's friendfhip I poffeffed in England, and my introduction to this part of the world was through his patronage. I happened, when a fchool-boy, to pick up a pleafing natural hiftory of Virginia, and my inclination from that day of feeing the weftern fide of the Atlantic never left me. In October, feventy-five, Dr. Franklin propofed giving me fuch materials as were in his hands, towards completing a hiftory of the prefent tranfactions, and feemed defirous of having the firft volume out the next fpring. I had then formed the outlines of Common Senfe, and finifhed nearly the firft part; and as I fuppofed the Doctor's defign in getting out a hiftory, was to open the new year with a new fyftem, I expected to furprife him with a production on that fubject, much earlier than he thought of; and without informing him of what I was doing, got it ready for the prefs as faft as I conveniently could, and fent him the firft pamphlet that was printed off.*

of England and his miniftry, as a fet of favages and brutes; and
thefe men, governed by the agony of a wounded mind, were for
trufting every thing to hope and Heaven, and bidding defiance at
once.　With others, it was a growing conviction that the fcheme of
the Britifh court was to create, ferment and drive on a quarrel for
the fake of confifcated plunder: Men of this caft ripened into independence in proportion as the evidence increafed.　While a third
clafs, conceived it was the true intereft of America, internally and
externally, to be her own mafter, gave their fupport to independence,
ftep by ftep, as they faw her abilities to maintain it enlarge.　With
many, it was a compound of all thefe reafons; while thofe who
were too callous to be reached by either, remained, and ftill remain
tories.

The *legal neceffity* of being independent, with feveral collateral
reafons, is pointed out in an elegant, mafterly manner, in a charge to
the grand jury for the diftrict of Charleftown, by the ,hon. William
Henry Drayton, efq. chief juftice of South-Carolina.　This performance, and the addrefs of the convention of New-York, are
pieces, in my humble opinion, of the firft rank in America.

The principal caufes why independence has not been fo univerfally
fupported as it ought, are *fear* and *indolence*, and the caufes why it
has been oppofed, are, *avarice*, *downright villany*, and *luft of perfonal
power*.　There is not fuch a being in America, as a tory from confcience; fome fecret defect or other is interwoven in the character of all
thofe, be they men or women, who can look with patience on the brutality, luxury, and debauchery of the Britifh court, and the violations
of their army here.　A woman's virtue muft fit very lightly on her
who can even hint a favourable fentiment in their behalf.　It is remarkable that the whole race of proftitutes in New-York were tories;
and the fchemes for fupporting the tory caufe, in this city, for which
feveral are now in gaol, and one hanged, were concerted and
carried on in common bawdy-houfes, affifted by thofe who kept
them.

The connexion between vice and meannefs is a fit object for fatire,
but when the fatire is a fact, it cuts with the irrefiftible power of a
diamond.　If a Quaker, in defence of his juft rights, his property and
the chaftity of his houfe, takes up a mufket, he is expelled the meeting;
but the prefent king of England, who feduced and took into keeping
a fifter of their fociety, is reverenced and fupported with repeated tef-
timonies, while the friendly noodle from whom fhe was taken (and

who is now in this city) continues a drudge in the fervice of his rival, as if proud of being cuckolded by a creature called a king.

Our fupport and fuccefs depend on fuch a variety of men and circumftances, that every one, who does but wifh well, is of fome ufe: There are men who have a ftrange awkwardnefs to arms, yet have hearts to rifk every fhilling in the caufe, or in fupport of thofe who have better talents for defending it. Nature, in the arrangement of mankind, has fitted fome for every fervice in life: Were all foldiers, all would ftarve and go naked, and were none foldiers, all would be flaves. As *difaffection* to independence is the badge of a tory, fo *affection* to it is the mark of a whig; and the different fervices of the whigs down from thofe who nobly contribute every thing, to thofe who have nothing to render but their wifhes, tend all to the fame centre, though with different degrees of merit and ability. The larger we make the circle, the more we fhall harmonize, and the ftronger we fhall be. All we want to fhut out, is difaffection, and, *that excluded*, we muft accept from each other fuch duties as we are beft fitted to beftow. A narrow fyftem of politics, like a narrow fyftem of religion, is calculated only to four the temper, and live at variance with mankind.

All we want to know in America is fimply this, who is for independence, and who is not? Thofe who are for it, will fupport it, and the remainder will undoubtly fee the reafonablenefs of their paying the charges; while thofe who oppofe or feek to betray it, muft expect the more rigid fate of the gaol and the gibbet. There is a baftard kind of generofity, which, by being extended to all men, is as fatal to fociety, on one hand, as the want of true generofity is on the other. A lax manner of adminiftering juftice, falfely termed moderation, has a tendency both to difpirit public virtue, and promote the growth of public evils. Had the late committee of fafety taken cognizance of the laft teftimony of the Quakers, and proceeded againft fuch delinquents as were concerned therein, they had, probably prevented the treafonable plans which have been concerted fince. When one villain is fuffered to efcape, it encourages another to proceed, either from a hope of efcaping likewife, or an apprehenfion that we dare not punifh. It has been a matter of general furprife, that no notice was taken of the incendiary publication of the Quakers, of the 20th of November laft: A publication evidently intended to promote fedition and treafon, and encourage the enemy, who were then within a day's march of this city, to proceed on and poffefs it. I here prefent the reader with a memorial, which was laid before the board of

fafety a few days after the teftimony appeared. Not a member of
that board, that I converfed with, but expreffed the higheft deteftation of the perverted principles and conduct of the Quaker junto,
and that the board would take the matter up; notwithftanding which,
it was fuffered to pafs away unnoticed, to the encouragement of new
acts of treafon, the general danger of the caufe, and the difgrace of
the ftate.

To the honourable the council of fafety of the ftate of Pennfylvania.

At a meeting of a reputable number of the inhabitants of the city
of Philadelphia, impreffed with a proper fenfe of the juftice of the
caufe which this continent is engaged in, and animated with a
generous fervour for fupporting the fame, it was refolved, that the
following be laid before the board of fafety :

" We profefs liberality of fentiment to all men ; with this diftinction only, that thofe who do not deferve it, would become wife and
feel to deferve it. We hold the pure doctrine of univerfal liberty of
confcience, and conceive it our duty to endeavour to fecure that facred
right to others, as well as to defend it for ourfelves ; for we undertake
not to judge of the religious rectitude of tenets, but leave the
whole matter to Him who made us.

" We perfecute no man, neither will we abet in the perfecution
of any man for religion fake ; our common relation to others, being
that of fellow-citizens and fellow-fubjects of one fingle community ;
and in this line of connexion we hold out the right hand of fellow-
fhip to all men. But we fhould conceive ourfelves to be unworthy
members of the FREE AND INDEPENDENT STATES OF
AMERICA, were we unconcernedly to fee or fuffer any treafonable
wound, public or private, directly or indirectly, to be given againft
the peace and fafety of the fame. We enquire not into the rank of
the offenders, nor their religious perfuafion ; we have no bufinefs
with either, our part being only to find them out, and exhibit them
to juftice.

" A printed paper, dated the 20th of November, and figned " *John
Pemberton*," whom we fuppofe to be an inhabitant of this city, has
lately been difperfed abroad, a copy of which accompanies this. Had
the framers and publifhers of that paper conceived it their duty, to
exhort the youth, and others, of their fociety, to a patient fubmiffion
under the prefent trying vifitations, and humbly to wait the event of
Heaven towards them, they had therein fhewn a Chriftian temper, and

we had been filent; but the anger and political virulence with which their inftructions are given, and the abufe with which they ftigmatize all ranks of men, not thinking like themfelves, leave no doubt on our minds from what fpirit their publication proceeded : And it is difgraceful to the pure caufe of truth, that men can dally with words of the moft facred import, and play them as mechanically off as if religion. confifted only in contrivance. We know of no inftance in which the Quakers have been compelled to bear arms, or to do any thing which might ftrain their confcience; wherefore their advice, " to withftand and refufe to fubmit to the arbitrary inftructions and ordinances of men," appear to us a falfe alarm, and could only be treafonably calculated to gain favour with our enemies, when they were feemingly on the brink of invading this ftate, or, what is ftill worfe, to weaken the hands of our defence, that their entrance into this city might be made practical and eafy.

" We difclaim all tumult and diforder in the punifhment of offenders; and wifh to be governed, not by temper but by reafon, in the manner of treating them. We are fenfible that our caufe has fuffered by the two following errors; firft, by ill-judged lenity to traitorous perfons in fome cafes ; and fecondly, by only a paffionate treatment of them in others. For the future we difown both, and wifh to be fteady in our proceedings, and ferious in our punifhments.

" Every ftate in America has by the repeated voice of its inhabitants, directed and authorifed the continental congrefs to publifh a formal declaration of independence of, and feparation from, the oppreffive king and parliament of Great Britain; and we look on every man an enemy who does not in fome line or other give his affiftance towards fupporting the fame ; at the fame time we confider the offence to be heightened to a degree of unpardonable guilt, when fuch perfons, under the fhew of religion, endeavour, either by writing, fpeaking, or otherwife, to fubvert, overturn, or bring reproach upon the independence of this continent as declared by congrefs.

" The publifhers of the paper, figned " John Pemberton," have called in a loud and paffionate manner on their friends and connexions, " to withftand and refufe" obedience to whatever " inftructions or ordinances" may be publifhed, not warranted by (what they call) " that happy conftitution under which they and others long en-" joyed tranquility and peace." If this be not treafon, we know not what may properly be called by that name.

" To us it is a matter of furprife and aftonifhment, that men with

the word "*peace, peace,*" continually on their lips fhould be fo fond of
living under, and fupporting a government, and at the fame time calling it "*happy,*" which is never better pleafed than when at war—
that hath filled India with carnage and famine—Africa with flavery—
and tampered with Indians and Negroes to cut the throats of the
freemen of America. We conceive it a difgrace to this ftate to harbour or wink at fuch palpable hypocrify. But as we feek not to hurt the
hair of any man's head, when we can make ourfelves fafe without, we
wifh fuch perfons to reftore peace to themfelves and us, by removing
themfelves to fome part of the king of Great Britain's dominions, as by
that means they may live unmolefted by us or we by them; for our fixt
opinion is, that thofe who do not deferve a place among us, ought not
to have one.

" We conclude, with requefting the council of fafety to take into
their confideration the paper figned " *John Pemberton* ;" and if it
fhall appear to them to be of a dangerous tendency, or of a treafonable nature, that they would commit the figner, together with
fuch other perfons as they can difcover were concerned therein, into
cuftody, until fuch time as fome mode of trial fhall afcertain the full
degree of their guilt and punifhment; in the doing of which, we wifh
their judges, whoever they may be, to difregard the man, his connexions, intereft, riches, poverty or principles of religion, and to attend
to the nature of his offence only."

The moft cavilling fectarian cannot accufe the foregoing with containing the leaft ingredient of perfecution. The free fpirit on which
the American caufe is founded, difdains to mix with fuch an impurity,
and leave it a rubbifh fit only for narrow and fufpicious minds to
grovel in. Sufpicion and perfecution are weeds of the fame dunghill,
and flourifh together. Had the Quakers minded their religion and
their bufinefs, they might have lived through this difpute in enviable
eafe, and none would have molefted them. The common phrafe with
thefe people is, " *Our principles are peace.*" To which may be replied,
and your practices are the reverfe ; for never did the conduct of men
oppofe their own doctrine more notorioufly than the prefent race of
the Quakers. They have artfully changed themfelves into a different
fort of people to what they ufed to be, and yet have the addrefs to
perfuade each other they are not altered; like antiquated virgins they
fee not the havoc deformity hath made upon them, but pleafantly
miftaking wrinkles for dimples, conceit themfelves yet lovely, and
wonder at the ftupid world for not admiring them.

Did no injury arife to the public by this apoftacy of the Quakers from themfelves, the public would have nothing to do with it; but as both the defign and confequences are pointed againft a caufe in which the whole community are interefted, it is therefore no longer a fubject confined to the cognizance of the meeting only, but comes as a matter of criminality before either the authority of the particular ftate *in which it is acted*, or of the continent *againft which* it operates.   Every attempt now to fupport the authority of the king and parliament of Great Britain over America, is treafon againft *every* ftate; therefore it is impoffible that any *one* can pardon or fcreen from punifhment an offender againft *all*.

But to proceed : While the infatuated tories of this and other ftates were laft fpring talking of commiffioners, accommodation, making the matter up, and the Lord knows what ftuff and nonfenfe, their *good* king and miniftry were glutting themfelves with the revenge of reducing America to *unconditional fubmiffion*, and folacing each other with the certainty of conquering it in *one campaign*.   The following quotations are from the parliamentary regifter of the debates of the houfe of lords, March 5th, 1776.

" The Americans," fays lord *Talbot*,* " have been obftinate,
" undutiful and ungovernable from the very beginning, from their
" firft early and infant fettlements ; and I am every day more and
" more convinced that this people will never be brought back to their
" duty, and the fubordinate relation they ftand in to this country,
" till *reduced to unconditional effectual fubmiffion ; no conceffion on our*
" *part, no lenity, no endurance*, will have any other effect but that of
" increafing their infolence."

" The ftruggle," fays lord *Townfend*,† " is now a ftruggle for
" power ; the die is caft, and the ONLY POINT which now re-
" mains to be determined, is, in what manner the war can be moft
" effectually profecuted and fpeedily finifhed, in order to procure that
" *unconditional fubmiffion*, which has been fo ably ftated by the noble
" Earl with the white ftaff" (meaning lord Talbot) ; " and I have
" no reafon to doubt that the meafures now purfuing will put an end
" to the war in the courfe of a SINGLE CAMPAIGN."
" Should it linger longer, we fhall then have reafon to expect that

* *Steward of the king's houfhold.*
† *Formerly general Townfend at Quebec, and late lord-lieutenant of Ireland.*

" fome foreign power will interfere, and take advantage of our
" domeftic troubles and civil diftractions."

Lord *Littleton*, " My fentiments are pretty well known.   I fhall
" only obferve now, that lenient meafures have had no other effect
" than to produce infult after infult; that the more we conceded,
" the higher America rofe in her demands, and the more infolent
" fhe has grown.   It is for this reafon that I am now for the moft
" effective and decifive meafures; and am of opinion, that no alter-
" native is left us, but to relinquifh America for ever, or finally
" determine to compel her to acknowledge the legiflative authority
" of this country; and it is the principle of an *unconditional fub-*
" *miffion* I would be for maintaining."

Can words be more expreffive than thefe.   Surely the tories will
believe the tory lords!   The truth is, they *do believe them*, and know
as fully as any whig on the continent knows, that the king and
miniftry never had the leaft defign of an accommodation with America, but an abfolute unconditional conqueft.   And the part which
the tories were to act, was, by downright lying, to endeavour to put
the continent off its guard, and to divide and fow difcontent in the
minds of fuch whigs as they might gain an influence over.   In fhort,
to keep up a diftraction here, that the force fent from England might
be able to conquer in " *one campaign*."   They and the miniftry
were, by a different game, playing into each others hands.   The cry
of the tories in England was, " *No reconciliation, no accommodation*,"
in order to obtain the greater military force; while thofe in America
were crying nothing but " *reconciliation and accommodation*," that the
force fent might conquer with the lefs refiftance.

But *this* " *fingle campaign*" is over, and America not conquered.
The whole work is yet to do, and the force much lefs to do it with.
Their condition is both defpicable and deplorable: Out of cafh—out
of heart, and out of hope.   A country furnifhed with arms and ammunition, as America now is, with three millions of inhabitants, and
three thoufand miles diftant from the neareft enemy that can approach
her, is able to look and laugh them in the face.

Howe appears to have two objects in view, either to go up the
North-river, or come to Philadelphia.

By going up the North-river, he fecures a retreat for his army
through Canada, but the fhips muft return if they return at all, the
fame way they went; and as our army would be in the rear, the
fafety of their paffage down is a doubtful matter.   By fuch a motion

he fhuts himfelf from all fupplies from Europe but through Canada, and expofes his army and navy to the danger of perifhing. The idea of his cutting off the communication between the Eaftern and Southern ftates, by means of the North-river, is merely vifionary. He cannot do it by his fhipping ; becaufe no fhip can lay long at anchor in any river within reach of the fhore ; a fingle gun would drive a firft rate from fuch a ftation. This was fully proved laft October at forts Wafhington and Lee, where one gun only, on each fide the river, obliged two frigates to cut and be towed off in an hour's time. Neither can he cut it off by his army ; becaufe the feveral pofts they muft occupy, would divide them almoft to nothing, and expofe them to be picked up by ours like pebbles on a river's bank ; but admitting he could, where is the injury ? Becaufe while his whole force is cantoned out, as centries over the water, they will be very innocently employed, and the moment they march into the country, the communication opens.

The moft probable object is Philadelphia, and the reafons are many. Howe's bufinefs in America is to conquer it, and in proportion as he finds himfelf unable to the tafk, he will employ his ftrength to diftrefs women and weak minds, in order to accomplifh through *their* fears what he cannot effect by his *own* force. His coming or attempting to come to Philadelphia is a circumftance that proves his weaknefs : For no general, that felt himfelf able to take the field and attack his antagonift, would think of bringing his army into a city in the fummer time ; and this mere fhifting the fcene from place to place, without effecting any thing, has feeblenefs and cowardice on the face of it, and holds him up in a contemptible light to any one who can reafon juftly and firmly. By feveral informations from New-York, it appears that their army in general, both officers and men, have given up the expectation of conquering America ; their eye now is fixt upon the fpoil. They fuppofe Philadelphia to be rich with ftores, and as they think to get more by robbing a town than by attacking an army, their movement towards this city is probable. We are not now contending againft an army of foldiers, but againft a band of thieves, who had rather plunder than fight, and have no other hope of conqueft than by cruelty.

They expect to get a mighty booty and ftrike another general panic by making a fudden movement and getting poffeffion of this city ; but unlefs they can march *out* as well as *in*, or get the entire command of the river, to remove off their plunder, they may probably be ftept with the ftolen goods upon them. They have never yet fucceeded wherever they have been oppofed but at fort Wafhington. At Charlefton their defeat was effectual. At Ticonderoga they ran away. In every fkirmifh at Kingfbridge and the White Plains they were obliged to retreat, and the inftant our arms were turned upon them in the Jerfeys, they turned likewife, and thofe that turned not were taken.

The neceffity of always fitting our internal police to the circumftances of the times we live in, is fomething fo ftrikingly obvious that no fufficient objection can be made againft it. The fafety of all focieties depend upon it; and where this point is not attended to, the confequences will either be a general languor or a tumult. The encouragement and protection of the good fubjects of any ftate, and the fuppreffion and punifhment of bad ones, are the principal objects for which all authority is inftituted, and the line in which it ought to operate. We have in this city a ftrange variety of men and characters, and the circumftances of the times require they fhould be publicly known; it is not the number of tories that hurt us, fo much as the not finding out who they are; men muft now take one fide or the other, and abide by the confequences: The Quakers, trufting to their fhort-fighted fagacity, have, moft unluckily for them, made their declaration in their laft teftimony, and we ought *now* to take them at their word. They have voluntarily read themfelves out of the continental meeting, and cannot hope to be reftored to it again, but by payment and penitence. Men whofe political principles are founded on avarice, are beyond the reach of reafon, and the only cure of toryifm of this caft, is to tax it. A fubftantial good drawn from a real evil, is of the fame benefit to fociety, as if drawn from a virtue; and where men have not public fpirit to render themfelves ferviceable, it ought to be the ftudy of government to draw the beft ufe poffible from their vices. When the governing paffion of any man or fet of men is once known, the method of managing them is eafy; for even mifers, whom no public virtue can imprefs, would become generous, could a heavy tax be laid upon covetoufnefs.

The tories have endeavoured to infure their property with the enemy, by forfeiting their reputation with us; from which may be juftly inferred, that their governing paffion is avarice. Make them as much afraid of lofing on one fide as the other, and you ftagger their toryifm; make them more fo, and you reclaim them; for their principle is to worfhip any power they are moft afraid of.

This method of confidering men and things together, opens into a large field for fpeculation, and affords me opportunity of offering fome obfervations on the ftate of our currency, fo as to make the fupport of it go hand in hand, with the fuppreffion of difaffection and the encouragement of public fpirit.

The thing which firft prefents itfelf in infpecting the ftate of the currency, is, that we have too much of it, and that there is a neceffity of reducing the quantity, in order to encreafe the value. Men are daily growing poor by the very means they take to get rich, for in the fame proportion that the prices of all goods on hand are raifed, the value of all money laid by is reduced. A fimple cafe will make this clear : Let a man have one hundred pounds cafh, and as many goods on hand as will to day fell for £.20 but not content with the prefent market price, he raifes them to 40, and by fo doing, obliges others in their own defence to raife cent. per cent. likewife ; in this cafe, it is evident that his hundred pounds laid by is reduced fifty pounds in value'; whereas, had the markets dropt cent. per cent. his goods would have fold but for ten, but his hundred pounds would have rifen in value to two hundred ; becaufe it would then purchafe as many goods again, or fupport his family as long again as before. And ftrange as it may feem, he is one hundred and fifty pounds the poorer for raifing his goods, to what he would have been had he lowered them ; becafe the forty pounds his goods fold for, is, by the general rife of the markets cent. per cent. rendered of no more value than the ten pounds would be had the market fallen in the fame proportion ; and confequently the whole difference of gain or lofs is on the different values of the hundred pounds laid by, viz. from fifty to two hundred. This rage for raifing goods is for feveral reafons much more the fault of the tories than the whigs ; and yet the tories (to their fhame and confufion ought they to be told of it) are by far the moft noify and difcontented. The greateft part of the whigs, by being now either in the army or employed in fome public fervice, are *buyers* only and not *fellers*, and as this evil has its origin in trade, it cannot be charged on thofe who are out of it.

But the grievance is now become too general to be remedied by partial methods, and the only effectual cure is to reduce the quantity of money: With half the quantity we fhould be richer than we are now, becaufe the value of it would be doubled, and confequently our attachment to it increafed ; for it is not the number of dollars a man has, but how far they will go, that makes him either rich or poor.

These two points being admitted, viz. that the quantity of money is too great, and that the prices of goods can be only effectually reduced by reducing the quantity of the money, the next point to be considered is, The method how to reduce it.

The circumstances of the times, as before observed, require that the public characters of all men should *now* be fully understood, and the only general method of ascertaining it is by an oath or affirmation, renouncing all allegiance to the king of Great-Britain, and to support the independency of the United States as declared by congress. Let at the same time, a tax of ten, fifteen or twenty per cent. per annum, to be collected quarterly, be levied on all property. These alternatives, by being perfectly voluntary, will take in all sorts of people. Here is the test ; here is the tax. He who takes the former, conscientiously proves his affection to the cause, and binds himself to pay his quota by the best *services* in his power, and is thereby justly exempt from the latter ; and those who choose the latter, pay their quota in money, to be excused from taking the former, or rather 'tis the price paid to us for their supposed, though mistaken, insurance with the enemy.

But this is only a part of the advantage which would arise by knowing the different characters of men. The whigs stake every thing on the issue of their arms, while the tories, by their disaffection, are sapping and undermining their strength ; and, of consequence, the property of the whigs is the more exposed thereby ; and whatever injury their estates may sustain by the movements of the enemy, must either be borne by themselves, who have done every thing which has *yet* been done, or by the tories, who have not only done nothing, but have by their disaffection, invited the enemy on.

In the present crisis we ought to know square by square, and house by house, who are in real allegiance with the United Independent States, and who are not. Let but the line be made clear and distinct, and all men will then know what they are to trust to. It would not only be good policy, but strict justice, to raise fifty or a hundred thousand pounds, or more, if it is necessary, out of the estates and property of the king of England's votaries, resident in Philadelphia, to be distributed, as a reward to those inhabitants of the city and state, who should turn out and repulse the enemy, should they attempt their march this way ; and likewise, to bind the property of all such persons to make good the damages which that of the whigs might sustain. In the undistinguishable mode of conducting a war, we frequently make reprifals at fea, on the veffels of perfons in England who are friends to our caufe compared with the refidentiary tories among us.

In every former publication of mine, from Common Senfe down to the laft Crifis, I have generally gone on the charitable fuppofition, that the tories were rather a miftaken than a criminal people, and have applied argument after argument with all the candour and temper I was capable of, in order to fet every part of the cafe clearly and fairly before them, and if poffible to reclaim them from ruin to reafou. I have done my duty by them and have now done with that doctrine, taking it for granted, that thofe who yet hold their difaffection, are, either a fet of avaricious mifcreants, who would facrifice the continent to fave themfelves, or a banditti of hungry traitors, who are hoping for a divifion of the fpoil. To which may be added, a lift of crown or proprietary dependants, who, rather than go without a portion of power, would be content to fhare it with the devil. Of fuch men there is no hope; and their obedience will only be according to the danger that is fet before them, and the power that is exercifed over them.

A time will fhortly arrive, in which, by afcertaining the characters of perfons now, we fhall be guarded againft their mifchiefs then; for in proportion as the enemy defpair of conqueft, they will be trying the arts of feduction and the force of fear by all the mifchiefs they can inflict. But in war we may be certain of thefe two things, viz. that cruelty in an enemy, and motions made with more than ufual parade, are always figns of weaknefs. He that can conquer, finds his mind too free and pleafant to be brutifh; and he that intends to conquer, never makes too much fhow of his ftrength.

We now know the enemy we have to do with. While drunk with the certainty of victory they difdained to be civil; and in proportion as difappointment makes them fober, and their apprehenfions of an European war alarm them, they will become cringing and artful; honeft they cannot be. But our anfwer to them, in either condition they may be in, is fhort and full, " As free and indepen-" dent ftates we are willing to make peace with you to-morrow, but " we can neither hear nor reply in any other character."

If Britain cannot conquer us, it proves, that fhe is neither able to govern nor protect us, and our particular fituation now is fuch, that any connexion with her would be unwifely exchanging a half-defeated enemy for two powerful ones. Europe, by every appearance and information, is now on the eve, nay, on the morning twilight of a war, and any alliance with *George the third* brings *France* and *Spain* upon our backs ; a feparation from him attach them to our fide ; therefore, the only read to *peace, honour* and commerce, is INDE-PENDENCE.

Written this fourth year of the UNION, *which GOD preferve.*

COMMON SENSE.

THE CRISIS.—NUMBER IV.

Philadelphia, September 12, 1777.

THOSE who expect to reap the bleffings of freedom, muft, like men, undergo the fatigues of fupporting it.   The event of yefterday is one of thofe kind alarms which is juft fufficient to roufe us to duty, without being of confequence enough to deprefs our fortitude.   It is not a field of a few acres of ground, but a caufe, that we are defending, and whether we defeat the enemy in one battle, or by degrees, the confequence will be the fame.

Look back at the events of laft winter and the prefent year, there you will find that the enemy's fucceffes have always contributed to reduce them.   What they have gained in ground, they paid fo dearly for in numbers, that their victories have in the end amounted to de-feats.   We have always been mafters at the laft pufh, and always fhall while we do our duty.   Howe has been once on the banks of the Delaware, and from thence driven back with lofs and difgrace : and why not be again driven from the Schuylkill? His condition and ours are very different.   He has every body to fight, we have only his one army to cope with, and which waftes away at every engage-ment; we can not only reinforce, but can redouble our numbers; he is cut off from all fupplies, and muft fooner or later inevitably fall into our hands.

Shall a band of ten or twelve thoufand robbers, who are this day fifteen hundred or two thoufand men lefs in ftrength than they were yefterday, conquer America, or fubdue even a fingle ftate? The thing cannot be, unlefs we fit down and fuffer them to do it.   Another fuch a brufh, notwithstanding we loft the ground, would, by ftill reducing the enemy, put them in a condition to be afterwards totally defeated.

Could our whole army have come up to the attack at one time, the confequences had probably been otherwife ; but our having different parts of the Brandywine-creek to guard, and the uncertainty which road to Philadelphia the enemy would attempt to take, naturally afforded them an opportunity of paffing with their main body at a place where only a part of ours could be pofted ; for it muft ftrike every thinking man with conviction, that it requires a much greater force to oppofe an enemy in feveral places, than is fufficient to defeat in any one place.

Men who are fincere in defending their freedom, will always feel concern at every circumftance which feems to make againft them ; it is the natural and honeft confequence of all affectionate attachments, and the want of it is a vice. But the dejection lafts only for a moment ; they foon rife out of it with additional vigour ; the glow of hope, courage and fortitude, will, in a little time fupply the place of every inferior paffion and kindle the whole heart into heroifm.

There is a myftery in the countenance of fome caufes, which we have not always prefent judgment enough to explain. It is diftreffing to fee an enemy advancing into a country, but it is the only place in which we can beat them, and in which we have always beaten them, whenever they made the attempt. The nearer any difeafe approaches to a crifis, the nearer it is to a cure. Danger and deliverance make their advances together, and it is only the laft pufh, that one or the other takes the lead.

There are many men who will do their duty when it is not wanted ; but a genuine public fpirit always appears moft when there is moft occafion for it. Thank God ! our army, though fatigued, is yet entire. The attack made by us yefterday, was under many difadvantages, naturally arifing from the uncertainty of knowing which route the enemy would take ; and from that circumftance, the whole of our force could not be brought up together time enough to engage all at once. Our ftrength is yet referved ; and it is evident that Howe does not think himfelf a gainer by the affair, otherwife he would this morning have moved down and attacked General Wafhington.

Gentlemen of the city and country, it is in your power, by a fpirited improvement of the prefent circumftance, to turn it to a real advantage. Howe is now weaker than before, and every fhot will contribute to reduce him. You are more immediately interefted than any other part of the continent ; your all is at ftake ; it is not fo with the general caufe ; you are devoted by the enemy to plunder and de-

ſtruction : It is the encouragement which Howe, the chief of plunderers, has promiſed his army.   Thus circumſtanced, you may ſave
yourſelves by a manly reſiſtance, but you can have no hope in any
other conduct.   I never yet knew our brave general, or any part of
the army, officers or men, out of heart, and I have ſeen them in circumſtances a thouſand times more trying than the preſent.   It is only
thoſe that are not in action, that feel languor and heavineſs, and the
beſt way to rub it off is to turn out, and make ſure work of it.

Our army muſt undoubtedly feel fatigue, and want a reinforcement
of reſt, though not of valour.   Our own intereſt and happineſs call upon
us to give them every ſupport in our power, and make the burden of
the day, on which the ſafety of this city depends, light as poſſible.
Remember, gentlemen, that we have forces both to the northward
and ſouthward of Philadelphia, and if the enemy be but ſtopt till
thoſe can arrive, this city will be ſaved, and the enemy finally routed.
You have too much at ſtake to heſitate.   You ought not to think
an hour upon the matter, but to ſpring to action at once.   Other
ſtates have been invaded, have likewiſe driven off the invaders.   Now
our time and turn is come, and perhaps the finiſhing ſtroke is reſerved
for us.   When we look back on the dangers we have been ſaved from,
and reflect on the ſucceſs we have been bleſſed with, it would be ſinful
either to be idle or deſpair.

I cloſe this paper with a ſhort addreſs to general Howe.   You, ſir,
are only lingering out the period that ſhall bring with it your defeat.
You have yet ſcarce began upon the war, and the farther you enter,
the faſter will your troubles thicken.   What you now enjoy is only a
reſpite from ruin ; an invitation to deſtruction ; ſomething that will
lead on to our deliverance at your expence.   We know the cauſe we
are engaged in, and though a paſſionate fondneſs for it may make us
grieve at every injury that threatens it, yet, when the moment of concern is over, the determination to duty returns.   We are not moved
by the gloomy ſmile of a worthleſs king, but by the ardent glow of
generous patriotiſm.   We fight not to enſlave, but to ſet a country
free, and to make room upon the earth for honeſt men to live in.   In
ſuch a cauſe we are ſure we are right; and we leave to you the deſpairing reflection of being the tool of a miſerable tyrant.

COMMON SENSE.

THE CRISIS.—NUMBER V.

TO GENERAL SIR WILLIAM HOWE.

Lancaſter, March 21, 1778.

To argue with a man who has renounced the uſe and authority of reaſon, and whoſe philoſophy conſiſts in holding humanity in contempt, is like adminiſtring medicine to the dead, or endeavouring to convert an atheiſt by ſcripture. Enjoy, ſir, your infenſibility of feeling and reflecting. It is the prerogative of animals. And no man will envy you thoſe honours, in which a ſavage only can be your rival and a bear your maſter.

As the generoſity of this country rewarded your brother's ſervices laſt war with an elegant monument in Weſtminſter-Abbey, it is conſiſtent that ſhe ſhould beſtow ſome mark of diſtinction upon you. You certainly deſerve her notice, and a conſpicuous place in the catalogue of extraordinary perſons. Yet it would be a pity to paſs you from the world in ſtate, and conſign you to magnificent oblivion among the tombs, without telling the future beholder why. Judas is as much known as John, yet hiſtory aſcribes their fame to very different actions.

Sir William hath undoubtedly merited a monument : But of what kind, or with what inſcription, where placed or how embelliſhed, is a queſtion that would puzzle all the heralds of St. James's in the profoundeſt mood of hiſtorical deliberation. We are at no loſs, ſir, to aſcertain your real character, but ſomewhat perplexed how to perpetuate its identity, and preſerve it uninjured from the transformations of time or miſtake. A ſtatuary may give a falſe expreſſion to your buſt, or decorate it with ſome equivocal emblems, by which you may happen to ſteal into reputation and impoſe upon the hereafter traditionary world. Ill nature or ridicule may conſpire, or a variety of accidents combine, to leſſen, enlarge, or change Sir William's fame; and no doubt but he who has taken ſo much pains to be ſingular in his conduct, would chooſe to be juſt as ſingular in his exit, his monument and his epitaph.

The uſual honours of the dead, to be ſure, are not ſufficiently ſublime to eſcort a character like you to the republic of duſt and aſhes ; for however men may differ in their ideas of grandeur or government here, the grave is nevertheleſs a perfect republic. Death

is not the monarch of the dead, but of the dying. The moment he
obtains a conquest he lofes a fubject, and, like the foolifh king you
ferve, will, in the end, war himfelf out of all his dominion.

As a proper preliminary towards the arrangement of your funeral
honours, we readily admit your new rank of *knighthood.* The title is
perfectly in character, and is your own, more by merit than creation.
There are knights of various orders, from the knight of the windmill
to the knight of the poft. The former is your patron for exploits,
and the latter will affift you in fettling your accounts. No honorary
title could be more happily applied! The ingenuity is fublime!
And your royal mafter hath difcovered more genius in fitting you
therewith, than in generating the moft finifhed figure for a button,
or defcanting on the properties of a button-mould.

But how, fir, fhall we difpofe of you? The invention of a ftatuary
is exhaufted, and Sir William is yet unprovided with a monument.
America is anxious to beftow her funeral favours upon you, and
wifhes to do it in a manner that fhall diftinguifh you from all the
deceafed heroes of the laft war. The *Egyptian method of embalming* is
not known to the prefent age, and hieroglyphical pageantry hath out-
lived the fcience of decyphering it. Some other method, therefore,
muft be thought of to immortalize the new knight of the windmill
and poft. Sir William, thanks to his ftars, is not oppreffed with
very delicate ideas. He has no ambition of being wrapped up and
handed about in myrrh, aloes and caffia. Lefs chargeable odours
will fuffice; and it fortunately happens, that the fimple genius of
America hath difcovered the art of preferving bodies and embellifhing
them too, with much greater frugality than the ancients. In a
balmage, fir, of humble tar, you will be as fecure as Pharaoh, and in
a hieroglyphic of feathers rival in finery all the mummies of Egypt.

As you have already made your exit from the moral world, and by
numberlefs acts both of paffionate and deliberate injuftice engraved
an " *Here Lyeth,*" on your deceafed honour, it muft be mere affec-
tation in you to pretend concern at the humours or opinions of
mankind refpecting you. What remains of you may expire at any
time. The fooner the better. For he who furvives his reputation,
lives out of fpite to himfelf, like a man liftening to his own reproach.

Thus entombed and ornamented, I leave you to the infpection of
the curious, and return to the hiftory of your yet furviving actions.
————The character of Sir William hath undergone fome extraordinary revolutions fince his arrival in America. It is now fixed and

known ; and we have nothing to hope from your candour or to fear from your capacity. Indolence and inability have too large a share in your compofition ever to fuffer you to be any thing more than the hero of little villanies and unfinifhed adventures. That, which to fome perfons appeared moderation in you at firft, was not produced by any real virtue of your own, but by a contraft of paffions dividing and holding you in perpetual irrefolution. One vice will frequently expel another, without the leaft merit in the man ; as powers in contrary directions reduce each other to reft.

It became you to have fupported a dignified folemnity of character; to have fhewn a fuperior liberality of foul ; to have won refpect by an obftinate perfeverance in maintaining order, and to have exhibited on all occafions, fuch an unchangeable gracioufnefs of conduct, that while we beheld in you the refolution of an enemy, we might admire in you the fincerity of a man. You came to America under the high-founding titles of commander and commiffioner ; not only to fupprefs what you called rebellion by arms, but to fhame it out of countenance, by the excellence of your example. Inftead of which, you have been the patron of low and vulgar frauds, the encourager of Indian cruelties; and have imported a cargo of vices blacker than thofe you pretended to fupprefs.

Mankind are not univerfally agreed in their determination of right and wrong ; but there are certain actions which the confent of all nations and individuals hath branded with the unchangeable name of MEANNESS. In the lift of human vices we find fome of fuch a refined conftitution, that they cannot be carried into practice without feducing fome virtue to their affiftance ; but *meannefs* hath neither alliance nor apology. It is generated in the duft and fweepings of other vices, and is of fuch a hateful figure that all the reft confpire to difown it. Sir William, the commiffioner of George the Third, hath at laft vouchfafed to give it rank and pedigree. He has placed the fugitive at the council board, and dubbed it companion of the order of knighthood.

The particular act of meannefs which I allude to in this defcription, is forgery. You, fir, have abetted and patronifed the forging and uttering counterfeit continental bills. In the fame New-York newfpapers in which your own proclamation under your mafter's authority was publifhed, offering, or pretending to offer, pardon and protection to the inhabitants of thefe ftates, there were repeated advertifements of counterfeit money for fale, and perfons who have come officially from you and under fanction of your flag, have been taken up in attempting to put them off.

A conduct fo bafely mean in a public character is without precedent or pretence. Every nation on earth, whether friends or enemies, will unite in defpifing you. 'Tis an incendiary war upon fociety which nothing can excufe or palliate—An improvement upon beggarly villany—and fhews an inbred wretchednefs of heart made up between the venomous malignity of a ferpent and the fpiteful imbecility of an inferior reptile.

The laws of any civilized country would condemn you to the gibbet without regard to your rank or titles, becaufe it is an action foreign to the ufage and cuftom of war ; and fhould you fall into our hands, which pray God you may, it will be a doubtful matter whether we are to confider you as a military prifoner or a prifoner for felony.

Befides, it is exceedingly unwife and impolitic in you, or any perfons in the Englifh fervice, to promote, or even encourage, or wink, at the crime of forgery in any cafe whatever.   Becaufe, as the riches of England, as a nation, are chiefly in paper, and the far greater part of trade among individuals is carried on by the fame medium, that is, by notes and drafts on one another, they, therefore, of all people in the world ought to endeavour to keep forgery out of fight, and, if poffible not to revive the idea of it.   It is dangerous to make men familiar with a crime which they may afterwards practife to much greater advantage againft thofe who firft taught them.   Several officers in the Englifh army have made their exit at the gallows for forgery on their agents ; for we all know, who knew any thing of England, that there is not a more neceffitous body of men, taking them generally, than what the Englifh officers are.   They contrive to make a fhew at the expence of the tailor, and appear clean at the charge of the wafher-women.

England hath at this time nearly two hundred million pounds fterling of public money in paper, for which fhe hath no real property, befides a large circulation of bank notes, bank-poft bills, and promiffory notes and drafts of private bankers, merchants and tradefmen.   She hath the greateft quantity of paper currency and the leaft quantity of gold and filver of any nation in Europe; the real fpecie, which is about fixteen millions fterling, ferves only as change in large fums, which are always made in paper, or for payment in fmall ones. Thus circumftanced, the nation is put to its wit's end, and obliged to be fevere almoft to criminalty, to prevent the practice and growth of forgery. Scarcely a feffion paffes at the Old Bailey, or an execution at Tyburn, but witneffeth this truth. Yet you, fir, regardlefs of the policy which her neceffity obliges her to adopt, have made your whole army intimate with the crime. And as all armies, at the conclufion of a war, are too apt to carry into practice the vices of the campaign, it will probably happen, that England will hereafter abound in forgeries, to which art, the practitioners were firft initiated under your authority in America. You, fir, have the honour of adding a new vice to the military catalogue; and the reafon, perhaps, why the invention was referved for you is, becaufe no General before was mean enough even to think of it.

That a man whofe foul is abforbed in the low traffic of vulgar vice, is incapable of moving in any fuperior region, is clearly fhewn in you by the event of every campaign. Your military exploits have been without plan, object or decifion. Can it be poffible that you or your employers can fuppofe the poffeffion of Philadelphia to be any ways equal to the expence or expectation of the nation which fupports you? What advantages does England derive from any atchievements of yours? To her it is perfectly indifferent what place, you are in, fo long as the bufinefs of conqueft is unperformed and the charge of maintaining you remains the fame.

If the principal events of the three campaigns be attended to, the balance will appear ftrongly againft you at the clofe of each; but the laft, in point of importance to us, hath exceeded the former two. It is pleafant to look back on dangers paft, and equally as pleafant to meditate on prefent ones when the way out begins to appear. That period is now arrived, and the long doubtful winter of war is changing to the fweeter profpects of victory and joy. At the clofe of the campaign in feventy-five, you were obliged to retreat from Bofton. In the fummer of feventy-fix, you appeared with a numerous fleet and army in the harbour of New-York. By what miracle the Continent was preferved in that feafon of danger is a fubject of admiration! If inftead of wafting your time againft Long-Ifland, you had run up the North-River and landed any where above New-York, the confequence muft have been, that either you would have compelled General Wafhington to fight you with very unequal numbers, or he muft have fuddenly evacuated the city with the lofs of nearly all the ftores of the army, or have furrendered for want of provifions, the fituation of the place naturally producing one or other of thefe events.

The preparations made to defend New-York were, neverthelefs, wife and military; becaufe your forces were then at fea, their numbers uncertain; ftorms, ficknefs, or a variety of accidents might have difabled their coming, or fo diminifhed them on their paffage, that thofe which furvived would have been incapable of opening the campaign with any profpect of fuccefs; in which cafe, the defence would have been fufficient and the place preferved; for cities that have been raifed from nothing with an infinitude of labour and expence, are not to be thrown away on the bare probability of their being taken. On thefe grounds, the preparations made to maintain New-York were as judicious as the retreat afterwards. While you, in the interim, let flip the *very* opportunity which feemed to put conqueft in your power.

Through the whole of that campaign you had nearly double the forces which General Wafhington immediately commanded. The principal plan, at that time, on our part, was to wear away the feafon with as little lofs as poffible, and to raife the army for the next year. Long-Ifland, New-York, Forts Wafhington and Lee were not defended, after your fuperior force was known, under any expectation of their being finally maintained, but as a range of out works, in the attacking of which, your time might be wafted, your numbers reduced, and your vanity amufed by poffeffing them on our retreat. It was intended to have withdrawn the garrifon from Fort Wafhington after it had anfwered the former of thofe purpofes, but the fate of that day put a prize into your hands without much honour to yourfelves.

Your progref through the Jerfeys was accidental; you had it not even in contemplation, or you would not have fent fo principal a part of your force to Rhode-Ifland before-hand. The utmoft hope of America in the year feventy-fix reached no higher than that fhe might not *then* be conquered. She had no expectation of defeating you in that campaign. Even the moft cowardly tory allowed, that, could fhe withftand the fhock of *that* fummer her independence would be paft a doubt. You had *then* greatly the advantage of her. You were formidable. Your military knowledge was fuppofed to be complete. Your fleets and forces arrived without an accident. You had neither experience nor reinforcements to wait for. You had nothing to do but to begin, and your chance lay in the firft vigourous onfet.

America was young and unfkilled. She was obliged to truft her defence to time and practice; and hath, by mere dint of perfeverance, maintained her caufe, and brought her enemy to a condition, in which, fhe is now capable of meeting him on any grounds.

It is remarkable that in the campaign of feventy-fix, you gained no more, notwithftanding your great force, than what was given you by confent of evacuation, except Fort Wafhington: While every advan-tage obtained by us was by fair and hard fighting. The defeat of Sir Peter Parker was complete. The conqueft of the Heffians at Trenton by the remains of a retreating army, which but a few days before you affected to defpife, is an inftance of heroic perfeverance very feldom to be met with. And the victory over the Britifh troops at Princeton, by a haraffed and wearied party, who had been en-gaged the day before and marched all night without refrefhment, is attended with fuch a fcene of circumftances and fuperiority of gene-ralfhip, as will ever give it a place on the firft line in the hiftory of great actions.

When I look back on the gloomy days of laft winter and fee America fufpended by a thread, I feel a triumph of joy at the recol-lection of her delivery, and a reverence for the characters which fnatched her from deftruction. To doubt *now* would be a fpecies of infidelity, and to forget the inftruments which faved us *then* would be ingratitude.

The clofe of that campaign left us with the fpirit of conquerors. The northern diftricts were relieved by the retreat of general Carleton over the lakes. The army under your command were hunted back and had their bounds prefcribed. The continent began to feel its military importance, and the winter paffed pleafantly away in prepa-rations for the next campaign.

However confident you might be on your firft arrival, the courfe of the year feventy-fix gave you fome idea of the difficulty, if not impoffibility, of conqueft. To this reafon I afcribe your delay in opening the campaign of feventy-feven. The face of matters, on the clofe of the former year, gave you no encouragement to purfue a difcretionary war as foon as the fpring admitted the taking the field: for though conqueft, in that cafe, would have given you a double portion of fame, yet the experiment was too hazardous. The mi-niftry, had you failed, would have fhifted the whole blame upon you, charged you with having acted without orders, and condemned at once both your plan and your execution.

To avoid thofe misfortunes, which might have involved you and your money accounts in perplexity and fufpicion, you prudently waited the arrival of a plan of operations from England, which was, that you should proceed for Philadelphia by the way of Chefapeak, and that Burgoyne, after reducing Ticonderago, should take his route by Albany, and, if neceffary, join you.

The fplendid laurels of the laft campaign have flourifhed in the north. In that quarter America hath furprized the world, and laid the foundation of her this year's glory. The conqueft of Ticonderoga (if it may be called a conqueft) has, like all your other victories, led on to ruin. Even the provifions taken in that fortrefs (which by general Burgoyne's return was fufficient in bread and flour for nearly 5000 men for ten weeks, and in beef and pork for the fame number of men for one month) ferved only to haften his overthrow, by enabling him to proceed for Saratoga, the place of his deftruction. A fhort review of the operations of the laft campaign will fhew the condition of affairs on both fides.

You have taken Ticonderoga and marched into Philadelphia. Thefe are all the events which the year hath produced on your part. A trifling campaign indeed, compared with the expences of England and the conqueft of the continent, On the other fide, a confiderable part of your northern force has been routed by the New-York militia under general Herkemer. Fort Stanwix hath bravely furvived a compounded attack of foldiers and favages, and the befiegers have fled. The battle of Bennington has put a thoufand prifoners into our hands, with all their arms, ftores, artillery and baggage. General Burgoyne in two engagements has been defeated; himfelf, his army, and all that were his and theirs are now ours. Ticonderoga and Independence are retaken, and not the fhadow of an enemy remains in all the northern diftricts. At this inftant we have upwards of eleven thoufand prifoners, between fixty and feventy pieces of brafs ordnance, befides fmall arms, tents, ftores, &c. &c.

In order to know the real value of thofe advantages we muft reverfe the fcene, and fuppofe general Gates and the force he commanded, to be at your mercy as prifoners, and general Burgoyne with his army of foldiers and favages to be already joined to you in Pennfylvania. So difmal a picture can fcarcely be looked at. It hath all the tracings and colourings of horror and defpair ; and excites the moft fwelling emotions of gratitude by exhibiting the miferies we are fo gracioufly preferved from.

I admire this diftribution of laurels around the continent. It 's the earneft of future union. South-Carolina has had her day of fuffering and of fame; and the other fouthern ftates have exerted themfelves in proportion to the force that invaded or infulted them.   Towards the clofe of the campaign in feventy-fix, thefe middle ftates were called upon and did their duty nobly.   They were witneffes to the almoft expiring flame of human freedom.   It was the clofe ftruggle of life and death.   The line of invifible divifion; and on which, the unabated fortitude of a Wafhington prevailed, and faved the fpark that has fince blazed in the north with unrivalled luftre.

Let me afk, fir, what great exploits have you performed? Through all the variety of changes and opportunities which this war hath produced, I know no one action of yours that can be ftiled mafterly.   You have moved in and out, backward and forward, round and round, as if valour confifted in a military jig.   The hiftory and figure of your movements would be truly ridiculous could they be juftly delineated.   They refemble the labours of a puppy purfuing his tail; the end is ftill at the fame diftance, and all the turnings round muft be done over again.

The firft appearance of affairs at Ticonderoga wore fuch an un-promifing afpect, that it was neceffary, in July, to detach a part of the forces to the fupport of that quarter, which were otherwife def-tined or intended to act againft you, and this, perhaps, has been the means of poftponing your downfal to another campaign.   The de-ftruction of one army at a time is work enough.   We know, fir, what we are about, what we have to do, and how to do it.

Your progrefs from Chefapeak was marked by no capital ftroke of policy or heroifm.   Your principal aim was to get General Wafh-ington between the Delaware and Schuylkill and between Philadel-phia and your army.   In that fituation, with a river on each of his flanks, which united about five miles below the city, and your army above him, you could have intercepted his reinforcements and fupplies, cut off all his communication with the country, and, if neceffary, have difpatched affiftance to open a paffage for General Burgoyne. This fcheme was too vifible to fucceed, for had General Wafhington fuffered you to command the open country above him, I think it a very reafonable conjecture that the conqueft of Burgoyne would not have taken place, becaufe you could, in that cafe, have relieved him. It was therefore neceffary, while that important victory was in fuf-pence, to trepan *you* into a fituation, in which you could only be on the defenfive, without the power of affording him affiftance.   The manœuvre had its effect and Burgoyne was conquered.

VOL. I.   P

There has been fomething unmilitary paffive in you from the time
of your paffing the Schuylkill and getting poffeffion of Philadelphia
to the clofe of the campaign. You miftook a trap for a conqueft,
the probability of which had been made known to Europe, and the
edge of your triumph taken off by our own information long before.

Having got you into this fituation, a fcheme for a general attack
upon you at Germantown was carried into execution on the fourth
of October, and though the fuccefs was not equal to the excellence
of the plan, yet the attempting it proved the genius of America to
be on the rife, and her power approaching to fuperiority. The obfcurity of the morning was your beft friend, for a fog is always favourable to a hunted enemy. Some weeks after this, you, likewife,
planned an attack on General Wafhington while at Whitemarfh.
Marched out with infinite parade, but on finding him preparing to
attack you the next morning, you prudently cut about and retreated
to Philadelphia with all the precipitation of a man conquered in imagination.

Immediately after the battle of Germantown, the probability of
Burgoyne's defeat gave a new policy to affairs in Pennfylvania, and
it was judged moft confiftent with the general fafety of America to
wait the iffue of the Northern campaign. Slow and fure is found
work. The news of that victory arrived in our camp on the 18th of
October, and no fooner did the fhout of joy and the report of the
thirteen cannon reach your ears, than you refolved upon a retreat, and
the next day, that is, on the 19th, withdrew your drooping army into
Philadelphia. This movement was evidently dictated by fear; and
carried with it a pofitive confeffion that you dreaded a fecond attack.
It was hiding yourfelf among women and children, and fleeping
away the choiceft part of a campaign in expenfive inactivity. An
army in a city can never be a conquering army. The fituation admits only of defence. It is mere fhelter; and every military power in
Europe will conclude you to be eventually defeated.

The time when you made this retreat was the very time you
ought to have fought a battle, in order to put yourfelf in a condition
of recovering in Pennfylvania what you had loft at Saratoga. And
the reafon why you did not, muft be either prudence or cowardice;
the former fuppofes your inability, and the latter needs no explanation.
I draw no conclufions, fir, but fuch as are naturally deduced from
known and vifible facts, and fuch as will always have a being while
the facts which produced them remain unaltered.

After this retreat a new difficulty arose which exhibited the power of Britain in a very contemptible light ; which was the attack and defence of Mud-Island. For several weeks did that little unfinished fortress stand out against all the attempts of Admiral and General Howe. It was the fable of Bender realized on the Delaware. Scheme after scheme, and force upon force were tried and defeated. The garrison, with scarce any thing to cover them but their bravery, survived in the midst of mud, shot and shells, and were at last obliged to give it up more to the powers of time and gunpowder than to the military superiority of the besiegers.

It is my sincere opinion that matters are in a much worse condition with you than what is generally known. Your master's speech at the opening of parliament is like a soliloquy on ill luck. It shows him to be coming a little to his reason, for sense of pain is the first symptom of recovery in profound stupefactions. His condition is deplorable. He is obliged to submit to all the insults of France and Spain, without daring to know or resent them ; and thankful for the most trivial evasions to the most humble remonstrances. The time *was* when he could not *deign* an answer to a petition from America, and the time now *is* when he dare not *give* an answer to an affront from France. The capture of Burgoyne's army will sink his consequence as much in Europe as in America. In his speech he expresses his suspicions at the warlike preparations of France and Spain, and as he has only the one army which you command to support his character in the world with, it remains very uncertain when, or in what quarter, it will be most wanted or can be best employed ; and this will partly account for the great care you take to keep it from action and attacks, for should Burgoyne's fate be yours, which it probably will, England may take her endless farewel not only of all America but of all the West-Indies.

Never did a nation invite destruction upon itself with the eagerness and ignorance with which Britain had done. Bent upon the ruin of a young and unoffending country, she hath drawn the sword that hath wounded herself to the heart, and in the agony of her resentment hath applied a poison for a cure. Her conduct towards America is a compound of rage and lunacy ; she aims at the government of it, yet preserves neither dignity nor character in her methods to obtain it. Were government a mere manufacture or article of commerce, immaterial by whom it should be made or sold, we might as well employ her as another, but when we consider it as the fountain from whence the general manners and morality of a country take their rife, that the perfons intrufted with the execution thereof are by their ferious example and authority to fupport thefe principles, how abominably abfurd is the idea of being hereafter governed by a fet of men who have been guilty of forgery, perjury, treachery, theft, and every fpecies of villany which the lowelt wretches on earth could practife or invent. What greater public curfe can befal any country than to be under fuch authority, and what greater blefling than to be delivered therefrom. The foul of any man of fentiment would rife in brave rebellion againft them and fpurn them from the earth.

The malignant and venomous tempered General Vaughan has amufed his favage fancy in burning the whole town of Kingfton, in York government, and the late Governer of that State, Mr. Tryon, in his letter to General Parfons, has endeavoured to juftify it, and declared his wifh to burn the houfes of every committee-man in the country. Such a confeffion from one who was once entrufted with the powers of civil government, is a reproach to the character. But it is the wifh and the declaration of a man whom anguifh and difappointment have driven to defpair, and who is daily decaying into the grave with conftitutional rottennefs.

There is not in the compafs of language a fufficiency of words to exprefs the bafenefs of your king, his miniftry and his army. They have refined upon villany till it wants a name. To the fiercer vices of former ages they have added the dregs and fcummings of the moft finifhed rafcality, and are fo completely funk in ferpentine deceit, that there is not left among them *one* generous enemy.

From fuch men and fuch mafters may the gracious hand of Heaven preferve America! And though the fufferings fhe now endures are heavy, and fevere, they are like ftraws in the wind compared to the weight of evils fhe would feel under the government of your king, and his penfioned parliament.

There is fomething in meannefs which excites a fpecies of refentment that never fubfides, and fomething in cruelty which ftirs up the heart to the higheft agony of human hatred; Britain hath filled up both thefe characters till no addition can be made, and hath not reputation left with us to obtain credit for the flighteft promife. The will of God hath parted us, and the deed is regiftered for eternity. When fhe fhall be a fpot fcarcely vifible among the nations, America fhall flourifh the favourite of Heaven and the friend of mankind.

For the domeftic happinefs of Britain and the peace of the world I with she had not a foot of land but what is circumscribed within her own island. Extent of dominion hath been her ruin, and instead of civilizing others hath brutalized herself. Her late reduction of India, under Clive and his successors, was not so properly a conquest as an extermination of mankind. She is the only power who could practise the prodigal barbarity of tying men to the mouths of loaded cannon and blowing them away. It happens that General Burgoyne, who made the report of that horrid transaction in the house of commons, is now a prisoner with us, and though an enemy, I can appeal to him for the truth of it, being confident that he neither can nor will deny it. Yet Clive received the approbation of the last parliament.

When we take a survey of mankind we cannot help cursing the wretch, who, to the unavoidable misfortunes of nature shall wilfully add the calamities of war. One wouldthink there were evils enough in the world without studying to increase them, and that life is sufficiently short without shaking the sand that measures it. The histories of Alexander, and Charles of Sweden, are the histories of human devils; a good man can not think of their actions without abhorrence nor of their deaths without rejoicings. To see the bounties of Heaven destroyed, the beautiful face of nature laid waste, and the choicest works of creation and art tumbled into ruin, would fetch a curse from the soul of piety itself. But in this country the aggravation is heightened by a new combination of affecting circumstances. America was young, and, compared with other countries, was virtuous. None but a Herod of uncommon malice would have made war upon infancy and innocence; and none but a people of the most finished fortitude dared under those circumstances, have resisted the tyranny. The natives, or their ancestors, had fled from the former oppressions of England, and with the industry of bees had changed a wilderness into a habitable world. To Britain they were indebted for nothing. The country was the gift of Heaven, and God alone is their Lord and Sovereign.

The time, sir, will come when you, in a melancholy hour, shall reckon up your miseries by your murders in America. Life, with you, begins to wear a clouded aspect. The vision of pleasurable delusion is wearing away, and changing to the barren wild of age and sorrow. The poor reflection of having served your king will yield you no consolation in your parting moments. He will crumble to the same undistinguished ashes with yourself, and have sins enough of his own to answer for. It is not the farcical benedictions of a bishop, nor the cringing hypocrify of a court of chaplains, nor the formality of an act of parliament, that can change guilt into innocence, or make the punifhment one pang the lefs. You may, perhaps, be unwilling to be ferious, but this deftruction of the goods of Providence, this havoc of the human race, and this fowing the world with mifchief, muft be accounted for to him who made and governs it. To us they are only prefent fufferings, but to him they are deep rebellions.

If there is a fin fuperior to every other it is that of wilful and offenfive war. Moft other fins are circumfcribed within narrow limits, that is, the power of one man cannot give them a very general extenfion, and many kinds of fins have only a mental exiftence from which no infection arifes; but he who is the author of a war, lets loofe the whole contagion of hell, and opens a vein that bleeds a nation to death. We leave it to England and Indians to boaft of thefe honours ; we feel no thirft for fuch favage glory; a nobler flame, a purer fpirit animates America. She hath taken up the fword of virtuous defence; fhe hath bravely put herfelf between Tyranny and Freedom, between a curfe and a bleffing, determined to expel the one, and protect the other.

It is the object only of war that makes it honourable. And if there were ever a *juft* war fince the world began, it is this which America is now engaged in. She invaded no land of yours. She hired no mercenaries to burn your towns, nor Indians to maffacre their inhabitants. She wanted nothing from you and was indebted for nothing to you ; and thus circumftanced, her defence is honourable and her profperity is certain.

Yet it is not on the *juftice* only, but likewife on the *importance* of this caufe that I ground my feeming enthufiaftical confidence of our fuccefs. The vaft extenfion of America makes her of too much value in the fcale of Providence, to be caft, like a pearl before fwine, at the feet of an European ifland; and of much lefs confequence would it be that Britain were funk in the fea than that America fhould mifcarry. There has been fuch a chain of extraordinary events in the difcovery of this country at firft, in the peopling and planting it afterwards, in the rearing and nurfing it to its prefent ftate, and in the protection of it through the prefent war, that no man can doubt, but Providence hath fome nobler end to accomplifh than the gratification of the petty elector of Hanover or the ignorant and infignificant king of Britain.

As the blood of the martyrs hath been the feed of the Chriftian church, fo the political perfecutions of England will and hath already enriched America with induſtry, experience, union and importance. Before the preſent era ſhe was a mere chaos of uncemented colonies, individually expoſed to the ravages of the Indians and the invaſion of any power that Britain ſhould be at war with. She had nothing ſhe could call her own. Her felicity depended upon accident. The convulſions of Europe might have thrown her from one conqueror to another, till ſhe had been the ſlave of all and ruined by every one ; for until ſhe had ſpirit enough to become her own maſter, there was no knowing to which maſter ſhe ſhould belong. *That* period, thank God, is paſt, and ſhe is no longer the dependant, diſunited colonies of Britain, but the Independent and United States of America, knowing no maſter but Heaven and herſelf. You or your king may call this " Deluſion," " Rebellion," or what name you pleaſe. To us it is perfectly indifferent. The iſſue will determine the character, and time will give it a name as laſting as his own.

You have now, ſir, tried the fate of three campaigns, and can fully declare to England, that nothing is to be got on your part but blows and broken bones, and nothing on hers but waſte of trade and credit and an increaſe of poverty and taxes. You are now only where you might have been two years ago, without the loſs of a ſingle ſhip, and yet not a ſtep the forwarder towards the conqueſt of the Continent ; becauſe, as I have already hinted, " An army in a city can never be a conquering army." The full amount of your loſſes ſince the beginning of the war exceeds twenty thouſand men, beſides millions of treaſure, for which you have nothing in exchange. Our expences, though great, are circulated within ourſelves. Yours is a direct ſinking of money, and that from both ends at once, firſt in hiring troops out of the nation, and in paying them afterwards, be-cauſe the money in neither caſe can return again to Britain. We are already in poſſeſſion of the prize, you only in ſuit for it. To us it is a real treaſure, to you it would be only an empty triumph. Our expences will repay themſelves with tenfold intereſt, while yours en-tail upon you everlaſting poverty.

Take a review, ſir, of the ground you have gone over, and let it teach you policy, if it cannot honeſty. You ſtand but on a very tottering foundation. A change of the miniſtry in England may probably bring your meaſures into queſtion and your head to the block. Clive, with all his ſucceſſes, had ſome difficulty in eſcaping, and yours being all a war of loſſes, will afford you leſs pretenſions, and your enemies more grounds for impeachment.

Go home, fir, and endeavour to fave the remains of your ruined country, by a juft reprefentation of the madnefs of her meafures. A few moments well applied may yet preferve her from political deftruction. I am not one of thofe who wifh to fee Europe in a flame, becaufe I am perfuaded fuch an event will not fhorten the war. The rupture, at prefent, is confined between the two powers of America and England. England finds fhe cannot conquer America, and America has no wifh to conquer England. You are fighting for what you can never obtain, and we defending what we mean never to part with. A few words, therefore, fettle the bargain. Let England mind her own bufinefs and we will mind ours. Govern yourfelves and we will govern ourfelves. You may then trade where you pleafe unmolefted by us, and we will trade where we pleafe unmolefted by you; and fuch articles as we can purchafe of each other better than elfewhere may be mutually done. If it were poffible that you could carry on the war for twenty years you muft ftill come to this point at laft, or worfe, and the fooner you think of it the better it will be for you.

My official fituation enables me to know the repeated infults which Britain is obliged to put up with from foreign powers, and the wretched fhifts fhe is driven to, to glofs them over. Her reduced ftrength and exhaufted coffers in a three years' war with America, have given a powerful fuperiority to France and Spain. She is not now a match for them——But if neither counfels can prevail on her to think, nor fufferings awaken her to reafon, fhe muft e'en go on, till the honour of England becomes a proverb of contempt, and Europe dub her the Land of Fools.

I am, Sir,
With every wifh for an honourable peace,
Your friend, enemy, and countryman,

COMMON SENSE.

To the Inhabitants of America.

WITH all the pleafure with which a man exchanges bad company for good, I take my leave of Sir William and return to you. It is now nearly three years fince the tyranny of Britain received its firft repulfe by the arms of America. A period, which has given birth to a new world, and erected a monument to the folly of the old.

I cannot help being sometimes surprised at the complimentary references which I have seen and heard made to antient histories and transactions. The wisdom, civil governments, and sense of honour of the States of Greece and Rome, are frequently held up as objects of excellence and imitation. Mankind have lived for very little purpose, if, at this period of the world, they must go two or three thousand years back for lessons and examples We do dishonourary injustice to ourselves by placing them in such a superior line. We have no just authority for it, neither can we tell why it is that we should suppose ourselves inferior.

Could the mist of antiquity be taken away, and men and things viewed as they then really were, it is more than probable that they would admire us, rather than we them. America has surmounted a greater variety and combination of difficulties than, I believe, ever fell to the share of any one people in the same space of time, and has replenished the world with more useful knowledge and sounder maxims of civil government than were ever produced in any age before. Had it not been for America there had been no such thing as freedom left throughout the whole universe. England hath lost hers in a long chain of right reasoning from wrong principles, and it is from this country now she must learn the resolution to redress herself, and the wisdom how.

The Grecians and Romans were strongly possessed of the *spirit* of liberty but *not* the *principle*, for at the time they were determined not to be slaves themselves, they employed their power to enslave the rest of mankind. But this distinguished era is blotted by no one misanthropical vice. In short, if the principle on which the cause is founded, the universal blessings that are to arise from it, the difficulties that accompanied it, the wisdom with which it has been debated, the fortitude by which it has been supported, the strength of the power we had to oppose, and the condition in which we undertook it, be all taken in one view, we may justly stile it the most virtuous and illustrious revolution that ever graced the history of mankind.

A good opinion of ourselves is exceedingly necessary in private life, but absolutely necessary in public life, and of the utmost importance in supporting national character. I have no notion of yielding the palm of the United States to any Grecians or Romans that were ever born. We have equalled the bravest in times of danger, and excelled the wisest in the construction of civil governments, *no one in America excepted.*

From this agreeable eminence let us take a review of prefent affairs. The fpirit of corruption is fo infeparably interwoven with Britifh politics, that their miniftry fuppofe all mankind are governed by the fame motive. They have no idea of a people fubmitting even to temporary inconvenience from an attachment to rights and privileges. Their plans of bufinefs are calculated *by* the hour and *for* the hour, and are uniform in nothing but the corruption which gives them birth. They never had, neither have they at this time, any regular plan for the conqueft of America by arms. They know not how to go about it, neither have they power to effect it if they could know. The thing is not within the compafs of human practicability, for America is too extenfive either to be fully conquered or *paffively* defended. But fhe may be *actively* defended by defeating or making prifoners of the army that invades her. And this is the only fyftem of defence that can be effectual in a large country.

There is fomething in a war carried on by invafion which makes it differ in circumftances from any other mode of war, becaufe he who conducts it cannot tell whether the ground he gains, be for him, or againft him, when he firft makes it. In the winter of feventy-fix General Howe marched with an air of victory through the Jerfeys, the confequence of which was his defeat, and General Burgoyne at Saratoga experienced the fame fate from the fame caufe. The Spaniards about two years ago were defeated by the Algerines in the fame manner, that is, their firft triumphs became a trap in which they were totally routed. And whoever will attend to the circumftances and events of a war carried on by invafion, will find, that any invader, in order to be finally conquered muft firft begin to conquer.

I confefs myfelf one of thofe who believe the lofs of Philadelphia to be attended with more advantages than injuries. The cafe ftood thus. The enemy imagined Philadelphia to be of more importance to us than it really was; for we all knew that it had long ceafed to be a port, not a cargo of goods had been brought into it for near a twelvemonth, nor any fixed manufactories, nor even fhip-building carried on in it; yet as the enemy believed the conqueft of it to be practicable, and to that belief added the abfurd idea that the foul of all America was centered there, and would be conquered there, it naturally follows, that their poffeffion of it, by not anfwering the end propofed, muft break up the plans they had fo foolifhly gone upon, and either oblige them to form a new one, for which their prefent ftrength is not fufficient, or to give over the attempt.

We never had fo fmall an army to fight againft, nor fo fair an opportunity of final fuccefs as *now*. The death wound is already given. The day is our own if we follow it up. The enemy by his fituation is within our reach, and by his reduced ftrength is within our power. The minifters of Britain may rage as they pleafe, but our part is to conquer their armies. Let them wrangle and welcome, but let it not draw our attention from the *one* thing needful. *Here, in this* fpot is our bufinefs to be accomplifhed, our felicity fecured. What we have now to do is as clear as light, and the way to do it is as ftraight as a line. It needs not to be commented upon, yet, in order to be perfectly underftood I will put a cafe that cannot admit of a miftake.

Had the armies under the Generals Howe and Burgoyne been united and taken poft at Germantown, and had the Northern army, under General Gates, been joined to that under General Wafhington at White Marfh, the confequence would have been a general action ; and if in that action we had killed and taken the fame number of officers and men, that is, between nine and ten thoufand, with the fame quantity of artillery, arms, ftores, &c. as have been taken at the Northward, and obliged General Howe with the remains of his army, that is, with the fame number he now commands, to take fhelter in Philadelphia, we fhould certainly have thought ourfelves the greateft heroes in the world; and fhould, as foon as the feafon permitted, have collected together all the force of the Continent and laid fiege to the city, for it requires a much greater force to befiege an enemy in a town than to defeat them in the field. The cafe *now* is juft the fame as if it had been produced by the means I have here fuppofed. Between nine and ten thoufand have been killed and taken, all their ftores are in our poffeffion, and General Howe, in confequence of that victory, has thrown himfelf for fhelter into Philadelphia He, or his trifling friend Galloway, may form what pretences they pleafe, yet no juft reafon can be given for their going into winter quarters fo early as the 19th of October but their apprehenfions of a defeat if they continued out, or their confcious inability of keeping the field with fafety. I fee no advantage which can arife to America by hunting the enemy from ftate to ftate. It is a triumph without a prize, and wholly unworthy the attention of a people determined to conquer. Neither can any ftate promife itfelf fecurity while the enemy remains in a condition to tranfport themfelves from one part of the Continent to another. Howe, likewife, cannot conquer where we have no army to oppofe, therefore any fuch removals in him are mean and cowardly,

and reduces Britain to a common pilferer. If he retreats from Philadelphia, he will be defpifed; if he ftays, he may be fhut up and ftarved
out, and the country, if he advances into it, may become his Saratoga.
He has his choice of evils and we of opportunities. If he moves early,
it is not only a fign but a proof that he expects no reinforcement,
and his delays will prove that he either waits for the arrival of a plan
to go upon, or force to execute it, or both; in *which* cafe, our ftrength
will increafe more than his, therefore in *any* cafe we cannot be wrong
if we do but proceed.

The particular condition of Pennfylvania deferves the attention of
all the other ftates. Her military ftrength muft not be eftimated by
the number of inhabitants. Here are men of all nations, characters,
profeffions and interefts. Here are the firmeft whigs, furviving, like
fparks in the ocean, unquenched and uncooled in the midft of dif-
couragement and difaffection. Here are men lofing their all with
cheerfulnefs, and collecting fire and fortitude from the flames of their
own eftates. Here are others fkulking in fecret, many making a market of the times, and numbers who are changing whig and tory with
the circumftances of every day.

It is by mere dint of fortitude and perfeverance that the whigs of
this ftate have been able to maintain fo good a countenance, and do
even what they have done. We want help, and the fooner it can
arrive the more effectual it will be. The invaded ftate, be it which
it may, will always feel an additional burden upon its back, and be
hard fet to fupport its civil power with fufficient authority: and this
difficulty will always rife or fall, in proportion as the other ftates throw
in their affiftance to the common caufe.

The enemy will moft probably make many manœuvres at the opening of this campaign, to amufe and draw off the attention of the feveral ftates from the *one thing needful*. We may expect to hear of alarms
and pretended expeditions to *this* place and *that* place, to the Southward, the Eaftward and the Northward, all intended to prevent our
forming into one formidable body. The lefs the enemy's ftrength
is, the more fubtleties of this kind will they make ufe of. Their exiftence depends upon it, becaufe the force of America, when collected,
is fufficient to fwallow their prefent army up. It is therefore our bufinefs to make fhort work of it, by bending our whole attention to *this
one principal point*, for the inftant that the main body under General
Howe is defeated, all the inferior alarms throughout the Continent,
like fo many fhadows, will follow his downfal.

The only way to finish a war with the least possible bloodshed, or perhaps without any, is to collect an army, against the power of which, the enemy shall have no chance. By not doing this, we prolong the war, and double both the calamities and the expences of it. What a rich and happy country would America be, were she, by a vigourous exertion, to reduce Howe as she has reduced Burgoyne. Her currency would rise to millions beyond its present value. Every man would be rich, and every man would have it in his power to be happy. And why not do these things? What is there to hinder? America is her own mistrefs and can do what she pleafes.

If we had not at this time a man in the field, we could, neverthelefs, raife an army in a few weeks fufficient to overwhelm all the force which General Howe at prefent commands. Vigour and determination will do any thing and every thing. We began the war with this kind of fpirit, why not end it with the fame? Here, gentlemen, is the enemy. Here is the army. The intereft, the happinefs, of all America is centered in this half ruined fpot. Come on and help us. Here are laurels, come and fhare them. Here are tories, come and help us to expel them. Here are whigs that will make you welcome, and enemies that dread your coming.

The worft of all policy is that of doing things by halves. Penny wife and pound foolifh, has been the ruin of thoufands. The prefent fpring, if rightly improved, will free us from all our troubles, and fave us the expence of millions. We have now only one army to cope with. No opportunity can be fairer; no profpect more promifing. I fhall conclude this paper with a few outlines of a plan, either for filling up the battalions with expedition, or for raifing an additional force, for any limited time, on any fudden emergency.

That in which every man is interefted, is every man's duty to fupport. And any burden which falls equally on all men, and, from which every man is to receive an equal benefit, is confiftent with the moft perfect ideas of liberty. I would wifh to revive fomething of that virtuous ambition which firft called America into the field. Then every man was eager to do his part, and perhaps the principal reafon why we have in any degree fallen therefrom, is, becaufe we did not fet a fufficient value by it at firft, but left it to blaze out of itfelf, inftead of regulating and preferving it by juft proportions of reft and fervice.

Suppofe any ftate whofe number of effective inhabitants was 80,000, fhould be required to furnifh 3,200 men towards the defence of the continent, on any fudden emergency.

First, Let the whole number of effective inhabitants be divided into hundreds ; then if each of those hundreds turn out four men, the whole number of 3,200 will be had.

Secondly, Let the names of each hundred men be entered in a book, and let four dollars be collected from each man, with as much more as any of the gentlemen, whose abilities can afford it, shall please to throw in, which gifts likewise shall be entered against the donors' names.

Thirdly, Let the fums fo collected be offered as a prefent, over and above the bounty of twenty dollars, to any four who may be inclined to propofe themfelves as volunteers : If more than four offer, the majority of the fubfcribers prefent fhall determine which ; if none offer, then four out of the hundred fhall be taken by lot, who fhall be entitled to the faid fums, and fhall either go, or provide others that will, in the fpace of fix days.

Fourthly, As it will always happen, that in the fpace of ground on which an hundred men fhall live, there will be always a number of perfons who, by age and infirmity, are incapable of doing perfonal fervice, and as fuch perfons are generally poffeffed of the greateft part of the property in any county, their portion of fervice, therefore, will be to furnifh each man with a blanket, which will make a regimental coat, jacket, and breeches, or clothes in lieu thereof, and another for a watch cloak, and two pair of fhoes—for however choice people may be of thefe things matters not in cafes of this kind —Thofe who live always in houfes can find many ways to keep themfelves warm, but it is a fhame and a fin to fuffer a foldier in the field to want a blanket while there is one in the country.

Should the clothing not be wanted, the fuperannuated or infirm perfons poffeffing property, may, in lieu thereof, throw in their money fubfcriptions towards increafing the bounty ; for though age will naturally exempt a perfon from perfonal fervice, it cannot exempt him from his fhare of the charge, becaufe the men are raifed for the defence of property and liberty, jointly.

There never was a fcheme againft which objections might not be raifed. But this alone is not a fufficient reafon for rejection. The only line to judge truly upon, is, to draw out and admit all the objections which can fairly be made, and place againft them all the contrary qualities, conveniencies and advantages, then by ftriking a balance you come at the true character of any fcheme, principle or pofition.

The mo ft material advantages of the plan here propofed are eafe,
expedition, and cheapnefs ; yet the men fo raifed get a much larger
bounty than is any where at prefent given ; becaufe all the expences,
extravagance, and confequent idlenefs of recruiting are faved or prevented.   The country incurs no new debt, nor intereft thereon ; the
whole matter being all fettled at once and entirely done with.   It is
a fubfcription anfwering all the purpofes of a tax, without either the
charge or trouble of collecting.   The men are ready for the field
with the greateft poffible expedition, becaufe it becomes the duty of
the inhabitants themfelves, in every part of the country, to find up
their proportion of men, inftead of leaving it to a recruiting ferjeant,
who, be he ever fo induftrious, cannot know always where to apply.

I do not propofe this as a regular digefted plan, neither will the
limits of this paper admit of any further remarks upon it.   I believe
it to be a hint capable of much improvement, and as fuch fubmit it
to the public.

COMMON SENSE.

THE CRISIS.—NUMBER VI.

TO THE EARL OF CARLISLE, GENERAL CLINTON,
AND WILLIAM EDEN, ESQ. BRITISH COMMISSI-
ONERS, AT NEW-YORK.

Philadelphia, October 20, 1778.

THERE is a dignity in the warm paffions of a whig, which is
never to be found in the cold malice of a tory.   In the one, nature
is only heated—in the other fhe is poifoned.   The inftant the former
has it in his power to punifh, he feels a difpofition to forgive ; but
the canine venom of the latter knows no relief but revenge.   This
general diftinction will, I believe, apply in all cafes, and fuit as well
the meridian of England as America.

As I prefume your laft proclamation will undergo the ftrictures of
other pens, I fhall confine my remarks to only a few parts thereof.
All that you have faid might have been comprifed in half the compafs.   It is tedious and unmeaning, and only a repetition of your
former follies, with here and there an offenfive aggravation.   Your
cargo of pardons will have no market—It is unfafhionable to look at

them—Even fpeculation is at an end. They are become a perfect drug, and no way calculated for the climate.

In the courfe of your proclamation you fay, " The policy as well as the BENEVOLENCE OF GREAT-BRITAIN, have thus far checked the extremes of war, when they tended to diftrefs a people ftill confidered as their fellow fubjects, and to defolate a country fhortly to become again a fource of mutual advantage." What you mean by " the BENEVOLENCE of Great-Britain" is to me inconceivable. To put a plain queftion : Do you confider yourfelves men or devils ? For until this point is fettled, no determinate fenfe can be put upon the expreffion. You have already equalled, and in many cafes excelled, the favages of either Indies ; and if you have yet a cruelty in ftore you muft have imported it unmixed with every human material from the original warehoufe of hell.

To the interpofition of Providence, and her bleffings on our endeavours, and not to BRITISH BENEVOLENCE, are we indebted for the fhort chain that limits your ravages. Remember you do not at this time, command a foot of land on the Continent of America. Staten-Ifland, York-Ifland, a fmall part of Long-Ifland, and Rhode-Ifland, circumfcribe your power ; and even thofe you held at the expence of the Weft-Indies. To avoid a defeat and prevent a defertion of your troops, you have taken up your quarters in holes and corners of inacceffible fecurity ; and in order to conceal what every one can conceive, you now endeavour to impofe your weaknefs upon us for an act of mercy. If you think to fucceed by fuch fhadewy devices, you are but infants in the political world ; you have the A, B, C, of ftratagem yet to learn, and are wholly ignorant of the people you have to contend with. Like men in a ftate of intoxication, you forget that the reft of the world have eyes, and that the fame ftupidity which conceals you from yourfelves, expofes you to their fatire and contempt.

The paragraph I have quoted, ftands as an introduction to the following : " But when that country (America) profeffes the unnatural defign, not only of eftranging herfelf from us, but of mortgaging herfelf and her refources to our enemies, the whole conteft is changed ; and the queftion is, how far Great-Britain may, by every means in her power, deftroy or render ufelefs, a connexion contrived for her ruin, and the aggrandizement of France. Under fuch circumftances. the laws of felf prefervation muft direct the conduct of Britain, and if the Britifh colonies are to become an acceffion to

France, will direct her to render that acceffion of as little avail as poffible to her enemy.

I confider you in this declaration, like madmen biting in the hour of death. It contains likewife a fraudulent meanncfs; for, in order to juftify a barbarous conclufion, you have advanced a falfe pofition. The treaty we have formed with France is open, noble and generous. It is true policy, founded on found philofophy, and neither a furrender or mortgage, as you would fcandaloufly infinuate. I have feen every article, and fpeak from pofitive knowledge. In France, we have found an affectionate friend, a faithful ally ; from Britain, nothing but tyranny, cruelty and infidelity.

But the happinefs is, that the mifchief you threaten, is not in your power to execute; and if it were, the punifhment would return upon you in a ten-fold degree. The humanity of America hath hitherto reftrained her from acts of retaliation, and the affection fhe retains for many individuals in England, who have fed, clothed, and comforted her prifoners, has, to the prefent day, warded off her refentment, and operated as a fcreen to the whole. But even thefe confiderations muft ceafe, when national objects interfere and oppofe them. Repeated aggravations will provoke a retort, and policy juftify the meafure. We mean now to take you ferioufly up upon your own ground and principle, and as you do, fo fhall you be done by.

You ought to know, gentlemen, that England and Scotland, are far more expofed to incendiary defolation than America, in her prefent ftate, can poffibly be. We occupy a country, with but few towns, and whofe riches confift in land and annual produce. The two laft can fuffer but little and that only within a very limited compafs. In Britain, it is otherwife. Her wealth lies chiefly in cities and large towns, the repofitories of manufactures and fleets of merchantmen.— There is not a nobleman's country-feat but may be laid in afhes by a fingle perfon. Your own may probably contribute to the proof: In fhort, there is no evil which cannot be returned when you come to incendiary mifchief.—The fhips in the Thames, may certainly be as eafily fet on fire, as the temporary bridge was a few years ago; yet of that affair no difcovery was ever made; and the lofs you would fuftain by fuch an event, executed at a proper feafon, is infinitely greater than any you can inflict. The Eaft-India houfe, and the bank, neither are, nor can be fecure from this fort of deftruction, and, as Dr. Price juftly obferves, a fire at the latter would bankrupt the nation. It has never been the cuftom of France and England, when at war, to make thofe havocs on each other, becaufe the eafe with which they could retaliate, rendered it as impolitic as if each had deftroyed his own.

But think not, gentlemen, that our diftance fecures you, or our invention fails us. We can much eafier accomplifh fuch a point than any nation in Europe. We talk the fame language, drefs in the fame habit, and appear with the fame manners as yourfelves. We can pafs from one part of England to another unfufpected; many of us are as well acquainted with the country as you are, and fhould you impolitically provoke our will, you will moft affuredly lament the effects of it. Mifchiefs of this kind require no army to execute them. The means are obvious, and the opportunities unguardable. I hold up a warning piece to your fenfes, if you have any left and " to the unhappy people likewife, whofe affairs are committed to you."* I call not with the rancour of an enemy, but with the earneftnefs of a friend, on the deluded people of England, left between your blunders and theirs, they fink beneath the evils contrived for us.

" He who lives in a glafs-houfe, fays the Spanifh proverb, fhould never begin throwing ftones." This, gentlemen, is exactly your cafe and you muft be the moft ignorant of mankind or fuppofe us fo, not to fee on which fide the balance of accounts will fall. There are many other modes of retaliation, which, for feveral reafons, I choofe not to mention. But be affured of this, that the inftant you put a threat in execution, a counter blow will follow it. If you openly profefs yourfelves favages, it is high time we fhould treat you as fuch, and if nothing but diftrefs can recover you to reafon, to punifh will become an office of charity.

While your fleet lay laft winter in the Delaware, I offered my fervice to the Pennfylvania navy-board then at Trenton, as one who would make a party with them, or any four or five gentlemen on an expedition down the river to fet fire to it, and though it was not then accepted, nor the thing perfonally attempted, it is more than probable, that your own folly will provoke a much more vulnerable part. Say not when the mifchief is done, that you had not warning, and remember that we do not begin it, but mean to repay it. Thus much for your favage and impolitic threat.

In another part of your proclamation you fay, " But if the honours of a military life are become the object of the Americans, let them feek thofe honours under the banners of their rightful fovereign, and

* General Clinton's letter to congrefs.

in fighting the battles of the united British empire, againſt our late mutual and natural enemies." Surely ! the union of abſurdity with madneſs was never marked in more diſtinguiſhable lines than theſe. Your rightful ſovereign as you call him, may do well enough for you, who dare not enquire into the humble capacities of the man; but we who eſtimate perſons and things by their real worth, cannot ſuffer our judgments to be ſo impoſed upon ; and, unleſs it is your wiſh to ſee him expoſed, it ought to be your endeavour to keep him out of ſight. The leſs you have to ſay about him the better. We have done with him, and that ought to be anſwer enough. You have been often told ſo. Strange ! that the anſwer muſt be ſo often repeated. You go a begging with your king as with a brat, or with ſome unſaleable commodity you were tired of; and though every body tells no, no, ſtill you keep hawking him about. But there is one that will have him in a little time, and as we have no inclination to diſappoint you of a cuſtomer, we bid nothing for him.

The impertinent folly of the paragraph I have juſt q uoted, deſerves no other notice than to be laughed at and thrown by, but the principle on which it is founded is deteſtable. We are invited to ſubmit to a man who has attempted by every cruelty to deſtroy us, and to join him in making war againſt France, who is already at war againſt him for our ſupport.

Can Bedlam, in concert with Lucifer, form a more mad and deviliſh requeſt? Were it poſſible a people could ſink into ſuch apoſtacy they would deſerve to be ſwept from the earth like the inhabitants of Sodom and Gomorrah. The propoſition is an univerſal affront to the rank which man holds in the creation and an indignity to him who placed him there. It ſuppoſes him made up without a ſpark of honour, and under no obligation to God or man.

What ſort of men or Chriſtians muſt you ſuppoſe the Americans to be, who, after ſeeing their moſt humble petitions inſultingly rejected; the moſt grievous laws paſſed to diſtreſs them in every quarter ; an undeclared war let looſe upon them, and Indians and Negroes invited to the ſlaughter: Who, after ſeeing their kinſmen murdered, their fellow citizens ſtarved to death in priſons, and their houſes and pro-perty deſtroyed and burned: Who, after the moſt ſerious appeals to Heaven; the moſt ſolemn abjuration by oath of all government connected with you, and the moſt heart-felt pledges and proteſtation of faith to each other; and who, after ſoliciting the friendſhip, and enter-ing into alliances with other nations, ſhould at laſt break through all thefe obligations, civil and divine, by complying with your horrid and infernal propofal. Ought we ever after to be confidered as a part of the human race? Or, ought we not rather to be blotted from the fociety of mankind, and become a fpectacle of mifery to the world? But there is fomething in corruption, which, like a jaundiced eye, transfers the colour of itfelf to the object it looks upon, and fees every thing ftained and impure ; for unlefs you were capable of fuch conduct yourfelves, you could never have fuppofed fuch a character in us. The offer fixes your infamy. It exhibits you as a nation without faith; with whom oaths and treaties are confidered as trifles, and the breaking them as the breaking of a bubble. Regard to decency or to rank might have taught you better, or pride infpired you, though virtue could not. There is not left a ftep in the degradation of character to which you can now defcend ; you have put your foot on the ground floor, and the key of the dungeon is turned upon you.

That the invitation may want nothing of being a complete monfter, you have thought proper to finifh it with an affertion which has no foundation, either in fact or philofophy ; and as Mr. Fergufon, your fecretary, is a man of letters, and has made civil fociety his ftudy, and publifhed a treatife on that fubject, I addrefs this part to him.

In the clofe of the paragraph which I laft quoted, France is ftiled the " natural enemy" of England, and by way of lugging us into fome ftrange idea, fhe is ftiled " the late mutual and natural enemy" of both countries. I deny that fhe ever was the natural enemy of either ; and that there does not exift in nature fuch a principle. The expreffion is an unmeaning barbarifm, and wholly unphilofophical, when applied to beings of the fame fpecies, let their ftation in the création be what it may. We have a perfect idea of a natural enemy when we think of the devil, becaufe the enmity is perpetual, unalterable, and unabateable. It admits neither of peace, truce, or treaty ; confequently the warfare is eternal, and therefore it is natural. But man with man cannot arrange in the fame oppofition. Their quarrels are accidental and equivocally created. They become friends or enemies as the change of temper, or the caft of intereft inclines them. The Creator of man did not conftitute them the natural enemy of each other. He has not made any one order of beings fo. Even wolves may quarrel, ftill they herd together. If any two nations are fo, then muft all nations be fo, otherwife it is not nature but cuftom, and the offence frequently originates with the accufer. England is as truly the natural enemy of France, as France is of England,

and perhaps more fo　　Separated from the reft of Europe, fhe has contracted an unfocial habit of manners, and imagines in others the jealoufy fhe creates in herfelf. Never long fatisfied with peace, fhe fuppofes the difcontent univerfal, and buoyed up with her own importance, conceives herfelf the only object pointed at. The expreffion has been often ufed, and always with a fraudulent defign; for, when the idea of a natural enemy is conceived, it prevents all other enquiries, and the real caufe of the quarrel is hidden in the univerfality of the conceit. Men ftart at the notion of a natural enemy, and afk no other queftion. The cry obtains credit like the alarm of a mad dog, and is one of thofe kind of tricks, which, by operating on the common paffions, fecures their intereft through their folly.

But we, fir, are not to be thus impofed upon. We live in a large world, and have extended our ideas beyond the limits and prejudices of an ifland. We hold out the right hand of friendfhip to all the univerfe, and we conceive there to be a fociality in the manners of France, which is much better difpofed to peace and negotiation than that of England, and until the latter becomes more civilized, fhe cannot expect to live long at peace with any power. Her common language is vulgar and offenfive, and children with their milk fuck in the rudiments of infult——' The arm of Britain! The mighty ' arm of Britain! Britain that fhakes the earth to its centre and ' its poles! The fcourge of France! The terror of the world! ' That governs with a nod, and pours down vengeance like a God.' This language neither makes a nation great or little; but it fhews a favagenefs of manners, and has a tendency to keep national animofity alive. The entertainments of the ftage are calculated to the fame end, and almoft every public exhibition is tinctured with infult. Yet England is always in dread of France. Terrified at the apprehenfion of an invafion. Sufpicious of being outwitted in a treaty and privately cringing, though fhe is publicly offending. Let her therefore, reform her manners and do juftice, and fhe will find the idea of a natural enemy, to be only a phantom of her own imagination.

Little did I think, at this period of the war, to fee a proclamation which could promife you no one ufeful purpofe whatever, and tend only to expofe you. One would think you were juft awakened from a four years' dream, and knew nothing of what had paffed in the interval. Is this a time to be offering pardons, or renewing the long forgotten fubjects of charters and taxation? Is it worth your while, after every force has failed you, to retreat under the fhelter of argu-

ment and perfuafion ? Or can you think that we with nearly half
your army prifoners, and in alliance with France, are to be begged
or threatened into fubmiffion by a piece of paper ? But as commiffioners, at a hundred pounds fterling a week each, you conceive yourfelves bound to do fomething, and the genius of ill fortune told you,
you muft write.

For my own part, I have not put pen to paper thefe feveral
months. Convinced of your fuperiority by the iffue of every campaign, I was inclined to hope, that that which all the reft of the
world now fee, would become vifible to you, and therefore felt unwilling to ruffle your temper by fretting you with repetitions and
difcoveries. There have been intervals of hefitation in your conduct,
from which it feemed a pity to difturb you, and a charity to leave
you to yourfelves. You have often ftopt, as if you intended to think,
but your thoughts have ever been too early or too late.

There was a time when Britain difdained to anfwer, or even hear
a petition from America. That time is paft, and fhe in her turn
is petitioning our acceptance. We now ftand on higher ground,
and offer her peace ; and the time will come when fhe, perhaps in
vain, will afk it from us. The latter cafe is as probable as the former
ever was. She cannot refufe to acknowledge our independence with
greater obftinacy than fhe before refufed to repeal her laws ; and if
America alone could bring her to the one, united with France fhe
will reduce her to the other. There is fomething in obftinacy which
differs from every other paffion, whenever it fails it never recovers,
but either breaks like iron, or crumbles fulkily away like a fractured
arch. Moft other paffions have their periods of fatigue and reft ;
their fuffering and their cure ; but obftinacy has no refource, and
the firft wound is mortal. You have already begun to give it up,
and you will, from the natural conftruction of the vice, find yourfelves
both obliged and inclined to do fo.

If you look back you fee nothing but lofs and difgrace. If you
look forward the fame fcene continues, and the clofe is an impenetra-
trable gloom. You may plan and execute little mifchiefs, but are
they worth the expence they coft you, or will fuch partial evils have
any effect on the general caufe ? Your expedition to Egg-Harbour,
will be felt at a diftance like an attack upon a hen-rooft, and expofe
you in Europe, with a fort of childifh phrenzy. Is it worth while
to keep an army to protect you in writing proclamations, or to get
once a year into winter-quarters ? Poffeffing yourfelves of towns is

not conqueſt, but convenience, and in which you will one day or other be trepanned. Your retreat from Philadelphia, was only a timely eſcape, and your next expedition may be leſs fortunate:

It would puzzle all the politicians in the univerſe to conceive what you ſtay for, or why you ſhould have ſtaid ſo long. You are proſecuting a war in which you confeſs you have neither object nor hope, and that conqueſt, could it be effected, would not repay the charges: In the mean while, the reſt of your affairs are running into ruin, and a European war kindling againſt you. In ſuch a ſituation, there is neither doubt or difficulty; the firſt rudiments of reaſon will determine the choice, for if peace can be procured with more advantages than even a conqueſt can be obtained, he muſt be an ideot indeed that heſitates.

But you are probably buoyed up by a ſet of wretched mortals, who, having deceived themſelves, are cringing with the duplicity of a ſpaniel for a little temporary bread. Thoſe men will tell you juſt what you pleaſe. It is their intereſt to amuſe, in order to lengthen out their protection. They ſtudy to keep you amongſt them for that very purpoſe; and in proportion as you diſregard their advice, and grow callous to their complaints, they will ſtretch into improbability, and pepper off their flattery the higher.—Characters like theſe, are to be found in every country, and every country will deſpiſe them.

COMMON SENSE.

THE CRISIS.—NUMBER VII.

TO THE PEOPLE OF ENGLAND.

Philadelphia, November 21, 1778.

THERE are ſtages in the buſineſs of ſerious life in which to amuſe is cruel, but to deceive is to deſtroy; and it is of little conſequence, in the concluſion, whether men deceive themſelves or ſubmit, by a kind of mutual conſent, to the impoſitions of each other. That England has long been under the influence of deluſion or miſtake, needs no other proof than the unexpected and wretched ſituation ſhe is now involved in: And ſo powerful has been the influence, that no

provifion was ever made or thought of againft the misfortune, becaufe the poffibility of its happening was never conceived.

The general and fuccefsful refiftance of America, the conqueft of
Burgoyne, and a war with France, were treated in parliament as the
dreams of a difcontented oppofition, or a diftempered imagination.
They were beheld as objects unworthy of a ferious thought, and the
bare intimation of them afforded the miniftry a triumph of laughter. Short triumph indeed! For every thing which has been predicted has happened, and all that was promifed have failed. A long
feries of politics fo remarkably diftinguifhed by a fucceffion of misfortunes, without one alleviating turn, muft certainly have fomething
in it fyftematically wrong. It is fufficient to awaken the moft credulous into fufpicion, and the moft obftinate into thought. Either
the means in your power are infufficient, or the meafures ill planned ;
either the execution has been bad, or the thing attempted impracticable ; or to fpeak more emphatically, either you are not able, or
Heaven is not willing. For, why is it that you have not conquered
us ? Who, or what has prevented you ? You have had every opportunity you could defire, and fucceeded to your utmoft wifh in
every preparatory means, Your fleets and armies have arrived in
America without an accident. No uncommon misfortune hath intervened. No foreign nation hath interfered until the time you had
allotted for victory was paft. The oppofition either in or out of
parliament, neither difconcerted your meafures, retarded or diminifhed your force. They only foretold your fate. Every minifterial fcheme was carried with as high a hand as if the whole nation
had been unanimous. Every thing wanted was afked for, and every
thing afked for was granted. A greater force was not within the
compafs of your abilities to fend, and the time you fent it was of all
others the moft favourable. You were then at reft with the whole
world befide. You had the range of every court in Europe uncontradicted by us. You amufed us with a tale of commiffioners of
peace, and under that difguife collected a numerous army and came
almoft unexpectedly upon us. The force was much greater than we
looked for ; and that which we had to oppofe it with, was unequal
in numbers, badly armed, and poorly difciplined ; befide which,
it was embodied only for a fhort time, and expired within a few
months after your arrival. We had governments to form ; meafures
to concert ; an army to raife and train, and every neceffary article to
import or to create. Our non-importation fcheme had exhaufted

ur ftores and your command by fea intercepted our fupplies. We were a people unknown, and unconnected with the political world, and ftrangers to the difpofition of foreign powers. Could you poffibly wifh for a more favourable conjunction of circumftances? Yet all thefe have happened and paffed away, and as it were left you with a laugh. They are likewife events of fuch an original nativity as can never happen again, unlefs a new world fhould arife from the ocean.

If any thing can be a leffon to prefumption, furely the circumftances of this war will have their effect. Had Britain been defeated by any European power, her pride would have drawn confolation from the importance of her conquerors; but in the prefent cafe, fhe is excelled by thofe fhe affected to defpife, and her own opinions retorting on herfelf, become an aggravation of her difgrace. Misfortune and experience are loft upon mankind when they produce neither reflection nor reformation. Evils, like poifons, have their ufes, and there are difeafes which no other remedy can reach. It has been the crime and folly of England to fuppofe herfelf invincible, and that, without acknowledging or perceiving that a full third of her ftrength was drawn from the country fhe is now at war with. The arm of Britain has been fpoken of as the arm of the Almighty, and fhe has lived of late as if fhe thought the whole world created for her diverfion. Her politics, inftead of civilizing, has tended to brutalize mankind, and under the vain unmeaning title of " Defender of the Faith," fhe has made war like an Indian againft the religion of humanity. Her cruelties in the Eaft-Indies will NEVER, NEVER be forgotten; and it is fomewhat remarkable that the produce of that ruined country, tranfported to America, fhould there kindle up a war to punifh the deftroyer. The chain is continued, though with a kind of myfterious uniformity both in the crime and the punifhment. The latter runs parallel with the former; and time and fate will give it a perfect illuftration.

Where information is withheld, ignorance becomes a reafonable excufe; and one would charitably hope that the people of England do not encourage cruelty from choice but from miftake. Their reclufe fituation, furrounded by the fea, preferves them from the calamities of war, and keeps them in the dark as to the conduct of their own armies. They fee not, therefore they feel not. They tell the tale that is told them and believe it, and accuftomed to no other news than their own, they receive it, ftript of its horrors and prepared for the palate of the nation, through the channel of the London Gazette. They are made to believe that their generals and armies differ from thofe of other nations, and have nothing of rudenefs or barbarity in them. They fuppofe them what they wifh them to be. They feel a difgrace in thinking otherwife, and naturally encourage the belief from a partiality to themfelves. There was a time when I felt the fame prejudices, and reafoned from the fame errors; but experience, fad and painful experience, has taught me better. What the conduct of former armies was I know not, but what the conduct of the prefent is I well know. It is low, cruel, indolent, and profligate: And had the people of America no other caufe for feparation than what the army has occafioned, that alone is caufe enough.

The field of politics in England is far more extenfive than that of news. Men have a right to reafon for themfelves, and though they cannot contradict the intelligence in the London Gazette, they may frame upon it what fentiments they pleafe. But the misfortune is, that a general ignorance has prevailed over the whole nation refpecting America. The miniftry and minority have both been wrong. The former was always fo ; the latter only lately fo. Politics to be executively right, muft have a unity of means and time, and a defect in either overthrows the whole. The miniftry rejected the plans of the minority while they were practicable, and joined in them when they became impracticable. From wrong meafures they got into wrong time, and have now completed the circle of abfurdity by clofing it upon themfelves.

It was my fate to come to America a few months before the breaking out of hoftilities. I found the difpofition of the people fuch, that they might have been led by a thread and governed by a reed. Their fufpicion was quick and penetrating, but their attachment to Britain was obftinate, and it was at that time a kind of treafon to fpeak againft it. They difliked the miniftry, but they efteemed the nation. Their idea of grievance operated without refentment, and their fingle object was reconciliation. Bad as I believed the miniftry to be, I never conceived them capable of a meafure fo rafh and wicked as the commencing of hoftilities; much lefs did I imagine the nation would encourage it. I viewed the difpute as a kind of law-fuit, in which I fuppofed the parties would find a way either to decide or fettle it. I had no thoughts of independence or of arms. The world could not then have perfuaded me that I fhould be either a foldier or an author. If I had any talents for either they were buried in me, and might ever have continued fo, had not the neceffity of the times dragged and driven them into action. I had formed my plan of life, and conceiving myfelf happy, wifhed every body elfe fo. But when the country, into which I had but juft put my foot, was fet on fire about my ears, it was time to ftir. It was time for every man to ftir. Thofe who had been long fettled had fomething to defend ; thofe who had juft come had fomething to purfue ; and the call and the concern was equal and univerfal. For in a country where all men were once ad-venturers, the difference of a few years in their arrival could make none in their right.

The breaking out of hoftilities opened a new fufpicion in the po-litics of America, which though at that time very rare, has been fince proved to be very right. What I allude to is, " A fecret and fixt determination in the Britifh cabinet to annex America to the crown of England as a conquered country." If this be taken as the object, then the whole line of conduct purfued by the miniftry, though rafh in its origin and ruinous in its confequences, is neverthelefs uniform and confiftent in its parts. It applies to every cafe and refolves every difficulty. But if taxation or any thing elfe be taken in its room, then is there no proportion between the object and the charge. No-thing but the whole foil and property of the country can be placed as a poffible equivalent againft the millions which the miniftry expended. No taxes raifed in America could poffibly repay it. A revenue of two millions fterling a year would not difcharge the fum and intereft accumulated thereon, in twenty years.

Reconciliation never appears to have been the wifh or the object of adminiftration, they looked on conqueft as certain and infallible, and under that perfuafion fought to drive the Americans into what they might ftile a general rebellion, and then crufhing them with arms in their hands, reap the rich harveft of a general confifcation, and filence them for ever. The dependants at court were too nume-rous to be provided for in England. The market for plunder in the Eaft-Indies was over ; and the profligacy of government required that a new mine fhould be opened, and that mine could be no other than America conquered and forfeited. They had no where elfe to go. Every other channel was drained ; and extravagance, with the thirft of a drunkard, was gaping for fupplies.

If the miniftry deny this to have been their plan, it becomes them to explain what was their plan. For either they have abufed us in coveting property they never laboured for, or they have abufed you in expending an amazing fum upon an incompetent object. Taxation, as I mentioned before, could never be worth the charge of obtaining it by arms; and any kind of formal obedience which America could have made, would have weighed with the lightnefs of a laugh againſt fuch a load of expence. It is therefore moſt probable, that the miniſtry will at laſt juſtify their policy by their diſhonefty, and openly declare, that their original defign was conqueſt : And in this cafe, it well becomes the people of England to confider how far the nation would have been benefited by the fuccefs.

In a general view there are few conqueſts that repay the charge of making them, and mankind are pretty well convinced that it can never be worth their while to go to war for profit fake. If they are made war upon, their country invaded, or their exiſtence at ſtake, it is their duty to defend and preferve themfelves, but in every other light and from every other caufe is war inglorious and deteſtable. But to return to the cafe in queſtion—

When conqueſts are made of foreign countries, it is fuppofed that the COMMERCE and DOMINION of the country which made them are extended. But this could neither be the object nor the confequence of the prefent war. You enjoyed the whole commerce before. It could receive no poſſible addition by a conqueſt, but on the contrary, muſt diminiſh as the inhabitants were reduced in numbers and wealth. You had the fame DOMINION over the country which you ufed to have, and had no complaint to make againſt her for breach of any part of the contract between you or her, or contending againſt any eſtabliſhed cuſtom, commercial, political or territorial. The country and commerce were both your own when you BEGAN to conquer, in the fame manner and form as they had been your own an hundred years before. Nations have fometimes been induced to make conqueſts for the fake only of reducing the power of their enemies, or bringing it to a balance with their own. But this could be no part of your plan. No foreign authority was claimed here, neither was any fuch authority fufpected by you, or acknowledged or imagined by us. What then, in the name of Heaven, could you go to war for ? or what chance could you poſſibly have in the event, but either to hold the fame country which you held before, and that in a much worfe condition, or to lofe with an amazing expence what you might have retained without a farthing charges.

War never can be the intereſt of a trading nation, any more

than quarrelling can be profitable to a man in bufinefs. But to make war with thofe who trade with us, is like fetting a bull-dog upon a cuftomer at the fhop-door. The leaft degree of common fenfe fhews the madnefs of the latter, and it will apply with the fame force of conviction to the former. Piratical nations, having neither commerce or commodities of their own to lofe, may make war upon all the world, and lucratively find their account in it. But it is quite otherwife with Britain. For befides the ftoppage of trade in time of war fhe expofes more of her own property to be loft, than fhe has the chance of taking from others. Some minifterial gentlemen in parliament have mentioned the greatnefs of her trade as an apology for the greatnefs of her'lofs. This is miferable politics indeed! becaufe it ought to have been given as a reafon for her not engaging in a war at firft. The coaft of America commands the Weft-India trade almoft as effectually as the coaft of Africa does that of the Streights ; and England can no more carry on the former without the confent of America, than fhe can the latter without a Mediterranean pafs.

In whatever light the war with America is confidered upon commercial principles, it is evidently the intereft of the people of England not to fupport it ; and why it has been fupported fo long againft the cleareft demonftrations of truth and national advantage, is to me, and muft be to all the reafonable world, a matter of aftonifhment. Perhaps it may be faid that I live in America, and write this from intereft. To this I reply, that my principles are univerfal. My attachment is to all the world, and not to any particular part, and if what I advance is right, no matter where or who it comes from. We have given the proclamation of your commiffioners a currency in our newfpapers, and I have no doubt you will give this a place in yours. To oblige and be obliged is fair.

Before I difmifs this part of my addrefs, I fhall mention one more circumftance in which I think the people of England have been equally miftaken; and then proceed to other matter.

There is fuch an idea exifting in the world, as that of NATIONAL HONOUR, and this falfely underftood, is oftentimes the caufe of war. In a Chriftian and philofophical fenfe, mankind feem to have ftood ftill at individual civilization, and to retain as nations all the original rudenefs of nature. Peace by treaty is only a ceffation of violence for a reformation of fentiment. It is a fubftitute for a principle that is wanting and ever will be wanting till the idea of

NATIONAL HONOUR be rightly underftood. As individuals we profefs ourfelves Chriftians, but as nations we are heathens, Romans, and what not. I remember the late admiral Saunders declaring in the houfe of commons, and that in the time of peace, " That the city of Madrid laid in afhes was not a fufficient atonement for the Spaniards taking off the rudder of an Englifh floop of war." I do not afk whether this is Chriftianity or morality, I afk whether it is decency? whether it is proper language for a nation to ufe? In private life we fhould call it by the plain name of bullying, and the elevation of rank cannot alter its character. It is I think exceedingly eafy to define what ought to be underftood by national honour; for that which is the beft character for an individual is the beft character for a nation; and wherever the latter exceeds or falls beneath the former, there is a departure from the line of true greatnefs.

I have thrown out this obfervation with a defign of applying it to Great-Britain. Her idea of national honour feems devoid of that benevolence of heart, that univerfal expanfion of philanthropy, and that triumph over the rage of vulgar prejudice, without which man is inferior to himfelf, and a companion of common animals. To know whom fhe fhall regard or diflike, fhe afks what country they are of, what religion they profefs, and what property they enjoy. Her idea of national honour feems to confift in national infult, and that to be a great people, is to be neither a Chriftian, a philofopher, or a gentleman, but to threaten with the rudenefs of a bear, and to devour with the ferocity of a lion. This perhaps may found harfh and uncourtly, but it is too true, and the more is the pity.

I mention this only as her general character. But towards America fhe has obferved no character at all; and deftroyed by her conduct what fhe affumed in her title. She fet out with the title of Parent, or Mother Country. The affociation of ideas which naturally accompany this expreffion, are filled with every thing that is fond, tender and forbearing. They have an energy particular to themfelves, and overlooking the accidental attachment of common affections, apply with peculiar foftnefs to the firft feelings of the heart. It is a political term which every mother can feel the force of, and every child can judge of. It needs no painting of mine to fet it off, for nature only can do it juftice.

But has any part of your conduct to America correfponded with the title you fet up? If in your general national character you are unpolifhed and fevere, in this you are inconfiftent and unnatural, and you muſt have exceeding falſe notions of national honour, to ſuppoſe that the world can admire a want of humanity, or that national honour depends on the violence of reſentment the inflexibility of temper, or the vengeance of execution.

I would willingly convince you, and that with as much temper as the times will ſuffer me to do, that as you oppoſed your own intereſt by quarrelling with us, ſo likewiſe your national honour, rightly conceived and underſtood, was no ways called upon to enter into a war with America ; had you ſtudied true greatneſs of heart, the firſt and faireſt ornament of mankind, you would have acted directly contrary to all that you have done, and the world would have aſcribed it to a generous cauſe ; beſides which, you had (though with the aſſiſtance of this country) ſecured a powerful name by the laſt war. You were known and dreaded abroad ; and it would have been wiſe in you to have ſuffered the world to have ſlept undiſturbed under that idea. It was to you a force exiſting without expence. It produced to you all the advantages of real power ; and you were ſtronger through the univerſality of that charm, than any future fleets and armies may probably make you. Your greatneſs was ſo ſecured and interwoven with your ſilence, that you ought never to have awakened mankind, and had nothing to do but to be quiet. Had you been true politicians you would have ſeen all this, and continued to draw from the magic of a name, the force and authority of a nation.

Unwiſe as you were in breaking the charm, you were ſtill more unwiſe in the manner of doing it. Samſon only told the ſecret, but you have performed the operation ; you have ſhaven your own head, and wantonly thrown away the locks. America was the hair from which the charm was drawn that infatuated the world. You ought to have quarrelled with no power ; but with her upon no account. You had nothing to fear from any condeſcenſion you might make. You might have humoured her, even if there had been no juſtice in her claims, without any riſk to your reputation ; for Europe, faſcinated by your fame, would have aſcribed it to your benevolence, and America, intoxicated by the grant, would have ſlumbered in her fetters.

But this method of ſtudying the progreſs of the paſſions, in order to aſcertain the probable conduct of mankind, is a philoſophy in politics which thoſe who preſide at St. James's have no conception of. They know no other influence than corruption, and reckon all their probabilities from precedent. A new caſe is to them a new world, and while they are feeking for a parallel they get loft. The talents of Lord Mansfield can be eftimated at beft no higher than thofe of a fophift. He underftands the fubtleties but not the elegance of nature; and by continually viewing mankind through the cold medium of the law, never thinks of penetrating into the warmer region of the mind. As for Lord North, it is his happinefs to have in him more philofophy than fentiment, for he bears flogging like a top and fleeps the better for it. His punifhment becomes his fuppoit, for while he fuffers the lafh for his fins he keeps himfelf up by twirling about. In politics, he is a good arithmetician, and in every thing elfe nothing at all.

There is one circumftance which comes fo much within Lord North's province as a financier, that I am furprized it fhould efcape him, which is the different abilities of the two countries in fupporting the expence; for, ftrange as it may feem, England is not a match for America in this particular. By a curious kind of revolution in accounts, the people of England feem to miftake their poverty for their riches; that is, they reckon their national debt as a part of their national wealth. They make the fame kind of error which a man would do, who after mortgaging his eftate, fhould add the money borrowed, to the full value of the eftate in order to count up his worth, and in this cafe he would conceit that he got rich by running into debt. Juft thus it is with England. The government owed at the beginning of this war onehu ndred and thirty-five millions fterling, and though the individuals to whom it was due, had a right to reckon their fhares as fo much private property, yet to the nation collectively it was fo much poverty. There is as effectual limits to public debts as to private ones, for when once the money borrowed is fo great as to require the whole yearly revenue to difcharge the intereft thereon, there is an end to a farther borrowing; in the fame manner as when the intereft of a man's debts amounts to the yearly income of his eftate, there is an end to his credit. This is nearly the cafe with England, the intereft of her prefent debt being at leaft equal to one half of her yearly revenue, fo that out of ten millions annually collected by taxes, fhe has but five fhe can call her own.

The very reverfe of this was the cafe with America; fhe began the war without any debt upon her, and in order to carry it on, fhe neither raifed money by taxes, nor borrowed it upon intereft, but created it; and her fituation at this time continues fo much the reverfe of yours that taxing would make her rich, whereas it would make you poor. When we fhall have funk the fum which we have created, we fhall then be out of debt, be juft as rich as when we began, and all the while we are doing it, fhall feel no difference, becaufe the value will rife as the quantity decreafes.

There was not a country in the world fo capable of bearing the expence of a war as America; not only becaufe fhe was not in debt when fhe began, but becaufe the country is young and capable of infinite improvement, and has an almoft boundlefs tract of new lands in ftore, whereas England has got to her extent of age and growth, and has no unoccupied land or property in referve. The one is like a young heir coming to a large improvable eftate; the other like an old man whofe chances are over, and his eftate mortgaged for half its worth.

In the fecond number of the Crifis, which I find has been re-publifhed in England, I endeavoured to fet forth the impracticability of conquering America. I ftated every cafe, that I conceived could poffibly happen, and ventured to predict its confequence. As my conclufions were drawn not artfully but naturally, they have all proved to be true. I was upon the fpot; knew the politics of America, her ftrength and refources, and by a train of fervices, the beft in my power to render, was honoured with the friendfhip of the congrefs, the army and the people. I confidered the caufe a juft one. I know and feel it a juft one, and under that confidence never made my own profit or lofs an object. My endeavour was to have the matter well underftood on both fides, and I conceived myfelf tendering a general fervice, by fetting forth to the one the impoffibility of being conquered, and to the other the impoffibility of conquering. Moft of the arguments made ufe of by the miniftry for fupporting the war, are the very arguments that ought to have been ufed againft fupporting it ; and the plans, by which they thought to conquer, are the very plans in which they were fure to be defeated. They have taken every thing up at the wrong end. Their ignorance is aftonifhing, and were you in my fituation you would fee it. They may perhaps have your confidence, but I am perfuaded they would make very indifferent members of congrefs. I know what England is, and what America is, and from the compound of knowledge, am better enabled to judge of the iffue, than what the king or any of his minifters can be.

In this number I have endeavoured to fhew the ill policy and difadvantages of the war. I believe many of my remarks are new. Thofe which are not fo, I have ftudied to improve and place in a manner that may be clear and ftriking. Your failure is, I am perfuaded, as certain as fate. America is above your reach. She is at leaft your equal in the world, and her independence neither refts upon your confent, nor can be prevented by your arms. In fhort, you fpend your fubftance in vain, and impoverifh yourfelves without a hope.

But fuppofe you had conquered America, what advantage collectively or individually, as merchants, manufacturers, or conquerors, could you have looked for. This is an object you feemed never to have attended to. Liftening for the found of victory, and led away by the phrenzy of arms, you neglected to reckon either the coft or the confequences. You muft all pay towards the expence; the pooreft among you muft bear his fhare, and it is both your right and your duty to weigh ferioufly the matter. Had America been conquered, fhe might have been parcelled out in grants to the favourites at court, but no fhare of it would have fallen to you. Your taxes would not have been leffened, becaufe fhe would have been in no condition to have paid any towards your relief. We are rich by a contrivance of our own, which would have ceafed as foon as you became mafters. Our paper money will be of no ufe in England, and filver and gold we have none. In the laft war you made many conquefts, but were any of your taxes leffened thereby ? On the contrary, were you not taxed to pay for the charge of making them, and have not the fame been the cafe in every war ?

To the parliament I beg to addrefs myfelf in a particular manner. They appear to have fuppofed themfelves partners in the chace, and to have hunted with the lion from an expectation of a right in the booty; but in this it is moft probable they would, as legiflators, have been difappointed. The cafe is quite a new one, and many unforefeen difficulties would have arifen thereon. The parliament claimed a legiflative right over America, and the war originated from that pretence. But the army is fuppofed to belong to the crown, and if America had been conquered through their means, the claim of the legiflature would have been fuffocated in the conqueft. Ceded or conquered countries are fuppofed to be out of the authority of par-
· liament. Taxation is exercifed over them by prerogative and not by law. It was attempted to be done in the Grenades a few years ago, and the only reafon why it was not done was becaufe the crown had made a prior relinquifhment of its claim. Therefore, parliament have been all this while fupporting meafures for the eftablifhment of their authority, in the iffue of which, they would have been triumphed

over by the prerogative. This might have opened a new and interefting oppofition between the parliament and the crown. The crown would have faid that it conquered for itfelf, and that to conquer for parliament was an unknown cafe. The parliament might have replied, that America not being a foreign country, but a country in rebellion, could not be faid to be conquered, but reduced; and thus continued their claim by difowning the term. The crown might have rejoined, that however America might be confidered at firft, fhe became foreign at laft by a declaration of independence and a treaty with France; and that her cafe being, by that treaty, put within the law of nations, was out of the law of parliament. The parliament might have maintained, that as their claim over America had never been furrendered, fo neither could it be taken away. The crown might have infifted, that though the claim of parliament could not be taken away, yet being an inferior it might be fuperceded; and that, whether the claim was withdrawn from the object, or the object taken from the claim, the fame feparation enfued ; and that America being fubdued after a treaty with France, was to all intents and purpofes a regal conqueft, and of courfe the fole property of the king. The parliament, as the legal delegates of the people, might have contended againft the term " inferior," and refted the cafe upon the antiquity of power, and this would have brought on a fet of very interefting and rational queftions.

First, What is the original fountain of power and honour in any country?

Secondly, Whether the prerogative does not belong to the people?

Thirdly, Whether there is any fuch thing as the Englifh conftitution?

Fourthly, Of what ufe is the crown to the people?

Fifthly, Whether he who invented a crown was not an enemy to mankind?

Sixthly, Whether it is not a fhame for a man to fpend a million a year and do no good for it, and whether the money might not be better applied?

Seventhly, Whether fuch a man is not better dead than alive?

Eighthly, Whether a congrefs conftituted like that of America, is not the moft happy and confiftent form of government in the world? —With a number of others of the fame import.

In fhort, the contention about the dividend might have diftracted the nation; for nothing is more common than to agree in the conqueſt and quarrel for the prize; therefore it is, perhaps, a happy circumſtance, that our ſucceſſes have prevented the diſpute.

If the parliament had been thrown out in their claim, which it is moſt probable they would, the nation likewiſe would have been thrown out in their expectation; for as the taxes would have been laid on by the crown without the parliament, the revenue ariſing therefrom, if any could have aroſe, would not have gone into the exchequer, but into the privy purſe, and ſo far from leſſening their taxes, would not even have been added to them, but ſerved only as pocket money to the crown. The more I reflect on this matter the more I am aſtoniſhed at the blindneſs and ill policy of my countrymen, whoſe wiſdom ſeems to operate without diſcernment, and their ſtrength without an object.

To the great bulwark of the nation, I mean the mercantile and manufacturing part thereof, I likewiſe preſent my addreſs. It is your intereſt to ſee America an independent country and not a conquered one. If conquered, ſhe is ruined; and if ruined, poor; conſequently the trade will be a trifle, and her credit doubtful. If independent, ſhe flouriſhes, and from her flouriſhing muſt your profits ariſe. It matters nothing to you who governs America, if your manufactures find a conſumption there. Some articles will conſequently be obtained from other places, and right they ſhould; but the demand of others will increaſe by the great influx of inhabitants which a ſtate of independence and peace will occaſion, and on the final event you may be enriched. The commerce of America is perfectly free, and ever will be ſo. She will conſign away no part of it to any nation. She has not to her friends, and certainly will not to her enemies, though it is probable that your narrow-minded politicians, thinking to pleaſe you thereby, may ſome time or other make ſuch an unneceſſary propoſal. Trade flouriſhes beſt when it is free, and it is weak policy to attempt to fetter it. Her treaty with France is on the moſt liberal and generous principles and the French in their conduct towards her have proved themſelves to be philoſophers, politicians and gentlemen.

To the miniſtry I likewiſe addreſs myſelf. You, gentlemen, have ſtudied the ruin of your country, from which it is not within your abilities to reſcue her. Your attempts to recover are as ridiculous as your plans which involved her are deteſtable. The commiſſioners being about to depart, will probably bring you this, and with it my fixth number to them; and in ſo doing they carry back more

COMMON SENSE than they brought, and you likewife will have more than when you fent them.

Having thus addreffed you feverally, I conclude by addreffing you collectively. It is a long lane that has no turning. A period of fixteen years of mifconduct and misfortune, is certainly long enough for any one nation to fuffer under ; and upon a fuppofition that war is not declared between France and you, I beg to place a line of conduct before you that will eafily lead you out of all your troubles. It has been hinted before, and cannot be too much attended to.

Suppofe America had remained unknown to Europe till the prefent year, and that Mr. Banks and Doctor Solander, in another voyage round the world, had made the firft difcovery of her in the felf fame condition fhe is now in, of arts, arms, numbers, and civilization. What I afk in that cafe, would have been your conduct towards her ? for THAT will point out what it ought to be now. The problems and their folutions are equal, and the right line of the one is the parallel of the other. The queftion takes in every circumftance that can poffibly arife. It reduces politics to a fimple thought, and is moreover a mode of inveftigation, in which, while you are ftudying your intereft, the fimplicity of the cafe will cheat you into good temper. You have nothing to do but to fuppofe you have found America, and fhe appears found to your hand, and while in the joy of your heart you ftand ftill to admire her, the path of politics rifes ftraight before you.

Were I difpofed to paint a contraft, I could eafily fet off what you have done in the prefent cafe againft what you would have done in THAT cafe, and by juftly oppofing them, conclude a picture that would make you blufh. But, as when any of the prouder paffions are hurt, it is much better philofophy to let a man flip into a good temper than to attack him in a bad one ; for that reafon, therefore, I only ftate the cafe, and leave yourfelves to reflect upon it.

To go a little back into politics, it will be found that the true intereft of Britain lay in propofing and promoting the independence of America immediately after the laft peace ; for the expence which Britain had then incurred by defending America as her own dominions, ought to have fhewn her the policy and neceffity of changing the STILE of the country, as the beft probable method of preventing future wars and expence, and the only method by which fhe could hold the commerce without the charge of fovereignty. Befides

which, the title she affumed of parent country, led to, and pointed
out, the propriety, wifdom and advantage of a feparation ; for as in
private life, children grow into men, and by fetting up for themfelves, extend and fecure the intereft of the whole family, fo in the
fettlement of colonies large enough to admit of maturity, the fame
policy fhould be purfued, and the fame confequences would follow.
Nothing hurts the affections both of parents and children fo much,
as living too clofely connected, and keeping up the diftinction too
long. Domineering will not do over thofe, who by a progrefs in
life are become equal in rank to their parents, that is, when they
have families of their own ; and though they may conceive themfelves the fubjects of their advice, will not fuppofe them the objects
of their government. I do not, by drawing this parallel, mean to
admit the title of PARENT COUNTRY, becaufe if due any
where, it is due to Europe collectively, and the firft fettlers from
England were driven here by profecution. I mean only to introduce
the term for the fake of policy, and to fhow from your title, the
line of your intereft.

When you faw the ftate of ftrength and opulence, and that by
her own induftry, which America had arrived at, you ought to have
advifed her to have fet up for herfelf, and propofed an alliance of
intereft with her, and in fo doing, you would have drawn, and that
at her own expence, more real advantage, and more military fupplies
and affiftance both of fhips and men, than from any weak and wrangling government you could exercife over her. In fhort, had you
ftudied only the domeftic politics of a family you would have learned
how to govern the ftate ; but, inftead of this eafy and natural line,
you flew out into every thing which was wild and outrageous, till by
following the paffion and ftupidity of the pilot, you wrecked the
veffel within fight of the fhore.

Having fhown what you ought to have done, I now proceed
to fhew the reafon why it was not done. The caterpillar circle of
the court, had an intereft to purfue diftinct from, and oppofed to
yours, for though by the independence of America and an alliance
therewith, the trade would have continued, if not increafed, as in
many articles neither country can go to a better market, and though
by defending and protecting herfelf, fhe would have been no expence
to you, and confequently your national charges would have de-
creafed, and your taxes might have been proportionably leffened
thereby; yet the ftriking off fo many places from the court calendar

was put in oppofition to the intereft of the nation. The lofs of thirteen government-fhips, with their appendages here and in England, is a fhocking found in the ear of a hungry courtier. Your prefent king and miniftry will be the ruin of you; and you had better rifk a revolution and call a congrefs, than be thus led on from madnefs to defpair, and from defpair to ruin. America has fet you the example, and you may follow it and be free.

I now come to the laft part, a war with France. This is what no man in his fenfes will advife you to, and all good men would wifh to prevent. Whether France will declare war againft you, is not for me in this place to mention, or to hint even if I knew it, but it muft be madnefs in you to do it firft. The matter is come now to a full crifis and peace is eafy if willingly fet about. Whatever you may think, France has behaved handfomely to you. She would have been unjuft to herfelf to have acted otherwife than fhe did; and having accepted our offer of alliance fhe gave you genteel notice of it. There was nothing in her conduct referved or indelicate, and while fhe announced her determination to fupport her treaty, fhe left you to give the firft offence. America on her part, has exhibited a character of firmnefs to the world. Unprepared and unarmed, without form or government, fhe fingly oppofed a nation that domineered over half the globe. The greatnefs of the deed demands refpect; and though you may feel refentment, you are compelled both to WONDER and ADMIRE.

Here I reft my arguments and finifh my addrefs. Such as it is, it is a gift and you are welcome. It was always my defign to dedicate a CRISIS to you, when the time fhould come that would properly MAKE IT A CRISIS; and when, likewife, I fhould catch myfelf in a temper to write it, and fuppofe you in a condition to read it. THAT time is now arrived, and with it the opportunity of conveyance. For the commiffioners—POOR COMMISSIONERS! having proclaimed, that " YET FORTY DAYS AND NINE-VEH SHALL BE OVERTHROWN" have waited out the date, and difcontented with their God, are returning to their gourd. And all the harm I wifh them is, that it may not WITHER about their ears, and that they may not make their exit in the belly of a whale.

COMMON SENSE.

P. S. Though in the tranquility of my mind I have concluded with a laugh, yet I have fomething to mention to the COMMIS-

SIONERS, which to them is ferious and worthy their attention. Their authority is derived from an act of parliament which likewife defcribes and LIMITS their OFFICIAL powers. Their commiffion, therefore, is only a recital, and perfonal inveftiture, of thofe powers, or a nomination and defcription of the perfons who are to execute them. Had it contained any thing contrary to, or gone beyond the line of, the written law from which it is derived and by which it is bound, it would, by the Englifh conftitution, have been treafon in the crown, and the king been fubject to an impeachment. He dared not, therefore, put in his commiffion what you have put in your proclamation, that is, he dared not have authorifed you in that commiffion to burn and deftroy, or to threaten to burn and deftroy any thing in America. You are both in the ACT and in the COMMISSION ftiled COMMISSIONERS FOR RESTORING PEACE, and the methods for doing it are there pointed out. Your laft proclamation is figned by you as commiffioners UNDER THAT ACT. You make parliament the patron of its contents. Yet in the body of it, you infert matters contrary both to the fpirit and letter of the act, and what likewife your king dared not have put in his commiffion to you. The ftate of things in England, gentlemen, is too ticklifh for you to run hazards. You are ACCOUNTABLE TO PARLIAMENT FOR THE EXECUTION OF THAT ACT ACCORDING TO THE LETTER OF IT. Your heads may pay for breaking it, for you certainly have broke it by exceeding it. And as a friend, who would wifh you to efcape the paw of the lion as well as the belly of the whale, I civilly hint to you, TO KEEP WITHIN COMPASS.

Sir Harry Clinton, ftrictly fpeaking, is as accountable as the reft; for though a general, he is likewife a commiffioner, acting under a fuperior authority. His firft obedience is to the act ; and his plea of being a general will not and cannot clear him as a commiffioner, for that would fuppofe the crown, in its fingle capacity, to have a power of difpenfing with an act of parliament. Your fituations, gentlemen, are nice and critical, and the more fo becaufe England is unfettled. Take heed? Remember the times of Charles the firft! For Laud and Stafford fell by trufting to a hope like yours.

Having thus fhewn you the danger of your proclamation, I now fhew you the folly of it. The means contradict your defign, You threaten to lay wafte in order to render America a ufelefs acquifition of alliance to France. I reply, that the more deftruction you commit (if you could do it) the more valuable to France you make that alliance. You can deftroy only houfes and goods ; and by fo doing you increafe our demand upon her for materials and merchandize; for the wants of one nation, provided it has FREEDOM and CRE-DIT, naturally produces riches to the other; and as you can neither ruin the land nor prevent the vegetation, you would encreafe the exportation of our produce in payment, which to her would be a new fund of wealth. In fhort, had you caft about for a plan on purpofe to enrich your enemies you could not have hit upon a better.

C. S.

THE CRISIS.—NUMBER VIII.

ADDRESSED TO THE PEOPLE OF ENGLAND.

"TRUSTING (fays the king of England in his fpeech of No-
" vember laft) in the Divine Providence, and in the juftice of my
" caufe, I am firmly refolved to profecute the war with vigour, and
" to make every exertion in order to compel our enemies to equi-
" table terms of peace and accommodation." To this declaration the United States of America and the confederated powers of Europe will reply, *if Britain will have war, fhe fhall have enough of it.*

Five years have nearly elapfed fince the commencement of hoftilities, and every campaign, by a gradual decay, has leffened your ability to conquer, without producing a ferious thought on your condition or your fate. Like a prodigal lingering in an habitual confumption, you feel the relics of life, and miftake them for recovery. New fchemes, like new medicines, have adminiftered frefh hopes and prolonged the difeafe inftead of curing it. A change of generals, like a change of phyficians, ferved only to keep the flattery alive, and furnifh new pretences for new extravagance.

" *Can Britain fail?*"* Has been proudly afked at the commencement of every enterprize, and that " *whatever fhe wills is fate?*"† has been given with the folemnity of prophetic confidence, and though

* *Whitehead's new-year's ode for 1776.*
† *Ode at the inftallation of Lord North for chancellor of the univerfity of Oxford.*

the queſtion has been conſtantly replied to by diſappointment, and the prediction falſified by misfortune, yet ſtill the inſult continued, and your catalogue of national evils increaſed therewith. Eager to per-ſuade the world of her power, ſhe conſidered deſtruction as the miniſter of greatneſs, and conceived that the glory of a nation, like that of an Indian, lay in the number of its ſcalps and the miſeries it inflicts.

Fire, ſword and want, as far as the arms of Britain could extend them, have been ſpread with wanton cruelty along the coaſt of Ame-rica; and while you, remote from the ſcene of ſuffering, had nothing to loſe and as little to dread, the information reached you like a tale of antiquity, in which the diſtance of time defaces the conception, and changes the ſevereſt ſorrows into converſable amuſement.

This makes the ſecond paper, addreſſed perhaps in vain to the peo-ple of England. That advice ſhould be taken wherever example has failed, or precept be regarded where warning is ridiculed, is like a picture of hope reſting on deſpair : But when time ſhall ſtamp with univerſal currency, the facts you have long encountered with a laugh, and the irreſiſtible evidence of accumulated loſſes, like the hand writing on the wall, ſhall add terror to diſtreſs, you will then, in a conflict of ſufferings, learn to ſympathiſe with others by feeling for your ſelves.

The triumphant appearance of the combined fleets in the channel and at your harbours' mouth, and the expedition of captain Paul Jones on the weſtern and eaſtern coaſt of England and Scotland, will, by placing you in the condition of an endangered country, read to you a ſtronger lecture on the calamities of invaſion, and bring to your minds a truer picture of promiſcuous diſtreſs, than the moſt finiſhed rhetoric can deſcribe or the keeneſt imagination conceive.

Hitherto you have experienced the expences, but nothing of the miſeries of war. Your diſappointments have been accompanied with no immediate ſuffering, and your loſſes came to you only by intelli-gence. Like fire at a diſtance, you heard not even the cry; you felt not the danger, you ſaw not the confuſion. To you every thing has been foreign but the taxes to ſupport it. You knew not what it was to be alarmed at midnight with an armed enemy in the ſtreets. You were ſtrangers to the diſtreſſing ſcene of a family in flight, and to the thouſand reſtleſs cares and tender ſorrows that inceſſantly aroſe. To ſee women and children wandering in the ſeverity of winter, with the broken remains of a well furniſhed houſe, and ſeeking ſhelter in every crib and hut, were matters you had no conception of. You knew not what it was to stand by and see your goods chopt for fuel, and your beds ript to pieces to make packages for plunder. The misery of others, like a tempestuous night, added to the pleasures of your own security. You even enjoyed the storm, by contemplating the difference of conditions and that which carried sorrow into the breasts of thousands, served but to heighten in you a species of tranquil pride.——Yet these are but the fainter sufferings of war, when compared with carnage and slaughter, the miseries of a military hospital, or a town in flames.

The people of America by anticipating distress had fortified their minds against every species you could inflict. They had resolved to abandon their homes, to resign them to destruction, and to seek new settlements rather than submit. Thus familiarised to misfortune, before it arrived, they bore their portion with the less regret: The justness of their cause was a continual source of consolation, and the hope of final victory, which never left them, served to lighten the load and sweeten the cup allotted them to drink.

But when their suffering shall become yours, and invasion be transferred upon the invaders, you will have neither their extended wilderness to fly to, their cause to comfort you, nor their hopes to rest on. Distress with them was sharpened by no self-reflection. They had not brought it on themselves. On the contrary, they had by every proceeding endeavoured to avoid it, and had descended even below the mark of congressional character to prevent a war. The national honour or the advantages of independence were matters, which at the commencement of the dispute, they had never studied, and it was only at the last moment that the measure was resolved on. Thus circumstanced, they naturally and conscientiously felt a dependence upon Providence. They had a clear pretension to it, and had they failed therein, infidelity had gained a triumph.

But your condition is the reverse of theirs. Every thing you suffer you have fought; nay, had you created mischiefs on purpose to inherit them, you could not have secured your title by a firmer deed. The world awakens with no pity at your complaints. You felt none for others; you deserve none for yourselves. Nature does not interest herself in cases like yours, but on the contrary turns from them with dislike and abandons them to punishment. You may now present memorials to what court you please, but so far as America is the object, none will listen. The policy of Europe and the propensity there is in every mind to curb insulting ambition, and bring cruelty to judgment, are unitedly againſt you; and where nature and intereſt reinforces each other, the compact is too intimate to be diſſolved.

Make but the caſe of others your own, and your own theirs, and you will then have a clear idea of the whole. Had France acted towards her colonies as you have done, you would have branded her with every epithet of abhorrence; and had you like her, ſtept in to ſuccour a ſtruggling people, all Europe muſt have echoed with your own applauſes. But entangled in the paſſion of diſpute, you ſee it not as you ought, and form opinions thereon which ſuit with no intereſt but your own. You wonder America does not riſe in union with you to impoſe on herſelf a portion of your taxes and reduce herſelf to unconditional ſubmiſſion. You are amazed that the ſouthern powers of Europe do not aſſiſt you in conquering a country which is afterwards to be turned againſt themſelves; and that the northern ones do not contribute to reinſtate you in America who already enjoy the market for naval ſtores by the ſeparation. You ſeem ſurpriſed that Holland does not pour in her ſuccours, to maintain you miſtreſs of the ſeas, when her own commerce is ſuffering by your act of navigation, or that any country ſhould ſtudy her own intereſts while yours is on the carpet.

Such exceſſes of paſſionate folly, and unjuſt as well as unwiſe reſentment, have driven you on, like Pharoah, to unpitied miſeries, and while the importance of the quarrel ſhall perpetuate your diſgrace, the flag of America will carry it round the world. The natural feelings of every rational being will take againſt you, and wherever the ſtory ſhall be told, you will have neither excuſe nor conſolation left. With an unſparing hand and an unſatiable mind, you have havocked the world, both to gain dominion and to loſe it; and while in a phrenzy of avarice and ambition, the eaſt and the weſt are doomed to tributary bondage, you rapidly earned deſtruction as the wages of a nation.

At the thoughts of a war at home every man amongſt you ought to tremble. The proſpect is far more dreadful there than in America. Here the party that was againſt the meaſures of the continent were in general a kind of neutrals who added ſtrength to neither army. There does not exiſt a being ſo devoid of ſenſe and ſentiment as to covet " UNCONDITIONAL SUBMISSION," and therefore no man in America could be with you in principle. Several might from a cowardice of mind, PREFER it to the hardſhips and dangers of OPPOSING it; but the ſame diſpoſition that gave them ſuch a choice, unfitted them to act either for or againſt. But England is rent into parties, with equal ſhares of reſolution. The principle which produced the war divides the nation. Their animoſities are in the higheſt ſtate of fermentation, and both ſides, by a call of the militia, are in arms. No human foreſight can diſcern, no concluſion can be formed, what turn a war might take, if once ſet on foot by an invaſion. She is not now in a fit diſpoſition, to make a common cauſe of her own affairs, and having no conqueſts to hope for abroad, and nothing but expences ariſing at home, her every thing is ſtaked upon a defenſive combat, and the further ſhe goes the worſe ſhe is off.

There are ſituations a nation may be in, in which peace or war, abſtracted from every other conſideration, may be politically right or wrong. When nothing can be loſt by a war, but what muſt be loſt without it, war is then the policy of that country ; and ſuch was the ſituation of America at the commencement of hoſtilities : But when no ſecurity can be gained by a war, but what may be accompliſhed by a peace, the caſe becomes reverſed, and ſuch now is the ſituation of England.

That America is beyond the reach of conqueſt, is a fact which experience has ſhewn and time confirmed, and this admitted, what, I aſk, is now the object of contention ? If there be any honour in purſuing ſelf-deſtruction with inflexible paſſion—if national ſuicide be the perfection of national glory, you may, with all the pride of criminal happineſs, expire unenvied and unrivalled.—But when the tumult of war ſhall ceaſe, and the tempeſt of preſent paſſions be ſucceeded by calm reflection, or when thoſe who ſurviving its fury, ſhall inherit from you a legacy of debts and misfortunes, when the yearly revenue ſhall ſcarcely be able to diſcharge the intereſt of the one, and no poſſible remedy be left for the other : ideas, far different to the preſent, will ariſe, and embitter the remembrance of former follies. A mind diſarmed of its rage, feels no pleaſure in contemplating a frantic quarrel. Sickneſs of thought, the ſure conſequence of conduct like yours, leaves no ability for enjoyment, no reliſh for reſentment; and though, like a man in a fit, you feel not the injury of the ſtruggle, nor diſtinguiſh between ſtrength and diſeaſe, the weakneſs will neverthelefs be proportioned to the violence, and the ſenſe of pain encreaſe with the recovery.

To what perſons or to whoſe ſyſtem of politics you owe your preſent ſtate of wretchedneſs, is a matter of total indifference to America.

They have contributed, however unwillingly, to set her above themselves, and she in the tranquility of conquest resigns the enquiry. The case now is not so properly who began the war, as who continues it. That there are men in all countries to whom a state of war is a mine of wealth, is a fact never to be doubted. Characters like these naturally breed in the putrefaction of distempered times, and after fattening on the disease they perish with it, or impregnated with the stench retreat into obscurity.

But there are several erroneous notions to which you likewise owe a share of your misfortunes, and which if continued will only increase your trouble and your losses. An opinion hangs about the gentlemen of the minority, that America would relish measures under THEIR administration, which she would not from the present cabinet. On this rock lord Chatham would have split had he gained the helm, and several of his survivers are steering the same course. Such distinctions in the infancy of the argument had some degree of foundation, but they now serve no other purpose than to lengthen out a war, in which the limits of a dispute, being fixt by the fate of arms, and guaranteed by treaties, are not to be changed or altered by trivial circumstances.

The ministry and many of the minority sacrifice their time in disputing on a question with which they have nothing to do, namely, whether America shall be independent or not? whereas the only question that can come under their determination is, whether they will accede to it or not? They confound a military question with a political one, and undertake to supply by a vote what they lost by a battle. Say, she shall not be independent, and it will signify as much as if they voted against a decree of fate, or say that she shall, and she will be no more independent than before. Questions, which when determined, cannot be executed, serve only to shew the folly of dispute and the weakness of disputants.

From a long habit of calling America your own, you suppose her governed by the same prejudices and conceits which govern yourselves. Because you have set up a particular denomination of religion to the exclusion of all others, you imagine she must do the same, and because you, with an unsociable narrowness of mind, have cherished enmity against France and Spain, you suppose her alliance must be defective in friendship. Copying her notions of the world from you, she formerly thought as you instructed, but now feeling herself free, and the prejudice removed, she thinks and acts upon a different fyftem. It frequently happens that in proportion as we are taught to diflike perfons and countries not knowing why, we feel an ardour of efteem upon the removal of the miftake : It feems as if fomething was to be made amends for, and we eagerly give into every office of friendfhip, to atone for the injury of the error.

But perhaps there is fomething in the extent of countries, which, among the generality of people, infenfibly communicates extenfion of the mind. The foul of an iflander in its native ftate feems bounded by the foggy confines of the water's edge, and all beyond affords to him matters only for profit or curiofity, not for friendfhip. His ifland is to him his world, and fixt to that, his every thing centres in it ; while thofe, who are inhabitants of a continent, by cafting their eye over a larger field, take in likewife a larger intellectual circuit, and thus approaching nearer to an acquaintance with the univerfe, their atmofphere of thought is extended, and their liberality fills a wider fpace. In fhort, our minds feem to be meafured by countries when we are men, as they are by places, when we are children, and until fomething happens to difentangle us from the prejudice, we ferve under it without perceiving it.

In addition to this, it may be remarked, that men who ftudy any univerfal fcience, the principles of which are univerfally known, or admitted, and applied without diftinction to the common benefit of all countries, obtain thereby a larger fhare of philanthropy than thofe who only ftudy national arts and improvements. Natural philofophy, mathematics and aftronomy, carry the mind from the country to the creation, and give it a fitnefs fuited to the extent. It was not Newton's honour, neither could it be his pride, that he was an Englifhman, but that he was a philofopher : The Heavens had liberated him from the prejudices of an ifland, and fcience had expanded his foul as boundlefs as his ftudies.

COMMON SENSE.

March, 1780.

THE CRISIS.—NUMBER IX.

Philadelphia, June 9, 1780.

HAD America purfued her advantages with half the fpirit fhe refifted her misfortunes, fhe would before now, have been a con

quering and a peaceful people ; but lulled in the lap of foft tranquility, fhe refted on her hopes, and adverfity only has convulfed
her into action. Whether fubtlety or fincerity, at the clofe of the
laft year, induced the enemy to an appearance for peace, is a point
not material to know : It is fufficient that we fee the effects it
has had on our politics, and that we fternly rife to refent the
delufion.

The war, on the part of America, has been a war of natural feelings. Brave in diftrefs; ferene in conqueft; drowfey while at reft ;
and in every fituation generoufly difpofed to peace. A dangerous
calm, and a moft heightened zeal, have, as circumftances varied, fucceeded each other. Every paffion, but that of defpair, has been
called to a tour of duty ; and fo miftaken has been the enemy, of our
abilities and difpofition, that when fhe fuppofed us conquered, we
rofe the conquerors. The extenfivenefs of the United States, and
the variety of their refources ; the univerfality of their caufe, the
quick operation of their feelings, and the fimilarity of their fentiments, have, in every trying fituation, produced a *fomething*, which,
favoured by Providence, and purfued with ardour, has accomplifhed
in an inftant the bufinefs of a campaign We have never deliberately
fought victory, but fnatched it ; and bravely undone in an hour, the
blotted operations of a feafon.

The reported fate of Charlefton, like the misfortunes of feventy-
fix, has at laft called forth a fpirit, and kindled up a flame, which
perhaps no other event could have produced. If the enemy has circulated a falfehood, they have unwifely aggravated us into life, and if
they have told us a truth, they have unintentionally done us a fervice.
We were returning with folded arms from the fatigues of war, and
thinking and fetting leifurely down to enjoy repofe. The dependence
that has been put upon Charlefton threw a drowfinefs over America.
We looked on the bufinefs done—the conflict over—the matter fettled
—or that all which remained unfinifhed would follow of itfelf. In this
ftate of dangerous relax, expofed to the poifonous infufions of the
enemy, and having no common danger to attract our attention, we
were extinguifhing by ftages the ardour we began with, and furren-
dering by peace-meals the virtue that defended us.

Afflicting as the lofs of Charlefton may be, yet if it univerfally
roufe us from the flumber of a twelve-months paft, and renew in us
the fpirit of former days, it will produce an advantage more important
than its lofs. America ever *is* what fhe *thinks* herfelf to be. Governed

by fentiment, and acting her own mind, fhe becomes, as fhe pleafes, the victor or the victim.

It is not the conqueft of towns, nor the accidental capture of garrifons, that can reduce a country fo extenfive as this. The fufferings of one part can never be relieved by the exertions of another, and there is no fituation the enemy can be in, that does not afford to us the fame advantages fhe feeks herfelf. By dividing her force, fhe leaves every poft attackable. It is a mode of war that carries with it a confeffion of weaknefs, and goes on the principle of diftrefs, rather than conqueft.

The decline of the enemy is vifible not only in their operations, but in their plans; Charlefton originally made but a fecondary object in the fyftem of attack, and it is now become their principal one, becaufe they have not been able to fucceed elfewhere. It would have carried a cowardly appearance in Europe had they formed their grand expedition in feventy-fix, againft a part of the continent where there was no army, or not a fufficient one to oppofe them; but failing year after year in their impreffions here, and to the eaftward and northward, they deferted their firft capital defign, and prudently contenting themfelves with what they can get, give a flourifh of honour to conceal difgrace.

But this piece-meal work is not conquering the continent. It is a difcredit in them to attempt it, and in us to fuffer it. It is now full time to put an end to a war of aggravations, which, on one fide, has no poffible object, and on the other, has every inducement which honour, intereft, fafety and happinefs can infpire. If we fuffer them much longer to remain among us, we fhall become as bad as themfelves. An affociation of vices will reduce us more than the fword, A nation hardened in the practice of iniquity knows better how to profit by it, than a young country newly corrupted. We are not a match for them in the line of advantageous guilt, nor they to us on the principles we bravely fet out with. Our firft days were our days of honour. They have marked the character of America wherever the ftory of her wars are told; and convinced of this, we have nothing to do, but wifely and unitedly to tread the well known track. The progrefs of a war is often as ruinous to individuals, as the iffue of it is to a nation; and it is not only neceffary that our forces be fuch, that we be conquerors in the end, but that by timely exertions we be fecure in the interim. The prefent campaign will afford an opportunity which has never prefented itfelf before, and the preparations for it are equally neceffary, whether Charlefton ftand or fall. Suppofe the firft, it is in that cafe only a failure of the enemy, not a defeat. All the conqueft a befieged town can hope for is, not to be conquered; and compelling an enemy to raife the fiege, is to the befieged a victory. But there muft be a probability amounting almoft to certainty, that would juftify a garrifon marching out to attack a retreat. Therefore fhould Charlefton not be taken, and the enemy abandon the fiege, every other part of the continent fhould prepare to meet them; and on the contrary, fhould it be taken, the fame preparations are neceffary, to balance the lofs, and put ourfelves in a condition to co-operate with our allies, immediately on their arrival.

We are not now fighting our battles alone, as we were in feventy-fix. England, from a malicious difpofition to America, has not only not declared war againft France and Spain, but the better to profecute her paffions here, has afforded thofe powers no military object, and avoids them, to diftrefs us. She will fuffer her Weft-India iflands to be over-run by France, and her fouthern fettlements taken by Spain, rather than quit the object that gratifies revenge. This conduct, on the part of Britain, has pointed out the propriety of France fending a naval and land force to co-operate with America on the fpot. Their arrival cannot be very diftant, nor the ravages of the enemy long. In the mean time the party neceffary to us needs no illuftration. The recruiting the army, and procuring the fupplies, are the two things needful, and a capture of either of the enemy's divifions will reftore to America peace and plenty.

At a crifis, big, like the prefent, with expectation and events, the whole country is called to unanimity and exertion. Not an ability ought now to fleep, that can produce but a mite to the general good, nor even a whifper to pafs that militates againft it. The neceffity of the cafe, and the importance of the confequences, admit no delay from a friend, no apology from an enemy. To fpare now, would be the height of extravagance, and to confult prefent cafe, would be to facrifice it, perhaps, for ever.

America, rich in patriotifm and produce, can want neither men nor fupplies, when a ferious neceffity calls them forth. The flow operation of taxes, owing to the extenfivenefs of collection, and their depreciated value before they arrived in the treafury, have, in many inftances thrown a burden upon government, which has been artfully interpreted by the enemy into a general decline throughout the country. Yet this, inconvenient as it may at firft appear, is not only remediable, but may be turned to an immediate advantage; for it makes no real difference, whether a certain number of men, or company of militia (and in this country every man is a militia-man) are directed by law to send a recruit at their own expence, or whether a tax is laid on them for that purpofe, and the man hired by government afterwards. The firft, if there is any difference, is both cheapeft and beft, becaufe it faves the expence which would attend collecting it as a tax, and brings the man fooner into the field than the modes of recruiting formerly ufed: And on this principle, a law has been paffed in this ftate for recruiting two men from each company of militia, which will add upwards of a thoufand to the force of the country.

But the flame, which has broke forth in this city fince the report from New-York of the lofs of Charlefton, not only does honour to the place, but, like the blaze of feventy-fix, will kindle into action the fcattered fparks throughout America.—The valour of a country may be learned by the bravery of its foldiery, and the general caft of its inhabitants, but confidence of fuccefs is beft difcovered by the active meafures purfued by men of property; and when the fpirit of enterprize becomes fo univerfal, as to act at once on all ranks of men, a war may then and not till then, be ftiled truly popular.

In feventy-fix the ardour of the enterprifing part was confiderably checked by the real revolt of fome, and the coolnefs of others. But in the prefent cafe there is a firmnefs in the fubftance and property of the country to the public caufe. An affociation has been entered into by the merchants, tradefmen and principal inhabitants of this city, to receive and fupport the new ftate money at the value of gold and filver; a meafure which, while it does them honour, will likewife contribute to their intereft, by rendering the operations of the campaign convenient and effectual.

Neither has the fpirit of exertion ftopt here. A voluntary fubfcription is likewife began to raife a fund of hard money, to be given as bounties to fill up the full quota of the Pennfylvania line. It has been the remark of the enemy, that every thing in America has been done by the force of government; but when fhe fees the individuals throwing in their voluntary aids, and facilitating the public meafures in concert with the eftablifhed powers of the country, it will convince her that the caufe of America ftands not on the will of a few, but on the broad foundation of property and popularity.

Thus aided, and thus fupported, difaffection will decline, and the withered head of tyranny expire in America. The ravages of the enemy will be fhort and limited, and like all their former ones will produce a victory over themfelves.

COMMON SENSE.

☞ At the time of writing this number of the Crifis, the lofs of Charlefton, though believed by fome, was more confidently difbelieved by others. But there ought to b no longer a doubt upon the matter. Charlefton is gone, and I believe for the want of a fufficient fupply of provifions. The man that does not now feel for the honour of the beft and nobleft caufe that ever a country engaged in, and exert himfelf accordingly, is no longer worthy a peaceable refidence among a people determined to be free.   C. S.

THE CRISIS EXTRAORDINARY.

(ON THE SUBJECT OF TAXATION.)

Philadelphia, October 6, 1780.

IT is impoffible to fit down and think ferioufly on the affairs of America, but the original principles on which fhe refifted, and the glow and ardour they infpired, will occur like the undefaced remembrance of a lovely fcene. To trace over in imagination the purity of the caufe, the voluntary facrifices made to fupport it, and all the various turnings of the war in its defence, is at once both paying and receiving refpect. The principles deferve to be remembered, and to remember them rightly is repoffeffing them. In this indulgence of generous recollection we become gainers by what we feem to give, and the more we beftow the richer we become.

So extenfively right was the ground on which America proceeded, that it not only took in every juft and liberal fentiment which could imprefs the heart, but made it the direct intereft of every clafs and order of men to defend the country. The war, on the part of Britain, was originally a war of covetoufnefs. The fordid and not the fplendid paffions gave it being. The fertile fields and profperous infancy of America appeared to her as mines for tributary wealth. She viewed the hive, and difregarding the induftry that had enriched it, thirfted for the honey. But in the prefent ftage of her affairs, the violence of temper is added to the rage of avarice ; and therefore, that which at the firft fetting out proceeded from purity of principle and public intereft, is now heightened by all the obligations of neceffity ; for it requires but little knowledge of human nature to difcern what would be the confequence, were America again reduced to the fubjection of Britain. Uncontrolled power, in the hands of an incenfed, imperious and rapacious conqueror, is an engine of dreadful execution, and woe be to that country over which it can be exercifed. The names of whig and tory would then be funk in the general term. of rebel, and the oppreffion, whatever it might be, would, with very few inftances of exception, light equally on all.

Britain did not go to war with America for the fake of dominion, becaufe fhe was then in poffeffion ; neither was it for the extenfion of trade and commerce, becaufe fhe had monopolized the whole and the country had yielded to it; neither was it to extinguifh what *fhe* might call rebellion, becaufe before fhe began no refiftance exifted. It could then be from no other motive than avarice, or a defign of eftablifhing, in the firft inftance, the fame taxes in America as are paid in England (which, as I fhall prefently fhow, are above eleven times heavier than the taxes we now pay for the prefent year 1780) or, in the fecond inftance, to confifcate the whole property of America, in cafe of refiftance and conqueft of the latter, of which fhe had then no doubt.

I fhall now proceed to fhow what the taxes in England are, and what the yearly expence of the prefent war is to her—What the taxes of this country amount to, and what the annual expence of defending it effectually will be to us ; and fhall endeavour concifely to point out the caufe of our difficulties, and the advantages on one fide, and the confequences on the other, in cafe we do, or do not, put ourfelves in an effectual ftate of defence. I mean to be open, candid and fincere. I fee a univerfal wifh to expel the enemy from the country, a murmuring becaufe the war is not carried on with more vigour, and my intention is to fhow as fhortly as poffible both the reafon and the remedy.

The number of fouls in England (exclufive of Scotland and Ireland) is feven millions,* and the number of fouls in America is three millions.

The amount of the taxes in England (exclufive of Scotland and Ireland) was, before the prefent war commenced, eleven millions fix hundred and forty-two thoufand fix hundred and fifty-three pounds fterling, which on an average is no lefs a fum than one pound thirteen fhillings

---

* *This is taking the higheft number that the people of England have been, or can be rated at.*

and three-pence fterling per head per annum, men, women and children ; befides county taxes, taxes for the fupport of the poor, and a
tenth of all the produce of the earth for the fupport of the bifhops and
clergy. * Nearly five millions of this fum went annually to pay the intereft of the national debt contracted by former wars, and the remaining fum of fix millions fix hundred and forty-two thoufand fix hundred
pounds was applied to defray the yearly expence of government, the
peace eftablifhment of the army and navy, placemen, penfioners, &c.
confequently the whole of the enormous taxes being thus appropriated
fhe had nothing to fpare out of them towards defraying the expences
of the prefent war or any other. Yet had fhe not been in debt at the beginning of the war as we were not, and like us had only a land and
not a naval war to carry on, her then revenue of eleven millions and

* *The following is taken from Dr. Price's ftate of the taxes of England, pages* 96, 97, 98.
An account of the money drawn from the public by taxes annually, being the medium of three years before the year 1776.

Amount of cuftoms in England,	£. 2,528,275
Amount of the excife in England,	4,649,892
Land tax at 3s.	1,300,000
Land tax at 1s. in the pound,	450,000
Salt duties,	218,739
Duties on ftamps, cards, dice, advertifements, bonds, leafes, indentures, newfpapers, almanacks, &c.	280,788
Duties on houfes and windows,	385,369
Poft office, feizures, wine licences, hackney coaches, &c.	250,000
Annual profits from lotteries,	150,000
Expence of collecting the excife in England,	297,887
Expence of collecting the cuftoms in England,	468,700
Intereft of loans on the land tax at 4s. expences of collection, militia, &c.	250,000
Perquifites, &c. on cuftom houfe officers, &c. fuppofed	250,000
Expence of collecting the falt duties in England 10 1-2 *per cent.*	27,000
Bounties on fifh exported,	18,000
Expence of collecting the duties on ftamps, cards, adver-tifements, &c. at 5 and 1-4 per cent.	18,000

Total, £.11,642,653

a half pounds fterling would defray all her annual expences of war and government within each year.

But this not being the cafe with her, fhe is obliged to borrow about ten million pounds fterling yearly, to profecute the war fhe is now engaged in (this year fhe borrowed twelve) and lay on new taxes to difcharge the intereft ; and allowing that the prefent war has coft her only fifty millions fterling, the intereft thereon at five per cent. will be two millions and an half, therefore the amount of her taxes now muft be fourteen millions, which on an average is no lefs than forty fhillings fterling per head, men, women, and children throughout the nation. Now as this expence of fifty millions was borrowed on the hopes of conquering America, and as it was avarice which firft induced her to commence the war, how truly wretched and deplorable would the condition of this country be, were fhe, by her own remiffnefs, to fuffer an enemy of fuch a difpofition, and fo circumftanced, to reduce her to fubjection.

I now proceed to the revenues of America.

I have already ftated the number of fouls in America to be three millions, and by a calculation I have made, which I have every reafon to believe is fufficiently right, the whole expence of the war, and the fupport of the feveral governments, may be defrayed for two million pounds fterling annually ; which on an average is thirteen fhillings and four pence per head, men, women, and children, and the peace eftablifhment at the end of the war, will be but three quarters of a million, or five fhillings fterling per head. Now, throwing out of the queftion every thing of honour, principle, happinefs, freedom and reputation in the world, and taking it up on the fimple ground of intereft, I put the following cafe.

Suppofe Britain was to conquer America, and as conquerors was to lay her under no other conditions than to pay the fame proportion towards her annual revenue which the people of England pay ; our fhare in that cafe, would be fix million pounds fterling yearly ; can it then be a queftion, whether it is beft to raife two millions to defend the country, and govern it ourfelves, and only three quarters of a million afterwards, or pay fix millions to have it conquered, and let the enemy govern it.

Can it be fuppofed that conquerors would choofe to put themfelves in a worfe condition than what they granted to the conquered? In England the tax on rum is five fhillings and one penny fterling per gallon, which is one filver dollar and fourteen coppers. Now would it not be laughable to imagine, that after the expence they have been at, they would let either whig or tory in America drink it cheaper than themfelves. Coffee which is fo confiderable an article of confumption and fupport here, is there loaded with a duty, which makes the price between five and fix fhillings fterling a pound, and a penalty of fifty pounds fterling on any perfon detected in roafting it in his own houfe. There is fcarce an article of life you can eat, drink, wear, or enjoy, that is not there loaded with a tax ; even the light from heaven is only permitted to fhine into their dwellings by paying eighteen pence fterling per window annually ; and the humbleft drink of life, fmall beer, cannot there be purchafed without a tax of nearly two coppers a gallon, befides a heavy tax upon the malt, and another on the hops before it is brewed, exclufive of a land tax on the earth which produces them. In fhort, the condition of that country in point of taxation is fo oppreffive, the number of her poor fo great, and the extravagance and rapacioufnefs of the court fo enormous, that were they to effect a conqueft of America, it is then only that the diftreffes of America would begin. Neither would it fignify any thing to a man whether he be whig or tory. The people of England and the miniftry of that country know us by no fuch diftinctions. What they want is clear folid revenue, and the modes they would take to procure it, would operate alike on all. Their manner of reafoning would be fhort, becaufe they would naturally infer that if we were able to carry on a war of five or fix years againft them, we were able to pay the fame taxes which they do.

I have already ftated that the expence of conducting the prefent war, and the government of the feveral ftates, may be done for two millions fterling and the eftablifhment in time of peace, for three quarters of a million.*

As to navy matters, they flourifh fo well, and are fo well attended in the hands of individuals, that I think it confiftent on every principle of real ufe and economy, to turn the navy into hard money (keeping only three or four packets) and apply it to promote the fervice of the army. We fhall not have a fhip the lefs ; the ufe of them, and the benefit from them, will be greatly increafed, and their expence faved.

---

* I have made the calculations in fterling, becaufe it is a rate generally known in all the ftates, and becaufe likewife, it admits of an eafy comparifon between our expences to fupport the war and thofe of the enemy. Four filver dollars and an half is one pound fterling, and three pence over.

We are now allied with a formidable naval power, from whom we derive the affiftance of a navy. And the line in which we can profecute the war, fo as to reduce the common enemy and benefit the alliance moft effectually, will be by attending clofely to the land fervice.

I eftimate the charge of keeping up and maintaining an army, officering them, and all expences included, fufficient for the defence of the country, to be equal to the expence of forty thoufand men at thirty pounds fterling per head, which is one million two hundred thoufand pounds.

I likewife allow four hundred thoufand pounds for continental expences at home and abroad.

And four hundred thoufand pounds for the fupport of the feveral ftate governments, the amount will then be,

	£.
For the army,	1,200,000
Continental expences at home and abroad,	400,000
Government of the feveral ftates,	400,000

Total, £. 2,000,000

I take the proportion of this ftate, Pennfylvania, to be an eighth part of the thirteen United States, the quota then for us to raife will be two hundred and fifty thoufand pounds fterling ; two hundred thoufand of which will be our fhare for the fupport and pay of the army and continental expences at home and abroad, and fifty thoufand pounds for the fupport of ftate government.

In order to gain an idea of the proportion in which the raifing fuch a fum will fall, I make the following calculation.

Pennfylvania contains three hundred and feventy-five thoufand inhabitants, men, women and children, which is likewife an eighth of the whole inhabitants of the whole United States : Therefore two hundred and fifty thoufand pounds fterling to be raifed among three hundred and feventy-five thoufand perfons, is, on an average, thirteen fhillings and four pence fterling per head, per annum, or fomething more than one fhilling fterling per month. And our proportion of three quarters of a million for the government of the country, in time of peace, will be ninety-three thoufand feven hundred and fifty pounds fterling, fifty thoufand of which will be for the government expences of the ftate, and forty-three thoufand feven hundred and fifty pounds for continental expences at home and abroad.

The peace eftablifhment then will, on an average, be five fhillings fterling per head. Whereas was England now to ftop, and the war

ceafe, her peace eftablifhment would continue the fame as it is now,
viz. forty fhillings per head ; therefore was our taxes neceffary for
carrying on the war as much per head as hers now is, and the difference to be only whether we fhould, at the end of the war, pay at the
rate of five fhillings per head, or forty fhillings per head, the cafe
needs no thinking of. But as we can fecurely defend and keep
the country for one third lefs than what our burden would be if
it was conquered, and fupport the governments afterward for
one eighth of what Britain would levy on us, and could I find a
mifer whofe heart never felt the emotion of a fpark of principle, even
that man, uninfluenced by every love but the love of money, and capable of no attachment but to his intereft, would and muft, from the
frugality which governs him, contribute to the defence of the country,
or he ceafes to be a mifer and becomes an ideot. But when we take
in with it every thing that can ornament mankind ; when the line of
our intereft becomes the line of our happinefs ; when all that can cheer
and animate the heart ; when fenfe of honour, fame, character, at home
and abroad, are interwoven not only with the fecurity but the increafe
of property, there exifts not a man in America, unlefs he be a hired
emiffary, who does not fee that his good is connected with keeping
up a fufficient defence.

I do not imagine that an inftance can be produced in the world of
a country putting herfelf to fuch an amazing charge to conquer and
enflave another as Britain has done. The fum is too great for her
to think of with any tolerable degree of temper ; and when we confider the burden fhe fuftains as well as the difpofition fhe has fhewn,
it would be the height of folly in us to fuppofe that fhe would not
reimburfe herfelf by the moft rapid means, had fhe once more America
within her power. With fuch an oppreffion of expence, what would
an empty conqueft be to her ! what relief under fuch circumftances
could fhe derive from a victory without a prize ? It was money, it was
revenue fhe firft went to war for, and nothing but *that* would fatisfy
her. It is not the nature of avarice to be fatisfied with any thing
elfe. Every paffion that acts upon mankind has a peculiar mode of
operation. Many of them are temporary and fluctuating ; they admit
of ceffation and variety. But avarice is a fixed uniform paffion. It
neither abates of its vigour nor changes its object ; and the reafon
why it does not is founded in the nature of things, for wealth has not
a rival where avarice is a ruling paffion. One beauty may excel another, and extinguifh from the mind of a man the pictured remembrance

of a former one: But wealth is the phœnix of avarice, and therefore cannot seek a new object, becaufe there is not another in the world.

I now pafs on to fhew the value of the prefent taxes, and compare them with the annual expence ; but this I fhall preface with a few explanatory remarks.

There are two diftinct things which make the payment of taxes difficult ; the one is the large and real value of the fum to be paid, and the other is the fcarcity of the thing in which the payment is to be made; and although thefe appear to be one and the fame, they are in feveral inftances not only different, but the difficulty fprings from different caufes.

Suppofe a tax was to be laid equal to one half of what a man's yearly income is, fuch a tax could not be paid becaufe the property could not be fpared ; and on the other hand, fuppofe a very trifling tax was laid to be collected in *pearls*, fuch a tax likewife could not be paid, becaufe it could not be had. Now any perfon may fee that thefe are diftinct cafes, and the latter of them is a reprefentation of ours.

That the difficulty cannot proceed from the former, that is, from the real value or weight of the tax is evident at firft view to any perfon who will confider it.

The amount of the quota of taxes for this ftate for the prefent year, 1780 (and fo in proportion for every other ftate) is twenty millions of dollars, which at feventy for one is but fixty-four thoufand two hundred and eighty pounds three fhillings fterling, and on an average is no more than three fhillings and five pence fterling per head per annum per man, woman and child, or three pence two-fifths per head per month. Now here is a clear pofitive fact, that cannot be contradicted, and which proves that the difficulty cannot be in the weight of the tax, for in itfelf it is a trifle and far from being adequate to our quota of the expence of the war. The quit-rents of one penny fterling per acre on only one half the ftate, come to upwards of fifty thoufand pounds, which is almoft as much as all the taxes of the prefent year, and as thofe quit-rents made no part of the taxes then paid, and are now difcontinued, the quantity of money drawn for public fervice this year, exclufive of the militia fines, which I fhall take notice of in the procefs of this work, is lefs than what was paid and payable in any year preceding the revolution, and fince the laft war ; what I mean is, that the quit-rents and taxes taken together came to a larger fum then, than the prefent taxes without the quit-rents do now.

My intention by thefe arguments and calculations is to place the difficulty to the right caufe, and fhew that it does not proceed from the weight or worth of the tax, but from the fcarcity of the medium in which it is paid ; and to illuftrate this point ftill farther, I fhall now fhew, that if the tax of twenty millions of dollars was of four times the real value it now is or nearly fo, which would be about two hundred and fifty thoufand pounds fterling, and would be our full quota, that this fum would have been raifed with more eafe, and lefs felt, than the prefent fum of only fixty-four thoufand two hundred and eighty pounds.

The convenience or inconvenience of paying a tax in money arifes from the quantity of money that can be fpared out of trade.

When the emiffions ftopt, the continent was left in poffeffion of two hundred millions of dollars, perhaps as equally difperfed as it was poffible for trade to do it. And as no more was to be iffued, the rife or fall of prices could neither increafe nor diminifh the quantity. It therefore remained the fame through all the fluctuations of trade and exchange

Now had the exchange ftood at twenty for one, which was the rate congrefs calculated upon when they quotad the ftates the latter end of laft year, trade would have been carried on for nearly four times lefs money than it is now, and confequently the twenty millions would have been fpared with much greater eafe, and when collected would have been of almoft four times the value they now are. And on the other end, was the depreciation to be ninety or one hundred for one, the quantity required for trade would be more than at fixty or feventy for one, and though the value of them would be lefs, the difficulty of fparing the money out of trade would be greater. And on thefe facts and arguments I reft the matter, to prove that it is not the want of property, but the fcarcity of the medium by which the proportion of property for taxation is to be meafured out, that makes the embarraffment we lie under. There is not money enough, and what is equally as true, the people will not let there be money enough.

While I am on the fubject of the currency, I fhall offer one remark which will appear true to every body, and can be accounted for by nobody, which is, that the better the times were, the worfe the money grew ; and the worfe the times were, the better the money ftood. It never depreciated by any advantage obtained by the enemy. The troubles of feventy-fix, and the lofs of Philadelphia in feventy feven, made no fenfible impreffion on it, and every one knows that the furrender of Charlefton did not produce the leaft alteration in the rate of exchange, which for long before, and for more than three months after, ftood at fixty for one. It feems as if the certainty of its being our own, made us carelefs of its value, and that the moft diftant thoughts of lofing it made us hug it the clofer, like fomething we were loth to part with ; or that we depreciate it for our paftime, which, when called to ferioufnefs by the enemy, we leave off to renew again at our leifure. In fhort our good luck feems to break us, and our bad make us whole.

Paffing on from this digreffion, I fhall now endeavour to bring into one view the feveral parts I have already ftated, and form thereon fome propofitions, and conclude.

I have placed before the reader, the average tax per head paid by the people of England ; which is forty fhillings fterling.

And I have fhewn the rate on an average per head, which will defray all the expences of the war to us, and fupport the feveral governments without running the country into debt, which is thirteen fhillings and four pence.

I have fhewn what the peace eftablifhment may be conducted for, viz. an eighth part of what it would be, if under the government of Britain.

And I have likewife fhewn what the average per head of the prefent taxes are, namely, three fhillings and five pence fterling, or three pence two-fifths per month ; and that their whole yearly value, in fterling, is only fixty-four thoufand two hundred and eighty pounds. Whereas our quota, to keep the payments equal with the expences, is two hundred and fifty thoufand pounds. Confequently, there is a deficiency of one hundred and eighty-five thoufand feven hundred and twenty pounds, and the fame proportion of defect, according to the feveral quotas, happens in every other ftate. And this defect is the caufe why the army has been fo indifferently fed, clothed and paid. It is the caufe, likewife, of the nervelefs ftate of the campaign, and the infecurity of the country. Now, if a tax equal to thirteen and four pence per head, will remove all thefe difficulties, make people fecure in their homes, leave them to follow the bufinefs of their ftores and farms unmolefted, and not only keep out, but drive out the enemy from the country ; and if the neglect of raifing this fum will let them in, and produce the evils which might be prevented—on which fide, I afk, does the wifdom, intereft and policy lie? Or, rather, would it not be an insult to reason to put the question? The sum, when proportioned out according to the several abilities of the people, can hurt no one, but an inroad from the enemy ruins hundreds of families.

Look at the destruction done in this city. The many houses totally destroyed, and others damaged; the waste of fences in the country round it, besides the plunder of furniture, forage and provision. I do not suppose that half a million sterling would reinstate the sufferers; and, does this, 1 ask, bear any proportion to the expence that would make us secure. The damage, on an average, is at least ten pounds sterling per head, which is as much as thirteen shillings and four pence per head comes to for fifteen years. The same has happened on the frontiers, and in the Jerseys, New-York, and other places where the enemy has been—Carolina and Georgia are likewise suffering the same fate.

That the people generally do not understand the insufficiency of the taxes to carry on the war, is evident, not only from common observation, but from the construction of several petitions, which were presented to the assembly of this state, against the recommendation of Congress of the 18th of March last, for taking up and funding the present currency at forty for one, and issuing new money in its stead. The prayer of the petition was, *That the currency might be appreciated by taxes* (meaning the present taxes) *and that part of the taxes be applied to the support of the army, if the army could not be otherwise supported.* Now it could not have been possible for such a petition to have been presented, had the petitioners known, that so far from *part* of the taxes being sufficient for the support of the army, the *whole* of them falls three-fourths short of the year's expences.

Before I proceed to propose methods by which a sufficiency of money may be raised, I shall take a short view of the general state of the country.

Notwithstanding the weight of the war, the ravages of the enemy, and the obstructions she has thrown in the way of trade and commerce, so soon does a young country out grow misfortune, that America has already surmounted many that once heavily oppressed her. For the first year or two of the war, we were shut up within our ports, scarce venturing to look towards the ocean. Now our rivers are beautified with large and valuable vessels, our stores filled with merchandize, and the produce of the country has a ready market, and an advantageous price. Gold and silver, that for a while seemed to have retreated again within the bowels of the earth, is once more rifen into circulation, and every day adds new ftrength to trade, commerce, and agriculture.   In a pamphlet written by Sir John Dalrymple, and difperfed in America in the year 1775, he afferted, that, *two twenty gun fhips, nay, fays he, tenders of thofe fhips, ftationed between Albemarl: found and Chefapeak bay would fhut up the trade of America for* 600 *miles.* How little did Sir John Dalrymple know of the abilities of America!

While under the government of Britain, the trade of this country was loaded with reftrictions.   It was only a few foreign ports we were allowed to fail to.   Now it is otherwife; and allowing that the quantity of trade is but half what it was before the war, the cafe muft fhew the vaft advantage of an open trade, becaufe the prefent quantity under her reftrictions could not fupport itfelf; from which I infer, that if half the quantity without the reftrictions can bear itfelf up nearly, if not quite, as well as the whole when fubject to them, how profperous muft the condition of America be when the whole fhall return open with all the world.   By trade I do not mean the employment of a merchant only, but the whole intereft and bufinefs of the country taken collectively.

It is not fo much my intention, by this publication, to propofe particular plans for raifing money, as it is to fhew the neceffity and the advantages to be derived from it.   My principal defign is to form the difpofition of the people to fuch meafures which I am fully perfuaded is their intereft and duty to adopt, and which needs no other force to accomplifh them than the force of being felt.   But as every hint may be ufeful, I fhall throw out a fketch, and leave others to make fuch improvements upon it as to them may appear reafonable.

The annual fum wanted is two millions, and the average rate in which it falls is thirteen fhillings and four pence per head.

Suppofe then that we raife half the fum and fixty thoufand pounds over.   The average rate thereof will be feven fhillings per head.

In this cafe we fhall have half the fupply we want and an annual fund of fixty thoufand pounds whereon to borrow the other million ; becaufe fixty thoufand pounds is the intereft of a million at fix per cent. and if at the end of another year we fhould be obliged, by the continuance of the war, to borrow another million, the taxes will be increafed to feven fhillings and fix pence ; and thus for every million borrowed, an additional tax equal to fix pence per head muft be levied.

The fum then to be raifed next year will be one million and fixty thoufand pounds: Cne half of which I would propofe fhould be raifed by duties on imported goods and prize goods, and the other half by a tax on landed property and houfes, or fuch other means as each ftate may devife.

But as the duties on imports and prize goods muft be the fame in all the ftates, therefore the rate per cent. or what other form the duty fhall be laid, muft be afcertained and regulated by Congrefs, and ingrafted in that form into the law of each ftate ; and the monies arifing therefrom carried into the treafury of each ftate. The duties to be paid in gold or filver.

There are many reafons why a duty on imports is the moft convenient duty or tax that can be collected ; one of which is, becaufe the whole is payable in a few places in a country, and it likewife operates with the greateft eafe and equality, becaufe as every one pays in proportion to what he confumes, fo people in general confume in proportion to what they can afford, and therefore the tax is regulated by the abilities which every man fuppofes himfelf to have, or in other words every man becomes his own affeffor, and pays by a little at a time when it fuits him to buy. Befides, it is a tax which people may pay or let alone by not confuming the articles ; and though the alternative may have no influence on their conduct, the power of choofing is an agreeable thing to the mind. For my own part, it would be a fatisfaction to me, was there a duty on all forts of liquors during the war, as in my idea of things it would be an addition to the pleafures of fociety, to know, that when the health of the army goes round, a few drops from every glafs become theirs. How often have I heard an emphatical wifh almoft accompanied with a tear, " *Oh, that our poor fellows in the field had fome of this !*" Why then need we fuffer under a fruitlefs fympathy, when there is a way to enjoy both the wifh and the entertainment at once ?

But the great national policy of putting a duty upon imports is, that it either keeps the foreign trade in our own hands, or draws fomething for the defence of the country from every foreigner who participates it with us.

Thus much for the firft half of the taxes, and as each ftate will beft devife means to raife the other half, I fhall confine my remarks to the refources of this ftate.

The quota then of this ftate of one million and fixty thoufand pounds will be one hundred and thirty three thoufand two hundred and fifty pounds, the half of which is fixty-fix thoufand fix hundred and twenty-five pounds; and fuppofing one fourth part of Pennfylvania inhabited, then a tax of one bufhel of wheat on every twenty acres of land, one with another, would produce the fum, and all the prefent taxes to ceafe. Whereas the tithes of the bifhops and clergy in England, exclufive of the taxes, are upwards of half a bufhel of wheat on *every fingle* acre of land, good and bad, throughout the nation.

In the former part of this paper I mentioned the militia fines, but referved fpeaking to the matter, which I fhall now do: The ground I fhall put it upon is, that two millions fterling a-year will fupport a fufficient army, and all the expences of war and government, without having recourfe to the inconvenient method of continually calling men from their employments, which of all others is the moft expenfive and the leaft fubftantial. I confider the revenues created by taxes as the firft and principal thing, and fines only as fecondary and accidental things. It was not the intention of the militia law to apply the militia fines to any thing elfe but the fupport of the militia, neither do they produce any revenue to the ftate, yet thefe fines amount to more than all the taxes; for taking the mufter-roll to be fixty thoufand men, the fine on forty thoufand who may not attend, will be fixty thoufand pounds fterling, and thofe who mufter, will give up a portion of time equal to half that fum, and if the eight claffes fhould be called within the year, and one third turn out, the fine on the remaining forty thoufand would amount to feventy-two millions of dollars, befides the fifteen fhillings on every hundred pounds property, and the charge of feven and an half per cent. for collecting in certain inftances, which on the whole would be upwards of two hundred and fifty thoufand pounds fterling.

Now if thofe very fines difable the country from raifing a fufficient revenue without producing an equivalent advantage, would it not be to the eafe and intereft of all parties to encreafe the revenue, in the manner I have propofed, or any better, if a better can be devifed, and ceafe the operation of the fines? I would ftill keep the militia as an organized body of men, and fhould there be a real neceffity to call them forth, pay them out of the proper revenues of the ftate, and encreafe the taxes a third or fourth per cent. on thofe who do not attend. My limits will not allow me to go farther into this matter, which I fhall therefore clofe with this remark; that fines are, of all modes of revenue, the moft unfuited to the mind of a free country. When a man pays a tax, he knows the public neceffity requires it, and therefore feels a pride in difcharging his duty ; but a fine feems an atonement for neglect of duty, and of confequence is paid with difcredit, and frequently levied with feverity.

I have now only one fubject more to fpeak to, with which I fhall conclude, which is, the refolve of congrefs of the 18th of March laft, for taking up and funding the prefent currency at forty for one, and iffuing new money in its ftead.

Every one knows I am not the flatterer of congrefs, but in this inftance *they are right ;* and if that meafure is fupported, the currency will acquire a value, which without it, it will not. But this is not all: It will give relief to the finances until fuch time as they can be properly arranged, and fave the country from being immediately double taxed under the prefent mode. In fhort, fupport that meafure, and it will fupport you.

I have now waded through a tedious courfe of difficult bufinefs, and over an untrodden path. The fubject on every point it could be viewed was entangled with perplexities, and enveloped in obfcurity, yet fuch are the refources of America, that fhe wants nothing but fyftem to fecure fuccefs.

COMMON SENSE.

THE CRISIS.—NUMBER X.

ON THE KING OF ENGLAND'S SPEECH.

OF all the innocent paffions which actuate the human mind, there is none more univerfally prevalent than curiofity. It reaches all mankind, and in matters which concern us, or concern us not, it alike provokes in us a defire to know.

Although the fituation of America, fuperior to every effort to enflave her, and daily rifing to importance and opulence, hath placed her above the region of anxiety, it ftill left her within the circle of curiofity ; and her fancy to fee the fpeech of a man who had proudly threatened to bring her to his feet, was vifibly marked with that tranquil confidence which cared nothing about its contents. It was enquired after with a fmile, read with a laugh, and difmiffed with difdain.

But, as justice is due, even to an enemy, it is right to say, that the speech is as well managed as the embarrassed condition of their affairs could well admit of; and though scarce a line of it is true, except the mournful story of Cornwallis, it may serve to amuse the deluded commons and people of England, for whom it was calculated.

"The war," says the speech, "is still unhappily prolonged by that "restless ambition which first excited our enemies to commence it, "and which still continues to disappoint my earnest wishes and dili- "gent exertions to restore the public tranquility."

How easy it is to abuse truth and language, when men, by habitual wickedness, have learned to set justice at defiance. That the very man who began the war, who, with the most sullen insolence refused to answer, and even to hear the humblest of all petitions, who hath encouraged his officers and his army in the most savage cruelties, and the most scandalous plunderings, who hath stirred up the Indians on one side, and the Negroes on the other, and invoked every aid of hell in his behalf, should now with an affected air of pity turn the tables from himself, and charge on another the wickedness that is his own, can only be equalled by the baseness of the heart that spoke it.

TO BE NOBLY WRONG IS MORE MANLY THAN TO BE MEANLY RIGHT, is an expression I once used on a former occasion, and it is equally applicable now. We feel something like respect for consistency even in error. We lament the virtue that is debauched into a vice, but the vice that affects a virtue, becomes the more detestable: And amongst the various assumptions of character, which hypocrisy has taught, and men have practised, there is none that raises a higher relish of disgust, than to see disappointed inveteracy twisting itself, by the most visible falshoods, into an appearance of piety it has no pretensions to.

"But I should not," continues the speech, "answer the trust "committed to the sovereign of a FREE PEOPLE, nor make a "suitable return to my subjects for their constant, zealous, and "affectionate attachment to my person, family and government, if I "consented to sacrifice, either to my own desire of peace, or "to their temporary ease and relief, THOSE ESSENTIAL "RIGHTS AND PERMANENT INTERESTS, upon the "maintenance and preservation of which, the future strength and "security of this country must principally depend."

That the man whose ignorance and obstinacy first involved and

ftill continues the nation in the moſt hopelefs and expenſive of all
wars, ſhould now meanly flatter them with the name of a FREE
PEOPLE, and make a merit of his crime, under the difguiſe of
their eſſential rights and permanent intereſts, is ſomething which dif-
graces even the character of perverſenefs. Is he afraid they will ſend
him to Hanover, or what does he fear? Why is the fycophant thus
added to the hypocrite, and the man who pretends to govern, funk
into the humble and fubmiſſive memorialiſt?

What thoſe eſſential rights and permanent intereſts are, on which
the future ſtrength and fecurity of England muſt principally DE-
PEND, are not ſo much as alluded to. They are words which impreſs nothing but the ear, and are calculated only for the ſound.

But if they have any reference to America, then do they amount to
the difgraceful confeſſion, that England, who once aſſumed to be her
protectreſs, is now become her DEPENDENT. The Britiſh king
and miniſtry are conſtantly holding up the vaſt importance which
America is of to England, in order to allure the nation to carry on
the war: Now whatever ground there is for this idea, it ought to
have operated as a reaſon for not beginning it; and therefore they
ſupport their preſent meaſures at their own difgrace, becauſe the
arguments they now uſe, are a direct reflexion on their former policy.

" The favourable appearance of affairs," continues the ſpeech, " in
" the Eaſt Indies and the ſafe arrival of the numerous commercial
" fleets of my kingdom muſt have given you fatisfaction."

That things are not QUITE ſo bad every where as in America
may be ſome cauſe of conſolation, but can be none for triumph. One
broken leg is better than two, but ſtill it is not joy: and let the appearance of affairs in the Eaſt-Indies be ever ſo favourable, they are
nevertheleſs worſe than at firſt, without a proſpect of their ever being
better. But the mournful ſtory of Cornwallis was yet to be told, and
it was neceſſary to give it the ſofteſt introduction poſſible.

" But in the courſe of this year," continues the ſpeech, " my affi-
" duous endeavours to guard the extenſive dominions of my crown,
" have not been attended with ſucceſs equal to the juſtice and upright-
" neſs of my views." ———What juſtice and uprightneſs there was
in beginning a war with America the world will judge of, and the
unequalled barbarity with which it has been conducted is not to be
worn from the memory by the cant of ſnivelling hypocriſy.

" And it is with GREAT CONCERN that I inform you that
" the events of war have been very unfortunate to my arms in Vir-

" ginia, having ended in the lofs of my forces in that province."——
And OUR great concern is that they are not all ferved in the fame
manner.

" No endeavours have been wanting on my part," fays the fpeech,
" to extinguifh that fpirit of rebellion which our enemies have found
" means to foment and maintain in the colonies; and to reftore to my
" DELUDED SUBJECTS in America that happy and profpe-
" rous condition which they formerly derived from a due obedience
" to the laws."

The expreffion of DELUDED SUBJECTS is become fo hack-
nied and contemptable, and the more fo when we fee them making
prifoners of whole armies at a time, that the pride of not being laughed
at would induce a man of common fenfe to leave it off. But the moft
offenfive falfehood in the paragraph, is the attributing the profperity
of America to a wrong caufe. It was the unremitted induftry of
the fettlers and their defcendants, the hard labour and toil of perfevering fortitude that were the true caufes of the profperity of America. The former tyranny of England ferved to people it, and
the virtue of the adventurers to improve it. Afk the man who with
his axe hath cleared a way in the wildernefs and now poffeffes an eftate,
what made him rich, and he will tell you the labour of his hands, the
fweat of his brow and the bleffing of heaven. Let Britain but leave
America to herfelf and fhe afks no more. She has rifen into greatnefs without the knowledge and againft the will of England, and has
a right to the unmolefted enjoyment of her own created wealth.

" I will order, " fays the fpeech, " the eftimates of the enfuing year
" to be laid before you. I rely on your wifdom and public fpirit for
" fuch fupplies as the circumftances of our affairs fhall be found to
" require. Among the many ill confequences which attend the con-
" tinuation of the prefent war, I muft fincerely regret the additional
" burdens which it muft unavoidably bring upon my faithful fub-
" jects."

Strange! That a nation muft run through fuch a labyrinth of trouble, and expend fuch a mafs of wealth to gain the wifdom which an
hour's reflection might have taught. The final fuperiority of America over every attempt which an ifland might make to conquer her,
was as naturally marked in the conftitution of things, as the future
ability of a giant over a dwarf is delineated in his features while an
infant. How far Providence, to accomplifh purpofes, which no human wifdom could forefee, permitted fuch extraordinary errors, will

be believed by some and doubted by others, and still a secret in the womb of time, must rest till futurity shall give it birth.

" In the prosecution of this great and important contest," says the speech, " in which we are engaged, I retain a firm confidence in the " PROTECTION OF DIVINE PROVIDENCE, and a per- " fect conviction in the justice of my cause, and I have no doubt, but, " that by the concurrence and support of my parliament, by the va- " lour of my fleets and armies, and by a vigourous, animated, and " united exertion of the faculties and resources of my people, I shall " be enabled to restore the blessings of a safe and honourable peace " to all my dominions."

The king of England is one of the readiest believers in the world. In the beginning of the contest he passed an act to put America out of the protection of the crown of England, and though Providence, for seven years together hath put him out of HER protection, still the man has no doubt. Like Pharoah on the edge of the Red sea, he sees not the plunge he is making, and precipitately drives acrofs the flood that is closing over his head.

I think it is a reasonable supposition, that this part of the speech was composed before the arrival of the news of the capture of Cornwallis: for it certainly has no relation to their condition at the time it was spoken. But, be this as it may, it is nothing to us. Our line is fixt. Our lot is cast. And America, the child of fate, is arriving at maturity. We have nothing to do but by a spirited and quick exertion, to stand prepared for war or peace. Too great to yield, and too noble to insult; superior to misfortune, and generous in success, let us untaintedly preferve the character we have gained, and show to future ages, an example of unequalled magnanimity. There is something in the cause and consequence of America that has drawn on her the attention of all mankind. The world has feen her brave. Her love of liberty ; her ardour in supporting it ; the justice of her claims, and the constancy of her fortitude has won her the esteem of Europe, and attached to her interest the first power of that country.

Her situation now is such, that to whatever point, past, present or to come she casts her eyes, new matter rises to convince her she is right. In her conduct towards her enemy, no reproachful sentiment lurks in secret. No fense of injustice is left upon the mind. Untainted with ambition and a stranger to revenge, her progress hath been marked by Providence, and she, in every stage of the conflict has blest her with success.

But let not America wrap herself up in delufive hope and fuppofe the bufinefs done. The leaft remifsnefs in preparation, the leaft relax in execution, will only ferve to prolong the war and increafe expences. If our enemies can draw confolation from misfortune and exert themfelves upon defpair, how much more ought we, who are to win a continent by the conqueft and have already an earneft of fuccefs.

Having in the preceding part made my remarks on the feveral matters which the fpeech contains, I fhall now make my remarks on what it does not contain.

There is not a fyllable in it refpecting alliances. Either the injuftice of Britain is too glaring, or her condition too defperate, or both, for any neighbouring power to come to her fupport. In the beginning of the conteft, when fhe had only America to contend with, fhe hired affiftance from Heffe and other fmaller ftates of Germany, and for nearly three years did America, young, raw, undifciplined and unprovided, ftand againft the power of Britain, aided by twenty thoufand foreign troops, and made a complete conqueft of one entire army. The remembrance of thofe things ought to infpire us with confidence and greatnefs of mind, and carry us through every remaining difficulty with content and chearfulnefs. What are the little fufferings of the prefent day, compared with the hardfhips that are paft. There was a time, when we had neither houfe nor home in fafety; when every hour was the hour of alarm and danger; when the mind, tortured with anxiety knew no repofe, and every thing but hope and fortitude, was bidding us farewel.

It is of ufe to look back upon thefe things; to call to mind the times of trouble and the fcenes of complicated anguifh that are paft and gone. Then every expence was cheap, compared with the dread of conqueft and the mifery of fubmiffion. We did not ftand debating upon trifles, nor contending about the neceffary and unavoidable charges of defence. Every one bore his lot of fuffering, and looked forward to happier days and fcenes of reft.

Perhaps one of the greateft dangers which any country can be expofed to arifes from a kind of trifling which fometimes fteals upon the mind when it fuppofes the danger paft; and this unfafe fituation marks at this time the peculiar crifis of America. What would fhe once have given, to have known that her condition at this day fhould be what it now is? and yet we do not feem to place a proper value upon it, nor vigoroufly purfue the neceffary meafures to fecure it. We know we cannot be defended, nor yet defend ourfelves, without trouble and expence. We have no right to expect it ; neither ought we to look for it. We are a people, who, in our fituation, differ from all the world. We form one common floor of public good, and, whatever is our charge, it is paid for our own intereft and upon our own account.

Misfortune and experience have now taught us fyftem and method ; and the arrangements for carrying on the war are reduced to rule and order. The quota of the feveral ftates are afcertained, and I intend in a future publication to fhew what they are, and the neceffity as well as the advantages of vigoroufly providing them.

In the mean time, I fhall conclude this paper with an inftance of *Britifh clemency*, from Smollet's Hiftory of England, volume the 11th, page 239, printed in London. It will ferve to fhow how difmal is the fituation of a conquered people, and that the only fecurity is an effectual defence.

We all know that the Stuart family and the houfe of Hanover oppofed each other for the crown of England. The Stuart family ftood firft in the line of fucceffion, but the other was the moft fuccefsful.

In July, 1745, Charles, the fon of the exiled king, landed in Scotland, collected a fmall force, at no time exceeding five or fix thoufand men, and made fome attempts to re-eftablifh his claim. The late duke of Cumberland, uncle to the prefent king of England, was fent againft him, and on the 16th of April following Charles was totally defeated at Culloden, in Scotland. Succefs and power are the only fituations in which clemency can be fhewn, and thofe who are cruel, becaufe they are victorious, can, with the fame facility, act any other degenerate characters.

" Immediately after the decifive action at Culloden, the duke of Cumberland took poffeffion of Invernefs ; where fix and thirty deferters, convicted by a court martial, were ordered to be executed : Then he detached feveral parties to ravage the country. One of thefe apprehended the lady Mackintofh, who was fent prifoner to Invernefs, plundered her houfe. and drove away her cattle, though her hufband was actually in the fervice of the government. The caftle of lord Lovat was deftroyed. The French prifoners were fent to Carlifle and Penrith : Kilmarnock, Balmerino, Cromartie, and his fon the lord Macleod, were conveyed by fea to London ; and thofe of an inferior rank were confined in different prifons. The marquis of Tullibardine together with a brother of the carl of Dunmore, and

Murray the pretender's fecretary, were feized and tranfported to the Tower of London, to which the earl of Traquair had been committed on fufpicion ; and the eldeft fon of lord Lovat was imprifoned in the caſtle of Edinburgh. In a word, all the gaols of Great-Britain, from the capital northwards, were filled with thofe unfortunate captives; and great numbers of them were crowded together in the holds of fhips, where they perifhed in the moft deplorable manner, for want of air and exercife. Some rebel chiefs efcaped in two French frigates that arrived on the coaft of Lochaber about the end of April, and en-gaged three veffels belonging to his Britannic majefty, which they obliged to retire. Others embarked on board a fhip on the coaft of Buchan, and were conveyed to Norway, from whence they travelled to Sweden. In the month of May, the duke of Cumberland ad-vanced with the army into the Highlands, as far as Fort-Auguſtus, where he encamped ; and fent off detachments on all hands, to hunt down the fugitives, and lay wafte the country with fire and fword. The caftles of Glengary and Lochiel were plundered and burned ; every houfe, hut, or habitation, met with the fame fate, without dif-tinction ; and all the cattle and provifion were carried off ; the men were either fhot upon the mountains, like wild beafts, or put to death in cold blood, without form of trial ; the women, after having feen their hufbands and fathers murdered, were fubjected to brutal viola--tion, and then turned out naked, with their children, to ftarve on the barren heaths. One whole family was inclofed in a barn, and confumed to afhes. Thofe minifters of vengeance were fo alert in the execution of their office, that in a few days there was neither houfe, cottage, man, nor beaft, to be feen within the compafs of fifty miles ; all was ruin, filence, and defolation."

I have here prefented the reader with one of the moft fhocking in-ftances of cruelty ever practifed, and I leave it to reft on his mind, that he may be fully impreffed with a fenfe of the deftruction he has efcaped in cafe Britain had conquered America ; and likewife, that he may fee and feel the neceffity, as well for his own perfonal fafety, as for the honour, the intereft, the happinefs of the whole community, to omit or delay no one preparation neceffary to fecure the ground we fo happily ftand upon.

TO THE PEOPLE OF AMERICA.

On the Expences, Arrangements and Difburfements for carrying on the War, and finifhing it with Honour and Advantage.

When any neceffity or occafion has pointed out the convenience of addreffing the public, I have never made it a confideration whether the fubject was popular or unpopular, but whether it was right or wrong; for that which is right will become popular, and that which is wrong, though by miftake it may obtain the cry or fafhion of the day, will foon lofe the power of delufion, and fink into difefteem.

A remarkable inftance of this happened in the cafe of Silas Deane; and I mention this circumftance with the greater eafe, becaufe the poifon of this hypocrify fpread over the whole country, and every man, almoft without exception, thought me wrong in oppofing him. The beft friends I then had, except Mr. Laurens, ftood at a diftance, and this tribute, which is due to his conftancy, I pay to him with refpect, and that the readier, becaufe he is not here to hear it. If it reaches him in his imprifonment, it will afford him an agreeable reflection.

" *As he rofe like a rocket, he would fall like the flick,*" is a metaphor which I applied to Mr. Deane in the firft piece which I publifhed refpecting him, and he has exactly fulfilled the defcription. The credit he fo unjuftly obtained from the public, he loft in almoft as fhort a time. The delufion perifhed as it fell, and he foon faw himfelf ftripped of popular fupport. His more intimate acquaintance began to doubt and to defert him long before he left America, and at his departure he faw himfelf the object of general fufpicion. When arrived in France, he endeavoured to effect by treafon what he had failed to accomplifh by fraud. His plans, fchemes and projects, together with his expectation of being fent to Holland to negociate a loan of money, had all mifcarried. He then began traducing and accufing America of every crime, which could injure her reputation. " That fhe was " a ruined country ; that fhe only meant to make a tool of France, " to get what money fhe could out of her, and then to leave her, and " accommodate with Britain." Of all which, and much more, Colonel Laurens and myfelf, when in France, informed Dr. Franklin, who had not before heard of it. And to compleat the character of a traitor, he has, by letters to this country fince, fome of which, in his own hand writing, are now in the poffeffion of Congrefs, ufed every expreffion and argument in his power to injure the reputation of France, and to advife America to renounce her alliance, and furrender up her independence.* Thus in France, he abufes America, and in his letters to America he abufes France; and is endeavouring to create difunion between the two countries, by the fame arts of double-dealing by which he caufed diffentions among the Commiffioners in Paris, and diftractions in America. But his life has been fraud, and his character is that of a plodding, plotting, cringing mercenary, capable of any difguife that fuited his purpofe. His final detection has very happily cleared up thofe miftakes, and removed thofe uneafineffes, which his unprincipled conduct occafioned. Every one now fees him in the fame light; for towards friends or enemies he acted with the fame deception and injuftice; and his name, like that of *Arnold*, ought now to be forgotten among us. As this is the firft time I have mentioned him fince my return from France, it is my intention it fhall be the laft. —From this digreffion, which for feveral reafons I thought neceffary to give, I now proceed to the purport of my addrefs.

I confider the war of America againft Britain as the country's war, the public's war, or the war of the people in their own behalf, for the fecurity of their natural rights, and the protection of their own property. It is not the war of Congrefs, the war of the Affemblies, or the war of Government, in any line whatever. The country firft, by a mutual compact, refolved to defend their rights and maintain their independence, *at the hazard of their lives and fortunes.* They elected their Reprefentatives, by whom they appointed their members to Congrefs, and faid, *act you for us, and we will fupport you.* This is the true ground and principle of the war on the part of America, and, confequently, there remains nothing to do, but for every one to fulfil his obligation.

It was next to impoffible that a new country, engaged in a new undertaking, could fet off fyftematically right at firft. She faw not the extent of the ftruggle fhe was involved in, neither could fhe avoid the beginning. She fuppofed every ftep fhe took, and every refolu-

---

* *Mr. William Marfhal, of this city, formerly a pilot, who had been taken at fea and carried to England, and got from thence to France, brought over letters from Mr. Deane to America, one of which was directed to* " Robert Morris, Efq." *Mr. Morris fent it unopened to Congrefs, and advifed Mr. Marfhal to deliver the others there, which he did. The letters were of the fame purport with thofe which have been already publifhed under the fignature of S. Deane, to which they had frequent reference.*

tion fhe formed, would bring her enemy to reafon, and clofe the conteft. Thofe failing, fhe was forced into new meafures ; and thefe,
like the former, being fitted to her expectations, and failing in their
turn, left her continually unprovided and without fyftem. The enemy likewife was induced to profecute the war, from the temporary expedients we adopted for carrying it on. We were continually expecting
to fee their credit exhaufted, and they were looking to fee our currency fail; and thus, between their watching us and we them, the
hopes of both have been deceived, and the childifhnefs of the expectation has ferved to increafe the expence.

Yet who, through this wildernefs of error, has been to blame ?
where is the man who can fay, the fault has not in part been his? They
were the natural unavoidable errors of the day. They were the errors of a whole country, which nothing but experience could detect,
and time remove. Neither could the circumftances of America admit of fyftem, till either the paper currency was fixed or laid afide. No
calculation of finance could be made on a medium failing without
reafon, and fluctuating without rule.

But there is one error which might have been prevented, and was
not ; and as it is not my cuftom to flatter, but to ferve mankind, I
will fpeak it freely. It certainly was the duty of every affembly on
the continent to have known, at all times, what was the condition of
its treafury, and to have afcertained at every period of depreciation,
how much the real worth of the taxes fell fhort of their nominal value. This knowledge, which might have been eafily gained, would
have enabled them to have kept their conftituents well informed, which
is one of the greateft duties of reprefentation. They ought to have
ftudied and calculated the expences of the war, the quota of each
State, and the confequent proportion that would fall on each man's
property for his defence ; and this muft eafily have fhewn to them,
that a tax of an hundred pounds could not be paid by a bufhel of ap-
ples or an hundred of flour, which was often the cafe two or three
years ago. But inftead of this, which would have been plain and upright dealing, the little line of temporary popularity, the feather of
an hour's duration, was too much purfued ; and in this involved condition of things, every State, for the want of a little thinking, or a
little information, fuppofed that it fupported the whole expences of
the war, when in fact it fell, by the time the tax was levied and collected, above three fourths fhort of its own quota.

Impreffed with a fenfe of the danger to which the country was expofed by this lax method of doing bufinefs, and the prevailing errors of the day, I publifhed, laft October was a twelvemonth, *The Crifis Extraordinary*, on the revenues of America, and the yearly expence of carrying on the war. My eftimation of the latter, together with the civil lift of congrefs, and the civil lift of the feveral ftates, was two million pounds fterling, which is very nearly nine millions of dollars.

Since that time, Congrefs have gone into a calculation, and have eftimated the expences of the war department and the civil lift of Congrefs (exclufive of the civil lift of the feveral governments) at eight millions of dollars; and as the remaining million will be fully fufficient for the civil lift of the feveral States, the two calculations are exceedingly near each other.

The fum of eight millions of dollars they have called upon the States to furnifh, and their quotas are as follows, which I fhall preface with the refolution itfelf.

By the United States in Congrefs affembled.

October 30th, 1781.

RESOLVED,

THAT the refpective States be called upon to furnifh the Treafury of the United States with their quotas of eighth millions of dollars, for the war department and civil lift for the enfuing year, to be paid quarterly, in equal proportions, the firft payment to be made on the firft day of April next.

Refolved, That a Committee, confifting of a member from each State, be appointed to apportion to the feveral States the quota of the above fum.

November 2d.

The Committee, appointed to afcertain the proportions of the feveral ftates of the monies to be raifed for the expences of the enfuing year, report the following refolutions:

That the fum of eight millions of dollars, as required to be raifed by the refolutions of the 30 th of October laft, be paid by the States in the following proportion.

New-Hampfhire,	- -	373,598
Maffachufetts.	- - -	1307,596
Rhode-Ifland,	- -	216,684
Connecticut	- - - -	747,196
New-York	- - -	373,598

New-Jerfey	-	-	485,679
Pennfylvania,		-	1,120,794
Delaware,	-	-	112,085
Maryland,	-	-	933,996
Virginia,	-	-	1,307,594
North-Carolina,		-	622,677
South-Carolina,	-	-	373,598
Georgia,		-	24,905

8,000,000 Dollars.

Refolved,

That it be recommended to the feveral States, to lay taxes for raifing their quotas of money for the United States, feparate from thofe laid for their own particular ufe.

On thefe refolutions I fhall offer feveral remarks.

Firft. On the fum itfelf, and the ability of the country.

Secondly. On the feveral quotas, and the nature of a union. And

Thirdly. On the manner of collection and expenditure.

Firft. On the fum itfelf, and the ability of the country. As I know my own calculation is as low as poffible, and as the fum called for by Congrefs, according to their calculation, agrees very nearly therewith, I am fenfible it cannot poffibly be lower. Neither can it be done for that, unlefs there is ready money to go to market with; and even in that cafe, it is only by the utmoft management and economy that it can be made to do.

By the accounts which were laid before the Britifh parliament laft fpring, it appeared that the charge of only fubfifting, that is feeding, their army in America, coft annually four millions pounds fterling, which is very nearly eighteen millions of dollars. Now if, for eight millions, we can feed, clothe, arm, provide for and pay, an army fufficient for our defence, the very comparifon fhows that, the money muft be well laid out.

It may be of fome ufe, either in debate or converfation, to attend to the progrefs of the expences of an army, becaufe it will enable us to fee on what part any deficiency will fall.

The firft thing is, to feed them and provide for the fick.

Secondly, to clothe them.

Thirdly, to arm and furnifh them.

Fourthly, to provide means for removing them from place to place. And,

Fifthly, to pay them.

The firſt and ſecond are abſolutely neceſſary to them as men. The third and fourth are equally as neceſſary to them as an army. And the fifth is their juſt due. Now if the ſum which ſhall be raiſed ſhould fall ſhort, either by the ſeveral acts of the States for raiſing it, or by the manner of collecting it, the deficiency will fall on the fifth head, the ſoldiers pay, which would be defrauding them, and eternally diſgracing ourſelves. It would be a blot on the councils, the country, and the revolution of America, and a man would hereafter be aſhamed to own he had any hand in it.

But if the deficiency ſhould be ſtill ſhorter, it would next fall on the fourth head, *the means of removing the army from place to place ;* and in this caſe, the army muſt either ſtand ſtill where it can be of no uſe, or ſeize on horſes, carts, waggons, or any means of tranſportation it can lay hold of; and in this inſtance the country ſuffers. In ſhort every attempt to do a thing for leſs than it can be done for, is ſure to become at laſt both a loſs and a diſhonour.

But the country cannot bear it ſay ſome. This has been the moſt expenſive doctrine that ever was held out, and coſt America millions of money for nothing. Can the country bear to be over-run, ravaged and ruined by an enemy, which will immediately follow where defence is wanting, and defence will ever be wanting where ſufficient revenues are not provided. But this is only one part of the folly. The ſecond is, that when the danger comes, invited in part by our not preparing againſt it, we have been obliged, in a number of inſtances, to expend double the ſums, to do that which at firſt might have been done for half the money. But this is not all. A third miſchief has been, that grain of all ſorts, flour, beef, fodder, horſes, carts, waggons, or whatever was abſolutely or immediately wanted, have been taken without pay. Now, I aſk, why was all this done, but from that extremely weak and expenſive doctrine, *that the country could not bear it ?* that is, that ſhe could not bear, in the firſt inſtance, that which would have ſaved her twice as much at laſt ; or, in proverbial language, that ſhe could not bear to pay a penny to ſave a pound ; the conſequence of which has been, that ſhe has paid a pound for a penny. Why are there ſo many unpaid certificates in almoſt every man's hands, but from the parſimony of not providing ſufficient revenues? Beſides, the doctrine contradicts itſelf; becauſe, if the whole country cannot bear it, how is it poſſible that a part ſhould ? and yet this has been the caſe: For thoſe things have been had; and they muſt be had; but the misfortune is, they have been had in a very unequal

manner and upon expenſive credit, whereas with ready money they
might have been purchaſed for half the price, and no body diſtreſſed.

But there is another thought which ought to ſtrike us, which is,
—How is the army to bear the want of food, clothing and other neceſſaries ? The man who is at home, can turn himſelf a thouſand ways,
and find as many means of eaſe, convenience or relief : But a ſoldier's
life admits of none of thoſe : Their wants cannot be ſupplied from
themſelves : For an army, though it is the defence of a ſtate, is at
the ſame time the child of a country, and muſt be provided for in
every thing.

And laſtly, The doctrine is falſe. There are not three millions
of people, in any part of the univerſe, who live ſo well, or have ſuch
a fund of ability as in America. The income of a common labourer, who is induſtrious, is equal to that of the generality of tradeſmen
in England. In the mercantile line, I have not heard of one who
could be ſaid to be a bankrupt ſince the war began, and in England
they have been without number. In America almoſt every farmer
lives on his own lands, and in England not one in a hundred does.
In ſhort, it ſeems as if the poverty of that country had made them
furious, and they were determined to riſk all to recover all.

Yet, notwithſtanding thoſe advantages on the part of America,
true it is, that had it not been for the operation of taxes for our neceſſary defence, we had ſunk into a ſtate of ſloth and poverty : For
there was more wealth loſt by neglecting to till the earth in the years
1776, 77 and 78, than the quota of the tax amounts to. That which
is loſt by neglect of this kind, is loſt for ever; whereas that which is
paid, and continues in that country, returns to us again; and at the
ſame time that it provides us with defence, it operates not only as a
ſpur but as a premium to our induſtry.

I ſhall now proceed to the ſecond head, viz. ON THE SEVE-
RAL QUOTAS, AND THE NATURE OF A UNION.

There was a time when America had no other bond of union, than
that of common intereſt and affection. The whole country flew to
the relief of Boſton, and, making her cauſe their own, participated
her cares and adminiſtered to her wants. The fate of war, ſince that
day, has carried the calamity in a ten-fold proportion to the ſouthward ; but in the mean time the union has been ſtrengthened by a
legal compact of the States, jointly and ſeverally ratified, and that
which before was choice, or the duty of affection, is now likewiſe the
duty of legal obligation.

The union of America is the foundation ftone of her independence; the rock on which it is built ; and is fomething fo facred in her conftitution, that we ought to watch every word we fpeak, and every thought we think, that we injure it not, even by miftake. When a multitude, extended, or rather fcattered, over a continent, in the manner we are, mutually agree to form one common centre whereon the whole fhall move; to accomplifh a particular purpofe, all parts muft act together and alike, or act not at all, and a floppage in any one is a floppage of the whole, at leaft for a time.

Thus the feveral States have fent Reprefentatives to affemble together in Congrefs, and they have empowered that body, which thus becomes their centre, and are no other than themfelves in reprefentation, to conduct and manage the war, while their conftituents at home attend to the domeftic cares of the country, their internal legiflation, their farms, profeffions or employments : For it is only by reducing complicated things to method and orderly connection that they can be underftood with advantage, or purfued with fuccefs.—Congrefs, by virtue of this delegation, eftimates the expence, and apportions it out to the feveral parts of the empire according to their feveral abilities; and here the debate muft end, becaufe each State has already had its voice, and the matter has undergone its whole portion of argument, and can no more be altered by any particular State, than a law of any State, after it has paffed, can be altered by an individual. For with refpect to thofe things which immediately concern the union, and for which the union was purpofely eftablifhed and is intended to fecure, each State is to the United States what each individual is to the State he lives in. And it is on this grand point, this movement upon one centre, that our exiftence as a nation, our happinefs as a people, and our fafety as individuals, depend.

It may happen that fome State or other may be fomewhat over or under rated, but this cannot be much. The experience which has been had upon the matter has nearly afcertained their feveral abilities. But even in this cafe, it can only admit of an appeal to the United States, but cannot authorife any State to make the alteration itfelf, any more than our internal government can admit an individual to do fo in the cafe of an act of affembly; for if one State can do it, then may another do the fame, and the inftant this is done the whole is undone.

Neither is it fuppofable that any fingle ftate can be judge of all the comparative reafons which may influence the collective body in quotaing out the continent. The circumstances of the several States are frequently varying, occasioned by the accidents of war and commerce, and it will often fall upon some to help others, rather beyond what their exact proportion at another time might be; but even this assistance is as naturally and politically included in the idea of a union, as that of any particular assigned proportion ; because we know not whose turn it may be next to want assistance, for which reason that is the wisest State which sets the best example.

Though in matters of bounden duty and reciprocal affection, it is rather a degeneracy from the honesty and ardour of the heart to admit any thing selfish to partake in the government of our conduct, yet in cases where our duty, our affections, and our interest all coincide, it may be of some use to observe their union. The United States will become heir to an extensive quantity of vacant land, and their several titles to shares and quotas thereof will naturally be adjusted according to their relative quotas, during the war, exclusive of that inability which may unfortunately arise to any State by the enemy holding possession of a part; but as this is a cold matter of interest, I pass it by, and proceed to my third head, viz.

ON THE MANNER OF COLLECTION AND EXPENDITURE.

It hath been our error, as well as our misfortune, to blend the affairs of each State, especially in money matters, with those of the United States; whereas it is to our ease, convenience and interest to keep them separate. The expences of the United States for carrying on the war, and the expences of each State for its own domestic government, are distinct things, and to involve them is a source of perplexity and a cloak for fraud. I love method, because I see and am convinced of its beauty and advantage. It is that which makes all business easy and understood, and without which every thing becomes embarrassed and difficult.

There are certain powers which the people of each State have delegated to their legislative and executive bodies, and there are other powers which the people of every State have delegated to Congress, among which is that of conducting the war, and, consequently, of managing the expences attending it; for how else can that be managed, which concerns every State, but by a delegation from each. When a State has furnished its quota, it has an undoubted right to know how it has been applied, and it is as much the duty of Congress to inform the State of the one, as it is the duty of the State to provide the other.

In the refolution of Congrefs already recited, it is recommended to the feveral States *to lay taxes for raifing their quotas of money for the United States, feparate from thofe laid for their own particular ufe.* This is a moft neceffary point to be obferved, and the diftinction fhould follow all the way through. They fhould be levied, paid and collected feparately, and kept feparate in every inftance. Neither have the civil officers of any State, or the government of that State, the leaft right to touch that money which the people pay for the fupport of their army and the war, any more than Congrefs has to touch that which each State raifes for its own ufe.

This diftinction will naturally be followed by another. It will occafion every State to examine nicely into the expences of its civil lift, and to regulate, reduce and bring it into better order than it has hitherto been; becaufe the money for that purpofe muft be raifed apart, and accounted for to the public feparately. But while the monies of both were blended, the neceffary nicety was not obferved, and the poor foldier, who ought to have been the firft, was the laft who was thought of.

Another convenience will be, that the people, by paying the taxes feparately, will know what they are for; and will likewife know that thofe which are for the defence of the country will ceafe with the war, or foon after. For although, as I have before obferved, the war is their own, and for the fupport of their own rights and the protection of their own property, yet they have the fame right to know, that they have to pay, and it is the want of not knowing that is often the caufe of diffatisfaction.

This regulation of keeping the taxes feparate has given rife to a regulation in the office of finance, by which it is directed,

" That the receivers fhall, at the end of every month, make out an exact account of the monies received by them refpectively, during fuch month, fpecifying therein the names of the perfons from whom the fame fhall have been received, the dates and the fums; which account they fhall refpectively caufe to be publifhed in one of the newf-papers of the State; to the end that every citizen may know how much of the monies collected from him, in taxes, is tranfmitted to the trea-fury of the United States for the fupport of the war; and alfo, that it may be known what monies have been at the order of the Superinten-dant of Finance. It being proper and neceffary, that in a free country the people fhould be as fully informed of the adminiftration of their affairs as the nature of things will admit."

It is an agreeable thing to fee a fpirit of order and economy taking place, after fuch a feries of errors and difficulties. A government or an adminiftration, who means and acts honeftly, has nothing to fear, and confequently has nothing to conceal; and it would be of ufe if a monthly or quarterly account was to be publifhed, as well of the expenditures as of the receipts. Eight millions of dollars muft be hufbanded with an exceeding deal of care to make it do, and therefore, as the management muft be reputable, the publication would be ferviceable.

I have heard of petitions which have been prefented to the Affembly of, this State (and probably the fame may have happened in other States) praying to have the taxes lowered. Now the only way to keep taxes low is, for the United States to have ready money to go to market with; and though the taxes to be raifed for the prefent year will fall heavy, and there will naturally be fome difficulty in paying them, yet the difficulty, in proportion as money fpreads about the country, will every day grow lefs, and in the end we fhall fave fome millions of dollars by it. We fee what a bitter, revengeful enemy we have to deal with, and any expence is cheap compared to their mercilefs paw. We have feen the unfortunate Carolineans hunted like partridges on the mountains, and it is only by providing means for our defence that we fhall not be in the fame condition. When we think or talk about taxes, we ought to recollect that we lie down in peace, and fleep in fafety; that we can follow our farms or ftores, or other occupations, in profperous tranquility; and that thefe ineftimable bleffings are procured to us by the taxes that we pay. In this view, our taxes are properly our infurance-money; they are what we pay to be made fafe, and in ftrict policy are the beft money we can lay out.

It was my intention to offer fome remarks on the impoft law of *five per cent.* recommended by Congrefs, and to be eftablifhed as a fund for the payment of the loan-office certificates and other debts of the United States; but I have already extended my piece beyond my intention. And as this fund will make our fyftem of finance compleat, and is ftrictly juft, and confequently requires nothing but honefty to do it, there needs but little to be faid upon it.

COMMON SENSE.

Philadelphia, March 5, 1782.

THE CRISIS.—NUMBER XI.

ON THE PRESENT STATE OF NEWS.

Philadelphia, May 22, 1782.

SINCE the arrival of two, if not three packets, in quick fucceffion, at New-York, from England, a variety of unconnected *news* has circulated through the country, and afforded as great a variety of fpeculation.

That fomething is the matter in the cabinet and councils of our enemies, on the other fide of the water, is certain—that they have run their length of madnefs, and are under the neceffity of changing their meafures may eafily be feen into ; but to what this change of meafures may amount, or how far it may correfpond with our intereft, happinefs and duty, is yet uncertain ; and from what we have hitherto experienced, we have too much reafon to fufpect them in every thing.

I do not addrefs this publication fo much to the people of America as to the Britifh miniftry, whoever they may be, for if it is their intention to promote any kind of negotiation, it is proper they fhould know beforehand, that the United States have as much honour as bravery ; and that they are no more to be feduced from their alliance than their allegiance ; that their line of politics is formed, and not dependaut, like that of their enemy, on chance and accident.

On our part, in order to know, at any time, what the Britifh gavernment will do, we have only to find out what they ought *not* to do, and this laft will be their conduct. For ever changing and for ever wrong ; too diftant from America to improve circumftances, and too unwife to forefee them ; fcheming without principle, and executing without probability, their whole line of management has hitherto been blunder and bafenefs. Every campaign is added to their lofs, and every year to their difgrace ; till unable to go on, and afhamed to go back, their politics have come to a halt, and all their fine profpects to a halter.

Could our affections forgive, or humanity forget, the wounds of an injured country—we might, under the influence of a momentary oblivion, ftand ftill and laugh. But they are engraven where no amufement can conceal them, and of a kind for which there is no recompence. Can ye reftore to us the beloved dead ? Can ye fay to the grave, Give up the murdered ? Can ye obliterate from our memories thofe who are no more ? Think not then to tamper with our feelings by infidious contrivance; nor fuffocate our humanity by feducing us to difhonour.

In March 1780, I publifhed part of the Crifis, Nº. VIII. in the newfpapers, but did not conclude it in the following papers, and the remainder has lain by me till the prefent day.

There appeared about that time fome difpofition in the Britifh cabinet to ceafe the further profecution of the war, and as I had formed my opinion, that whenever fuch a defign fhould take place, it would be accompanied with a difhonourable propofition to America, refpecting France, I had fupprefied the remainder of that number, not to expofe the bafenefs of any fuch propofition. But the arrival of the next news from England, declared her determination to go on with the war, and confequently as the political object I had then in view was not become a fubject, it was unneceffary in me to bring it forward, which is the reafon it was never publifhed.

The matter which I allude to in the unpublifhed part I fhall now make a quotation of, and apply it as the more enlarged ftate of things, at this day, fhall make convenient or neceffary.

It was as follows :

"By the fpeeches which have appeared from the Britifh parliament, it is eafy to perceive to what impolitic and imprudent exceffes their paffions and prejudices have, in every inftance, carried them, during the prefent war. Provoked at the upright and honourable treaty between America and France, they imagined nothing more was neceffary to be done to prevent its final ratification, than to promife, through the agency of their commiffioners (Carlifle, Eden and Johnfton) a repeal of their once offenfive acts of parliament. The vanity of the conceit was as unpardonable as the experiment was impolitic. And fo convinced am I of their wrong ideas of America, that I fhall not wonder, if in their laft ftage of political phrenzy, they propofe to her to break her alliance with France, and enter into one with them. Such a propofition, fhould it ever be made, and it has already been more than once hinted in parliament, would difcover fuch a difpofition to perfidioufnefs, and fuch difregard of honour and morals, as would add the finifhing vice to national corruption.—I do not mention this to put America on the watch, but to put England on her guard, that fhe do not, in the loofenefs of

her heart, envelope in difgrace every fragment of reputation."—
Thus far the quotation.

By the complexion of fome part of the news which has tranfpired
through the New-York papers, it feems probable that this infidious
era in the British politics is beginning to make its appearance.. I
wifh it may not ; for that which is a difgrace to human nature,
throws fomething of a fhade over all the human character, and the
individual feels his fhare of the wound that is given to the whole.

The policy of Britain has ever been to divide America in fome
way or other. In the beginning of the difpute, fhe practifed every
art to prevent or deftroy the union of the States, well knowing that
could fhe once get them to ftand fingly, fhe could conquer them unconditionally. Failing in this project in America, fhe renewed it in
Europe ; and after the alliance had taken place, fhe made fecret offers
to France to induce her to give up America, and what is ftill more
extraordinary, fhe at the fame time made propofitions to Doctor
Franklin, then in Paris, the very court to which fhe was fecretly
applying, to draw off America from France. But this is not all.

On the 14th of September, 1778, the Britifh court, through their
fecretary, lord Weymouth, made application to the marquis D'Alma-
dovar the Spanifh ambaffador at London, to " afk the MEDIATI-
ON," for thefe were the words of the court of Spain, for the purpofe
of negociating a peace with France, leaving America (as I fhall hereafter fhew) out of the queftion. Spain readily offered her mediation,
and likewife the city of Madrid as the place of conference, but withal,
propofed that the United States of America fhould be invited to the
treaty and confidered as independent during the time the bufinefs was
negociating. But this was not the view of England. She wanted
to draw France from the war, that fhe might uninterruptedly pour
out all her force and fury upon America : and being difappointed in
this plan, as well through the open and generous conduct of Spain,
as the determination of France, fhe refufed the mediation fhe had folicited.

I fhall now give fome extracts from the juftifying memorial of the
Spanifh court, in which fhe has fet the conduct and character of
Britain, with refpect to America, in a clear and ftriking point of
light.

The memorial, fpeaking of the refufal of the Britifh court to meet
in conference, with commiffioners from the United States, who were
to be confidered as independent during the time of the conference, fays,

" It is a thing very extraordinary and even ridiculous, that the court of London, who treats the colonies as independent, not only in acting, but of right, during the war, fhould have a repugnance to treat them as fuch only in acting during a truce of fufpenfion of hoftilities. The convention of Saratoga : the reputing general Burgoyne as a lawful prifoner, in order to fufpend his trial; the exchange and liberating other prifoners made from the colonies ; the having named commiffioners to go and fupplicate the Americans, at their own doors, requeft peace of them, and treat with them and the congrefs; and finally, by a thoufand other acts of this fort, authorifed by the court of London, which have been, and are true figns of the acknowledgment of their independence.

" In aggravation to all the foregoing, at the fame time the Britifh cabinet anfwered the king of Spain in the terms already mentioned ; they were infinuating themfelves at the court of France by means of fecret emiffaries, and making very great offers to her to abandon the colonies and make peace with England. But there is yet more: for at this fame time the Englifh miniftry were treating by means of another certain emiffary with doctor Franklin, minifter plenipotentiary from the colonies, refiding at Paris, to whom they made various propofals to difunite them from France, and accommodate matters with England."

" From what has been obferved it evidently follows, that the whole of the Britifh politics was, to difunite the two courts of Paris and Madrid, by means of the fuggeftions and offers fhe feparately made to them; and alfo to feparate the colonies from their treaties and engagements entered into with France, and induce them to arm againft the houfe of Bourbon, or MORE PROBABLY TO OPPRESS THEM WHEN THEY FOUND FROM BREAKING THEIR ENGAGEMENTS, THEY STOOD ALONE AND WITHOUT PROTECTORS."

" This therefore, is the net they laid for the American ftates ; that is to fay, to tempt them with flattering and very magnificent promifes to come to an accommodation with them, exclufive of any intervention of Spain or France, that the Britifh miniftry might always remain the arbiters of the fate of the colonies.

" But the Catholic king (the king of Spain) faithful on the one part to the engagements which bind him to the moft Chriftian king (the king of France) his nephew; juft and uprighton the other, to his own fubjects, whom he ought to protect and guard againft fo many infults; and finally, full of humanity and compaffion for the Americans and other individuals who fuffer in the prefent war; he is determined to purfue and profecute it, and to make all the efforts in his power, until he can obtain a folid and permanent peace, with full and fatisfactory fecurities that it fhall be obferved."

Thus far the memorial; a tranflation of which into Englifh, may be feen in full, under the head of STATE PAPERS, in the Annual Regifter, for 1779, page 367.

The extracts I have here given, ferve to fhew the various endeavours and contrivances of the enemy to draw France from her connection with America, and to prevail on her to make a feparate peace with England, leaving America totally out of the queftion, and at the mercy of a mercilefs, unprincipled enemy. The opinion, likewife, which Spain has formed of the Britifh cabinet character, for meannefs and perfidioufnefs, is fo exactly the opinion of America, refpecting it, that the memorial, in this inftance, contains our own fentiments and language: for people, however remote, who think alike will unavoidably fpeak alike.

Thus we fee the infidious ufe which Britain endeavoured to make of the propofitions for peace under the mediation of Spain.—I fhall now proceed to the fecond propofition under the mediation of the emperor of Germany and the emprefs of Ruffia; the general out-line of which was, that a congrefs of the feveral powers at war fhould meet at Vienna, in 1781, to fettle preliminaries of peace.

I could wifh myfelf at liberty to make ufe of all the information I am poffeffed of on this fubject, but as there is a delicacy in the matter, I do not conceive it prudent, at leaft at prefent, to make references and quotations in the fame manner as I have done with refpect to the mediation of Spain, who publifhed the whole proceedings herfelf; and therefore, what comes from me, on this part of the bufinefs, muft reft on my own credit with the public, affuring them, that when the whole proceedings, relative to the propofed congrefs at Vienna, fhall appear, they fhall find my account not only true but ftudioufly moderate.

We know that at the time this mediation was on the carpet, the expectations of the Britifh king and miniftry ran high with refpect to the conqueft of America. The Englifh packet which was taken with the mail on board, and carried into l'Orient in France, contained letters from lord G. Germaine to fir Henry Clinton, which expreffed in the fulleft terms the minifterial idea of a total conqueft. Copies of thofe letters were fent to congrefs and publifhed in the newfpapers of laft year. Colonel Laurens brought over the originals, fome of which, figned in the hand writing of the then fecretary, Germaine, are now in my poffeffion.

Filled with thefe high ideas, nothing could be more infolent towards America than the language of the Britifh court on the propofed mediation. A peace with France and Spain fhe anxioufly folicited; but America, as before, fhould be left to her mercy, neither would fhe hear any propofition for admitting an agent from the United States into the congrefs of Vienna.

On the other hand, France, with an open, noble and manly determination, and the fidelity of a good ally, would hear no propofition for a feparate peace, nor even meet in congrefs at Vienna, without an agent from America: and likewife, that the independent character of the United States, reprefented by the agent, fhould be fully and unequivocally defined and fettled before any conference fhould be entered on. The reafoning of the court of France on the feveral propofitions of the two Imperial courts, which relate to us, is rather in the ftile of an American than an ally, and fhe advocated the caufe of America as if fhe had been America herfelf.—Thus the fecond mediation, like the firft, proved ineffectual.

But fince that time a reverfe of fortune has overtaken the Britifh arms, and all their high expectations are dafhed to the ground. The noble exertions to the fouthward under general Greene; the fuccefsful operations of the allied arms in the Chefapeak ; the lofs of moft of their iflands in the Weft-Indies and Minorca in the Mediterranean; the perfevering fpirit of Spain againft Gibraltar ; the expected capture of Jamaica; the failure of making a feparate peace with Holland, and the expence of an hundred millions fterling, by which all thefe fine loffes were obtained, have read them a loud leffon of difgraceful misfortune, and neceffity has called on them to change their ground.

In this fituation of confufion and defpair their prefent councils have no fixt character. It is now the hurricane months of Britifh politics. Every day feems to have a ftorm of its own, and they are fcudding under the bare poles of hope. Beaten, but not humble; condemned, but not penitent; they act like men trembling at fate and catching at a ftraw.—From this convulfion, in the entrails of their politics, it is more than probable, that the mountain groaning in labour, will bring forth a moufe as to its fize, and a monfter in its make. They will try on America the fame infidious arts they tried on France and Spain.

We fometimes experience fenfations to which language is not equal. The conception is too bulky to be born alive, and in the torture of thinking we ftand dumb. Our feelings imprifoned by their magnitude, find no way out—and, in the ftruggle of expreffion every finger tries to be a tongue. The machinery of the body feems too little for the mind, and we look about for helps to fhew our thoughts by.— Such muft be the fenfation of America, whenever Britain, teeming · with corruption, fhall propofe to her to facrifice her faith.

But, exclufive of the wickednefs, there is a perfonal offence contained in every fuch attempt. It is calling us villains ; for no man afks another to act the villain unlefs he believes him inclined to be one. No man attempts to feduce a truly honeft women. It is the fuppofed loofenefs of her mind that ftarts the thoughts of feduction, and he who offers it calls her a proftitute. Our pride is always hurt by the fame propofitions which offend our principles ; for when we are fhocked at the crime we are wounded by the fufpicion of our compliance.

Could I convey a thought that might ferve to regulate the public mind, I would not make the intereft of the alliance the bafis of defending it. All the world are moved by intereft, and it affords them nothing to boaft of. But I would go a ftep higher, and defend it on the ground of honour and principle. That our public affairs have flourifhed under the alliance—that it was wifely made and has been nobly executed—that by its affiftance we are enabled to preferve our country from conqueft and expel thofe who fought our deftruction— that it is our true intereft to maintain it unimpaired, and that while we do fo no enemy can conquer us ;—are matters which experience has taught us, and the common good of ourfelves, abftracted from principles of faith and honour, would lead us to maintain the connection.

But over and above the mere letter of the alliance, we have been nobly and generoufly treated, and have had the fame refpect and attention paid us, as if we had been an old eftablifhed country. To oblige and be obliged is fair work among mankind, and we want an opportunity of fhewing to the world that we are a people fenfible of kindnefs and worthy of confidence.—Character is to us, in our prefent circumftances, of more importance than intereft. We are a young nation, juft ftepping upon the ftage of public life, and the eye of the world is upon us to fee how we act. We have an enemy that is watching to deftroy our reputation, and who will go any length to

gain fome evidence againft us, that may ferve to render our conduct
fufpected, and our character odious; becaufe, could fhe accomplifh this,
wicked as it is, the world would withdraw from us, as from a people
not to be trufted, and our talk would then become difficult.

There is nothing fets the character of a nation in a higher or lower
light with others, than the faithfully fulfilling, or perfidioufly breaking
of treaties.--They are things not to be tampered with; and fhould
Britain, which feems very probable, propofe to feduce America into
fuch an act of bafenefs, it would merit from her fome mark of unufual
deteftation. It is one of thofe extraordinary inftances in which we
ought not to be contented with the bare negative of congrefs, becaufe
it is an affront on the multitude as well as on the government. It
goes on the fuppofition that the public are not honeft men, and that
they may be managed by contrivance, though they cannot be conquered by arms. But, let the world and Britain know, that we are
neither to be bought nor fold. That our mind is great and fixt; our
profpect clear; and that we will fupport our character as firmly as
our independence.

But I will go ftill farther, general Conway, who made the motion
in the Britifh parliament, for difcontinuing offenfive war in America,
is a gentleman of an amiable character. We have no perfonal quarrel
with him. But he feels not as we feel; he is not in our fituation, and
that alone, without any other explanation, is enough.

The Britifh parliament fuppofes they have many friends in America,
and that when all chance of conqueft is over, they will be able to draw
her from her alliance with France. Now, if I have any conception
of the human heart, they will fail in this more than in any thing they
have yet tried.

This part of the bufinefs is not a queftion of policy only but of honour and honefty; and the propofition will have in it fomething
fo vifibly low and bafe that their partizans, if they have any, will be
afhamed of it. Men are often hurt by a mean action who are not
ftartled at a wicked one, and this will be fuch a confeffion of inability,
fuch a declaration of fervile thinking, that the fcandal of it will ruin all
their hopes.

In fhort, we have nothing to do but to go on with vigour and determination. The enemy is yet in our country. They hold New-
York, Charlefton and Savannah, and the very being in thofe places is
an offence, and a part of offenfive war, and until they can be driven
from them or captured in them it would be folly in us to liften to an

idle tale.—I take it for granted that the Britifh miniftry are finking under the impoffibility of carrying on the war. Let them then come to a fair and open peace with France, Spain, Holland and America in the manner fhe ought to do; but until then we can have nothing to fay to them.

COMMON SENSE.

A SUPERNUMERARY CRISIS.

TO SIR GUY CARLETON.

IT is the nature of compaffion to affociate with misfortune ; and I addrefs this to you in behalf even of an enemy, a captain in the Britifh fervice, now on his way to the head-quarters of the American army, and unfortunately doomed to death for a crime not his own— A fentence fo extraordinary, an execution fo repugnant to every human fenfation, ought never to be told without the circumftances which produced it : and as the deftined victim is yet in exiftence, and in your hands reft his life or death, I fhall briefly ftate the cafe, and the melancholy confequence.

Captain Huddy, of the Jerfey militia, was attacked in a fmall fort on Tom's River, by a party of refugees in the Britifh pay and fervice, was made prifoner together with his company, carried to New-York and lodged in the provoft of that city : about three weeks after which, he was taken out of the provoft down to the water-fide, put into a boat and brought again upon the Jerfey fhore, and there, contrary to the practice of all nations but favages, was hung up on a tree, and left hanging till found by our people, who took him down and buried him.

The inhabitants of that part of the country where the murder was committed, fent a deputation to General Wafhington with a full and certified ftatement of the fact. Struck, as every human breaft muft be, with fuch brutifh outrage, and determined both to punifh and prevent it for the future, the General reprefented the cafe to General Clinton, who then commanded, and demanded that the refugee officer who ordered and attended the execution, and whofe name is Lippincut, fhould be delivered up as a murderer ; and in cafe of refufal, that the perfon of fome Britifh officer fhould fuffer in his ftead.

The demand, though not refufed, has not been complied with; and
the melancholy lot (not by felcdion, but by cafting lots) has fallen
upon captain Afgill, of the guards, who, as I have already mentioned, is on his way from Lancaster to camp, a martyr to the general
wickednefs of the caufe he engaged in, and the ingratitude of thofe
he has ferved.

The firft reflection which arifes on this black bufinefs is, what fort
of men muft Englifhmen be, and what fort of order and difcipline do
they preferve in their army, when in the immediate place of their head-
quarters, and under the eye and nofe of their commander in chief,
a prifoner can be taken at pleafure from his confinement, and his
death made a matter of fport.

The hiftory of the moft favage Indians does not produce inftances
exactly of this kind. They, at leaft, have a formality in their punifhments. With them it is the horridnefs of revenge, but with your
army it is the ftill greater crime, the horridnefs of diverfion.

The Britifh generals who have fucceeded each other, from the time
of general Gage to yourfelf, have all affected to fpeak in language they
have no right to. In their proclamations, their addreffes, their letters
to general Wafhington, and their fupplications to congrefs (for they deferve no other name) they talk of Britifh honour, Britifh generofity and
Britifh clemency, as if thofe things were matters of fact; whereas, we
whofe eyes are open, who fpeak the fame language with yourfelves,
many of whom were born on the fame fpot with you, and who can no
more be miftaken in your words than in your actions, can declare to all
the world, that fo far as our knowledge goes, there is not a more deteftable character, nor a meaner or more barbarous enemy, than the
prefent Britifh one. With us, you have forfeited all pretenfions of
reputation, and it is only holding you like a wild beaft, afraid of your
keepers, that you can be made manageable.—But to return to the
point in queftion.

Though I can think no man innocent who has lent his hand to
deftroy the country which he did not plant, and to ruin thofe he could
not enflave, yet abftracted from all ideas of right and wrong on the
original queftion, captain Afgill, in the prefent cafe, is not the guilty
man. The villain and the victim are here feparated characters. You
hold the one and we the other. You difown, or affect to difown and
reprobate the conduct of Lippincut, yet you give him a fanctuary;
and by fo doing you as effectually become the executioner of Afgill,
as if you put the rope on his neck, and difmiffed him from the world.

Whatever your feelings on this extraordinary occafion may be, are beft known to yourfelf, Within the grave of our own mind lies buried the fate of Afgill. He becomes the corpfe of your will, or the furvivor of your juftice. Deliver up the one, and you fave the other; withhold the one, and the other dies by your choice.

On our part the cafe is exceeding plain; AN OFFICER HAS BEEN TAKEN FROM HIS CONFINEMENT AND MURDERED, AND THE MURDERER IS WITHIN YOUR LINES. Your army have been guilty of a thoufand inftances of equal cruelty, but they have been rendered equivocal, and fheltered from perfonal detection. Here the crime is fixt; and is one of thofe extraordinary cafes which can neither be denied nor palliated, and to which the cuftom of war does not apply; for it never could be fuppofed that fuch a brutal outrage would ever be committed. It is an original in the hiftory of civilized barbarians, and is truly Britifh.

On your part, you are accountable to us for the perfonal fafety of the prifoners within your walls. Here can be no miftake; they can neither be fpies nor fufpected as fuch; your fecurity is not endangered, nor your operations fubjected to mifcarriage, by men immured within a dungeon. They differ in every circumftance from men in the field, and leave no pretence for feverity of punifhment. But if to the difmal condition of captivity with you, muft be added the conftant apprehenfions of death; if to be imprifoned is fo nearly to be entombed; and, if after all, the murderers are to be protected and thereby the crime encouraged, wherein do you differ from Indians, either in conduct or character?

We can have no idea of your honour, or your juftice, in any future tranfaction, of what nature it may be, while you fhelter within your lines an outrageous murderer, and facrifice in his ftead an officer of your own. If 'you have no regard to us, at leaft fpare the blood which it is your duty to fave. Whether the punifhment will be greater on him, who, in this cafe, innocently dies; or, on him whom fad neceffity forces to retaliate, is, in the nicety of fenfation, an undecided queftion? It refts with you to prevent the fufferings of both. You have nothing to do but to give up the murderer, and the matter ends.

But to protect him, be he who he may, is to patronize his crime, and to trifle it off by frivolous and unmeaning enquiries is to promote it. There is no declaration you can make, no promife you can give that will obtain credit.   It is the man and not the apology that is demanded.

You fee yourfelf preffed on all fides to fpare the life of your own officer, for die he will if you withhold juftice.   The murder of captain Huddy is an offence not to be borne with, and there is no fecurity we can have that fuch actions or fimilar ones fhall not be repeated, but by making the punifhment fall upon yourfelves.   To deftroy the laft fecurity of captivity, and to take the unarmed, the unrefifting prifoner to private and fportive execution, is carrying barbarity too high for filence.   The evil MUST be put an end to; and the choice of perfons refts with you.   But if your attachment to the guilty is ftronger than to the innocent, you invent a crime that muft deftroy your character, and if the caufe of your king needs to be fo fupported, for ever ceafe, fir, to torture our remembrance with the wretched phrafes of Britifh honour, Britifh generofity, and Britifh clemency.

From this melancholy circumftance, learn, fir, a leffon of morality. The refugees are men whom your predeceffors have inftructed in wickednefs, the better to fit them to their mafter's purpofe.   To make them ufeful they have made them vile, and the confequence of their tutored villany is now defcending on the heads of their encouragers. They have been trained like hounds to the fcent of blood, and cherifhed in every fpecies of diffolute barbarity.   Their ideas of right and wrong are worn away in the conftant habitude of repeated infamy, till like men practifed in executions they feel not the value of another's life.

The tafk before you though painful is not difficult ; give up the murderer, and fave your officer, as the firft outfet of a neceffary reformation.

                                        COMMON SENSE.

Philadelphia, May 31, 1782.

THE CRISIS.—NUMBER XII.

TO THE EARL OF SHELBURNE.

MY LORD,

A SPEECH, which has been printed in feveral of the Britifh and New-York newfpapers, as coming from your lordfhip, in anfwer to one from the duke of Richmond, of the 10th of July laft, contains expreffions and opinions fo new and fingular, and fo enveloped in myfterious reafoning, that I addrefs this publication to you, for the purpofe of giving them a free and candid examination. The fpeech I allude to is in thefe words :

" His lordfhip faid, it had been mentioned in another place, that
" he had been guilty of inconfiftence. To clear himfelf of this, he
" afferted that he ftill held the fame principles in refpect to American
" independence which he at firft imbibed. He had been, and yet was
" of opinion, whenever the parliament of Great-Britain acknow-
" ledges that point, the fun of England's glory is fet for ever.
" Such were the fentiments he poffeffed on a former day, and fuch
" the fentiments he continued to hold at this hour. It was the
" opinion of lord Chatham, as well as many other able ftatefmen.
" Other noble lords, however, think differently ; and as the majority
" of the cabinet fupport them, he acquiefced in the meafure, diffent-
" ing from the idea ; and the point is fettled for bringing the matter
" into the full difcuffion of parliament, where it will be candidly,
" fairly, and impartially debated. The independence of America
" would end in the ruin of England ; and that a peace patched up
" with France, would give that proud enemy the means of yet
" trampling on this country. The fun of England's glory he
" wifhed not to fee fet for ever ; he looked for a fpark at leaft to
" be left, which might in time light us up to a new day. But if
" independence was to be granted, if parliament deemed that mea-
" fure prudent, he forefaw, in his own mind, that England was un-
" done. He wifhed to God that he had been deputed to congrefs,
" that he might plead the caufe of that country as well as of this,
" and that he might exercife whatever powers he poffeffed as an
" orator, to fave both from ruin, in a conviction to congrefs, that,
" if their independence was figned, their liberties was gone for ever.

" Peace, his lordihip added, was a defirable object, but it muſt be
" an honourable peace, and not an humiliating one, dictated by
" France, or infiſted on by America. It was very true, this king-
" dom was not in a flouriſhing ſtate, it was impoveriſhed by war.
" But if we were not rich, it was evident that France was poor.
" If we were ſtraitened in our finances, the enemy were exhauſted
" in their reſources. This was a great empire ; it abounded with
" brave men, who were able and willing to fight in a common
" cauſe ; the language of humiliation ſhould not, therefore, be the
" language of Great-Britain. His lordſhip ſaid, that he was not
" aſhamed nor afraid of thoſe expreſſions going to America. There
" were numbers, great numbers there, who were of the ſame way of
" thinking, in reſpect to that country being dependant on this, and
" who, with his lordſhip, perceived ruin and independence linked to-
" gether."

Thus far the ſpeech ; on which I remark—That his lordſhip is a
total ſtranger to the mind and ſentiments of America ; that he has
wrapped himſelf up in fond deluſion, that ſomething leſs than independence may, under his adminiſtration, be accepted ; and he wiſhes
himſelf ſent to congreſs, to prove the moſt extraordinary of all doc-
trines, which is, that *independence*, the ſublimeſt of all human conditions, is loſs of liberty.

In anſwer to which we may ſay, that in order to know what the
contrary word *dependence* means, we have only to look back to thoſe
years of ſevere humiliation, when the mildeſt of all petitions could obtain no other notice than the haughtieſt of all inſults ; and when the baſe
terms of unconditional ſubmiſſion were demanded, or undiſtinguiſhable
deſtruction threatened. It is nothing to us that the miniſtry have
been changed, for they may be changed again. The guilt of government is the crime of a whole country ; and the nation that can, though
but for a moment, think and act as England has done, can never afterwards be believed or truſted, There are caſes in which it is as im-
poſſible to reſtore character to life, as it is to recover the dead. It is
a phœnix that can expire but once, and from whoſe aſhes there is no
reſurrection. Some offences are of ſuch a ſlight compoſition, that
they reach no farther than the temper, and are created or cured by a
thought. But the ſin of England has ſtruck the heart of America,
and nature has not left it in our power to ſay we can forgive.

Your lordſhip wiſhes for an opportunity to plead before congreſs
the cauſe of England and America, and to ſave, as you ſay, both from ruin.

That the country, which, for more than feven years has fought our deftruction, fhould now cringe to folicit our protection, is adding the wretchednefs of difgrace to the mifery of difappointment; and if England has the leaft fpark of fuppofed honour left, that fpark muft be darkened by afking, and extinguifhed by receiving, the fmalleft favour from America: for the criminal who owes his life to the grace and mercy of the injured, is more executed by living than he who dies.

But a thoufand pleadings, even from your lordfhip, can have no effect. Honour, intereft, and every fenfation of the heart, would plead againft you. We are a people who think not as you think ; and what is equally true, you cannot feel as we feel. The fituations of the two countries are exceedingly different. We have been the feat of war; you have feen nothing of it. The moft wanton deftruction has been committed in our fight; the moft infolent barbarity has been acted on our feelings. We can look round and fee the remains of burnt and deftroyed houfes, once the fair fruit of hard induftry, and now the ftriking monuments of Britifh brutality. We walk over the dead whom we loved, in every part of America, and remember by whom they fell. There is fcarcely a village but brings to life fome melancholy thought, and reminds us of what we have fuffered, and of thofe we have loft by the inhumanity of Britain. A thoufand images arife to us, which, from fituation, you cannot fee, and are accompa-nied by as many ideas which you cannot know ; and therefore your fuppofed fyftem of reafoning would apply to nothing, and all your expectations die of themfelves.

The queftion, whether England fhall accede to the independence of America, and which your lordfhip fays is to undergo a parliamen-tary difcuffion, is fo very fimple, and compofed of fo few cafes, that it fcarcely needs a debate.

It is the only way out of an expenfive and ruinous war, which has no object, and without which acknowledgment there can be no peace.

But your lordfhip fays, " *The fun of Great-Britain will fet when-ever fhe acknowledges the independence of America.*" Whereas the me-taphor would have been ftrictly juft, to have left the fun wholly out of the figure, and have afcribed her not acknowledging it to the in-fluence of the moon.

But the expreffion, if true, is the greateft confeffion of difgrace that could be made, and furnifhes America with the higheft notions of fo-vereign independent importance. Mr. Wedderburne, about the year 1776, made ufe of an idea of much the fame kind,—" *Relinquifh*

" *America! says he—What is it but to defire a giant to fhrink fponta-*
" *neoufly into a dwarf.*"

Alas! are thofe people who call themfelves Englifhmen, of fo little
internal confequence, that when America is gone, or fhuts her eyes
upon them, their fun is fet, they can fhine no more, but grope about
in obfcurity, and contract into infignificant animals? Was America,
then, the giant of the empire, and England only her dwarf in waiting?
Is the cafe fo ftrangely altered, that thofe who once thought we could
not live without them, now declare they cannot exift without us? Will
they tell to the world, and that from their firft minifter of ftate, that
America is their all in all; that it is by her importance only they can
live, and breath, and have a being? Will they, who threatened to bring
us to their feet, bow themfelves at ours, and own that without us they
are not a nation? Are they become fo unqualified to debate on independence, that they have loft all idea of it in themfelves, and are calling to the rocks and mountains of America to cover their infignificance? Or, if America is loft, is it manly to fob over it like a child for
its rattle, and invite the laughter of the world by declarations of difgrace? Surely, the more confiftent conduct would be, to bear it without complaint; and to fhew that England, without America, can preferve her independence, and a fuitable rank with other European
powers. You were not contented while you had her, and to weep
for her now is childifh.

But lord Shelburne thinks that fomething may yet be done. What
that fomething is, or how it is to be accomplifhed, is a matter in obfcurity. By arms there is no hope. The experience of nearly eight
years, with the expence of an hundred million pounds fterling, and the
lofs of two armies, muft pofitively decide that point. Befides, the
Britifh have loft their intereft in America with the difaffected. Every
part of it has been tried. There is no new fcene left for delufion:
and the thoufands who have been ruined by adhering to them, and
have now to quit the fettlements they had acquired, and be conveyed
like tranfports to cultivate the deferts of Auguftine and Nova-Scotia,
has put an end to all further expectations of aid.

If you caft your eyes on the people of England, what have they to
confole themfelves with for the millions expended? or, what encouragement is there left to continue throwing good money after bad?
America can carry on the war for ten years longer, and all the charges
of government included, for lefs than you can defray the charges
of war and government for one year. And I, who know both coun-

tries, know well, that the people of America can afford to pay their
ſhare of the expence much better than the people of England can.
Beſides, it is their own eſtates and property, their own rights, liberties
and government, they are defending; and were they not do it, they
would deſerve to loſe all, and none would pity them.   The fault
would be their own, and their puniſhment juſt.

The Britiſh army in America care not how long the war laſts.
They enjoy an eaſy and indolent life.   They fatten on the folly of
one country and the ſpoils of another; and, between their plunder and
their pay, may go home rich.   But the caſe is very different with
the labouring farmer, the working tradeſman, and the neceſſitous poor
in England, the ſweat of whoſe brow goes day after day to feed, in
prodigality and ſloth, the army that is robbing both them and us.
Removed from the eye of that country that ſuppports them, and diſ-
tant from the government that employs them, they cut and carve for
themſelves, and there is none to call them to account.

But England will be ruined, ſays lord Shelburne, if America is independent.

Then, I ſay, is England already ruined, for America is already
independent :   and if lord Shelburne will not allow this, he immediately denies the fact which he infers.   Beſides, to make England
the mere creature of America, is paying too great a compliment to
us, and too little to himſelf.

But the declaration is a rhapſody of inconſiſtence.   For to ſay,
as lord Shelburne has numberleſs times ſaid, that the war againſt
America is ruinous, and yet to continue the proſecution of that ruinous
war for the purpoſe of avoiding ruin, is a language which cannot be
underſtood.   Neither is it poſſible to ſee how the independence of
America is to accompliſh the ruin of England after the war is over,
and yet not affect it before.   America cannot be more independent of
her, nor a greater enemy to her, hereafter than ſhe now is ; nor
England derive leſs advantages from her than at preſent : why then
is ruin to follow in the beſt ſtate of the caſe, and not in the worſt ?
and if not in the worſt, why is it to follow at all ?

That a nation is to be ruined by peace and commerce, and fourteen or fifteen millions a-year leſs expences than before, is a new doctrine in politics.   We have heard much clamour of national ſavings
and economy ; but ſurely the true economy would be, to ſave the
whole charge of a ſilly, fooliſh, and headſtrong war ; becauſe, compared with this, all other retrenchments are bawbles and trifles.

But is it possible that lord Shelburne can be serious in supposing the least advantage can be obtained by arms, or that any advantage can be equal to the expence or the danger of attempting it? Will not the capture of one army after another satisfy him, but all must become prisoners? Must England ever be the sport of hope and the victim of delusion? Sometimes our currency was to fail; another time our army was to disband: then whole provinces were to revolt. Such a general said this and that; another wrote so and so; lord Chatham was of this opinion; and lord somebody else of another. To-day 20,000 Russians and 20 Russian ships of the line were to come; to-morrow the empress was abused without mercy or decency—Then the emperor of Germany was to be bribed with a million of money, and the king of Prussia was to do wonderful things. At one time it was, Lo here! and then it was, Lo there! Sometimes this power, and sometimes that power, was to engage in the war, just as if the whole world was as mad and foolish as Britain. And thus, from year to year, has every straw been catched at, and every Will-with-a-wisp led them a new dance.

This year a still newer folly is to take place. Lord Shelburne wishes to be sent to congress, and he thinks that something may be done.

Are not the repeated declarations of congress, and which all America supports, that they will not even hear any proposals whatever, until the unconditional and unequivocal independence of America is recognised; are not, I say, these declarations answer enough?

But for England to receive any thing from America now, after so many insults, injuries and outrages, acted towards us, would shew such a spirit of meanness in her, that we could not but despise her for accepting it. And so far from lord Shelburne coming here to solicit it, it would be the greatest disgrace we could do them to offer it. England would appear a wretch indeed, at this time of day, to ask or owe any thing to the bounty of America. Has not the name of Englishman blots enough upon it, without inventing more? Even Lucifer would scorn to reign in heaven by permission, and yet an Englishmen can creep for only an entrance into America. Or, has a land of liberty so many charms, that to be a door-keeper in it is better than to be an English minister of state?

But what can this expected something be? or, if obtained, what can it amount to, but new disgraces, contentions and quarrels? The people of America have for years accustomed themselves to think and fpeak fo freely and contemptuoufly of Englifh authority, and the inveteracy is fo deeply rooted, that a perfon invefted with any authority from that country, and attempting to exercife it here, would have the life of a toad under a harrow. They would look on him as an interloper, to whom their compaffion permitted a refidence. He would be no more than the Mungo of a farce ; and if he difliked that, he muft fet off. It would be a ftation of degradation, debafed by our pity, and defpifed by our pride, and would place England in a more contemptible fituation than any fhe has yet fuffered by the war. We have too high an opinion of ourfelves, ever to think of yielding again the leaft obedience to outlandifh authority ; and for a thoufand reafons, England would be the laft country in the world to yield it to. She has been treacherous, and we know it. Her character is gone, and we have feen the funeral.

Surely fhe loves to fifh in troubled waters, and drink the cup of contention, or fhe would not now think of mingling her affairs with thofe of America. It would be like a foolifh dotard taking to his arms the bride that defpifes him, or who has placed on his head the enfigns of her difguft. It is kiffing the hand that boxes his ears, and propofing to renew the exchange. The thought is as fervile as the war was wicked, and fhows the laft fcene of the drama as inconfiftent as the firft.

As America is gone, the only act of manhood is to *let her go.* Your lordfhip had no hand in the feparation, and you will gain no honour by temporifing politics. Befides, there is fomething fo exceedingly whimfical, unfteady, and even infincere in the prefent conduct of England, that fhe exhibits herfelf in the moft difhonourable colours.

On the fecond of Auguft laft general Carlton and admiral Digby wrote to general Wafhington in thefe words :

" The refolution of the houfe of commons, of the 27th of February " laft, has been placed in your excellency's hands, and intimations " given at the fame time that further pacific meafures were likely to " follow. Since which, until the prefent time, we have had no di- " rect communications from England ; but a mail is now arrived, " which brings us very important information. We are acquainted, " fir, *by authority*, that negociations for a general peace have already " commenced at Paris, and that Mr. Grenville is invefted with full " powers to treat with all the parties at war, and is now at Paris in " the execution of his commiffion. And we are farther, fir, made " acquainted, *that his majefty, in order to remove any obftacles to that*

" *peace which he so ardently wishes to restore, has commanded his minif-*
" *ters to direct Mr. Grenville, that the independence of the Thirteen*
" *United Provinces, should be proposed by him in the first instance, instead*
" *of making it a condition of a general treaty.*"

Now, taking your present measures into view, and comparing
them with the declaration in this letter, pray, what is the word of
your king, or his ministers, or the parliament, good for? Must we
not look upon you as a confederated body of faithless, treacherous
men, whose assurances are fraud, and their language deceit? What
opinion can we possibly form of you, but that you are a lost, abandoned, profligate nation, who sport even with your own character,
and are to be held by nothing but the bayonet or the halter?

To say, after this, *that the sun of Great-Britain will be set whenever
she acknowledges the independence of America,* when the not doing it is
the unqualified lie of government, can be no other than the language
of ridicule, the jargon of inconsistency. There were thousands in
America who predicted the delusion, and looked upon it as a trick of
treachery, to take us from our guard, and draw off our attention from
the only system of finance, by which we can be called, or deserve to be
called, a sovereign, independent people. The fraud, on your part,
might be worth attempting, but the sacrifice to obtain it is too high.

There are others who credited the assurance, because they thought
it impossible that men who had their characters to establish, would
begin it with a lie. The prosecution of the war by the former ministry was savage and horrid; since which it has been mean, trickish, and
delusive. The one went greedily into the passion of revenge, the
other into the subtleties of low contrivance; till, between the crimes
of both, there is scarcely left a man in America, be he whig or tory,
who does not despise or detest the conduct of Britain.

The management of lord Shelburne, whatever may be his views, is
a caution to us, and must be to the world, never to regard British
assurances. A perfidy so notorious cannot be hid. It stands even in
the public papers of New-York, with the names of Carlton and
Digby affixed to it. It is a proclamation that the king of England
is not to be believed: that the spirit of lying is the governing principle
of the ministry. It is holding up the character of the house of commons to public infamy, and warning all men not to credit them.
Such is the consequence which lord Shelburne's management has
brought upon his country.

After the authorised declarations contained in Carlton and

Digby's letter, you ought, from every motive of honour, policy, and prudence, to have fulfilled them, whatever might have been the event. It was the least atonement you could possibly make to America, and the greateft kindnefs you could do to yourfelves; for you will fave millions by a general peace, and you will lofe as many by continuing the war.

COMMON SENSE.

Philadelphia, October 29, 1782.

P. S. The manufcript copy of this letter is fent your lordfhip, by the way of our head-quarters, to New-York, inclofing a late pamphlet of mine, addreffed to the Abbe Raynal, which will ferve to give your lordfhip fome idea of the principles and fentiments of America.

C. S.

THE LAST CRISIS.—NUMBER XIII.

Philadelphia, April 19, 1783.

"THE times that tried men's fouls,"* are over—and the greateft and completeft revolution the world ever knew, glorioufly and happily accomplifhed.

But to pafs from the extremes of danger to fafety—from the tumult of war, to the tranquility of peace, though fweet in contemplation, requires a gradual compofure of the fenfes to receive it. Even calmnefs has the power of ftunning, when it opens too inftantly upon us. The long and raging hurricane that fhould ceafe in a moment, would leave us in a ftate rather of wonder than enjoyment; and fome moments of recollection muft pafs, before we could be capable of tafting the full felicity of repofe. There are but few inftances, in which the mind is fitted for fudden tranfitions: It takes in its pleafures by reflection and comparifon, and thofe muft have time to act, before the relifh for new fcenes is complete.

In the prefent cafe—the mighty magnitude of the object—the various uncertainties of fate it has undergone—the numerous and complicated dangers we have fuffered or efcaped—the eminence we now

* *" Thefe are the times that try men's fouls. Crifis, No. I. publifhed December 19, 1796.*

ſtand on, and the vaſt proſpect before us, muſt all conſpire to impreſs us with contemplation.

To ſee it in our power to make a world happy—to teach mankind the art of being ſo—to exhibit on the theatre of the univerſe, a cha-, racter hitherto unknown—and to have, as it were, a new creation entruſted to our hands, are honours that command reflection, and can neither be too highly eſtimated, nor too gratefully received.

In this pauſe then of recollection—while the ſtorm is ceaſing, and the long agitated mind vibrating to a reſt, let us look back on the ſcenes we have paſſed, and learn from experience what is yet to be done.

Never, I ſay, had a country ſo many openings to happineſs as this. Her ſetting out into life, like the riſing of a fair morning, was un-. clouded and promiſing. Her cauſe was good. Her principles juſt and liberal. Her temper ſerene and firm. Her conduct regulated by the niceſt ſteps, and every thing about her wore the mark of honour.

It is not every country (perhaps there is not another in the world) that can boaſt ſo fair an origin. Even the firſt ſettlement of America correſponds with the character of the revolution. Rome, once the proud miſtreſs of the univerſe, was originally a band of ruffians. Plunder and rapine made her rich, and her oppreſſion of millions made her great. But America needs never be aſhamed to tell her birth, nor relate the ſtages by which ſhe roſe to empire.

The remembrance then of what is paſt, if it operates rightly, muſt inſpire her with the moſt laudable of all ambition, that of adding to the fair fame ſhe began with. The world has ſeen her great in adver-ſity. Struggling, without a thought of yielding, beneath accumulated difficulties. Bravely, nay proudly, encountering diſtreſs, and riſing in reſolution as the ſtorm encreaſed. All this is juſtly due to her, for her fortitude has merited the character. Let then the world ſee that ſhe can bear proſperity: and that her honeſt virtue in time of peace, is equal to the braveſt virtue in time of war.

She is now deſcending to the ſcenes of quiet and domeſtic life. Not beneath the cypreſs ſhade of diſappointment, but to enjoy, in her own land, and under her own vine, the ſweet of her labours, and the reward of her toil—In this ſituation, may ſhe never forget that a fair national reputation, is of as much importance as independence. That it poſſeſſes a charm which wins upon the world, and makes even enemies civil.—That it gives a dignity which is often ſuperior to power, and commands a reverence where pomp and ſplendour fail.

It would be a circumftance ever to be lamented and never to be forgotten, were a fingle blot, from any caufe whatever, fuffered to fall on a revolution, which to the end of time muft be an honour to the age that accomplifhed it : and which has contributed more to enlighten the world, and diffufe a fpirit of freedom and liberality among mankind, than any human event (if this may be called one) that ever preceded it.

It is not among the leaft of the calamities of a long continued war, that it unhinges the mind from thofe nice fenfations which at other times appear fo amiable. The continual fpectacle of woe, blunts the finer feelings, and the neceffity of bearing with the fight, renders it familiar. In like manner, are many of the moral obligations of fociety weakened, till the cuftom of acting by neceffity, becomes an apology where it is truly a crime. Yet let but a nation conceive rightly of its character, and it will be chaftly juft in protecting it. None ever began with a fairer than America, and none can be under a greater obligation to preferve it.

The debt which America has contracted, compared with the caufe fhe has gained, and the advantages to flow from it, ought fcarcely to be mentioned. She has it in her choice to do, and to live, as happily, as fhe pleafes. The world is in her hands. She has no foreign power to monopolize her commerce, perplex her legiflation, or control her profperity. The ftruggle is over, which muft one day have happened, and, perhaps, never could have happened at a better time.*

* *That the revolution began at the exact period of time beft fitted to the purpofe, is fufficiently proved by the event—But the great hinge on which the whole machine turned is the UNION OF THE STATES: and this union was naturally produced by the inability of any one ftate to fupport itfelf againft any foreign enemy without the affiftance of the reft.*

Had the ftates feverally been lefs able than they were when the war began, their united ftrength would not have been equal to the undertaking, and they muft in all human probability, have failed—And on the other hand, had they feverally been more able. they might not have feen, or, what is more, might not have felt the neceffity of uniting ; and either by attempting to ftand alone, or in fmall confederacies, would have been feparately conquered.

Now, as we cannot fee a time (and many years muft pafs away before it can arrive) when the ftrength of any one ftate, or feveral united, can be equal to the whole of the prefent United States, and as we have feen the

And inftead of a domineering mafter, fhe has gained an *ally,* whofe exemplary greatnefs, and univerfal liberality, have extorted a confef-fion even from her enemies.

With the bleffings of peace, independence, and an univerfal com-merce, the ftates individually and collectively, will have leifure and opportunity to regulate and eftablifh their domeftic concerns, and to put it beyond the power of calumny to throw the leaft reflection on their honour. Character is much eafier kept than recovered, and that man, if any fuch there be, who, from any finifter views, or little-nefs of foul, lends unfeen his hand to injure it, contrives a wound it will never be in his power to heal.

As we have eftablifhed an inheritance for pofterity, let that inheri-tance defcend, with every mark of an honourable conveyance. The little it will coft, compared with the worth of the ftates, the greatnefs

extreme difficulty of collectively profecuting the war to a fuccefsful iffue, and preferving our national importance in the world, therefore, from the ex-perience we have had and the knowledge we have gained, we muft, unlefs we make a wafte of wifdom, be ftrongly impreffed with the advantage, as well as the neceffity of ftrengthening that happy union which has been our falvation, and without which we fhould have been a ruined people.

While I was writing this note, I caft my eye on the pamphlet COMMON SENSE, *from which I fhall make an extract, as it applies exactly to the cafe. It is as follows :*

" *I have never met with a man, either in England or America, who* " *hath not confeffed his opinion that a feparation between the countries* " *would take place one time or other: And there is no inftance in which* " *we have fhewn lefs judgment, than in endeavouring to defcribe, what* " *we call, the ripenefs or fitnefs of the continent for independence.*

" *As all men allow the meafure, and differ only in their opinion of the* " *time, let us, in order to remove miftakes, take a general furvey of things,* " *and endeavour, if poffible, to find out the* VERY TIME. *But we need not* " *to go far, the enquiry ceafes at once, for,* THE TIME HATH FOUND US. " *The general concurrence, the glorious union of all things prove the fact.*

" *It is not in numbers, but in a union, that our great ftrength lies. The* " *continent is juft arrived at that pitch of ftrength, in which no fingle co-* " *lony is able to fupport itfelf; and the whole, when united, can accomplifh* " *the matter ; and either more or lefs than this, might be fatal in its ef-* " *fects.''*

of the object, and the value of national character, will be a profitable exchange.

But that which must more forcibly strike a thoughtful penetrating mind, and which includes and renders eafy all inferior concerns, is the UNION OF THE STATES. On this, our great national character depends. It is this which muft give us importance abroad and fecurity at home. It is through this only that we are, or can be nationally known in the world. It is the flag of the United States which renders our ships and commerce fafe on the feas, or in a foreign port. Our Mediterranean paffes muft be obtained under the fame ftile. All our treaties whether of alliance, peace or commerce, are formed under the fovereignty of the United States, and Europe knows us by no other name or title.

The divifion of the empire into ftates is for our own convenience, but abroad this diftinction ceafes. The affairs of each ftate are local. They can go no farther than to itfelf. And were the whole worth of even the richeft of them expended in revenue, it would not be fufficient to fupport fovereignty againft a foreign attack. In fhort, we have no other national fovereignty than as United States. It would even be fatal for us if we had—too expenfive to be maintained, and impoffible to be fupported. Individuals or individual ftates may call themfelves what they pleafe ; but the world, and efpecially the world of enemies, is not to be held in awe by the whiftling of a name. Sovereignty muft have power to protect all the parts that compofe and conftitute it : and as UNITED STATES we are equal to the importance of the title, but otherwife we are not. Our union well and wifely regulated and cemented, is the cheapeft way of being great— the eafieft way of being powerful, and the happieft invention in government which the circumftances of America can admit of—Becaufe it collects from each ftate, that which, by being inadequate, can be of no ufe to it, and forms an aggregate that ferves for all.

The ftates of Holland are an unfortunate inftance of the effects of individual fovereignty. Their disjointed condition expofes them to numerous intrigues, loffes, calamities and enemies; and the almoft impoffibility of bringing their meafures to a decifion, and that decifion into execution, is to them, and would be to us, a fource of endlefs misfortune.

It is with confederated ftates as with individuals in fociety ; fomething muft be yielded up to make the whole fecure. In this view of things we gain by what we give, and draw an annual intereft greater than the capital.—I ever feel myself hurt when I hear the union, that great palladium of our liberty and fafety, the leaft irreverently fpoken of. It is the moft facred thing in the conftitution of America, and that which every man fhould be moft proud and tender of. Our citizenfhip in the United States is our national character. Our citizenfhip in any particular ftate is only our local diftinction. By the latter we are known at home, by the former to the world. Our great title is, AMERICANS—our inferior one varies with the place.

So far as my endeavours could go, they have all been directed to conciliate the affections, unite the interefts and draw and keep the mind of the country together ; and the better to affift in this foundation-work of the revolution, I have avoided all places of profit or office, either in the ftate I live in, or in the United States; kept myfelf at a diftance from all parties and party connections, and even difregarded all private and inferior concerns: and when we take into view the great work we have gone through, and feel, as we ought to feel, the juft importance of it, we fhall then fee, that the little wranglings and indecent contentions of perfonal parley, are as difhonourable to our characters, as they are injurious to our repofe.

It was the caufe of America that made me an author. The force with which it ftruck my mind, and the dangerous condition the country appeared to me in, by courting an impoffible and an unnatural reconciliation with thofe who were determined to reduce her, inftead of ftriking out into the only line that could cement and fave her, A DECLARATION OF INDEPENDENCE, made it impoffible for me, feeling as I did, to be filent : and if, in the courfe of more than feven years, I have rendered her any fervice, I have likewife added fomething to the reputation of literature, by freely and difintereftedly employing it in the great caufe of mankind, and fhewing there may be genius without proftitution.

Independence always appeared to me practicable and probable ; provided the fentiment of the country could be formed and held to the object : and there is no inftance in the world, where a people fo extended, and wedded to former habits of thinking, and under fuch a variety of circumftances, were fo inftantly and effectually pervaded, by a turn in politics, as in the cafe of independence, and who fupported their opinion, undiminifhed, through fuch a fucceffion of good and ill fortune, till they crowned it with fuccefs.

But as the fcenes of war are clofed, and every man preparing for home and happier times, I therefore take my leave of the fubject. I have moft fincerely followed it from beginning to end, and through all its turns and windings : and whatever country I may hereafter be in, I fhall always feel an honeft pride at the part I have taken and acted, and a gratitude to Nature and Providence for putting it in my power to be of fome ufe to mankind.

COMMON SENSE.

A SUPERNUMERARY CRISIS.

TO THE PEOPLE OF AMERICA.

IN " *Rivington's New-York Gazette*," of December 6th, is a publication, under the appearance of a letter from London, dated September 30th ; and is on a fubject which demands the attention of the United States.

The Public will remember, that a treaty of commerce between the United States and England was fet on foot laft fpring, and that until the faid treaty could be completed, a bill was brought into the Britifh parliament, by the then chancellor of the exchequer, Mr. Pitt, to admit and legalize (as the cafe then required) the commerce of the United States into the Britifh ports and dominions. But neither the one nor the other has been completed. The commercial treaty is either broken off, or remains as it began ; and the bill in parliament has been thrown afide. And in lieu thereof, a felfifh fyftem of Englifh politics has ftarted up, calculated to fetter the commerce of America, by engroffing to England the carrying trade of the American produce to the Weft-India iflands.

Among the advocates for this laft meafure is Lord Sheffield, a Member of the Britifh Parliament, who has publifhed a pamphlet entituled, " *Obfervations on the Commerce of the American States.*" The pamphlet has two objects; the one is, to allure the Americans to purchafe Britifh manufactures; and the other, to fpirit up the Britifh Parliament to prohibit the Citizens of the United States from trading to the Weft-India Iflands.

Viewed in this light, the pamphlet, though in fome parts dextroufly written, is an abfurdity. It offends, in the very act of endeavouring to ingratiate; and his Lordfhip, as a politician, ought not to have fuffered the two objects to have appeared together. The letter alluded to contains extracts from the pamphlet, with high encomiums on Lord Sheffield, for laborioufly endeavouring (as the letter ftiles it) " to " fhew the mighty advantages of retai ing the carrying trade."

Since the publication of this pamphlet in England, the commerce of the United States to the Weft-Indies in American veffels, h s been prohibited ; and all intercourfe, except in Britifh bottoms, the property of, and navigated by Britifh fubjects, cut off.

That a country has a right to be as foolifh as it pleafes, has been proved by the practice of England for many years paft : In her ifland fituation, fequeftered from the world, fhe forgets that her whifpers are heard by other nations; and in her plans of politics and commerce, fhe feems not to know, that other vetes are neceffary befides her own. America would be equally as foolifh as Britain, were fhe to fuffer fo great a degradation on her flag, and fuch a ftroke on the freedom of her commerce, to pafs without a balance.

We admit the right of any nation to prohibit the commerce of another into its own dominions, where there are no treaties to the contrary; but as this right belongs to one fide, as well as the other, there is always a way left to bring avarice and infolence to reafon.

But the ground of fecurity which Lord Sheffield has chofen to erect his policy upon, is of a nature which ought, and I think muft awaken, in every American, a juft and ftrong fenfe of national dignity. Lord Sheffield appears to be fenfible, that in advifing the Britifh nation and Parliament to engrofs to themfelves fo great a part of the carrying trade of America, he is attempting a meafure which cannot fucceed, if the politics of the United States be properly directed to counteract the affumption.

But, fays he, in his pamphlet, " *It will be a long time before the* " *American States can be brought to act as a nation, neither are they to* " *be feared as fuch by us.*"

What is this more or lefs than to tell us, that while we have no national fyftem of commerce, the Britifh will govern our trade by their own laws and proclamations as they pleafe. The quotation difclofes a truth too ferious to be overlooked, and too mifchievous not to be remedied.

Among other circumftances which led them to this difcovery, none could operate fo effectually, as the injudicious, uncandid and indecent oppofition made by fundry perfons in a certain ftate, to the recommendations of Congrefs laft winter, for an import duty of five per cent. It could not but explain to the British a weaknefs in the national power of America, and encourage them to attempt reftrictions on her trade, which otherwife they would not have dared to hazard. Neither is there any ftate in the union, whofe policy was more mifdirected to its intereft than the ftate I allude to, becaufe her principal fupport is the carrying trade, which Britain, induced by the want of a well-centered power in the United States to protect and fecure, is now attempting to take away. It fortunately happened (and to no ftate in the union more than the ftate in queftion) that the terms of peace were agreed on before the oppofition appeared, ctherwife, there needs not a doubt, that if the fame idea of the diminifhed authority of America had occurred to them at that time as has occurred to them fince, but they would have made the fame grafp at the fifheries, as they have done at the carrying trade.

It is furprifing that an authority which can be fuppcrted with fo much eafe, and fo little expence, and capable of fuch extenfive advantages to the country, fhould be cavilled at by thofe whofe duty it is to watch over it, and whofe exiftence as a people depends upon it. But this, perhaps, will ever be the cafe, till fome misfortune awakens us into reafon, and the inftance now before us is but a gentle beginning of what America muft expect, unlefs fhe guards her union with nicer care and ftricter honour. United, fhe is formidable, and that with the leaft poffible charge a nation can be fo : Separated, fhe is a medley of individual nothings, fubject to the fport of foreign nations.

It is very probable that the ingenuity of commerce may have found out a method to evade and fupercede the intentions of the Britifh, in interdicting the trade with the Weft-India iflands. The language of both being the fame, and their cuftoms well underftood, the veffels of one country may, by deception, pafs for thofe of another. But this would be a practice too debafing for a fovereign people to ftoop to, and too profligate not to be difcountenanced. An illicit trade, under any fhape it can be placed, cannot be carried on without a violation of truth. America is now fovereign and independent, and ought to act all her affairs in a regular ftile of character. She has the fame right to fay that no Britifh veffel fhall enter her ports, or that no Britifh manufactures fhall be imported, but in American bottoms, the property of, and navigated by American fubjects, as Britain has to fay the fame thing refpecting the Weft-Indies. Or fhe may lay a duty of ten, fifteen or twenty fhillings per ton (exclufive of other duties) on every Britifh veffel coming from any port of the Weft-Indies, where fhe is not admitted to trade, the faid tonnage to continue as long on her fide as the prohibition continues on the other.

But it is only by acting in union, that the ufurpations of foreign nations on the freedom of trade can be counteracted, and fecurity extended to the commerce of America. And when we view a flag, which to the eye is beautiful, and to contemplate its rife and origin infpires a fenfation of fublime delight, our national honour muft unite with our intereft to prevent injury to the one, or infult to the other.

COMMON SENSE.

New-York, December 9, 1783.

BEING

AN EXAMINATION

INTO

The Claim of Virginia to the vacant Weſtern Territory,

AND OF THE

Right of the United States to the ſame.

TO WHICH ARE ADDED,

PROPOSALS

FOR

LAYING OFF A NEW STATE,

TO BE APPLIED AS A FUND FOR CARRYING ON THE WAR,
OR REDEEMING THE NATIONAL DEBT.

———————

WRITTEN IN THE YEAR 1780.

THE PREFACE.

THE following pages are on a fubject hitherto little underftood but highly intereſting to the United States.

They contain an inveftigation of the claims of Virginia to the vacant weſtern territory, and of the right of the United States to the fame; with fome outlines of a plan for laying out a new ſtate, to be applied as a fund, for carrying on the war, or redeeming the national debt.

The reader, in the courſe of this publication, will find it ſtudiouſly plain, and, as far as I can judge, perfectly candid. What materials I could get at I have endeavoured to place in a clear line, and deduce ſuch arguments therefrom as the fubject required. In the profecution of it, I have confidered myfelf as an advocate for the right of the ſtates, and taken no other liberty with the fubject than what a counfel would, and ought to do, in behalf of a client.

I freely confefs that the refpect I had conceived, and ſtill preferve, for the character of Virginia, was a conſtant check upon thofe fallies of imagination, which are fairly and advantageouſly indulged againſt an enemy, but ungenerous when againſt a friend.

If there is any thing I have omitted or miſtaken, to the injury of the intentions of Virginia or her claims, I ſhall gladly rectify it; or if there is any thing yet to add, ſhould the fubject require it, I ſhall as cheerfully undertake it; being fully convinced, that to have matters fairly difcuſſed, and properly underſtood, is a principal means of preferving harmony and perpetuating friendſhip.

THE AUTHOR.

PUBLIC GOOD.

WHEN we take into view the mutual happiness and united interefts of the ftates of America, and confider the important confequences to arife from a ftrict attention of each, and of all, to every thing which is juft, reafonable, and honourable; or the evils that will follow from an inattention to thofe principles; there cannot, and ought not, to remain a doubt, but that the governing rule of *right* and mutual good muft in all public cafes finally prefide.

The hand of Providence has caft us into one common lot, and accomplifhed the independence of America, by the unanimous confent of the feveral parts, concurring at once in time, manner and circumftances. No fuperiority of intereft, at the expence of the reft, induced the one, more than the other, into the meafure. Virginia and Maryland, it is true, might forefee, that their ftaple commodity, tobacco, by being no longer monopolized by Britain, would bring them a better price abroad: for as the tax on it in England was treble its firft purchafe from the planter, and they being now no longer compelled to fend it under that obligation, and in the reftricted manner they formerly were; it is eafy to fee, that the article, from the alteration of the circumftances of trade, will, and daily does, turn out to them with additional advantages.

But this being a natural confequence, produced by that common freedom and independence of which all are partakers, is therefore an advantage they are intitled to, and on which the reft of the ftates can congratulate them without feeling a wifh to leffen, but rather to extend it. To contribute to the encreafed profperity of another, by the fame means which occafion our own, is an agreeable reflection; and the more valuable any article of export becomes, the more riches will be introduced into and fpread over the continent.

Yet this is an advantage which thofe two ftates derive from the independence of America, fuperior to the local circumftances of the reſt ; and of the two it more particularly belongs to Virginia than Maryland, becauſe the ſtaple commodity of a conſiderable part of Maryland is flour, which, as it is an article that is the growth of Europe as well as of America, cannot obtain a foreign market but by underſelling, or at leaſt by limiting it to the current price abroad. But tobacco commands its own price. It is not a plant of almoſt univerſal growth, like wheat. There are but few ſoils and climes that produce it to advantage, and before the cultivation of it in Virginia and Maryland, the price was from four to ſixteen ſhillings ſterling a pound in England.*

But the condition of the vacant weſtern territory of America makes a very different caſe to that of the circumſtances of trade in any of the ſtates. Thoſe very lands, formed, in contemplation, the fund by which the debt of America would in a courſe of years be redeemed. They were conſidered as the common right of all ; and it is only till lately that any pretenſion of claims had been made to the contrary.

That difficulties and differences will ariſe in communities, ought always to be looked for. The oppoſition of intereſts, real or ſuppoſed ; the variety of judgments ; the contrariety of temper ; and, in ſhort, the whole compoſition of man, in his individual capacity, is tinctured with a diſpoſition to contend ; but in his ſocial capacity there is either a right which, being proved, terminates the diſpute, or a reaſonableneſs in the meaſure, where no direct right can be made out, which decides or compromiſes the matter.

As I ſhall have frequent occaſion to mention the word *right*, I wiſh to be clearly underſtood in my definition of it. There are various ſenſes in which this term is uſed, and cuſtom has, in many of them, afforded it an introduction contrary to its true meaning. We are ſo naturally inclined to give the utmoſt degree of force to our own caſe, that we call every pretenſion, however founded, *a right*; and by this means the term frequently ſtands oppoſed to juſtice and reaſon.

After Theodore was elected king of Corſica, not many years ago, by the mere choice of the natives, for their own convenience in oppoſing the Genoeſe, he went over into England, run himſelf into debt, got himſelf into jail, and on his releaſe therefrom by the benefit of an act of inſolvency, he ſurrendered up, what he called *his* kingdom of Corſica, as a part of his perſonal property, for the uſe of his creditors;

---

* See ſir Dalby Thomas's Hiſtorical Account of the Riſe and Growth of the Weſt-India Colonies.

fome of whom may hereafter call this a charter, or by any other name more fafhionable, and ground thereon what they may term a *right* to the fovereignty and property of Corfica   But does not juftice abhor fuch an action, both in him and them, under the proftituted name of a *right*, and muft not laughter be excited where ever it is told?

A right, to be truly fo, muft be right in itfelf: yet many things have obtained the name of rights, which are originally founded in wrong.   Of this kind are all rights by mere conqueft, power or violence.   In the cool moments of reflection we are obliged to allow, that the mode by which fuch right is obtained, is not the beft fuited to that fpirit of univerfal juftice which ought to prefide equally over all mankind.   There is fomething in the eftablifhment of fuch a right that we wifh to flip over as eafily as poffible, and fay as little about as can be.   But in the cafe of a *right founded in right* the mind is carried cheerfully into the fubject, feels no compunction, fuffers no diftrefs, fubjects its fenfations to no violence, nor fees any thing in its way which requires an artificial fmoothing.

From this introduction I proceed to examine into the claims of Virginia; firft as to the right, fecondly as to the reafonablenefs, and laftly as to the confequences.

The name, *Virginia*, originally bore a different meaning to what in does now.   It ftood in the place of the word North-America, and feems to have been intended as a name comprehenfive of all the Englifh fettlements or colonies on the continent, and not defcriptive of any one as diftinguifhing it from the reft.   All to the fouthward of Chefapeake, as low as the gulf of Mexico, was called South-Virginia, and all to the northward North-Virginia, in a fimilar line of diftinction, as we now call the whole continent North and South-America.*

The firft charter or patent was to fir Walter Rawleigh by Queen Elizabeth, of England, in the year 1583, and had neither name nor bounds.   Upon fir Walter's return, the name *Virginia* was given to the whole country, including the now United States.   Confequently the prefent Virginia, either as a province or a ftate, can fet up no exclufive claim to the weftern territory under this patent, and that for two reafons; firft, becaufe the words of the patent run *to fir Walter Rawleigh, and fuch perfons as he fhould nominate, themfelves and their fuccefors*; which is a line of fucceffion Virginia does not pretend to ftand in; and fecondly, becaufe a prior queftion would arife, namely,

* *Oldmixon's Hiftory of Virginia.*

Vol. I.   G g

who are to be underſtood by Virginians under this patent ? and the anſwer would be, all the inhabitants of America, from New-England to Florida.

This patent, therefore, would deſtroy their excluſive claim, and inveſt the right collectively in the thirteen ſtates.

But it unfortunately happened, that the ſettlers under this patent, partly from miſconduct, the oppoſition of the Indians, and other cala-mities, diſcontinued the proceſs, and the patent became extinct.

After this, James the firſt, who, in the year 1602, ſucceeded Eliza-beth, iſſued a new patent, which I come next to deſcribe.

This patent differed from the former in this eſſential point, that it had limits, whereas the other had none: the former was intended to promote diſcoveries wherever they could be made, which accounts why no limits were affixed, and this to ſettle diſcoveries already made, which likewiſe aſſigns a reaſon why limits ſhould be deſcribed.

In this patent were incorporated two companies, called the South-Virginia company, and the North-Virginia company, and ſometimes the London company, and the Plymouth company.

The South-Virginia or London company was compoſed chiefly of London adventurers; the North-Virginia or Plymouth company was made up of adventurers from Plymouth in Devonſhire, and other per-ſons of the weſtern parts of England.

Though they were not to fix together, yet they were allowed to chooſe their places of ſettlement any where on the coaſt of America, then called Virginia, between the latitudes of 34 and 45 degrees, which was a range of 760 miles: the ſouth company was not to go below 34 degrees, nor the north company above 45 degrees. But the pa-tent expreſſed, that as ſoon as they had made their choice, each was to become limited to 50 miles each way on the coaſt, and 100 up the country ; ſo that the grant to each company was a ſquare of 100 miles, and no more. The North-Virginia or Plymouth company ſettled to the eaſtward, and in the year 1614 changed the name, and called that part New-England. The South-Virginia or London company ſettled near Cape Henry.

This then cannot be the patent of boundleſs extent, and that for two reaſons; firſt, becauſe the limits are deſcribed, namely, a ſquare of 100 miles ; and ſecondly, becauſe there were two companies of equal rights included in the ſame patent.

Three years after this, that is, in the year 1609, the South-Virginia company applied for new powers from the crown of England, which were granted them in a new patent, and the boundaries of the grant enlarged; and this is the charter or patent on which fome of the prefent Virginians ground their pretenfion to boundlefs territory.

The firft reflection that prefents itfelf on this enlargement of the grant is, that it muft be fuppofed to bear fome intended degree of reafonable comparifon to that which it fuperfeded. The former could not be greater than a fquare of one hundred miles; and this new one being granted in the lieu of that, and that within the fpace of three years, and by the fame perfon, James the firft, who was never famed either for profufion or generofity, cannot, on a review of the time and circumftances of the grant, be fuppofed a very extravagant or very extraordinary one. If a fquare of one hundred miles was not fufficiently large, twice that quantity was as much as could well be expected or folicited: but to fuppofe that he, who had caution enough to confine the firft grant within moderate bounds, fhould in fo fhort a fpace as three years, fuperfede it by another grant of many million times greater content, is, on the face of the affair, a circumftantial nullity.

Whether this patent or charter was in exiftence or not at the time the revolution commenced, is a matter I fhall hereafter fpeak to, and confine myfelf in this place to the limits which the faid patent or charter lays down. The words are as follow :

" Beginning from the cape or point of land called Cape or Point " Comfort, thence all along the fea coaft to the NORTHWARD " 200 miles and from the faid point or Cape Comfort, all along the " fea coaft to the *fouthward* 200 miles; and all that fpace or circuit " of land lying from the fea coaft of the precinct aforefaid up into the " land throughout, from fea to fea, WEST and *northweft.*"

The firft remark I fhall offer on the words of this grant is, that they are uncertain, obfcure and unintelligible, and may be conftrued into fuch a variety of contradictory meanings as to leave at laft no meaning at all.

Whether the two hundred miles each way, from Cape Comfort were to be on a *ftraight* line, or afcertained by following the indented *line of the coaft*, that is, " *all along the fea coaft,*" in and out as the coaft lay, cannot now be fully determined; becaufe, as either will admit of fuppofition, and nothing but fuppofition can be produced, therefore neither can be taken as pofitive. Thus far may be faid, that had it been intended to be a ftraight line, the word *ftraight* ought to have been inferted, which would have made the matter clear; but as no inference

can well be drawn to the advantage of that which does *not appear*
against that which *does*, therefore the omiffion implies negatively in
favour of the coaſt indented line, or that the 400 miles were to be
traced on the windings of the coaſt, that is, " *all long the ſea coaſt.*"

But what is meant by the words " *weſt and northweſt*" is ſtill more
unintelligible.   Whether they mean a weſt line and a northweſt line,
or whether they apply to the general lying of the land from the Atlantic, without regard to lines, cannot again be determined.   But if
they are ſuppoſed to mean lines to be run, then a new difficulty of
more magnitude than all the reſt ariſes ; namely, from which end of
the extent on the coaſt is the weſt line and the northweſt line to be ſet
off? as the difference in the content of the grant, occaſioned by tranſpoſing them is many hundred millions of acres ; and either includes
or excludes a far greater quantity of land then the whole thirteen
United States contain.

In ſhort, there is not a boundary in this grant that is clear, fixt
and defined.   The coaſt line is uncertain, and that being the baſe on
which the others are to be formed, renders the whole uncertain.   But
even if this line was admitted, in either ſhape, the other boundaries
would ſtill be on ſuppoſition, till it might be ſaid there is no boundary
at all, and conſequently no charter; for words which deſcribe nothing
can give nothing.

The advocates for the Virginia claim, laying hold of theſe ambi-
guities, have explained the grant thus :

Four hundred miles on the ſea coaſt, and from the South point a
weſt line to the great South Sea, and from the north point a northweſt line to the ſaid South Sea   The figure which theſe lines produce will be thus :

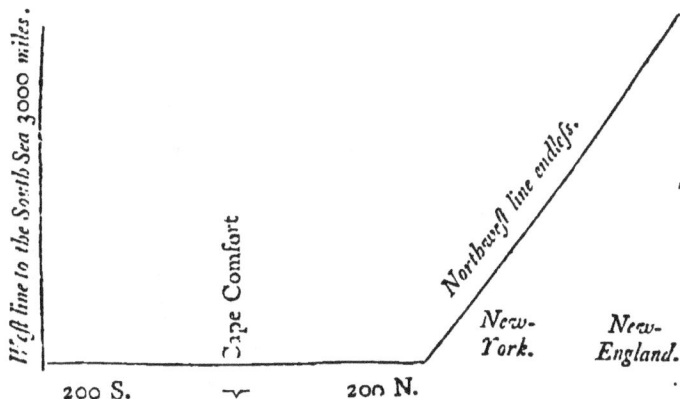

But why, I afk, muft the weft land line be fet off from the fouth point, any more than from the north point ? The grant or patent does not fay from which it fhall be, neither is it clear that a line is the thing intended by the words: but admitting it is, on what grounds do the claimants proceed in making this choice ? the anfwer, I prefume, is eafily given, namely, becaufe it is the moft beneficial explanation to themfelves they can poffibly make ; as it takes in many thoufand times more extent of country than any other explanation would. But this, though it be a very good reafon to them, is a very bad reafon to us ; and though it may do for the claimants to hope upon, will not anfwer to plead upon ; efpecially to the very people, who, to confirm the partiality of the claimants' choice, muft relinquifh their own right and intereft.

Why not fet off the weft land line from the north end of the coaft line, and the northweft line from the fouth end of the fame ? There is fome reafon why this fhould be the conftruction, and none why the other fhould.

Firft, becaufe, if the line of two hundred miles each way from Cape Comfort, be traced by following the indented line of the coaft, which feems to be the implied intention of the words, and a weft line be fet off from the north end, and a northweft line from the fouth end, thefe lines will all unite (which the other conftruction never can) and form a complete triangle, the content of which will be about twenty-nine or thirty millions of acres, or fomething larger than Pennfylvania : and

Secondly, becaufe this conftruction is following the order of the lines as expreffed in the grant ; for the *firft* mentioned *coaft* line, which is that to the *northward* of Cape Comfort, and the *firft* mentioned *land* line, which is the *weft* line, have a numerical relation, being the firft mentioned of each; and implies, that the weft line was to be fet off from the *north* point and *not* from the fouth point: and confequently the *two laft* mentioned of each have the fame numerical relation, and again implies that the *northweft* line was to be fet off from the *fouth* point, and not from the *north* point. But why the claimants fhould break through the order of the lines, and, contrary to implication, join the *firft* mentioned of the *one*, to the laft mentioned of the other, and thereby produce a fhapelefs monfter, for which there is no name nor any parallel in the world, either as to extent of foil and fovereignty, is a conftruction that cannot be fupported.

The figure produced by following the order of the lines is as follows.

N. B. If the reader will caft his eye again over the words of the patent on page 235, he will perceive the numerical relation alluded to, by obferving, that the firft mentioned coaft line and the firft mentioned land line are diftinguifhed by CAPITALS. And the laft mentioned of each by *italics*, which I have chofen to do to illuftrate the explanation.

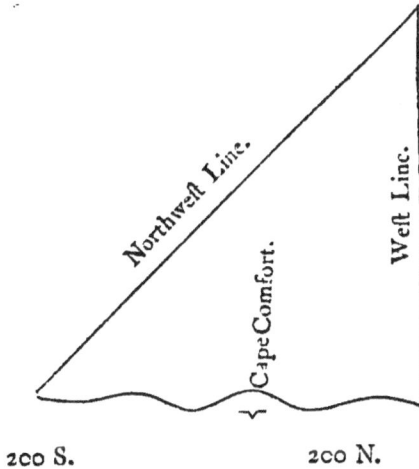

Northweft Line.

Weft Line.

CapeComfort.

2oo S.   2oo N.

I prefume that if four hundred miles be traced by following the inflexes of any fea fhore, that the two extremes will not be more than three hundred miles diftant from each other, on a ftraight line. Therefore to find the content of a triangle whofe bafe is three hundred miles, multiply the length of the bafe into half the perpendicular, which, in this cafe, is the weft line, and the product will be anfwer :

300   miles length of the bafe.

150   half the perpendicular (fuppofing it a right angled
                                 triangle).

15000

300

45,000 content of the grant in fquare miles.

640 acres in a fquare mile.

1800000

270000

28,800,000 content in fquare acres.

Now will any one undertake to fay, that this explanation is not as fairly drawn (if not more fo) from the words themfelves, as any other that can be offered, becaufe it is not only juftified by the exact words of the patent, grant, or charter, or any other name by which it may be called, but by their implied meaning ; and is likewife of fuch a content, as may be fuppofed to have been intended ; whereas the claimants' explanation is without bounds, and beyond every thing that is reafonable. Yet after all, who can fay what were the precife meaning of terms and expreffions fo loofely formed, and capable of fuch a variety of contradictory interpretations ?

Had the order of the lines been otherwife than they are in the patent, the reafonablenefs of the thing muft have directed the manner in which they fhould be connected : but as the claim is founded in unreafonablenefs, and that unreafonablenefs endeavoured to be fupported by a tranfpofition of the lines, there remains no pretence for the claim to ftand on.

Perhaps thofe who are interefted in the claimants' explanation will fay that as the South Sea is fpoken of, the lines muft be as they explain them, in order to reach it.

To this I reply ; firft, that no man then knew how far it was from the Atlantic to the South Sea, as I fhall prefently fhow, but believed it to be but a fhort diftance : and,

Secondly, that the uncertain and ambiguous manner in which the South Sea is alluded to (for it is not mentioned by name, but only " *from fea to fea*"), ferves to perplex the patent, and not to explain it : and as no right can be founded on an ambiguity, but on fome proof cleared of ambiguity, therefore the allufive introduction of " fea to fea" can yield no fervice to the claim.

There is likewife an ambiguous mention made of *two lands* in this patent, as well as of two *feas* ; viz. and all that " *fpace or circuit of land* lying from the fea coaft of the precinct aforefaid up into the land *throughout from fea to fea*."

On which I remark, that the two *lands* here mentioned have the appearance of a major and a minor, or the greater out of which the lefs is to be taken : and the term from " *fea to fea*" may be faid to apply defcriptively to the *land throughout*, and not to the *fpace or circuit of land patented to the company* : in a fimilar manner that the former patent defcribed a major of 706 miles extent, out of which the minor, or fquare of one hundred miles, was to be chofen.

But to fuppofe, that becaufe the South Sea is darkly alluded to, it muſt therefore (at whatever diſtance it might be, which then nobody knew, or for whatever purpoſe it might be introduced) be made a certain boundary, and that without regard to the reaſonableneſs of the matter, or the order in which the lines are arranged, which is the only implication the patent gives for ſetting off the land lines, is a ſuppoſition that contradicts every thing which is reaſonable.

The figure produced by following the order of the lines will be compleat in itſelf, let the diſtance to the South Sea be more or leſs ; becauſe, if the *land throughout from ſea to ſea* had not been ſufficiently extenſive to admit the weſt land line and and the northweſt land line to cloſe, the South Sea, in that caſe, would have eventually become a boundary : but if the extent of the *land throughout from ſea to ſea*, was ſo great, that the lines cloſed without reaching the ſaid South Sea, the figure was compleat without it.

Wherefore, as the order of the lines, when raiſed on the indented coaſt line, produces a regular figure of reaſonable dimenſions, and of about the ſame content, though not of the ſame ſhape, which Virginia now holds within the Allegany Mountains ; and by tranſpoſing them another figure is produced, for which there is no name, and cannot be compleated, as I ſhall preſently explain, and of an extent greater than one half of Europe, it is needleſs to offer any other arguments to ſhew that the order of the lines muſt be the rule, if any rule can be drawn from the words, for aſcertaining from which point the weſt line and northweſt line were to be ſet off. Neither is it poſſible to ſuppoſe any other rule could be followed ; becauſe a northweſt line ſet off two hundred miles above Cape Comfort, would not only never touch the South Sea, but would form a ſpiral line of infinite windings round the globe, and after paſſing over the northern parts of America and the frozen ocean, and then into the northern parts of Aſia, would, when eternity ſhould end and not before, terminate in the north-pole.

This is the only manner in which I can expreſs the effect of a northweſt line, ſet off as above; becauſe as its direction muſt always be between the north and the weſt, it conſequently can never get into the pole nor yet come to a reſt, and on the principle that matter or ſpace is capable of being eternally divided, muſt proceed on for ever.

But it was a prevailing opinion, at the time this patent was obtained, that the South Sea was at no great diſtance from the Atlantic, and therefore it was needleſs, under that ſuppoſition to regard which way the lines ſhould be run ; neither need we wonder at this error in the

English government respecting America then, when we see so many and such glaring ones now, for which there are less excuse.

Some circumstances favoured this mistake. Admiral sir Francis Drake not long before this, had, from the top of a mountain in the isthmus of Darien, which is the centre of North and South America, seen both the South Sea and the Atlantic; the width of the part of the continent where he then was, not being above 70 miles, whereas its width opposite Chesapeake-bay is as great, if not greater, than in any other part, being from *sea to sea*, about the distance it is from America to England. But this could not then be known, because only two voyages had been made across the South Sea; the one by the ship in which Magellan sailed, who died in his passage, and which was the first ship that sailed round the world, and the other by sir Francis Drake: but as neither of these sailed into a northern latitude in that ocean, high enough to fix the longitude of the western coast of America from the eastern, the distance across was entirely on supposition, and the errors they then ran into appear laughable to us who now know what the distance is.

That the company expected to come at the South Sea without much trouble or travelling, and that the great body of land which intervened, so far from being their view in obtaining the charter, became their disappointment, may be collected from a circumstance mentioned in Stith's History of Virginia.

He relates, that, in the year 1608, which was at the time the company were soliciting this patent, they fitted up in England " a barge " for captain Newport," (who was afterwards one of the joint deputy governors under the very charter we are now treating of) " which, for convenience of carriage, might be taken into five pieces, " and with which he and his company were instructed to go up " James River as far as the falls thereof, to discover the country of the " Monakins, and from thence they were to proceed, *carrying their* " *barge beyond the falls to convey them to the South Sea ;* being ordered " not to return without a lump of gold, or a certainty of the said " sea."

And Hutchinson, in his History of New-England, which was called North-Virginia at the time this patent was obtained, says, " the geo- " graphy of this part of America was less understood than at present. " A line to the Spanish settlements was imagined much shorter than " it really was. Some of Chaplain's people, in the beginning of the " last century, who had been but a few days march from Quebec, re-

" turned with great joy, fuppofing that from the top of a high moun-
" tain, they had difcovered *the South Sea*."

From thefe matters, which are evidences on record, it appears that
the adventurers had no knowledge of the diftance it was to the South
Sea, but fuppofed it to be no great way from the Atlantic; and alfo
that great extent of territory was not their object, but a fhort communication with the fouthern ocean, by which they might get into the
neighbourhood of the Gold Coaft, and likewife carry on a commerce
with the Eaft-Indies.

Having thus fhewn the confufed and various interpretations this
charter is fubject to, and that it may be made to mean any thing and
nothing; I now proceed to fhow, that, let the limits of it be more or
lefs, the prefent Virginia does not, and cannot, as a matter of right,
inherit under it.

I fhall open this part of the fubject by putting the following cafe :

Either Virginia ftands in fucceffion to the London company, to
whom the charter was granted, or to the crown of England. If to
the London company, then it becomes her, as an outfet in the matter,
to fhew who they were, and likewife that they were in poffeffion to
the commencement of the revolution.—If to the crown, then the
charter is of confequence fuperfeded; becaufe the crown did not poffefs territories by charter, but by prerogative without charter. The
notion of the crown chartering to itfelf is a nullity; and in this cafe,
the unpoffeffed lands, be they little or much, are in the fame condition
as if they never had been chartered at all; and the fovereignty of them
devolves to the fovereignty of the United States.

The charter or patent of 1609 as well as that of 1606 was to fir
Thomas Gates, fir George Summers, the Reverend Richard Hack-
luit, prebend of Weftminfter, and others; and the government was
then proprietary. Thofe proprietors, by virtue of the charter of
1709, chofe lord Delaware for their governor, and fir Thomas
Gates, fir George Summers, and captain Newport (the perfon who
was to go with a boat to the South Sea,) joint deputy governors.

Was this the form of government either as to foil or conftitution
at the time the prefent revolution commenced? if not, the charter was
not in *being;* for it matters not to us how it came to be *out of being,* fo
long as the prefent Virginians, or their anceftors, neither are nor were
fufferers by the change then made.

But fuppofe it could be proved to be in being, which it cannot,
becaufe *being* in a charter is power, it would only prove a right in be-

half of the London company of adventurers, but how that right is
to be difpofed of is another queftion. We are not defending the
right of the London company, deceafed 150 years ago, but taking up
the matter at the place where we found it, and fo far as the authority
of the crown of England was exercifed when the revolution commenced.

The charter was a contract between the crown of England and
thofe adventurers for their own emolument, and not between the
crown and the people of Virginia; and whatever was the occafion of
the contract becoming void, or furrendered up, or fuperfeded, makes
no part of the queftion now. It is fufficient that when the United
States fucceeded to fovereignty they found no fuch contract in exiftence or even in litigation. They found Virginia under the authority
of the crown of England, both as to foil and government, fubject to
quit-rents to the crown and not to the company, and had been fo
for upwards of 150 years: and that an inftrument or deed of writing,
of a private nature, as all proprietary contracts are fo far as land is
concerned, and which is now only hiftorically known, and in which
Virginia was no party, and to which no fucceffion in any line can be
proved, and has ceafed for 150 years, fhould now be raked from oblivion and held up as a charter whereon to affume a right to boundlefs
territory, and that by a perverfion of the order of it, is fomething
very fingular and extraordinary.

If there was any innovation on the part of the crown, the conteft
refted between the crown and the proprietors, the London company,
and not between Virginia and the faid crown. It was not her charter;
it was the company's charter, and the only parties in the cafe were
the crown and the company.

But why, if Virginia contends for the immutability of charters, has
fhe felected this in preference to the two former ones? All her arguments arifing from this principle muft go to the firft charter and not to
the laft; but by placing them to the laft, inftead of the firft, fhe admits
a fact againft her principle; becaufe, in order to eftablifh the laft, fhe
proves the firft to be vacated by the fecond in the fpace of 23 years,
the fecond to be vacated by the third in the fpace of 3 years; and why
the third fhould not be vacated by the fourth form of government,
iffuing from the fame power with the former two and which took
place about 25 years after, and continued in being for 150 years fince,
and under which all her public and private bufinefs was tranfacted,
her purchafes made, her warrants for furvey and patents for land obtained, is too myfterious to account for.

Either the re-affumption of the London company's charter into the hands of the crown was an ufurpation, or it was not. If it was, then, ftrictly fpeaking, is every thing which Virginia has done under that ufurpation illegal, and fhe may be faid to have lived in the moft curious fpecies of rebellion ever known ; rebellion againft the London company of adventurers. For if the charter to the company (for it was not to the Virginians) ought to be in being now, it ought to have been in being then ; and why fhe fhould admit its vacation then and reject it now, is unaccountable ; or why fhe fhould efteem her purchafes of lands good which were then made contrary to this char-
and now contend for the operation of the fame charter to poffefs lands by, are circumftances which cannot be reconciled.

But whether the charter, as it is called, ought to be extinct or not, cannot make a queftion with us. All the parties concerned in it are deceafed, and no fucceffors, in any regular line of fucceffion, appear to claim. Neither the London company of adventurers, their heirs or affigns, were in poffeffion of the exercife of this charter at the commencement of the revolution ; and therefore the ftate of Virginia does not, in point of fact, fucceed to and inherit from the company.

But fay they, we fucceed to and inherit from the crown of England, which was the immediate poffeffor of the fovereignty at the time we entered, and had been fo for 150 years.

To fay this, is to fay there is no charter at all. A charter is an affurance from one party to another, and cannot be from the fame party to itfelf.

But before I enter further on this cafe I fhall concifely ftate how this charter came to be re-affumed by the power which granted it, the crown of England.

I have already ftated that it was a proprietary charter, or grant, to fir Thomas Gates and others, who were called the London company, and fometimes the South-Virginia company, to diftinguifh them from thofe who fettled to the eaftward (now New England) and were then called the North-Virginia or Plymouth company.

Oldmixon's Hiftory of Virginia (in his account of the Britifh empire in America) publifhed in the year 1708, gives a concife progrefs of the affair. He attributes it to the mifconduct, contentions and mifmanagement of the proprietors, and their innovations upon the Indians, which had fo exafperated them, that they fell on the fettlers and deftroyed at one time 334 men, women and children.

" Some time after this maffacre, fays he, feveral gentlemen in England procured grants of land from the company, and others came over on their private accounts to make fettlements; among the former was one captain Martin, who was named to be of the council. This man raifed fo many differences among them, that new diftractions followed, which the Indians obferving, took heart and once more fell upon the fettlers on the borders, deftroying, without pitying either age, fex, or condition.

" Thefe and other calamities being chiefly imputed to the mif-management of the proprietors, whofe loffes had fo difcouraged moft of their beft members, that they fold their fhares, and Charles the firft on his acceffion to the throne diffolved the company, and took the colony into his own immediate direction. He appointed the governor and council himfelf, ordered all patents and procefs to iffue in his own name, and referved a quit-rent of two fhillings fterling for every hundred acres."

Thus far our author. Now it is impoffible for us at this diftance of time to fay what were all the exact caufes of the change; neither have we any bufinefs with it. The company might furrender it, or they might not, or they might forfeit it by not fulfilling conditions, or they might fell it, or the crown might, as far as we know, take it from them. But what are either of thefe cafes to Virginia, or any other which can be produced. She was not a party in the matter. It was not her charter, neither can fhe ingraft any right upon it, or fuffer any injury under it.

If the charter was vacated it muft have been by the London company; if it was furrendered it muft be by the fame; and if it was fold nobody elfe could fell it, and if it was taken from them nobody elfe could lofe it; and yet Virginia calls this her charter, which it was not within her power to hold, to fell, to vacate, or to lofe.

But if fhe puts her right upon the ground that it never was fold, furrendered, loft, or vacated, by the London company, fhe admits that if they *had* fold, furrendered, loft, or vacated it, that it would have become extinct, and to her no charter at all. And in this cafe, the only thing to prove is the fact, which is, has this charter been the rule of government, and of purchafing or procuring unappropriated lands in Virginia, from the time it was granted to the time of the revolution? Anfwer—the charter has not been the rule of government, nor of purchafing and procuring lands, neither has any lands been purchafed or procured under its fanction or authority for upwards of 150 years.

But if she goes a step further, and says, that they could not vacate, surrender, sell, or lose it, by any act they could do, so neither
could they vacate, surrender, sell, or lose that of 1606, which was
three years prior to this ; and this argument, so far from establishing
the charter of 1609, would destroy it ; and in its stead confirm the
preceding one which limited the company to a square of 100 miles.
And if she still goes back to that of sir Walter Rawleigh, *that* only
places her in the light of Americans in common with all.

The only fact that can be clearly proved is, that the crown of
England exercised the power of dominion and government in Virginia,
and of the disposal of the lands, and that the charter had neither been
the rule of government or purchasing land for upwards of 150 years,
and this places Virginia in succession to the crown and not to the
company.   Consequently it proves a lapse of the charter into the
hands of the crown by some means or other.

Now to suppose that the charter could return into the hands of
the crown and yet remain in force, is to suppose that a man could
be bound by a bond of obligation to himself.

Its very *being* in the hands of the crown from which it issued, is
a cessation of its existence ; and an effectual unchartering all that
part of the grant which was not before disposed of.   And consequently the state of Virginia standing thus in succession to the crown,
can be entitled to no more extent of country as a state under the
union, than what it possessed as a province under the crown.   And
all lands exterior to these bounds, as well of Virginia as the rest of
the states, devolve, in the order of succession, to the sovereignty of
the United States, for the benefit of all.

And this brings the case to what were the limits of Virginia as a
province under the crown of England.

Charter it had none.   Its limits then rested at the discretion of
the authority to which it was subject.   Maryland and Pennsylvania
became its boundary to the eastward and northward, and North-Carolina to the southward, therefore the boundary to the westward
was the only principal line to be ascertained.

As Virginia from a proprietary soil and government was become
what then bore the name of a royal one, the extent of the province,
as the order of things then stood (for something must always be admitted whereon to form a beginning) was wholly at the disposal of
the crown of England, who might enlarge, or diminish, or erect new
governments to the westward, by the same authoritative right that Vir-

ginia now can divide a county into two; if too large, or too inconvenient.

To fay, as has been faid, that Pennfylvania, Maryland and North-Carolina, were taken out of Virginia, is no more than to fay, they were taken out of America; becaufe Virginia was the common name of all the country, north and fouth: and to fay they were taken out of the chartered limits of Virginia, is likewife to fay nothing ; becaufe after the diffolution or extinction of the proprietary company, there was nobody to whom any provincial limits became chartered. The extinction of the company was the extinction of the chartered limits. The patent could not furvive the company, becaufe it was to them a right, which, when they expired ceafed to be any body's elfe in their ftead.

But to return to the weftern boundary of Virginia at the commencement of the revolution.

Charters, like proclamations, were the fole act of the crown, and if the former were adequate to fix limits to the lands which it gave away, fold, or otherwife difpofed of, the latter were equally adequate to fix limits or divifions to thofe which it retained; and therefore, the weftern limits of Virginia, as the proprietary company was extinct and confequently the patent with it, muft be looked for in the line of proclamations.

I am not fond of quoting thefe old remains of former arrogance, but as we muft begin fomewhere, and as the ftates have agreed to regulate the right of each ftate to territory, by the condition each ftood in with the crown of England at the commencement of the revolution, we have no other rule to go by; and any rule which can be agreed on is better than none.

From the proclamation then of 1763, the weftern limits of Virginia, as a province under the crown of England, are defcribed fo as not to extend beyond the heads of any of the rivers which empty themfelves into the Atlantic, and confequently the limits did not pafs over the Allegany Mountain.

Extract from the proclamation of 1763 fo far as refpects boundary:

" AND WHEREAS it is *juft* and *reafonable*, and *effential to our interest*, and the fecurity of our colonies, that the feveral nations or tribes of Indians, with whom we are connected, and who live under our protection, fhould not be molefted or difturbed in the poffeffion of fuch parts of our dominions and territories, *as, not having being ceded to, or purchafed by us, are referved to them or any of them as their hunt-*

ing grounds ; we do therefore, with the advice of our privy council, declare it to be our royal will and pleafure that no governor, or commander in chief, in any of our colonies of Quebec, Eaft Florida, or Weft-Florida, do prefume upon any pretence whatever, to grant warrants of furvey, or pafs any patents for lands beyond the bounds of their refpective governments, as defcribed in their commiffions: As ALSO that no governor or commander in chief of our colonies or plantations in America, do prefume, for the prefent, and until our further pleafure be known, to grant warrants of furvey or pafs patents for any lands *beyond the heads or fources of any of the rivers which fall into the Atlantic ocean from the weft or northweft,* or upon any lands whatever, *which not having been ceded to, or purchafed by us, as aforefaid, are referved unto the faid Indians or any of them.*

"And we do further declare it to be our royal will and pleafure, for the prefent, as aforefaid, to referve under our fovereignty, protection and dominion, *for the ufe of the faid Indians all the lands and territories,* not included within the limits of our faid three new governments, or within the limits of the territory granted to the Hudfon's-Bay company; as alfo, *all the lands and territories lying to the weftward of the fources of the rivers, which fall into the fea from the weft and northweft as aforefaid;* and we do hereby ftrictly forbid, on pain of our difpleafure, all our loving fubjects from making any purchafes or fettlements whatever, or taking poffeffion of any of the lands above referved, without our efpecial leave and licence for that purpofe firft obtained.

"And we do further ftrictly enjoin and require all perfons whatever, who have either wilfully or inadvertently feated themfelves upon any lands within the countries above defcribed, or upon any other lands, *which, not having been ceded to, or purchafed by us,* are ftill referved to the faid Indians, as aforefaid, forthwith to remove themfelves from fuch fettlements."

It is eafy for us to underftand, that the frequent and plaufible mention of the Indians was only fpecioufnefs to create an idea of the humanity of government. The object and intention of the proclamation was the weftern boundary, which is here fignified not to extend beyond the heads of the rivers: and thefe, then, are the weftern limits which Virginia had as a province under the crown of Britain.

And agreeable to the intention of this proclamation and the limits defcribed thereby, lord Hillfborough, then fecretary of ftate in England, addreffed an official letter of the 31ft of July, 1770, to lord Bottetourt, at that time governor of Virginia, which letter was laid before the council of Virginia by Mr. prefident Nelfon, and by him anfwered on the 18th of October in the fame year, of which the following are extracts :

" On the evening of the day your lordfhip's letter to the governor was delivered to me (as it contains matters of great variety and importance), it was read in council, and, together with the feveral papers inclofed, it hath been maturely confidered, and I now trouble your lordfhip with theirs as well as my own opinion upon the fubject of them.

" We do not prefume to fay to whom our gracious fovereign fhall grant his vacant lands," and " with refpect to the eftablifhment of a *new colony on the back of Virginia*, it is a fubject of too great political importance for me to prefume to give an opinion upon, however, permit me, my lord, to obferve, that when that part of the country fhall become fufficiently populated it may be a wife and prudent meafure."

On the death of lord Bottetourt, lord Dunmore was appointed to the government, and he, either from ignorance of the fubject, or other motives, made a grant of fome lands on the Ohio to certain of his friends and favourites, which produced the following letter from lord Dartmouth, who fucceeded lord Hillfborough as fecretary of ftate :

" I think fit to inclofe your lordfhip a copy of lord Hillfborough's letter to lord Bottetourt, of the 31ft of July, 1770, the receipt of which was acknowledged by Mr. prefident Nelfon, a few days before lord Bottetourt's death, and appears by his anfwer to it, to have been laid before the council. That board, therefore, could not be ignorant of what has paffed here upon Mr. Walpole's application, nor of the king's exprefs command, contained in lord Hillfborough's letter, that no lands fhould be granted beyond the limits of the royal proclamation of 1763, until the king's further pleafure was fignified ; and I have only to obferve, that it muft have been a very extraordinary neglect in them not to have informed your lordfhip of that letter and thofe orders."

On thefe documents I fhall make no remarks. They are their own evidence, and fhew what the limits of Virginia were while a Britifh province ; and as there was then no other authority by which they could be fixed, and as the grant to the London company could not be a grant to any but themfelves, and of confequence ceafed to be when they ceafed to exift, it remained a matter of choice in the crown, on its re-affumption of the lands, to limit or divide them into feparate governments, as it judged beft, and from which there was not, and could not, in the order of government, be any appeal. Neither was Virginia, as a province, affected by it, becaufe the monies, in any cafe, arifing from the fale of lands, did not go into her treafury; and whether to the crown or to the proprietors was to her indifferent. And it is likewife evident, from the fecretary's letter, and the prefident's anfwer, that it was in contemplation to lay out a new colony on the back of Virginia, between the Allegany Mountains and the Ohio.

Having thus gone through the feveral charters, or grants, and their relation to each other, and fhewn that Virginia cannot ftand in fucceffion to a private grant, which has been extinct for upwards of 150 years—and that the weftern limits of Virginia, at the commencement of the revolution, were at the heads of the rivers emptying themfelves into the Atlantic, none of which are beyond the Allegany Mountains; I now proceed to the fecond part, namely,

The reafonablenefs of her claims.

Virginia, as a Britifh province, ftood in a different fituation with the crown of England to any of the other provinces, becaufe fhe had no afcertained limits, but fuch as arofe from the laying off new provinces and the proclamation of 1763. For the fame name, Virginia, as I have before mentioned, was the general name of all the country, and the dominion out of which the feveral governments were laid off: and in ftrict propriety, conformable to the origin of names, the province of Virginia was taken out of the dominion of Virginia. For the term. *dominion*, could not appertain to the province, which retained the name of Virginia, but to the crown, and from thence was applied to the whole country, and fignified its being an appendage to the crown of England, as they now fay, " *our dominion of Wales.*"

It is not poffible to fuppofe there could exift an idea that Virginia, as a Britifh province, was to be extended to the South Sea at the diftance of three thoufand miles. The dominion, as appertaining at that time to the crown, might be claimed to extend fo far, but as a province the thought was not conceivable, nor the practice poffible.

And it is more than probable, that the deception made ufe of to obtain the patent of 1609 by reprefenting the South Sea to be near where the Allegany Mountains are, was one caufe of its becoming extinct; and it is worthy of remarking, that no hiftory (at leaft that I have met with) mentions any difpute or litigation, between the crown and the company in confequence of the extinction of the patent, and the re-affumption of the lands; and therefore the negative evidence corroborating with the positive, make it, as certain as such a case can possibly be, that either the company received a compensation for the patent, or quitted it quietly, ashamed of the imposition they had acted, and their subsequent mal-administration. Men are not inclined to give up a claim where there is any ground to contend on, and the silence in which the patent expired is a presumptive proof that its fate, from whatever cause, was just.

There is one general policy which seems to have prevailed with the English in laying off new governments, which was, not to make them larger than their own country, that they might the easier hold them manageable : This was the case with every one except Canada, the extension of whose limits was for the politic purpose of recognizing new acquisition of territory, not immediately convenient for colonization.

But, in order to give this matter a chance through all its cases, I will admit what no man can suppose, which is, that there is an English charter that fixes Virginia to extend from the Atlantic to the South Sea, and contained within a due west line, set off two hundred miles below Cape Comfort, and a northwest line, set off two hundred miles above it. Her side, then, on the Atlantic (according to an explanation given in Mr. Bradford's paper of September 29, 1779, by an advocate for the Virginia claims) will be four hundred miles ; her side to the south three thousand ; her side to the west four thousand ; and her northwest line about five thousand ; and the quantity of land contained within these dimensions will be almost 4,000,000,000, that is four thousand million of acres, which is more than ten times the quantity contained within the present United States, and above an hundred times greater than the kingdom of England.

To reason on a case like this, is such a waste of time, and such an excess of folly, that it ought not to be reasoned upon. It is impossible to suppose that any patent to private persons could be so intentionally absurd, and the claim, grounded thereon, is as wild as any thing the imagination of man ever conceived.

But if, as I before mentioned, there was a charter which bore such an explanation, and that Virginia stood in succession to it, what would that be to us, any more than the will of Alexander, had he taken it in his head to have bequeathed away the world ? Such a charter, or grant must have been obtained by imposition and a false representation of the country, or granted in error, or both ; and in any of, or all, these cases, the United States must reject the matter as something they cannot know, for the merits will not bear an argument, and the pretenfion of right ftands upon no better ground.

Our cafe is an original one; and many matters attending it muft be determined on their own merits and reafonablenefs. The territory of the reft of the ftates is, in general, within known bounds of moderate extent, and the quota which each ftate is to furnifh towards the expence and fervice of the war, muft be afcertained upon fome rule of comparifon. The number of inhabitants of each ftate formed the firft rule; and it was naturally fuppofed that thofe numbers bore nearly the fame proportion to each other, which the territory of each ftate did. Virginia, on this fcale, would be about one fifth larger than Pennfylvania, which would be as much dominion as any ftate could manage with happinefs and convenience.

When I firft began this fubject, my intention was to be extenfive on the merits, and concife on the matter of right; inftead of which, I have been extenfive on the matter of right, and concife on the merits of reafonablenefs: and this alteration in my defign arofe, confequentially, from the nature of the fubject; for as a reafonable thing the claim can be fupported by no argument, and therefore needs none to refute it; but as there is a ftrange propenfity in mankind to fhelter themfelves under the fanction of a right, however unreafonable that fuppofed right may be, I found it muft conducive to the intereft of the cafe, to fhew, that the right ftands upon no better grounds than the reafon. And fhall therefore proceed to make fome obfervations on,
The confequences of the claim.

The claim being unreafonable in itfelf and ftanding on no ground of right, but fuch as, if true, muft from the quarter it is drawn be offenfive, has a tendency to create difguft and four the minds of the reft of the ftates. Thofe lands are capable, under the management of the United States, of repaying the charges of the war, and fome of them, as I fhall hereafter fhow, may, I prefume, be made an immediate advantage of.

I diftinguifh three different defcriptions of lands in America at the commencement of the revolution. Proprietary or chartered lands, as was the cafe in Pennfylvania: Crown lands, within the defcribed limits of any of the crown governments; and crown refiduary lands, that were without, or beyond the limits of any province; and thofe laft were held in referve whereon to erect new governments and lay out new provinces; as appears to have been the defign by lord Hillfborough's letter and the prefident's anfwer, wherein he fays " with

" refpect to the eftablifhment of a *new* colony on the *back* of Vir-
" ginia, it is a fubject of too great political importance for me to
" prefume to give an opinion upon; however, permit me, my lord,
" to obferve, that when that part of the country, fhall become popu-
" lated it may be a wife and prudent meafure."

The expreffion is a " *new colony* on the *back* of Virginia;" and referred to lands between the heads of the rivers and the Ohio. This
is a proof that thofe lands were not confidered within, but beyond, the
limits of Virginia as a colony; and the other expreffion in the letter
is equally defcriptive, namely, " *We do not prefume to fay to whom*
" *our gracious fovereign fhall grant his vacant lands.*" Certainly then,
the fame right, which, at that time, refted in the crown, refts now in
the more fupreme authority of the United States; and therefore, addreffing the prefident's letter to the circumftances of the revolution,
it will run thus:

" We do not prefume to fay to whom the *fovereign United States*
fhall grant their vacant lands, and with refpect to the fettlement of a
new colony on the *back* of Virginia, it is a matter of too much political
importance for me to give an opinion upon ; however, permit me to
obferve, that when that part of the country fhall become populated
it may be a wife and prudent meafure."

It muft occur to every perfon, on reflection, that thofe lands are
too diftant to be within the government of any of the prefent ftates;
and, I may prefume to fuppofe, that were a calculation juftly made,
Virginia has loft more by the decreafe of taxables, than fhe has gained
by what lands fhe has made fale of ; therefore, fhe is not only doing
the reft of the ftates wrong in point of equity, but herfelf and them an
injury in point of ftrength, fervice and revenue.

It is only the United States, and not any fingle ftate, that can lay off
new ftates and incorporate them in the union by reprefentation ; therefore, the fituation which the fettlers on thofe lands will be in, under
the affumed right of Virginia, will be harzardous and diftreffing, and
they will feel themfelves at laft like aliens to the commonwealth of
Ifrael, their habitations unfafe and their title precarious.

And when men reflect on that peace, harmony, quietude and fecurity, which is neceffary to profperity, efpecially in making new fettlements, and think that when the war fhall be ended, their happinefs
and fafety will depend on a union with the ftates, and not a fcattered
people, unconnected with, and politically unknown to the reft, they
will feel but little inclination to put themfelves in a fituation, which

however folitary and reclufe, it may appear at prefent, will then be uncertain and unfafe and their troubles will have to begin where thofe of the United States fhall end.

It is probable that fome of the inhabitants of Virginia may be inclined to fuppofe, that the writer of this, by taking up the fubject in the manner he has done, is arguing unfriendly againft their intereft. To this he wifhes to reply ;

That the moft extraordinary part of the whole is, that Virginia fhould countenance fuch a claim. For it is worthy of obferving, that, from the beginning of the conteft with Britain, and long after, there was not a people in America who difcovered, through all the variety and multiplicity of public bufinefs, a greater fund of true wifdom, fortitude, and diftintereftednefs, than the then colony of Virginia. They were loved—They were reverenced. Their inveftigation of the affumed rights of Britain had a fagacity which was uncommon. Their reafonings were piercing, difficult to be equalled and impoffible to be refuted, and their public fpirit was exceeded by none. But fince this unfortunate land-fcheme has taken place, their powers feem to be abforbed ; a torpor has overfhaded them and every one afks, What is become of Virginia ?

It feldom happens that the romantic fchemes of extenfive dominion are of any fervice to a government, and never to a people. They affuredly end at laft in lofs, trouble, divifion and difappointment. And was even the title of Virginia good, and the claim admiffible, fhe would derive more lafting and real benefit by participating it, than by attempting the management of an object fo infinitely beyond her reach. Her fhare with the reft, under the fupremacy of the United States, which is the only authority adequate to the purpofe, would be worth more to her, than what the whole would produce under the management of herfelf alone. And that for feveral reafons :

Firft, becaufe her claim not being admiffible nor yet manageable, fhe cannot make a good title to the purchafers, and confequently can get but little for the lands.

Secondly, becaufe the diftance the fettlers will be at from her, will immediately put them out of all government and protection, fo far, at leaft as relates to Virginia : and by this means fhe will render her frontiers a refuge to defperadoes, and a hiding-place from juftice ; and the confequence will be perpetual unfafety to her own peace, and that of the neighbouring ftates.

Thirdly, becaufe her quota of expence for carrying on the war, admitting her to engrofs fuch an immenfity of territory, would be greater than fhe can either fupport or fupply, and could not be lefs, upon a reafonable rule of proportion, than nine-tenths of the whole. And,

Laftly, becaufe fhe muft fooner or later relinquifh them, and therefore to fee her own intereft wifely at firft, is preferable to the alternative of finding it out by misfortune at laft.

I have now gone through my examination of the claims of Virginia, in every cafe which I propofed; and for feveral reafons wifh the lot had fallen to another perfon.

But as this is a moft important matter, in which all are interefted, and the fubftantial good of Virginia not injured but promoted, and as few men have leifure, and ftill fewer have inclination, to go into intricate inveftigation, I have at laft ventured on the fubject.

The fucceffion of the United States to the vacant weftern territory is a right they originally fat out upon; and in the pamphlet *Common Senfe*, I frequently mentioned thofe lands as a national fund for the benefit of all; therefore refuming the fubject, where I then left off, I fhall conclude with concifely reducing to fyftem what I then only hinted.

In my laft piece, *The Crifis Extraordinary*, I eftimated the annual amount of the charge of war and the fupport of the feveral governments at two million pounds fterling, and the peace eftablifhment at three quarters of a million, and, by a comparifon of the taxes of this country with thofe of England, proved that the whole yearly expence to us, to defend the country, is but a third of what Britain would have drawn from us by taxes, had fhe fucceeded in her attempt to conquer; and our peace eftablifhment only an eighth part; and likewife fhewed, that it was within the ability of the ftates to carry on the whole of the war by taxation, without having recourfe to any other modes or funds. To have a clear idea of taxation is neceffary to every country, and the more funds we can difcover and organize, the lefs will be the hope of the enemy, and the readier their difpofition to peace, which it is now *their* intereft more than *ours* to promote.

I have already remarked, that only the United States and not any particular ftate can lay off new ftates and incorporate them in the union by reprefentation; keeping, therefore, this idea in view, I afk, might not a fubftantial fund be quickly created by laying off a new fiate, fo as to contain between twenty and thirty millions of acres, and opening a land-office in all the countries in Europe for hard money, and in this country for fupplies in kind, at a certain price.

The tract of land that feems beft adapted to anfwer this purpofe is contained between the Allegany Mountain and the river Ohio, as far north as the Pennfylvania line, thence extending down the faid river to the falls thereof, thence due fouth into the latitude of the North-Carolina line, and thence caft to the Allegany Mountain aforefaid— I, the more readily, mention this tract, becaufe it is fighting the enemy at their own weapons, as it includes the fame ground on which a new colony would have been erected, for the emolument of the crown of England, as appears by lord Hillfborough's and Dartmouth's letters, had not the revolution prevented its being carried into execution.

It is probable there may be fome fpots of private property within this tract, but to incorporate them into fome government will render them more profitable to the owners, and the condition of the fcattered fettlers more eligible and happy than at prefent.

If twenty millions of acres of this new ftate be patented and fold at twenty pounds fterling per hundred acres, they will produce four million pounds fterling, which, if applied to continental expences only, will fupport the war for three years, fhould Britain be fo unwife to herfelf to profecute it againft her own direct intereft and againft the intereft and policy of all Europe. The feveral ftates will then have to raife taxes for their internal government only, and the continental taxes as foon as the fund begins to operate, will leffen, and if fufficiently productive, will ceafe.

Lands are the real riches of all the habitable world, and the natural funds of America. The funds of other countries are, in general, artificially conftructed; the creatures of neceffity and contrivance; dependant upon credit, and always expofed to hazard and uncertainty. But lands can neither be annihilated nor lofe their value; on the contrary, they univerfally rife with population, and rapidly fo; when under the fecurity of effectual government. But this it is impoffible for Virginia to give, and, therefore, that which is capable of defraying the expences of the empire, will, under the management of any fingle ftate, produce only a fugitive fupport to wandering individuals.

I fhall now enquire into the effects which the laying out a new ftate, under the authority of the United States, will have upon Virginia.

It is the very circumstance she ought to, and must, wish for, when she examines the matter through all its cases and consequences.

The present settlers being beyond her reach, and her supposed authority over them remaining in herself, they will appear to her as revolters, and she to them as oppressors; and this will produce such a spirit of mutual dislike, that in a little time a total disagreement will take place, to the disadvantage of both.

But under the authority of the United States the matter is manageable, and Virginia will be eased of a disagreeable consequence.

Besides this, a sale of the lands, continentally, for the purpose of supporting the expence of the war, will save her a greater share of taxes, than what the small sale she could make herself, and the small price she could get for them, would produce.

· She would likewise have two advantages which no other state in the union enjoys; first, a frontier state for her defence against the incursions of the Indians; and the second is, that the laying out and peopling a new state on the back of an old one, situated as she is, is doubling the quantity of its trade.

The new state, which is here proposed to be laid out, may send its exports down the Mississippi, but its imports must come through Chesapeak Bay, and consequently Virginia will become the market for the new state; because, though there is a navigation from it, there is none into it, on account of the rapidity of the Mississippi.

There are certain circumstances that will produce certain events whether men think of them or not. The events do not depend upon thinking, but are the natural consequence of acting; and according to the system which Virginia has gone upon, the issue will be, that she will get involved with the back settlers in a contention about *rights* till they dispute with her own claims; and, soured by the contention, will go to any other state for their commerce; both of which may be prevented, a perfect harmony established, the strength of the states encreased, and the expences of the war defrayed, by settling the matter now on the plan of a general right; and every day it is delayed the difficulty will be encreased and the advantages lessened.

But if it should happen, as it possibly may, that the war should end before the money which the new state may produce be expended, the remainder of the lands therein may be set apart to reimburse those, whose houses have been burnt by the enemy, as this is a species of suffering which it was impossible to prevent, because houses are not

moveable property: and it ought not to be, that becaufe we cannot
do every thing, that we ought not to do what we can.

Having faid thus much on the fubject, I think it neceffary to remark, that the profpect of a new fund, fo far from abating our endeavours in making every immediate provifion for the fupply of the army,
ought to quicken us therein; for fhould the ftates fee it expedient to
go upon the meafure, it will be at leaft a year before it can be productive. I the more freely mention this, becaufe, there is a dangerous
fpecies of popularity, which, I fear, fome men are feeking from their
conftituents by giving them grounds to believe, that if they are elected they will lighten the taxes; a meafure, which, in the prefent ftate
of things, cannot be done without expofing the country to the ravages of the enemy by difabling the army from defending it.

Where knowledge is a duty, ignorance is a crime; and if any man
whofe duty it was to know better has encouraged fuch an expectation, he has either deceived himfelf or them: befides, no country can
be defended without expence, and let any man compare his portion
of temporary inconveniences arifing from taxations, with the real diftreffes of the army for the want of fupplies, and the difference is not
only fufficient to ftrike him dumb, but make him thankful that worfe
confequences have not followed.

In advancing this doctrine, I fpeak with an honeft freedom to the
country; for as it is their good to be defended, fo it is their intereft to
provide that defence, at leaft, till other funds can be organized.

As the laying out new ftates will fome time or other be the bufinefs
of the country, and as it is yet a new bufinefs to us; and as the influence of the war has fcarcely afforded leifure for reflecting on diftant circumftances, I fhall throw together a few hints for facilitating
that meafure, whenever it may be proper for adopting it.

The United States now ftanding on the line of fovereignty, the vacant territory is their property collectively, but the perfons by whom
it may hereafter be peopled will have an equal right with ourfelves;
and therefore, as new ftates fhall be laid off and incorporated with the
prefent, they will become partakers of the remaining territory with us
who are already in poffeffion. And this confideration ought to
heighten the value of lands to new emigrants; becaufe, in making
th purchafes, they not only gain an immediate property, but become
initia ed into the right and heirfhip of the ftates to a property in
referve, which is an additional advantage to what any purchafers under the late government of England enjoyed.

The fetting off the boundary of any new ftate will naturally be the firft ftep, and as it muft be fuppofed not to be peopled at the time it is laid off, a conftitution muft be formed, by the United States, as the rule of government in any new ftate, for a certain term of years (perhaps ten) or until the ftate become peopled to a certain number of inhabitants ; after which, the whole and fole right of modelling their government to reft with themfelves.

A queftion may arife, whether a new ftate fhould immediately pof-fefs an equal right with the prefent ones in all cafes which may come before congrefs.

This, experience will beft determine ; but at firft view of the matter it appears thus ; that it ought to be immediately incorporated into the union on the ground of a family right, fuch a ftate ftanding in the line of a younger child of the fame ftock ; but as new emigrants will have fomething to learn when they firft come to America, and a new ftate requiring aid rather than capable of giving it, it might be moft conve-nient to admit its immediate reprefentation into congrefs, there to fit, hear and debate, on all queftions and matters, but not to vote on any till after the expiration of feven years.

I fhall in this place take the opportunity of renewing a hint which I formerly threw out in the pamphlet *Common Senfe*, and which the fe-veral ftates will, fooner or later, fee the convenience, if not the necef-fity, of adopting ; which is, that of electing a continental convention, for the purpofe of forming a continental conftitution, defining and defcribing the powers and authority of congrefs.

Thofe of entering into treaties, and making peace, they naturally poffefs, in behalf of the ftates, for their feparate as well as their united good, but the internal control and dictatorial powers of congrefs are not fufficiently defined, and appear to be too much in fome cafes, and too little in others ; and therefore, to have them marked legally out will give additional energy to the whole, and new confidence to the feveral parts.

ADDRESSED TO THE

ABBE RAYNAL,

ON THE

AFFAIRS OF *NORTH-AMERICA*.

IN WHICH

THE MISTAKES IN THE ABBE'S ACCOUNT

OF THE

REVOLUTION OF *AMERICA*

ARE CORRECTED AND CLEARED UP.

By THOMAS PAINE, M. A.

OF THE UNIVERSITY OF PENNSYLVANIA, AND AUTHOR OF THE PAMPHLET

AND OTHER PUBLICATIONS, ENTITLED, OR SIGNED,

"COMMON SENSE."

INTRODUCTION.

A LONDON tranflation of an original work in French, by the
Abbe Raynal, which treats of the revolution of North-America,
having been re-printed in Philadelphia and other parts of the continent, and as the diftance at which the Abbe is placed from the
American theatre of war and politics, has occafioned him to miftake
feveral facts, or, mifconceive the caufes or principles by which they
were produced ; the following tract, therefore, is publifhed with a
view to rectify them, and prevent even accidental errors intermixing
with hiftory, under the fanction of time and filence.

The editor of the London edition has entitled it, " *The Revolution
of America*, by the ABBE RAYNAL," and the American printers
have followed the example. But I have underftood, and I believe
my information juft, that the piece, which is more properly reflexions
on the revolution, was unfairly purloined from the printer which the
Abbe employed, or from the manufcript copy, and is only part of a
larger work then in the prefs, or preparing for it. The perfon who
procured it, appears to have been an Englifhman, and though, in an
advertifement prefixt to the London edition, he has endeavoured to
glofs over the embezzlement with profeffions of patriotifm, and to
foften it with high encomiums on the author, yet the action, in any
view, in which it can be placed, is illiberal and unpardonable.

" In the courfe of his travels," fays he, " the tranflator happily
" fucceeded in obtaining a copy of this exquifite little piece, which
" has not yet made its appearance from any prefs. He publifhes a
" French edition, in favour of thofe who feel its eloquent reafoning
" more forcibly in its native language, at the fame time with the
" following tranflation of it ; in which he has been defirous, perhaps

" in vain, that all the warmth, the grace, the ftrength, the dignity
" of the original, fhould not be loft. And he flatters himfelf, that
" the indulgence of the illuftrious hiftorian will not be wanting to a
" man, who, of his own motion, has taken the liberty to give this
" compofition to the public, only from a ftrong perfuafion, that its
" momentous argument will be ufeful, in a critical conjuncture, to
" that country which he loves with an ardour, that can be exceeded
" only by the nobler flame, which burns in the bofom of the philan-
" thropic author, for the freedom and happinefs of all the countries
" upon earth."

This plaufibility of fetting off a difhonourable action, may pafs for
patriotifm and found principles with thofe who do not enter into its
demerits, and whofe intereft is not injured nor their happinefs affected
thereby. But it is more than probable, notwithftanding the declarations it contains, that the copy was obtained for the fake of profiting by the fale of a new and popular work, and that the profeffions
are but a garb to the fraud.

It may with propriety be remarked, that in all countries where
literature is protected, and it never can flourifh where it is not, the
works of an author are his legal property ; and to treat letters in
any other light than this, is to banifh them from the country or
ftrangle them in the birth.—The embezzlement from the Abbe
Raynal, was, it is true, committed by one country upon another,
and therefore fhows no defect in the laws of either. But it is neverthelefs a breach of civil manners and literary juftice ; neither can it be
any apology, that becaufe the countries are at war, literature fhall
be entitled to depredation.*

But the foreftalling the Abbe's publication by London editions,

---

* *The ftate of literature in America muft one day become a fubject of
legiflative confideration. Hitherto it hath been a difinterefted volunteer
in the fervice of the revolution, and no man thought of profits : but when
peace fhall give time and opportunity for ftudy, the country will deprive
itfelf of the honour and fervice of letters and the improvement of fcience,
unlefs fufficient laws are made to prevent depredations on literary property.
—It is well worth remarking, that Ruffia, who but a few years ago
was fcarcely known in Europe, owes a large fhare of her prefent greatnefs to the clofe attention fhe has paid, and the wife encouragement fhe has
given, to every branch of fcience and learning ; and we have almoft the
fame inftance in France, in the reign of Lewis the XIV.*

both in French and English, and thereby not only defrauding him
and throwing an expensive publication on his hands by anticipating
the fale, are only the fmaller injuries which fuch conduct may occafion. A man's opinions, whether written or in thought, are his own
until he pleafes to publifh them himfelf; and it is adding cruelty to
injuftice, to make him the author of what future reflection, or better
information, might occafion him to fupprefs or amend. There are
declarations and fentiments in the Abbe's piece, which, for my own
part, I did not expect to find, and fuch as himfelf, on a revifal,
might have feen occafion to change; but the anticipated piracy effectually prevented him the opportunity, and precipitated him into
difficulties, which, had it not been for fuch ungenerous fraud, might
not have happened.

This mode of making an author appear before his time, will appear ftill more ungenerous, when we confider how exceedingly few
men there are in any country, who can at once, and without the aid
of reflection and revifal, combine warm paffions with a cool temper,
and the full expanfion of the imagination with the natural and neceffary gravity of judgment, fo as to be rightly balanced within themfelves, and to make a reader feel, fancy, and underftand juftly at the
fame time. To call three powers of the mind into action at once,
in a manner that neither fhall interrupt, and that each fhall aid and
vigorate the other, is a talent very rarely poffeffed.

It often happens that the weight of an argument is loft by the wit
of fetting it off; or the judgment difordered by an intemperate ir-
ritation of the paffions : yet a certain degree of animation muft be
felt by the writer, and raifed in the reader, in order to intereft the
attention; and a fufficient fcope given to the imagination, to enable
it to create in the mind a fight of the perfons, characters and circumftances of the fubject : for without thefe the judgment will feel little
or no excitement to office, and its determinations will be cold, flug-
gifh, and imperfect. But if either or both of the two former are
raifed too high, or heated too much, the judgment will be joftled
from its feat, and the whole matter, however important in itfelf, will
diminifh into a pantomime of the mind, in which we create images
that promote no other purpofe than amufement.

The Abbe's writings bear evident marks of that extenfion and ra-
pidnefs of thinking and quicknefs of fenfation, which of all others
require revifal, and the more particularly fo, when applied to the
living characters of nations or individuals in a ftate of war. The

leaft mifinformation or mifconception leads to fome wrong conclufion, and an error believed becomes the progenitor of others.—And as the Abbe has fuffered fome inconveniences in France by miftating certain circumftances of the war, and the characters of the parties therein, it becomes fome apology for him that thofe errors were precipitated into the world by the avarice of an ungenerous enemy.

LETTER

ABBE RAYNAL.

To an author of fuch diftinguifhed reputation as the Abbe Raynal, it might very well become me to apologize for the prefent undertaking ; but, as *to be right* is the firft wifh of philofophy, and the firft principle of hiftory, he will, I prefume, accept from me a declaration of my motives, which are thofe of doing juftice, in preference to any complimental apology, I might otherwife make.—— The Abbe, in the courfe of his work, has, in fome inftances, extolled without a reafon, and wounded without a caufe. He has given fame where it was not deferved, and withheld it where it was juftly due ; and appears to be fo frequently in and out of temper with his fubjects and parties, that few or none of them are decifively and uniformly marked.

It is yet too foon to write the hiftory of the revolution, and whoever attempts it precipitately, will unavoidably miftake characters and circumftances, and involve himfelf in error and difficulty. Things, like men, are feldom underftood rightly at firft fight. But the Abbe is wrong even in the foundation of his work ; that is, he has mifconceived and miftated the caufes which produced the rupture between England and her then colonies, and which led on, ftep by ftep, unftudied and uncontrived on the part of America, to a revolution, which has engaged the attention, and affected the intereft, of Europe.

To prove this, I fhall bring forward a paffage, which, though placed towards the latter part of the Abbe's work, is more intimately

connected with the beginning; and in which, fpeaking of the original
caufe of the difpute, he declares himfelf in the following manner—
" None," fays he, " of thofe energetic caufes, which have pro-
" duced fo many revolutions upon the globe, exifted in North-Ame-
" rica. Neither religion nor laws had there been outraged. The
" blood of martyrs or patriots had not there ftreamed from fcaffolds.
" Morals had not there been infulted. Manners, cuftoms, habits,
" no object dear to nations, had there been the fport of ridicule.
" Arbitrary power had not there torn any inhabitant from the arms
" of his family and his friends, to drag him to a dreary dungeon.
" Public order had not been there inverted. The principles of ad-
" miniftration had not been changed there ; and the maxims of go-
" vernment had there always remained the fame. The whole quef-
" tion was reduced to the knowing whether the mother country had,
" or had not, a right to lay, directly or indirectly, a flight tax upon
" the colonies."

On this extraordinary paffage, it may not be improper, in general
terms, to remark, that none can feel like thofe who fuffer; and that
for a man to be a competent judge of the provocative, or as the Abbe
ftiles them, the energetic caufes of the revolution, he muft have re-
fided in America.

The Abbe in faying that the feveral particulars he has enumerated,
did not exift in America, and neglecting to point out the particular
period, in which he means they did not exift, reduces thereby his declaration to a nullity, by taking away all meaning from the paffage.
They did not exift in 1763, and they all exifted before 1776; confequently as there was a time when they did *not*, and another, when
they *did* exift, the *time when* conftitutes the effence of the fact, and not
to give it, is to withhold the only evidence, which proves the declaration right or wrong, and on which it muft ftand or fall. But the declaration as it now appears, unaccompanied by time, has an effect in
holding out to the world, that there was no real caufe for the revolution, becaufe it denies the exiftence of all thofe caufes, which are fuppofed to be juftifiable, and which the Abbe ftiles energetic.

I confefs myfelf exceedingly at a lofs to find out the time to which
the Abbe alludes; becaufe, in another part of the work, in fpeaking
of the ftamp act, which was paffed in 1764, he ftyles it " an *ufurpation*
of the Americans' *moft precious and facred rights*." Confequently he
here admits the moft energetic of all caufes, that is, *an ufurpation of
their moft preci us and facred rights*, to have exifted in America twelve

years before the declaration of independence, and ten years before the breaking out of hoflilities.—The time, therefore, in which the paragraph is true, muft be antecedent to t e ftamp act, but as at that time there was no revolution nor any idea of one, it confequently applies without a meaning; and as it cannot, on the Abbe's own principle, be applied to any time *after* the ftamp act, it is therefore a wandering folitary paragraph, connected with nothing and at variance with every thing.

The ftamp act, it is true, was repealed in two years after it was paffed, but it was immediately followed by one of infinitely more mifchievous magnitude; I mean the declaratory act, which afferted the right, as it was ftyled, of the Britifh parliament, " *:o bind America in all cafes whatfoever.*"

If then the ftamp act was an ufurpation of the Americans' moft precious and facred rights, the declaratory act left them no right at all; and contained the full grown feeds of the moft defpotic government ever exercifed in the world. It placed America not only in the loweft, but in the bafeft ftate of vaffalage; becaufe it demanded an unconditional fubmiffion in every thing, or as the act expreffes it, *in all cafes whatfoever:* And what renders this act the more offenfive, is, that it appears to have been paffed as an act of mercy; truly then may it be faid, that *the tender mercies of the wicked are cruel.*

All the original charters from the crown of England, under the faith of which, the adventurers from the old world fettled in the new, were by this act difplaced from their foundations; becaufe, contrary to the nature of them, which was that of a compact, they were now made fubject to repeal or alteration at the mere will of one party only. The whole condition of America was thus put into the hands of the parliament or the miniftry, without leaving to her the leaft right in any cafe whatfoever.

There is no defpotifm to which this iniquitous law did not extend; and though it might have been convenient in the execution of it, to have confulted manners and habits, the principle of the act made all tyranny legal. It ftopt no where. It went to every thing. It took in with it the whole life of a man, or, if I may fo exprefs it, an eternity of circumftances. It is the nature of law to require obedience, but this demanded fervitude; and the condition of an American, under the operation of it, was not that of a fubject, but a vaffal. Tyranny has often been eftablifhed *without* law and fometimes *againft* it, but the hiftory of mankind does not produce another in-france, in which it has been eftablifhed *by* law. It is an audacious outrage upon civil government, and cannot be too much expofed, in order to be fufficiently deteſted.

Neither could it be faid after this, that the legiſlature of that country any longer made laws for this, but that it gave out commands; for wherein differed an act of parliament conſtructed on this principle, and operating in this manner, over an unreprefented people, from the orders of a military eftablifhment.

The parliament of England, with refpect to America, was not feptennial but *perpetual.* It appeared to the latter a body always in being. Its election or its expiration were to her the fame as if its members fucceeded by inheritance, or went out by death, or lived for ever, or were appointed to it as a matter of office. Therefore, for the people of England to have any juft conception of the mind of America, refpecting this extraordinary act, they muft fuppofe all election and expiration in that country to ceafe for ever, and the prefent parliament, its heirs, &c. to be perpetual; in this cafe, I afk, what would the moft clamorous of them think, were an act to be paffed, declaring the right of *fuch a parliament* to bind *them* in all cafes whatfoever? For this word *whatfoever* would go as effectually to their *magna charta, bill of rights, trial by juries,* &c. as it went to the charters and forms of government in America.

I am perfuaded, that the gentleman to whom I addrefs thefe remarks, will not, after the paffing this act, fay, " that the *principles* of " adminiftration had not been *changed* in America, and that the max- " ims of government had there been *always the fame.*" For here is, in principle, a total overthrow of the whole ; and not a fubverfion only, but an annihilation of the foundation of liberty, and abfolute domination eftablifhed in its ftead.

The Abbe likewife ftates the cafe exceedingly wrong and injurioufly, when he fays, " that *the whole* queftion was reduced to the " knowing whether the mother country had, or had not, a right to " lay, directly or indirectly, a flight tax upon the colonies."—This was *not the whole* of the queftion; neither was the *quantity* of the tax the object either to the miniftry or to the Americans. It was the principle, of which the tax made but a part, and the quantity ftill lefs, that formed the ground on which America oppofed.

The tax on tea, which is the tax here alluded to, was neither more or lefs than an experiment to eftablifh the practice of the declaratory law upon; modelled into the more fafhionable phrafe *of the univerfal fupremacy of parliament.* For until this time the declaratory law had lain dormant, and the framers of it had contented themfelves with barely declaring an opinion.

Therefore the *whole* queftion with America, in the opening of the difpute, was, fhall we be bound in all cafes whatfoever by the Britifh parliament, or fhall we not? For fubmiffion to the tea or tax act implied an acknowledgment of the declaratory act, or, in other words, of the univerfal fupremacy of parliament, which as they never intended to do, it was neceffary they fhould oppofe it, in its firft ftage of execution.

It is probable the Abbe has been led into this miftake by perufing detached pieces in fome of the American newfpapers; for, in a cafe where all were interefted, every one had a right to give his opinion; and there were many, who, with the beft intentions, did not choofe the beft, nor indeed the true ground, to defend their caufe upon. They felt themfelves right by a general impulfe, without being able to feparate, analyze and arrange the parts.

I am fomewhat unwilling to examine too minutely into the whole of this extraordinary paffage of the Abbe, left I fhould appear to treat it with feverity ; otherwife I could fhew that not a fingle declaration is juftly founded : For inftance, the reviving an obfolete act of the reign of Henry the eighth, and fitting it to the Americans, by authority of which they were to be feized and brought from America to England, and there imprifoned and tried for any fuppofed offences, was, in the worft fenfe of the words, *to tear them, by the arbitrary power of parliament, from the arms of their families and friends, and drag them not only to dreary but diftant dungeons.* Yet this act was contrived fome years before the breaking out of hoftilities. And again, though the blood of martyrs and patriots had not ftreamed on the fcaffolds, it ftreamed in the ftreets, in the maffacre of the inhabitants of Bofton, by the Britifh foldiery in the year 1770.

Had the Abbe faid that the caufes which produced the revolution in America were originally *different* from thofe which produced revolutions in other parts of the globe, he had been right. Here the value and quality of liberty, the nature of government and the dignity of man, were known and underftood, and the attachment of the Americans to thefe principles, produced the revolution as a natural and almoft unavoidable confequence. They had no particular family to fet up or pull down. Nothing of perfonality was incorporated with their caufe. They ftarted even-handed with each other, and went no faster into the several stages of it, than they were driven by the unrelenting and imperious conduct of Britain. Nay, in the last act, the declaration of independence, they had nearly been too late; for had it not been declared at the exact time it was, I see no period in their affairs since, in which it could have been declared with the same effect, and probably not at all.

But the object being formed before the reverse of fortune took place, that is, before the operations of the gloomy campaign of 1776, their honour, their interest, their every thing called loudly on them to maintain it; and that glow of thought and energy of heart, which even a distant prospect of independence inspires, gave confidence to their hopes and resolution to their conduct, which a state of dependence could never have reached. They looked forward to happier days and scenes of rest, and qualified the hardships of the campaign by contemplating the establishment of their new born system.

If on the other hand we take a review of what part Britain has acted, we shall find every thing which ought to make a nation blush. The most vulgar abuse, accompanied by that species of haughtiness, which distinguishes the hero of a mob from the character of a gentleman; it was equally as much from her manners as from her injustice that she lost the colonies. By the latter she provoked their principles, by the former she wore out their temper; and it ought to be held out as an example to the world, to shew, how necessary it is to conduct the business of government with civility. In short, other revolutions may have originated in caprice or generated in ambition; but here, the most unoffending humility was tortured into rage, and the infancy of existence made to weep.

A union so extensive, continued and determined, suffering with patience and never in despair, could not have been produced by common causes. It must be something capable of reaching the whole soul of man and arming it with perpetual energy. In vain is it to look for precedents among the revolutions of former ages, to find out, by comparison, the causes of this. The spring, the progress, the object, the consequences, nay, the men, their habits of thinking, and all the circumstances of the country are different. Those of other nations are, in general, little more than the history of their quarrels. They are marked by no important character in the annals of events; mixt in the mass of general matters, they occupy but a common page; and while the chief of the successful partizans stept into power, the plundered multitude sat down and sorrowed. Few, very few of them are

LETTER TO ABBE RAYNAL. 273

accompanied with reformation, either in government or manners; many of them with the moſt confummate profligacy. Triumph on the one ſide and miſery on the other were the only events. Pains, puniſhments, torture, and death were made the buſineſs of mankind, until compaſſion, the faireſt aſſociate of the heart, was driven from its place, and the eye, accuſtomed to continual cruelty, could behold it without offence.

But as the principles of the preſent revolution differed from thoſe which preceded it, ſo likewiſe has the conduct of America both in government and war. Neither the foul finger of diſgrace nor the bloody hand of vengeance has hitherto put a blot upon her fame. Her victories have received luſtre from a greatneſs of lenity; and her laws been permitted to ſlumber, where they might juſtly have awakened to puniſh. War, ſo much the trade of the world, has here been only the buſineſs of neceſſity; and when the neceſſity ſhall ceaſe, her very enemies muſt confeſs, that as ſhe drew the ſword in her juſt defence, ſhe uſed it without cruelty and ſheathed it without revenge.

As it is not my deſign to extend theſe remarks to a hiſtory, I ſhall now take my leave of this paſſage of the Abbe, with an obſervation, which, until ſomething unfolds itſelf to convince me otherwiſe, I cannot avoid believing to be true;—which is, that it was the fixt determination of the Britiſh cabinet to quarrel with America at all events.

They (the members who compoſed the cabinet) had no doubt of ſucceſs, if they could once bring it to the iſſue of a battle, and they expected from a conqueſt, what they could neither propoſe with decency, nor hope for by negociation. The charters and conſtitutions of the colonies were become to them matters of offence, and their rapid progreſs in property and population were diſguſtingly beheld as the growing and natural means of independence. They ſaw no way to retain them long but by reducing them in time. A conqueſt would at once have made them both lords and landlords; and put them in poſſeſſion both of the revenue and the rental. The whole trouble of government would have ceaſed in a victory, and a final end been put to remonſtrance and debate. The experience of the ſtamp act had taught them how to quarrel with the advantages of cover and convenience, and they had nothing to do but to renew the ſcene, and put contention into motion. They hoped for a rebellion, and they made one. They expected a declaration of independence and they were not diſappointed. But after this, they looked for victory, and they obtained a defeat.....

VOL. I.   M m

If this be taken as the generating caufe of the conteft, then is every part of the conduct of the Britifh miniftry confiftent from the commencement of the difpute, until the figning the treaty of Paris, after which, conqueft becoming doubtful, they retreated to negociation; and were again defeated.

Though the Abbe poffeffes and difplays great powers of genius; and is a mafter of ftyle and language, he feems not to pay equal attention to the office of an hiftorian. His facts are coldly and carelefsly ftated. They neither inform the reader nor intereft him. Many of them are erroneous, and moft of them defective and obfcure. It is undoubtedly both an ornament and a ufeful addition to hiftory, to accompany it with maxims and reflections. They afford likewife an agreeable change to the ftyle and a more diverfified manner of expreffion; but it is abfolutely neceffary that the root from whence they fpring, or the foundation on which they are raifed, fhould be well attended to, which in this work they are not. The Abbe haftens through his narrations as if he was glad to get from them, that he may enter the more copious field of eloquence and imagination.   -

The actions of Trenton and Princeton, in New-Jerfey, in December 1776, and January following, on which the fate of America ftood for a while trembling on the point of fufpence, and from which the moft important confequences followed, are comprifed within a fingle paragraph, faintly conceived, and barren of character, circumftance and defcription.

" On the 25th of December," fays the Abbe, " they (the Ame-
" ricans) croffed the Claware, and fell *accidentally* upon Trenton;
" which was occupied by fifteen hundred of the twelve thoufand
" Heffians, fold in fo bafe a manner by their avaricious mafter, to
" the king of Great-Britain. This corps was *maffacred*, taken, or
" difperfed. Eight days after, three Englifh regiments were, in like
" manner, driven, from Princeton, but after having better fupported
" their reputation than the foreign troops in their pay."

This is all the account which is given of thefe moft interefting events. The Abbe has preceded them by two or three pages on the military operations of both armies, from the time of general Howe's arriving before New-York from Halifax, and the vaft reinforcements of Britifh and foreign troops with lord Howe from England. But in thefe, there is fo much miftake, and fo many omiffions, that, to fet them right, muft be the bufinefs of hiftory and not of a letter. The action of Long-Ifland is but barely hinted at, and the operations at the White-plains wholly omitted: as are likewise the attack and loss of Fort Washington, with a garrison of about two thousand five hundred men, and the precipitate evacuation of Fort Lee, in consequence thereof; which losses were in a great measure the cause of the retreat through the Jersies to the Delaware, a distance of about ninety miles. Neither is the manner of the retreat described; which, from the season of the year, the nature of the country, the nearness of the two armies (sometimes within sight and shot of each other, for such a length of way) the rear of the one employed in pulling down bridges, and the van of the other, in building them up, must necessarily be accompanied with many interesting circumstances.

It was a period of distresses. A crisis rather of danger than of hope. There is no description can do it justice; and even the actors in it, looking back upon the scene, are surprised how they got through; and at a loss to account for those powers of the mind and springs of animation, by which they withstood the force of accumulated misfortune.

It was expected, that the time for which the army was inlisted, would carry the campaign so far into the winter, that the severity of the season, and the consequent condition of the roads, would prevent any material operation of the enemy, until the new army could be raised for the next year. And I mention it, as a matter worthy of attention, by all future historians, that the movements of the American army, until the attack upon the Hessian post at Trenton, the 26th of December, are to be considered as operating to effect no other principal purpose than delay, and to wear away the campaign under all the disadvantages of an unequal force, with as little misfortune as possible.

But the loss of the garrison at Fort Washington on the 16th of November, and the expiration of the time of a considerable part of the army, so early as the 30th of the same month, and which were to be followed by almost daily expirations afterwards, made retreat the only final expedient. To these circumstances may be added the forlorn and destitute condition of the few that remained; for the garrison of Fort Lee, which composed almost the whole of the retreat, had been obliged to abandon it so instantaneously, that every article of stores and baggage was left behind, and in this destitute condition, without tent or blanket, and without any other utensils to dress their provision, than what they procured by the way, they performed a march of about ninety miles, and had the address and management to prolong it to the space of nineteen days.

By this unexpected or rather unthought of turn of affairs, the country was in an instant surprised into confusion, and found an enemy within its bowels, without an army to oppose him. There were no succours to be had, but from the free-will offering of the inhabitants. All was choice and every man reasoned for himself.

It was in this situation of affairs, equally calculated to confound or to inspire, that the gentleman, the merchant, the farmer, the tradesman and the labourer mutually turned from all the conveniences of home, to perform the duties of private soldiers and undergo the severities of a winter campaign. The delay, so judiciously contrived on the retreat, afforded time for the volunteer reinforcements to join general Washington on the Delaware.

The Abbe is likewise wrong in saying, that the American army fell *accidentally* on Trenton. It was the very object for which general Washington crossed the Delaware in the dead of the night and in the midst of snow, storms, and ice; and which he immediately re-crossed with his prisoners, as soon as he had accomplished his purpose. Neither was the intended enterprize a secret to the enemy, information having been sent of it by letter, from a British officer at Princeton, to colonel Rolle, who commanded the Hessians at Trenton, which letter was afterwards found by the Americans. Nevertheless the post was completely surprised. A small circumstance, which had the appearance of mistake on the part of the Americans, led to a more capital and real mistake on the part of Rolle.

The case was this. A detachment of twenty or thirty Americans had been sent across the river, from a post a few miles above, by an officer unacquainted with the intended attack; these were met by a body of Hessians, on the night to which the information pointed, which was Christmas night, and repulsed. Nothing farther appearing, and the Hessians, mistaking this for the advanced party, supposed the enterprize disconcerted, which at that time was not begun, and under this idea, returned to their quarters; so that, what might have raised an alarm, and brought the Americans into an ambuscade, served to take off the force of an information and promote the success of the enterprise. Soon after day-light general Washington entered the town, and after a little opposition, made himself master of it, with upwards of nine hundred prisoners.

This combination of equivocal circumstances, falling within what the Abbe stiles, " *the wide empire of chance*," would have afforded a fine field for thought, and I wish, for the fake of that elegance of reflexion he is fo capable of uing, that he had known it.

But the action at Princeton was accompanied by a still greater embarraffment of matters, and followed by more extraordinary confequences. The Americans, by a happy ftroke of generalfhip, in this inftance, not only deranged and defeated all the plans of the Britifh, in the intended moment of execution, but drew from their pofts the enemy they were not able to drive, and obliged them to clofe the campaign. As the circumftance is a curiofity in war, and not well underftood in Europe, I fhall, as concifely as I can, relate the principal parts ; they may ferve to prevent future hiftorians from error, and recover from forgetfulnefs a feene of magnificent fortitude.

Immediately after the furprife of the Heffians at Trenton, general Wafhington re-croffed the Delaware ; which at this place is about three quarters of a mile over, and re-affumed his former poft on the Pennfylvania fide. Trenton remained unoccupied, and the enemy were pofted at Princeton, twelve miles diftant, on the road towards New-York. The weather was now growing very fevere, and as there were very few houfes near the fhore where general Wafhington had taken his ftation, the greateft part of his army remained out in the woods and fields. Thefe, with fome other circumftances, induced the re-croffing the Delaware and taking poffeffion of Trenton. It was undoubtedly a bold adventure, and carried with it the appearance of defiance, efpecially when we confider the panic-ftruck condition of the enemy on the lofs of the Heffian poft. But in order to give a juft idea of the affair, it is neceffary, I fhould defcribe the place.

Trenton is fituated on a rifing ground, about three quarters of a mile diftant from the Delaware, on the eaftern or Jerfey fide ; and is cut into two divifions by a fmall creek or rivulet, fufficient to turn a mill which is on it, after which it empties itfelf at nearly right angles into the Delaware. The upper divifion, which is to to the northeaft, contains about feventy or eighty houfes, and the lower about forty or fifty. The ground on each fide this creek, and on which the houfes are, is likewife rifing, and the two divifions prefent an agreeable profpect to each other, with the creek between, on which there is a fmall ftone bridge of one arch.

Scarcely had general Wafhington taken poft here, and before the feveral parties of militia, out on detachments, or on their way, could be collected, than the British, leaving behind them a strong garrison at Princeton, marched suddenly and entered Trenton at the upper or northeast quarter. A party of the Americans skirmished with the advanced party of the British, to afford time for removing the stores and baggage, and withdrawing over the bridge.

In a little time the British had possession of one half of the town, general Washington of the other; and the creek only separated the two armies. Nothing could be a more critical situation than this, and if ever the fate of America depended on the event of a day, it was now. The Delaware was filling fast with large sheets of driving ice, and was impassible; so that no retreat into Pennsylvania could be effected, neither is it possible, in the face of an enemy, to pass a river of such extent. The roads were broken and rugged with the frost, and the main road was occupied by the enemy.

About four o'clock a party of the British approached the bridge, with a design to gain it, but were repulsed. They made no more attempts, though the creek itself is passable any where between the bridge and the Delaware. It runs in a rugged natural made ditch, over which a person may pass with little difficulty, the stream being rapid and shallow. Evening was now coming on, and the British, believing they had all the advantages they could wish for, and that they could use them when they pleased, discontinued all further operations, and held themselves prepared to make the attack next morning.

But the next morning produced a scene as elegant as it was unexpected. The British were under arms and ready to march to action, when one of their light-horse from Princeton came furiously down the street, with an account that general Washington had that morning attacked and carried the British post at that place, and was proceeding on to seize the magazine at Brunswick; on which the British, who were then on the point of making an assault on the evacuated camp of the Americans, wheeled about, and in a fit of consternation marched for Princeton.

This retreat is one of those extraordinary circumstances, that in future ages may probably pass for fable. For it will with difficulty be believed, that two armies, on which such important consequences depended, should be crouded into so small a space as Trenton, and that the one, on the eve of an engagement, when every ear is supposed to be open, and every watchfulness employed, should move completely from the ground, with all its stores, baggage, and artillery, unknown and even unfufpected by the other. And fo entirely were the Britifh deceived, that when they heard the report of the cannon and fmall arms at Princeton, they fuppofed it to be thunder, though in the depth of winter.

General Wafhington, the better to cover and difguife his retreat from Trenton, had ordered a line of fires to be lighted up in front of his camp. Thefe not only ferved to give an appearance of going to reft, and continuing that deception, but they effectually concealed from the Britifh whatever was acting behind them, for flame can no more be feen through than a wall, and in this fituation, it may with fome propriety be faid, they became a pillar of fire to the one army, and a pillar of a cloud to the other: after this, by a circuitous march of about eighteen miles, the Americans reached Princeton early in the morning.

The number of prifoners taken were between two and three hundred, with which general Wafhington immediately fet off. The van of the Britifh army from Trenton entered Princeton about an hour after the Americans had left it, who continuing their march for the remainder of the day, arrived in the evening at a convenient fituation, wide of the main road to Brunfwick, and about fixteen miles diftant from Princeton.—But fo wearied and exhaufted were they, with the continual and unabated fervice and fatigue of two days and a night, from action to action, without fhelter and almoft without refrefhment, that the bare and frozen ground, with no other covering than the fky, became to them a place of comfortable reft. By thefe two events, and with but a little comparative force to accomplifh them, the Americans clofed with advantage, a campaign, which, but a few days before, threatened the country with deftruction. The Britifh army, apprehenfive for the fafety of their magazines at Brunfwick, eighteen miles diftant, marched immediately for that place, where they arrived late in the evening, and from which they made no attempts to move, for nearly five months.

Having thus ftated the principal outlines of thefe two moft interefting actions, I fhall now quit them, to put the Abbe right in his miftated account of the debt and paper money of America, wherein, fpeaking of thefe matters, he fays,

" Thefe ideal riches were rejected. The more the multiplication " of them was urged by want, the greater did their depreciation " grow. The congrefs was indignant at the affront given to its " money, and declared all thofe to be traitors to their country,

" who fhould not receive it as they would have received gold it-
" felf.

" Did not this body know, that prepoffeffions are no more to be
" controlled than feelings are ? Did it not perceive that, in the
" prefent crifis, every rational man would he afraid of expofing his
" fortune ? Did it not fee, that at the beginning of a republic, it
" permitted to itfelf the exercife of fuch acts of defpotifm as are un-
" known even in the countries which are moulded to, and become
" familiar with, fervitude and oppreffion ? Could it pretend that it
" did not punifh a want of confidence with the pains which would
" have been fearcely merited by revolt and treafon ? Of all this
" was the congrefs well aware. But it had no choice of means.
" Its defpifed and defpicable fcraps of paper were actually thirty
" times below their original value, when more of them were ordered
" to be made. On the 13th of September, 1779, there was of this
" paper among the public, to the amount of 35,544,155l. The
" flate owed moreover 8,385,356l. without reckoning the particular
" debts of fingle provinces."

In the above recited paffages, the Abbe fpeaks as if the United
States. had contracted a debt of upwards of forty million pounds
flerling, befides the debts of the individual flates. After which,
fpeaking of foreign trade with America, he fays, that " thofe coun-
" tries in Europe, which are truly commercial ones, knowing that
" North-America had been reduced to contract debts, at the epoch
" even of her greateft profperity, wifely thought that, in her prefent
" diftrefs, fhe would be able to pay but very little, for what might
" be carried to her."

I know it muft be extremely difficult to make foreigners underfland the nature and circumflances of our paper money, becaufe there
are natives, who do not underfland it themfelves. But with us its
fate is now determined. Common confent has configned it to reft
with that kind of regard, which the long fervice of inanimate things
infenfibly obtains from mankind. Every ftone in the bridge, that
has carried us over, feems to have a claim upon our efteem. But
this was a corner ftone, and its ufefulnefs cannot be forgotten.
There is fomething in a grateful mind, which extends itfelf even to
things that can neither be benefited by regard, nor fuffer by neglect :
—But fo it is ; and almoft every man is fenfible of the effect.

But to return. The paper money, though iffued from congrefs
under the name of dollars, did not come from that body always at

that value. Thofe which were iffued the firft year, were equal to gold and filver. The fecond year lefs, the third ftill lefs, and fo en, for nearly the fpace of five years: at the end of which, I imagine, that the whole value, at which Congrefs might pay away the feveral emiffions, taking them together, was about ten or twelve millions pounds fterling.

Now as it would have taken ten or twelve millions fterling of taxes to carry on the war for five years, and, as while this money was iffuing and likewife depreciating down to nothing, there were none, or few valuable taxes paid ; confequently the event to the public was the fame, whether they funk ten or twelve millions of expended money, by depreciation, or paid ten or twelve millions by taxation ; for as they did not do both, and chofe to do one, the matter which, in a general view, was indifferent. And therefore, what the Abbe fuppofes to be a debt, has now no exiftence ; it having been paid, by every body confenting to reduce, at his own expence, from the value of the bills continually paffing among themfelves, a fum, equal to nearly what the expence of the war was for five years.

Again. The paper money having now ceafed, and the depreciation with it, and gold and filver fupplied its place, the war will now be carried on by taxation, which will draw from the public a confiderable lefs fum than what the depreciation drew ; but as while they pay the former, they do not fuffer the latter, and as when they fuffered the latter, they did not pay the former, the thing will be nearly equal, with this moral advantage, that taxation occafions frugality and thought, and depreciation produced diffipation and careleffnefs.

And again. If a man's portion of taxes comes to lefs than what he loft by the depreciation, it proves the alteration is in his favour. If it comes to more, and he is juftly affeffed, it fhews that he did not fuftain his proper fhare of depreciation, becaufe the one was as operatively his tax as the other.

It is true, that it never was intended, neither was it forefeen, that the debt contained in the paper currency fhould fink itfelf in this manner ; but as by the voluntary conduct of all and of every one it has arrived at this fate, the debt is paid by thofe who owed it. Perhaps nothing was ever fo univerfally the act of a country as this. Government had no hand in it. Every man depreciated his own money by his own confent, for fuch was the effect, which the raifing the nominal value of goods produced. But as by fuch reduction he fuftained a lofs equal to what he muft have paid to fink it by taxation, therefore the line of juftice is to confider his lofs by the depreciation as his tax for that time, and not to tax him when the war is over, to make that money good in any other perfon's hands, which became nothing in his own.

Again. The paper currency was iffued for the exprefs purpofe of carrying on the war. It has performed that fervice, without any other material charge to the public, while it lafted. But to fuppofe as fome did, that, at the end of the war, it was to grow into gold or filver, or become equal thereto, was to fuppofe that we were to *get* two hundred millions of dollars by *going to war*, inftead of *paying* the coft of carrying it on.

But if any thing in the fituation of America, as to her currency or her circumftances, yet remains not underftood, then let it be remembered, that this war is the public's war; the people's war; the country's war. It is *their* independence that is to be fupported; *their* property that is to be fecured; *their* country that is to be faved. Here, government, the army, and the people, are mutually and reciprocally one. In other wars, kings may lofe their thrones, and their dominions; but here, the lofs muft fall on the majefty of the multitude, and the property they are contending to fave. Every man being fenfible of this, he goes to the field, or pays his portion of the charge, as the fovereign of his own poffeffions; and when he is conquered a monarch falls.

The remark, which the Abbe in the conclufion of the paffage has made, refpecting America contracting debts in the time of her profperity (by which he means, before the breaking out of hoftilities), ferves to fhow, though he has not made the application, the very great commercial difference between a dependant and an independent country. In a ftate of dependance, and with a fettered commerce, though with all the advantages of peace, her trade could not balance itfelf, and fhe annually run into debt. But now, in a ftate of independence, though involved in war, fhe requires no credit; her ftores are full of merchandize, and gold and filver are become the currency of the country. How thefe things have eftablifhed themfelves are difficult to account for: But they are facts, and facts are more powerful than arguments.

As it is probable this letter will undergo a republication in Europe, the remarks here thrown together will ferve to fhew the extreme folly of Britain in refting her hopes of fuccefs on the extinction of our paper currency. The expectation is at once fo childifh and for-

lorn, that it places her in the laughable condition of a famished lion
watching for prey at a fpider's web.

From this account of the currency, the Abbe proceeds to state the
condition of America in the winter 1777, and the spring following;
and clofes his obfervations with mentioning the treaty of alliance,
which was figned in France, and the propofitions of the Britifh miniftry, which were rejected in America. But in the manner in
which the Abbe has arranged his facts, there is a very material error,
that not only he, but other European hiftorians have fallen into; none
of them having affigned the true caufe why the Britifh propofals were
rejected, and all of them have affigned a wrong one.

In the winter 1778, and spring following, congrefs were affembled
at York-town, in Pennfylvania, the Britifh were in poffeffion of Philadelphia, and general Wafhington with the army were encamped
in huts at the Valley-Forge, twenty-five miles diftant therefrom. To
all, who can remember, it was a feafon of hardfhip, but not defpair;
and the Abbe, fpeaking of this period and its inconveniences, fays,

" A multitude of privations, added to fo many other misfortunes,
" might make the Americans regret their former tranquility, and in-
" cline them to an accommodation with England. In vain had the peo-
" ple been bound to the new government by the facrednefs of oaths
" and the influence of religion. In vain had endeavours been ufed
" to convince them that it was impoffible to treat fafely with a coun-
" try, in which one parliament might overturn, what fhould have been
" eftablifhed by another. In vain had they been threatened with the
" eternal refentment of an exafperated and vindictive enemy.   It was
" poffible that thefe diftant troubles might not be balanced by the
" weight of prefent evils.

" So thought the Britifh miniftry, when they fent to the new
" world public agents, authorized to offer every thing except inde-
" pendence to thefe very Americans, from whom they had two years
" before exacted an unconditional fubmiffion. It is not improbable
" but, that by this plan of conciliation, a few months fooner, fome
" effect might have been produced. But at the period, at which it
" was propofed by the court of London, it was rejected with difdain,
" becaufe this meafure appeared but as an argument of fear and weak-
" nefs. The people were already re-affured. The congr. . the
" generals, the troops, the bold and fkilful men, in each colory had
" poffeffed themfelves of the authority ; every thing had recovered
" its firft fpirit. *This was the effect of a treaty of friendfhip and com-*

" *merce between the United States and the court of Verfailles, signed the*
" *6th of February*, 1778."

On this passage of the Abbe's I cannot help remarking, that, to unite time with circumstance, is a material nicety in history; the want of which frequently throws it into endless confusion and mistake, occasions a total separation between causes and consequences, and connects them with others they are not immediately, and sometimes not at all, related to.

The Abbe, in saying that the offers of the British ministry " were " rejected with disdain," is *right*, as to the *fact*, but *wrong* as to the *time*; and this error in the time, has occasioned him to be mistaken in the cause.

The signing the treaty of Paris the 6th of February, 1778, could have no effect on the mind or politics of America, until it was *known in America*; and therefore, when the Abbe says, that the rejection of the British offers was in consequence of the alliance, he must mean, that it was in consequence of the alliance, *being known* in America; which was not the case: and by this mistake he not only takes from her the reputation, which her unshaken fortitude in that trying situation deserves, but is likewise led very injuriously to suppose, that had she *not known* of the treaty, the offers would probably have been accepted; whereas she knew nothing of the treaty at the time of the rejection, and consequently did not reject them on that ground.

The propositions or offers above mentioned were contained in two bills brought into the British parliament by lord North on the 17th of February, 1778. Those bills were hurried through both houses with unusual haste, and before they had gone through all the customary forms of parliament, copies of them were sent over to lord Howe and general Howe, then in Philadelphia, who were likewise commissioners. General Howe ordered them to be printed in Philadelphia, and sent copies of them by a flag to general Washington, to be forwarded to congress at York-town, where they arrived the 21st of April, 1778. Thus much for the arrival of the bills in America.

Congress, as is their usual mode, appointed a committee from their own body, to examine them and report thereon. The report was brought in the next day (the twenty-second), was read, and unanimously agreed to, entered on their journals, and published for the information of the country. Now this report must be the rejection to which the Abbe alludes, because congress gave no other formal opinion on those bills and propositions: And on a subsequent appli-

*ation from the Britifh commiffioners, dated the 27th of May, and received at York-town the 6th of June, congrefs immediately referred them for an anfwer to their printed refolves of the 22d of April. Thus much for the rejection of the offers.

On the 2d of May, that is, eleven days after the above rejection was made, the treaty between the United States and France arrived at York-town; and until this moment congrefs had not the leaft notice or idea, that fuch a meafure was in any train of execution. But left this declaration of mine fhould pafs only for affertion, I fhall fupport it by proof, for it is material to the character and principle of the revolution to fhow, that no condition of America, fince the declaration of independence, however trying and fevere, ever operated to produce the moft diftant idea of yielding it up either by force, diftrefs, artifice or perfuafion. And this proof is the more neceffary, becaufe it was the fyftem of the Britifh miniftry at this time, as well as before and fince, to hold out to the European powers that America was unfixt in her refolutions and policy; hoping by this artifice to leffen her reputation in Europe, and weaken the confidence which thofe powers or any of them might be inclined to place in her.

At the time thefe matters were tranfacting, I was fecretary in the foreign department of congrefs. All the *political* letters from the American commiffioners refted in my hands, and all that were officially written went from my office; and fo far from congrefs knowing any thing of the figning the treaty, at the time they rejected the Britifh offers, they had not received a line of information from their commiffioners at Paris on any fubject whatever for upwards of a twelve-month. Probably the lofs of the port of Philadelphia and the navigation of the Delaware, together with the danger of the feas, covered at this time with Britifh cruifers, contributed to the difappointment.

One packet, it is true, arrived at York-town in January preceding, which was about three months before the arrival of the treaty; but, ftrange as it may appear, every letter had been taken out, before it was put on board the veffel which brought it from France, and blank white paper put in their ftead.

Having thus ftated the time when the propofals from the Britifh commiffioners were firft received, and likewife the time when the treaty of alliance arrived, and fhewn that the rejection of the former was eleven days prior to the arrival of the latter, and without the leaft knowledge of fuch circumftance have taken place or being about

to take place; the rejection, therefore, muſt, and ought to be attributed to the fixt unvaried ſentiments of America reſpecting the enemy
ſhe is at war with, and her determination to ſupport her independence
to the laſt public effort, and not to any new circumſtance in her favour, which at that time ſhe did not and could not know of.

Beſides, there is a vigour of determination and ſpirit of defiance in
the language of the rejection (which I here ſubjoin), which derive
their greateſt glory by appearing before the treaty was known ; for
that, which is bravery in diſtreſs becomes inſult in proſperity: And
the treaty placed America on ſuch a ſtrong foundation, that had ſhe
then known it, the anſwer which ſhe gave, would have appeared rather as an air of triumph, than as the glowing ſerenity of fortitude.

Upon the whole, the Abbe appears to have entirely miſtaken the
matter; for inſtead of attributing the rejection of the propoſitions to
our knowledge of the treaty of alliance; he ſhould have attributed the
origin of them in the Britiſh cabinet, to *their knowledge* of that event.
And then the reaſon why they were hurried over to America in the
ſtate of bills, that is, before they were paſſed into acts, is eaſily accounted for, which is, that they might have the chance of reaching
America before any knowledge of the treaty ſhould arrive, which they
were lucky enough to do, and there met the fate they ſo richly merited.
That theſe bills were brought into the Britiſh parliament after the
treaty with France was ſigned, is proved from the dates: The treaty
being on the 6th, and the bills the 17th of February. And that the
ſigning the treaty was known in parliament, when the bills were
brought in, is likewiſe proved by a ſpeech of Mr. Charles Fox, on
the ſaid 17th of February, who, in reply to lord North, informed the
houſe of the treaty being ſigned, and challenged the miniſter's knowledge of the ſame fact.*

* *In* CONGRESS, *April 22d,* 1788.
" *The committee to whom was referred the general's letter of the* 18*th,*
containing a certain printed paper ſent from Philadelphia, purporting to be the
draught of a bill for declaring the intentions *of the parliament of Great-*
Britain, as to the exerciſe *of what they are pleaſed to term their right of*
impoſing taxes within theſe United States ; and alſo the draught of a bill
to enable the king of Great-Britain to appoint commiſſioners, with powers
to treat, conſult and agree upon the means of quieting certain diſorders within
the ſaid ſtates, beg leave to obſerve.
" *That the ſaid paper being induſtriouſly circulated by emiſſaries of the*

Though I am not furprifed to fee the Abbe miftaken in matters
of hiftory, acted at fo great a diftance from his fphere of immediate obfervation, yet I am more than furprifed to find him wrong

*enemy, in a partial and fecret manner, the fame ought to be forthwith printed
for the public information.*

"*The committee cannot afcertain whether the contents of the faid paper
have been framed in Philadelphia, or in Great-Britain, much lefs whether
the fame are really and truly intended to be brought into the parliament of
that kingdom, or whether the faid parliament will confer thereon the ufual
folemnities of their laws. But are inclined to believe this will happen, for
the following reafons :*

"*1ft. Becaufe their general hath made divers feeble efforts to fet on
foot fome kind of treaty during the laft winter, though, either from a miftaken idea of his own dignity and importance, the want of information,
or fome other caufe, he hath not made application to thofe who are invefted
with a proper authority.*

"*2dly. Becaufe they fuppofe that the fallacious idea of a ceffation of
hoftilities will render thefe ftates remifs in their preparations for war.*

"*3dly. Becaufe believing the Americans wearied with war, they fuppofe
we will accede to their terms for the fake of peace.*

"*4thly. Becaufe they fuppofe that our negociations may be fubject to a like
corrupt influence with their debates.*

"*5thly. Becaufe they expect from this ftep the fame effects they did from
what one of their minifters thought proper to call his conciliatory motion,
viz. that it will prevent foreign powers from giving aid to thefe ftates ;
that it will lead their own fubjects to continue a little longer the prefent war ;
and that it will detach fome weak men in America from the caufe of freedom and virtue.*

"*6thly. Becaufe their king, from his own fhewing, hath reafon to
apprehend that his fleets and armies, inftead of being employed againft the
territories of thefe ftates, will be neceffary for the defence of his own dominions. And,*

"*7thly. Becaufe the impracticability of fubjugating this country being
every day more and more manifeft, it is their intereft to extricate themfelves
from the war upon any terms.*

"*The committee beg leave further to obferve, that, upon a fuppofition
the matters contained in the faid paper will really go into the Britifh ftatute books, they ferve to fhew, in a clear point of view, the weaknefs and
wickednefs of the enemy.*

(or at least what appears fo to me) in the well-enlightened field of philofophical reflection. Here the materials are his own ; created by himfelf ; and the error therefore, is an act of the mind.

" Their weaknefs.

" 1ft. *Becaufe they formerly declared, not only that they had a right to bind the inhabitants of thefe ftates in all cafes whatfoever, but alfo that the faid inhabitants fhould* abfolutely *and* unconditionally *fubmit to the exercife of that right. And this fubmiffion they have endeavoured to exact by the fword. Receding from this claim, therefore, under the prefent circumftances, fhews their inability to enforce it.*

" 2dly. *Becaufe their prince hath heretofore rejected the humbleft petitions of the reprefentatives of America, praying to be confidered as fubjects, and protected in the enjoyment of peace, liberty and fafety ; and hath waged a moft cruel war againft them, and employed the favages to butcher innocent women and children. But now the fame prince pretends to treat with thofe very reprefentatives, and grant to the* arms *of America what he refufed to her* prayers.

" 3dly. *Becaufe they have uniformly laboured to conquer this continent, rejecting every idea of accommodation propofed to them, from a confidence in their . . n ftrength. Wherefore it is evident, from the change in their mode of attack, that they have loft this confidence. And,*

" 4thly. *Becaufe the conftant language, fpoken not only by their minifters, but by the moft public and authentic acts of the nation, hath been, that it is incompatible with their dignity to treat with the Americans while they have arms in their hands. Notwithftanding which, an offer is now about to be made for treaty.*

" *The wickednefs and infincerity of the enemy appear from the following confiderations :*

" 1ft. *Either the* bills *now to be paffed contain a direct or indirect ceffion of a part of their former claims, or they do not. If they do, then it is acknowledged that they have facrificed many brave men in an unjuft quarrel. If they do not, then they are calculated to deceive America into terms, to which neither argument before the war, nor force fince, could procure her affent.*

" 2dly. *The firft of thefe* bills *appears, from the title, to be a declaration of the intentions of the Britifh parliament concerning the exercife of the right of impofing taxes within thefe ftates. Wherefore, fhould thefe ftates treat under the faid bill, they would indirectly acknowledge that right, to obtain which acknowledgment the prefent war hath been avowedly undertaken and profecuted on the part of Great-Britain.*

Hitherto my remarks have been confined to circumstances ; the order in which they arose, and the events they produced. In

" 3*dly*. *Should such pretended right be so acquiesced in, then, of consequence, the same might be exercised whenever the British parliament should find themselves in a different temper and disposition ; since it must depend upon those, and such like contingencies, how far men will act according to their former* intentions.

" 4*thly*. *The said first bill, in the body thereof, containeth no new matter, but is precisely the same with the motion before-mentioned, and liable to all the objections which lay against the said motion, excepting the following particular, viz.* that by the motion actual taxation was to be suspended, so long as America should give as much as the said parliament might think proper : *Whereas*, by the proposed bill, it is to be suspended, as long as future parliaments continue of the same mind with the present.

" 5*thly*. *From the second bill it appears, that the British king may, if he pleases, appoint commissioners to* treat and agree *with those, whom they please, about a variety of things therein mentioned.* But such treaties and agreements are to be of no validity without the concurrence of the said parliament, except so far as they relate to the suspension of hostilities, and of certain of their acts, the granting of pardons, and the appointing of governors to these sovereign, free and independent states. Wherefore the said parliament have reserved to themselves, in express words, the power of setting aside any such treaty, and taking the advantage of any circumstances which may arise to subject this continent to their usurpations.

" 6*thly*. *The said bill, by holding forth a tender of pardon, implies a criminality in our justifiable resistance, and consequently, to treat under it would be an implied acknowledgment, that the inhabitants of these states were, what Britain has declared them to be,* Rebels.

" 7*thly*. *The inhabitants of these states being claimed by them as subjects. they may infer, from the nature of the negociation now pretended to be set on foot, that the said inhabitants would of right be afterwards bound by such laws as they should make. Wherefore any agreement entered into on such negociation might at any future time be repealed. And*,

" 8*thly*. *Because the said bill purports, that the commissioners therein mentioned may treat with private individuals ; a measure highly derogatory to the dignity of national character.*

" *From all which it appears evident to your committee, that the said bills are intended to operate upon the hopes and fears of the good people of these states, so as to create divisions among them, and a defection from the* thefe, my information being better than the Abbe's, my tafk was eafy. How I may fucceed in controverting matters of fentiment and

common caufe, now by the bleffing of Div'ne Providence drawing near to a favourable iffue. That they are the fequel of that infidious plan, which from the days of the flamp act down to .he prefent time, hath involved this country in contention and bloodfhed. And that, as in other cafes fo in this, although circumftances may force them at times to recede from their unjuf-tifiable claims, there can be no doubt but they will as heretofore, upon the firft favourable occafion, again difplay that luft of domination, which hath rent in twaih the mighty empire of Britain.

" *Upon the whole matter, the committee beg leave to report it as their opinion, that as the Americans united in this arduous conteft upon princi-ples of common intereft, for the defence of common rights and priveleges, which union hath been cemented by common calamities and by mutual good offices and affection, fo the great caufe for which they contend, and in which all mankind are interefted, muft derive its fuccefs from the continuance of that union. Wherefore any man or body of men, who fhould prefume to make any feparate or partial convention or agreement with commiffioners under the crown of Great-Britain, or any of them, ought to be confidered and treated as open and avowed enemies of the United States.*

" *And further your committee beg leave to report it as their opinion, that thefe United States cannot with propriety, hold any conference or treaty with any commiffioners on the part of Great-Britain, unlefs they fhall, as a preliminary thereto, either withdraw their fleets and armies, or elfe, in pofitive and exprefs terms, acknowledge the independence of the faid ftates.*

" *And inafmuch as it appears to be the defign of the enemies of thefe ftates to lull them into a fatal fecurity—to the end that they may act with becoming weight and importance, it is the opinion of your committee, that the feveral ftates be called upon to ufe the moft ftrenuous exertions to have their refpective quotas of continental troops in the field as foon as poffible, and that all the militia of the faid ftates be held in readinefs, to act as occa-fion may require.*"

The following is the anfwer of congrefs to the fecond application of the commiffioners :

" York-Town, June 6, 1778.

" SIR,

" *I have had the honour of laying your letter of the 3d inftant, with the acts of the Britifh parliament which came inclofed, before congrefs ;*

*pinion, with one whom years, experience, and long establihed reputation have placed in a superior line, I am lefs confident in ; but as they fall within the fcope of my obfervations it would be improper to pafs them over.

From this part of the Abbe's work to the latter end, I find feveral expreffions, which appear to me to ftart, with a cynical complexion, from the path of liberal thinking, or at leaft they are fo involved as to lofe many of the beauties which diftinguifh other parts of the performance.

The Abbe having brought his work to the period when the treaty of alliance between France and the United States commenced, proceeds to make fome remarks thereon.

" In fhort," fays he, " philofophy' whofe firft fentiment is the defire " to fee all governments juft and all people happy, in cafting her eyes " upon this alliance of a monarchy, with a people, who are defend- " ing their liberty, *is curious to know its motive. She fees, at once,* " *too clearly, that the happinefs of mankind has no part in it.*"

Whatever train of thinking or of temper the Abbe might be in, when he penned this expreffion, matters not. They will neither qualify the fentiment, nor add to its defect. If right, it needs no apology ; if wrong, it merits no excufe. It is fent into the world as an opinion of philofophy, and may be examined without regard to the author.

It feems to be a defect, connected with ingenuity, that it often

and I am inftructed to acquaint you, fir, that they have already expreffed their fentiments upon bills, not effentially different from thofe acts, in a publication of the 22d of April laft.

" *Be affured, fir, when the king of Great-Britain fhall be ferioufly difpofed to put an end to the unprovoked and cruel war waged againft thefe United States, congrefs will readily attend to fuch terms of peace, as may confift with the honour of independent nations, the intereft of their conftituents, and the facred regard they mean to pay to treaties. I have the honour to be, fir,*

Your moft obedient, and
moft humble fervant,
HENRY LAURENS,
Prefident of congrefs."

His Excellency
Sir Henry Clinton, K. B. Philadelphia.

employs itself more in matters of curiofity, than ufefulnefs. Man muft be the privy counfellor of fate, or fomething is not right. He muft know the fprings, the whys and wherefores of every thing, or he fits down unfatisfied. Whether this be a crime, or only a caprice of humanity, I am not enquiring into. I fhall take the paffage as I find it, and place my objections againft it.

It is not fo properly the *motives* which *produced* the alliance, as the *confequences* which are to be *produced from it*, that mark out the field of philofophical reflection. In the one we only penetrate into the barren cave of fecrecy, where little can be known, and every thing may be mifconceived; in the other, the mind is prefented with a wide extended profpect of vegetative good, and fees a thoufand bleffings budding into exiftence.

But the expreffion, even within the compafs of the Abbe's meaning, fets out with an error, becaufe it is made to declare that, which no man has authority to declare. Who can fay that the happinefs of mankind made *no part of the motives* which produced the alliance? To be able to declare this, a man muft be poffeffed of the mind of all the parties concerned, and know that their motives were fomething elfe.

In proportion as the independence of America became contemplated and underftood, the local advantages of it to the immediate actors, and the numerous benefits it promifed to mankind, appeared to be every day increafing; and we faw not a temporary good for the prefent race only, but a continued good to all pofterity; thefe motives, therefore, added to thofe which preceded them, became the motives on the part of America, which led her to propofe and agree to the treaty of alliance, as the beft effectual method of extending and fecuring happinefs; and therefore, with refpect to us, the Abbe is wrong.

France, on the other hand, was fituated very differently to America. She was not acted upon by neceffity to feek a friend, and therefore her motive in becoming one, has the ftrongeft evidence of being good, and that which is fo, muft have fome happinefs for its object. With regard to herfelf, fhe faw a train of conveniences worthy her attention. By leffening the power of an enemy, whom at the fame time, fhe fought neither to deftroy nor diftrefs, fhe gained an advantage without doing an evil, and created to herfelf a new friend by affociating with a country in misfortune. The fprings of thought that lead to actions of this kind, however political they may be, are neverthelefs naturally beneficent ; for in all caufes, good or bad, it is neceffary there fhould be a fitnefs in the mind, to enable it to act in character with the object : Therefore as a bad caufe cannot be profecuted with a good motive, fo nether can a good caufe be long fupported by a bad one ; and as no man acts without a motive, therefore in the prefent inftance, as they cannot be bad, they muft be admitted to be good. But the Abbe fets out upon fuch an extended fcale, that he overlooks the degrees by which it is meafured, and rejects the beginning of good, becaufe the end comes not out at once.

It is true that bad motives may in fome degree be brought to fupport a good caufe or profecute a good object ; but it never continues long, which is not the cafe with France ; for either the object will reform the mind, or the mind corrupt the object, or elfe not being able, either way, to get into unifon, they will feparate in difguft : And this natural, though unperceived progrefs of affociation or contention between the mind and the object, is the fecret caufe of fidelity or defection. Every object a man purfues, is, for the time, a kind of miftrefs to his mind : if both are good or bad, the union is natural ; but if they are in reverfe, and neither can feduce nor yet reform the other, the oppofition grows into diflike and a feparation follows.

When the caufe of America firft made her appearance on the ftage of the univerfe, there were many, who, in the ftyle of adventurers and fortune-hunters, were dangling in her train, and making their court to her with every profeffion of honour and attachment. They were loud in her praife and oftentatious in her fervice. Every place echoed with their ardour or their anger, and they feemed like men in love. But, alas! they were fortune-hunters. Their expectations were excited, but their minds were unimpreffed ; and finding her not to their purpofe, nor themfelves reformed by her influence, they ceafed their fuit, and in fome inftances deferted and betrayed her.

There were others, who at firft beheld her with indifference, and unacquainted with her character were cautious of her company. They treated her as one, who, under the fair name of Liberty, might conceal the hideous figure of Anarchy, or the gloomy monfter of Tyranny. They knew not what fhe was. If fair, fhe was fair indeed. But ftill fhe was fufpected, and though born among us appeared to be a ftranger.

Accident with fome, and curiofity with others, brought on a diftant acquaintance. They ventured to look at her. They felt an inclination to fpeak to her. One intimacy led to another, till the fufpicion wore away and a change of fentiment ftole gradually upon the mind ; and having no felf-intereft to ferve, no paffion of difhonour to gratify, they became enamoured of her innocence, and unaltered by misfortune or uninfluenced by fuccefs, fhared with fidelity in the varieties of her fate.

This declaration of the Abbe's refpecting motives, has led me, unintendedly, into a train of metaphyfical reafoning ; but there was no other avenue by which it could fo properly be approached. To place prefumption againft prefumption, affertion againft affertion, is a mode of oppofition that has no effect ; and therefore the more eligible method was to fhew, that the declaration does not correfpond with the natural progrefs of the mind, and the influence it has upon our conduct.—I fhall now quit this part and proceed to what I have before ftated, namely, that it is not fo properly the motives which produced the alliance, as the confequences to be produced from it, that mark out the field of philofophical reflection.

It is an obfervation I have already made in fome former publications, that the circle of civilization is yet incomplete. A mutuality of wants have formed the individuals of each country into a kind of national fociety, and here the progrefs of civilization has ftopt. For it is eafy to fee, that nations with regard to each other (notwith-ftanding the ideal civil law, which every one explains as it fuits him) are like individuals in a ftate of nature. They are regulated by no fixt principle, governed by no compulfive law, and each does inde-pendently what it pleafes or what it can.

Were it poffible we could have known the world when in a ftate of barbarifm, we might have concluded that it never could be brought into the order we now fee it. The untamed mind was then as hard, if not harder, to work upon in its individual ftate, than the national mind is in its prefent one. Yet we have feen the accomplifhment of the one, why then fhould we doubt that of the other ?

There is a greater fitnefs in mankind to extend and complete the civilization of nations with each other at this day, than there was to begin it with the unconnected individuals at firft ; in the fame manner that it is fomewhat eafier to put together the materials of a machine after they are formed, than it was to form them from original matter. The prefent condition of the world differing fo exceedingly from what it formerly was, has given a new caft to the mind of man, more than what he appears to be fenfible of. The wants of the individual which firft produced the idea of fociety, are now augmented into the wants of the nation, and he is obliged to feek from another country what before he fought from the next perfon.

Letters, the tongue of the world, have in fome meafure brought all mankind acquainted, and by an extenfion of their ufes are every day promoting fome new friendfhip. Through them diftant nations become capable of converfation, and lofing by degrees the awkward-nefs of ftrangers, and the morofenefs of fufpicion, they learn to know and underftand each other. Science, the partifan of no country, but the beneficent patronefs of all, has liberally opened a temple where all may meet. Her influence on the mind, like the fun on the chilled earth, has long been preparing it for higher cultivation and further improvement. The philofopher of one country fees not an enemy in the philofopher of another: He takes his feat in the temple of fcience, and afks not who fits befide him.

This was not the condition of the barbarian world. Then the wants of man were few and the objects within his reach. While he could acquire thefe, he lived in a ftate of individual independence; the confequence of which was, there were as many nations as perfons, each contending with the other, to fecure fomething which he had, or to obtain fomething which he had not. The world had then no bufinefs to follow, no ftudies to exercife the mind. Their time was divided between floth and fatigue. Hunting and war were their chief occupations; fleep and food their principal enjoyments.

Now it is otherwife. A change in the mode of life has made it neceffary to be bufy; and man finds a thoufand things to do now which before he did not. Inftead of placing his ideas of greatnefs in the rude atchievements of the favage, he ftudies arts, fciences, agri-culture and commerce, the refinements of the gentleman, the princi-ples of fociety, and the knowledge of the philofopher.

There are many things which in themfelves are neither morally good nor bad, but they are productive of confequences, which are ftrongly marked with one or other of thefe characters. Thus com-merce, though in itfelf a moral nullity, has had a confiderable influ-ence in tempering the human mind. It was the want of objects in the ancient world, which occafioned in them fuch a rude and perpetual turn for war. Their time hung on their hands without the means of employment. The indolence they lived in afforded leifure for mif-chief, and being all idle at once, and equal in their circumftances, they were eafily provoked or induced to action.

But the introduction of commerce furnished the world with objects, which, in their extent, reach every man and give him something to think about and something to do ; by these his attention is mechanically drawn from the pursuits, which a state of indolence and an unemployed mind occasioned, and he trades with the same countries, which former ages, tempted by their productions, and too indolent to purchase them, would have gone to war with.

Thus, as I have already observed, the condition of the world being materially changed by the influence of science and commerce, it is put into a fitness not only to admit of, but to defire, an extenfion of civilization. The principal and almost only remaining enemy, it now has to encounter, is *prejudice*; for it is evidently the intereft of mankind to agree and make the beft of life. The world has undergone its divifions of empire, the feveral boundaries of which are known and fettled. The idea of conquering countries, like the Greeks and Romans, does not now exift : and experience has exploded the notion of going to war for the fake of profit. In fhort, the objects for war are exceedingly diminifhed, and there is now left fcarcely any thing to quarrel about, but what arifes from that demon of fociety, prejudice, and the confequent fullennefs and nutractablenefs of the temper.

There is fomething exceedingly curious in the conftitution and operation of prejudice. It has the fingular ability of accommodating itfelf to all the poffible varieties of the human mind. Some paffions and vices are but thinly fcattered among mankind, and find only here and there a fitnefs of reception. But prejudice, like the fpider, makes every where its home. It has neither tafte nor choice of place, and all that it requires is room. There is fcarcely a fituation, except fire or water, in which a fpider will not live. So, let the mind be as naked as the walls of an empty and forfaken tenement, gloomy as a dungeon, or ornamented with the richeft abilities of thinking, let it be hot, cold, dark, or light, lonely or inhabited, ftill prejudice, if undifturbed, will fill it with cobwebs, and live, like the fpider, where there feems nothing to live on. If the one prepares her food by poifoning it to her palate and her ufe, the other does the fame ; and as feveral of our paffions are ftrongly charactered by the animal world, prejudice may be denominated the fpider of the mind.

Perhaps no two events ever united fo intimately and forcibly to combat and expel prejudice, as the revolution of America and the alliance with France. Their effects are felt, and their influence already extends as well to the old world as the new. Our ftyle and manner of thinking have undergone a revolution, more extraordinary than the political revolution of the country. We fee with other eyes; we hear with other ears; and think with other thoughts, than thofe we formerly ufed. We can look back on our own prejudices, as if they had been the prejudices of other people. We now fee and know they were prejudices and nothing elfe; and relieved from their fhackles enjoy a freedom of mind, we felt not before. It was not all the argument, however powerful, nor all the reafoning, however elegant, that could have produced this change, fo neceffary to the ex-tenfion of the mind, and the cordiality of the world, without the two circumftances of the revolution and the alliance.

Had America dropt quietly from Britain, no material change, in fentiment, had taken place. The fame notions, prejudices, and con-ceits, would have governed in both countries, as governed them before, and ftill the flaves of error and education, they would have travelled on in the beaten track of vulgar and habitual thinking. But brought about by the means it has been, both with regard to ourfelves, to France, and England, every corner of the mind is fwept of its cob-webs, poifon, and duft, and made fit for the reception of generous hap-pinefs.

Perhaps there never was an alliance on a broader bafis, than that between America and France, and the progrefs of it is worth attend-ing to. The countries had been enemies, not properly of themfelves, but through the medium of England. They, originally, had no quarrel with each other, nor any caufe for one, but what arofe from the intereft of England and her arming America againft France. At the fame time, the Americans at a diftance from, and unacquainted with the world, and tutored in all the prejudices which governed thofe who governed them, conceived it their duty to act as they were taught. In doing this, they expended their fubftance, to make con-quefts, not for themfelves but for their mafters, who in return treated them as flaves.

A long fucceffion of infolent feverity, and the feparation finally occafioned by the commencement of hoftilities at Lexington, on the 19th of April, 1775, naturally produced a new difpofition of think-ing. As the mind clofed itfelf towards England, it opened itfelf tow-ards the world, and our prejudices like our oppreffions underwent, though lefs obferved, a mental examination; until we found the for-mer as inconfiftent with reafon and benevolence, as the latter were repugnant to our civil and political rights.

While we were thus advancing by degrees into the wide field of extended humanity, the alliance with France was concluded. An alliance not formed for the mere purpofe of a day, but on juft and generous grounds, and with equal and mutual advantages; and the eafy affectio.... manner in which the parties have fince communicated, has made it an alliance not of courts only but of countries. There is now an union of mind as well as of intereft; and our hearts as well as our profperity call on us to fupport it.

The people of England not having experienced this change, had likewife no idea of it. They were hugging to their bofoms the fame prejudices we were trampling beneath our feet; and they expected to keep a hold upon America, by that narrownefs of thinking, which America difdained. What they were proud of, we defpifed; and this is a principal caufe why all their negociations, conftructed on this ground, have failed. We are now really another people, and cannot again go back to ignorance and prejudice. The mind once enlightened cannot again become dark. There is no poffibility, neither is there any term to exprefs the fuppofition by, of the mind, unknowing any thing it already knows; and therefore all attempts on the part of England, fitted to the former habit of America, and on the expectation of their applying now, will be like perfuading a feeing man to become blind, and a fenfible one to turn an ideot. The firft of which is unnatural, and the other impoffible.

As to the remark which the Abbe makes on the one country being a monarchy and the other a republic, it can have no effential meaning. Forms of government have nothing to do with treaties. The former are the internal police of the countries feverally; the latter, their external police jointly: and fo long as each performs its part, we have no more right or bufinefs to know how the one or the other conducts its domeftic affairs, than we have to enquire into the private concerns of a family.

But had the Abbe reflected for a moment, he would have feen, that courts or the governing powers of all countries, be their forms what they may, are relatively republics with each other. It is the firft and true principle of alliancing. Antiquity may have given precedence, and power will naturally create importance, but their equal right is never difputed. It may likewife be worthy of remarking, that a monarchical country can fuffer nothing in its popular happinefs by allyingwith a republican one; and republican governments have never been deftroyed by their external connections, but by fome internal convulfion or contrivance. France has been in alliance with the republic of Swifferland for more than two hundred years, and ftill Swifferland retains her original form as entire as if fhe had been allied with a republic like herfelf; therefore this remark of the Abbe goes to nothing. Befides it is beft mankind fhould mix. There is ever fomething to learn·either of manners or principle; and it is by a free communication, without regard to domeftic matters, that friendfhip is to be extended, and prejudice deftroyed all over the world.

But notwithftanding the Abbe's high profeffions in favour of liberty, he appears fometimes to forget himfelf, or that his theory is rather the child of his fancy than of his judgment: For in almoft the fame inftant that he cenfures the alliance as not originally or fufficiently calculated for the happinefs of mankind, he, by a figure of implication, accufes France for having acted fo generoufly and unrefervedly in concluding it. "Why did they (fays he, meaning the "court of France) tie themfelves down by an inconfiderate treaty to "conditions with the Congrefs, which they might themfelves have "held in dependence by ample and regular fupplies."

When an author undertakes to treat of public happinefs, he ought to be certain that he does not miftake paffion for right, nor imagination for principle. Principle, like truth, needs no contrivance. It will ever tell its own tale, and tell it the fame way. But where this is not the cafe, every page muft be watched, recollected, and compared, like an invented ftory.

I am furprifed at this paffage of the Abbe. It means nothing or it means ill; and in any cafe it fhews the great difference between fpeculative and practical knowledge. A treaty according to the Abbe's language would have neither duration nor affection; it might have lafted to the end of the war, and then expired with it. But France, by acting in a ftyle fuperior to the little politics of narrow thinking, has eftablifhed a generous fame and won the love of a country fhe was before a ftranger to. She had to treat with a people who thought as nature taught them; and, on her own part, fhe wifely faw, there was no prefent advantage to be obtained by unequal terms, which could balance the more lafting ones that might flow from a kind and generous beginning.

From this part the Abbe advances into the fecret tranfactions of the two cabinets of Verfailles and Madrid refpecting the independence of America; through which I mean not to follow him. It is a circumftance fufficiently ftriking without being commented on, that the former union of America with Britain produced a power, which in her hands, was becoming dangerous to the world : And there is no improbability in suppofing, that had the latter known as much of the ftrength of the former, before fhe began the quarrel as fhe has known fince, that inftead of attempting to reduce her to unconditional fubmiffion, fhe would have propofed to her the conqueft of Mexico. But from the countries feparately, Spain has nothing to apprehend, though from their union fhe had more to fear than any other power in Europe,

The part which I fhall more particularly confine myfelf to, is that wherein the Abbe takes an opportunity of complimenting the Britifh miniftry with high encomiums of admiration, on their rejecting the offered mediation of the court of Madrid, in 1779.

It muft be remembered that before Spain joined France in the war, fhe undertook the office of a mediator and made propofals to the Britifh king and miniftry fo exceedingly favourable to their intereft, that had they been accepted, would have become inconvenient, if not inadmiffible, to America. Thefe propofals were neverthelefs rejected by the Britifh cabinet ; on which the Abbe fays,—

" It is in fuch a circumftance as this; it is in the time when noble
" pride elevates the foul fuperior to all terror ; when nothing is feen
" more dreadful than the fhame of receiving the law, and when there
" is no doubt or hefitation which to choofe, between ruin and dif-
" honour; it is then, that the greatnefs of a nation is difplayed. I
" acknowledge however that men, accuftomed to judge of things by
" the event, call great and perilous refolutions, heroifm or madnefs,
" according to the good or bad fuccefs with which they have been
" attended. If then, I fhould be afked, what is the name which
" fhall in years to come be given to the firmnefs, which was in this mo-
" ment exhibited by the Englifh, I fhall anfwer that I do not know.
" But that which it deferves I know. I know that the annals of the
" world hold out to us but rarely, the auguft and majeftic fpectacle of
" a nation, which choofes rather to renounce its duration than its
" glory."

In this paragraph the conception is lofty and the expreffion elegant, but the colouring is too high for the original, and the likenefs falls through an excefs of graces. To fit the powers of thinking and the turn of language to the fubject, fo as to bring out a clear conclufion that fhall hit the point in queftion and nothing elfe, is the true criterion of writing. But the greater part of the Abbe's writings (if he will pardon me the remark) appear to me uncentral and burdened with variety. They reprefent a beautiful wildernefs without paths; in which the eye is diverted by every thing, without being particularly directed to any thing ; and in which it is agreeable to be loft, and difficult to find the way out.

Before I offer any other remark on the fpirit and compofition of the above paffage, I fhall compare it with the circumftance it alludes to. The circumftance then does not deferve the encomium. The rejection was not prompted by her fortitude but her vanity. She did not view it as a cafe of defpair or even of extreme danger, and confequently the determination to renounce her duration rather than her glory, cannot apply to the condition of her mind. She had then high expectations of fubjugating America, and had no other naval force againft her than France; neither was fhe certain that rejecting the mediation of Spain would combine that power with France. New mediations might arife more favourable than thofe fhe had refufed. But if they fhould not, and Spain fhould join, fhe ftill faw that it would only bring out her naval force againft France and Spain, which was not wanted and could not be employed againft America, and habits of thinking had taught her to believe herfelf fuperior to both.

But in any cafe to which the confequence might point, there was nothing to imprefs her with the idea of renouncing her duration. It is not the policy of Europe to fuffer the extinction of any power, but only to lop off or prevent its dangerous encreafe. She was likewife freed by fituation from the internal and immediate horrors of invafion; was rolling in diffipation and looking for conquefts; and though fhe fuffered nothing but the expence of war, fhe ftill had a greedy eye to magnificent reimburfement.

But if the Abbe is delighted with high and ftriking fingularities of character, he might, in America, have found ample field for encomium. Here was a people, who could not know what part the world would take for, or againft them; and who were venturing on an untried fcheme, in oppofition to a power, againft which more formidable nations had failed. They had every thing to learn but the principles which fupported them, and every thing to procure that was neceffary for their defence. They have at times feen themfelves as low as diftrefs could make them, without fhewing the leaft ftagger in their fortitude ; and been raifed again by the moft unexpected events, without difcovering an unmanly difcompofure of joy. To hefitate or to defpair are conditions equally unknown in America. Her mind was prepared for every thing; becaufe her original and final re-folution of fucceeding or perifhing included all poffible circumftances.

The rejection of the Britifh propofitions in the year 1778, circum-ftanced as America was at that time, is a far greater inftance of un-fhaken fortitude than the refufal of the Spanifh mediation by the court of London: And other hiftorians, befides the Abbe, ftruck with the vaftnefs of her conduct therein, have, like himfelf, attributed it to a circumftance, which was then unknown, the alliance with France. Their error fhews their idea of its greatnefs; becaufe, in order to ac-count for it, they have fought a caufe fuited to its magnitude, with-out knowing that the caufe exifted in the principles of the country.*

But this paffionate encomium of the Abbe is defervedly fubject to moral and philofophical objections. It is the effufion of wild think-ing, and has a tendency to prevent that humanity of reflection which the criminal conduct of Britain enjoins on her as a duty.—It is a laudanum to courtly iniquity.—It keeps in intoxicated fleep the confcience of a nation; and more mifchief is effected by wrapping up guilt in fplendid excufe, than by directly patronizing it.

Britain is now the only country which holds the world in difturb-ance and war; and inftead of paying compliments to the excefs of her crimes, the Abbe would have appeared much more in character, had he put to her, or to her monarch, this ferious queftion—

Are there not miferies enough in the world, too difficult to be encountered and too pointed to be borne, without ftudying to enlarge the lift and arming it with new deftruction? Is life fo very long that it is neceffary, nay even a duty, to fhake the fand and haften out the period of duration? Is the path fo elegantly fmooth, fo decked

---

* Extract from "A fhort Review of the prefent Reign," in England. Page 45, in the new Annual Regifter, for the year 1780.

"The commiffioners, who, in confequence of lord North's conciliatory bills, went over to America, to propofe terms of peace to the colonies, were wholly unfuccefsful. The conceffions which formerly would have been received with the utmoft gratitude, were rejected with difdain. Now was the time of American pride and haughtinefs. It is proba-ble, however, that it was not pride and haughtinefs alone that dictated the refolutions of congrefs, but a diftruft of the fincerity of the offers of Britain, a determination not to give up their independence, and, above all, the engagements into which they had entered by their late treaty with France."

on every fide and carpeted with joys, that wretchednefs is wanted to enrich it as a foil? Go afk thine aching heart, when forrow from a thoufand caufes wounds it, go afk thy fickened felf, when every medicine fails, whether this be the cafe or not?

Quitting my remarks on this head, I proceed to another, in which the Abbe has let loofe a vein of ill nature, and, what is ftill worfe, of injuftice.

After cavilling at the treaty, he goes on to characterize the feveral parties combined in the war. " Is it poffible," fays the Abbe, " that a ftrict union fhould long fubfift amongft confederates of cha-
" racters fo oppofite as the hafty, light, difdainful Frenchman, the
" jealous, haughty, fly, flow, circumfpective Spaniard, and the Ame-
" rican, who is fecretly fnatching looks at the mother country, and
" would rejoice, were they compatible with his independence, at the
" difafters of his allies?"

To draw foolifh portraits of each other, is a mode of attack and reprifal, which the greater part of mankind are fond of indulging. The ferious philofopher fhould be above it, more efpecially in cafes from which no poffible good can arife, and mifchief may, and where no received provocation can palliate the offence.—The Abbe might have invented a difference of character for every country in the world, and they in return might find others for him, till in the war of wit all real character is loft. The pleafantry of one nation or the gravity of another may, by a little pencilling, be diftorted into whimfical features, and the painter become as much laughed at as the painting.

But why did not the Abbe look a little deeper and bring forth the excellencies of the feveral parties?—Why did he not dwell with pleafure on that greatnefs of character, that fuperiority of heart, which has marked the conduct of France in her conquefts, and which has forced an acknowledgment even from Britain?

There is one line, at leaft (and many others might be difcovered) in which the confederates unite; which is, that of a rival eminence in their treatment of their enemies. Spain in her conqueft of Minorca and the Bahama-Iflands, confirms this remark. America has been invariable in her lenity from the beginning of the war, notwithftanding the high provocations fhe has experienced. It is England only who has been infolent and cruel.

But why muft America be charged with a crime undeferved by her conduct, more fo by her principles, and which, if a fact, would be fatal to her honour. I mean the want of attachment to her allies,

or rejoicing in their difasters. She, it is true, has been affiduous in
shewing to the world that she was not the aggressor towards England,
and that the quarrel was not of her seeking, or, at that time, even of
her wishing. But to draw inferences from her candour, and even
from her justification, to stab her character by (and I see nothing
else from which they can be supposed to be drawn) is unkind and unjust.

Does her rejection of the British propositions in 1778, before she
knew of any alliance with France, correspond with the Abbe's description of her mind ? Does a single instance of her conduct since
that time justify it ?—But there is a still better evidence to apply to,
which is, that of all the mails, which, at different times, have been way-
laid on the road, in divers parts of America, and taken and carried into
New-York, and from which the most secret and confidential private letters, as well as those from authority, have been published, not one of
them, I repeat it, not a single one of them, gave countenance to such
charge.

This is not a country where men are under government restraint in
speaking ; and if there is any kind of restraint, it arises from a fear
of popular resentment. Now, if nothing in her private or public
correspondence favours such a suggestion, and if the general disposition of the country is such as to make it unsafe for a man to show an
appearance of joy at any disaster to her ally, on what grounds, I ask,
can the accusation stand ? What company the Abbe may have kept
in France, we cannot know ; but this we know, that the account
he gives does not apply to America.

Had the Abbe been in America at the time the news arrived of
the disaster of the fleet under count de Grasse in the West-Indies,
he would have seen his vast mistake. Neither do I remember any
instance, except the loss of Charleston, in which the public mind
suffered more severe and pungent concern, or underwent more agita-
tions of hope and apprehension as to the truth or falshood of the report. Had the loss been all our own, it could not have had a deeper
effect, yet it was not one of these cases which reached to the independence of America.

In the geographical account which the Abbe gives of the thirteen
states, he is so exceedingly erroneous, that to attempt a particular
refutation would exceed the limits I have prescribed to myself.
And as it is a matter neither political, historical, nor sentimental,
and which can always be contradicted by the extent and natural circumstances of the country, I shall pass it over ; with this additional

remark, that I never yet faw an European defcription of America that was true, neither can any perfon gain a juft idea of it, but by coming to it.

Though I have already extended this letter beyond what I at firft propofed, I am, neverthelefs, obliged to omit many obfervations, I originally defigned to have made. I wifh there had been no occafion for making any. But the wrong ideas which the Abbe's work had a tendency to excite, and the prejudicial impreffions they might make, muft be an apology for my remarks, and the freedom with which they are done.

I obferve the Abbe has made a fort of epitome of a confiderable part of the pamphlet *Common Senfe*, and introduced it in that form into his publication. But there are other places where the Abbe has borrowed freely from the faid pamphlet without acknowledging it. The difference between fociety and government, with which the pamphlet opens, is taken from it, and in fome expreffions almoft lite-rally, into the Abbe's work as if originally his own ; and through the whole of the Abbe's remarks on this head, the idea in Common Senfe is fo clofely copied and purfued, that the difference is only in words, and in the arrangement of the thoughts, and not in the thoughts themfelves. *

* COMMON SENSE.	*ABBE RAYNAL.*
" *Some writers have fo con-founded fociety with government, as to leave little or no diftinction be-tween them ; whereas they are not only different, but have different ori-gins.*"	" *Care muft be taken not to con-found together fociety with govern-ment. That they may be known diftinctly, their origin fhould be con-fidered?*"
" *Society is produced by our wants and governments by our wickednefs ; the former promotes our happinefs pofitively ; by unit-ing our affections—the latter nega-tively, by reftraining our vices.*"	" *Society originates in the wants of men, government in their vices. Society tends always to good ; go-vernment ought always to tend to the repreffing of evil.*"

In the following paragraphs there is lefs likenefs in the language, but the ideas in the one are evidently copied from the other.

| " *In order to gain a clear and juft idea of the defign and end of go-vernment, let us fuppofe a fmall* | " *Man thrown, as it were, by chance upon the globe, furrounded by all the evils of nature, obliged* |

But as it is time I should come to the conclusion of my letter, I shall forbear all further observations on the Abbe's work, and take a concise view of the state of public affairs, since the time in which that performance was published.

number of persons, meeting in some sequestered part of the earth, unconnected with the rest ; they will then represent the peopling of any country or of the world. In this state of natural liberty, society will be their first thought. A thousand motives will excite them thereto. The strength of one man is so unequal to his wants, and his mind so unfitted for perpetual solitude, that he is soon obliged to seek assistance of another, who, in his turn, requires the same. Four or five united would be able to raise a tolerable dwelling in the midst of a wilderness ; but one man might labour out the common period of life, without accomplishing any thing ; when he had felled his timber, he could not remove it, nor erect it after it was removed ; hunger, in the mean time would urge him from his work, and every different want call him a different way. Disease, nay even misfortune, would be death ; for though neither might be immediately mortal, yet either of them would disable him from living, and reduce him to a state in which he might rather be said to perish than to die.— Thus necessity, like a gravitating power, would form our newly arrived emigrants into society, the reciprocal blessings of which, would supersede and render the obligations of

continually to defend and protect his life against the storms and tempests of the air, against the inundations of water, against the fire of volcanoes, against the intemperance of frigid and torrid zones, against the sterility of the earth which refuses him aliment, or its baneful fecundity, which makes poison spring up beneath his feet ; in short against the claws and teeth of savage beasts, who dispute with him his habitation and his prey, and, attacking his person, seem resolved to render themselves rulers of this globe, of which he thinks himself to be the master : Man, in this state, alone and abandoned to himself, could do nothing for his preservation. It was necessary, therefore, that he should unite himself, and associate with his like, in order to bring together their strength and intelligence in common stock. It is by this union that he has triumphed over so many evils, that he has fashioned this globe to his use, restrained the rivers, subjugated the seas, insured his subsistence, conquered a part of the animals in obliging them to serve him, and driven others far from his empire, to the depths of deserts or of woods, where their number diminishes from age to age.—What a man alone would not have been able to effect, men have executed in con-

A mind habited to actions of meannefs and injuftice, commits them without reflection, or with a very partial one; for on what other ground than this, can we account for the declaration of war againft the Dutch. To gain an idea of the politics which actuated the Britifh miniftry to this meafure, we muft enter into the opinion which they, and the Englifh in general, had formed of the temper of the Dutch nation; and from thence infer what their expectation of the confequences would be.

Could they have imagined that Holland would have ferioufly made a common caufe with France, Spain, and America, the Britifh miniftry would never have dared to provoke them. It would have been a madnefs in politics to have done fo; unlefs their views were to haften on a period of fuch emphatic diftrefs, as fhould juftify the conceffions which they faw they muft one day or other make to the world, and for which they wanted an apology to themfefves.—There is a temper in fome men which feeks a pretence for fubmiffion. Like a fhip difabled in action, and unfitted to continue it, it waits the approach of a ftill larger one to ftrike to, and feels relief at the opportunity. Whether this is greatnefs or littlenefs of mind, I am not enquiring into. I fhould fuppofe it to be the latter, becaufe it proceeds from the want of knowing how to bear misfortune in its original ftate.

But the fubfequent conduct of the Britifh cabinet has fhewn that this was not their plan of politics, and confequently their motives muft be fought for in another line.

law and government unneceffary, while they remained perfectly juft to each other. But as nothing but heaven is impregnable to vice, it will unavoidably happen, that in proportion as they furmount the firft difficulties of emigration, which bound them together in a common caufe, they will begin to relax in their duty and attachment to each other, and this remiffnefs will point out the neceffity of eftablifhing fome form of government to fupply the defect of moral virtue."

cert; and altogether they preferve their work. Such is the origin, fuch the advantages, and the end of fociety.—Government owes its birth to the neceffity of preventing and repreffing the injuries which the affociated individuals had to fear from one another. It is the centinel who watches, in order that the common labourers be not difturbed."

The truth is, that the British had formed a very humble opinion of the Dutch nation. They looked on them as a people who would submit to any thing; that they might insult them as they liked, plunder them as they pleafed, and still the Dutch dared not to be provoked.

If this be taken as the opinion of the British cabinet, the meafure is eafily accounted for; becaufe it goes on the fuppofition, that when, by a declaration of hoftilities, they had robbed the Dutch of fome millions fterling (and to rob them was popular) they could make peace with them again whenever they pleafed, and on almoft any terms the British minifry fhould propofe. And no fooner was the plundering committed, than the accommodation was fet on foot, and failed.

When once the mind lofes the fenfe of its own dignity, it lofes, likewife, the ability of judging of it in another. And the American war has thrown Britain into fuch a variety of abfurd fituations, that, arguing from herfelf, fhe fees not in what conduct national dignity confifts in other countries. From Holland fhe expected duplicity and fubmiffion, and this miftake arofe from her having acted, in a number of inftances during the prefent war, the fame character her-felf.

To be allied to, or connected with Britain, feems to be an unfafe and impolitic fituation. Holland and America are inftances of the reality of this remark. Make thofe countries the allies of France or Spain, and Britain will court them with civility, and treat them with refpect; make them her own allies, and fhe will infult and plunder them. In the firft cafe, fhe feels fome apprehenfions at offending them, becaufe they have fupport at hand; in the latter, thofe appre-henfions do not exift. Such, however, has hitherto been her con-duct.

Another meafure which has taken place fince the publication of the Abbe's work, and likewife fince the time of my beginning this letter, is the change in the British miniftry. What line the new ca-binet will purfue refpecting America, is at this time unknown; nei-ther is it very material, unlefs they are ferioufly difpofed to a general and honourable peace.

Repeated experience has fhewn, not only the impracticability of conquering America, but the ftill higher impoffibility of conquering her mind, or recalling her back to her former condition of thinking. Since the commencement of the war, which is now approaching to eight years, thoufands and tens of thoufands have advanced, and are daily advancing into the firft ftage of manhood, who know nothing of Britain but as a barbarous enemy, and to whom the independence of America appears as much the natural and eftablifhed government of the country, as that of England does to an Englifhman. And on the other hand, thoufands of the aged, who had Britifh ideas, have dropped, and are daily dropping, from the ftage of bufinefs and life. The natural progrefs of generation and decay operates every hour to the difadvantage of Britain. Time and death, hard enemies to contend with, fight conftantly againft her intereft; and the bills of mortality, in every part of America, are the thermometers of her decline. The children in the ftreets are from their cradle bred to confider her as their only foe. Tney hear of her cruelties; of their fathers, uncles, and kindred killed; they fee the remains of burnt and deftroyed houfes, and the common tradition of the fchool they go to, tells them, *thofe things were done by the Britifh.*

Thefe are circumftances which the mere Englifh ftate politician, who confiders man only in a ftate of manhood, does not attend to. He gets entangled with parties coeval or equal with himfelf at home, and thinks not how faft he rifing generation in America is growing beyond his knowledge of them, or they of him. In a few years all perfonal remembrance will be loft, and who is king or minifter in England, will be little known and fcarcely enquired after.

The new Britifh adminiftration is compofed of perfons who have ever been againft the war, and who have conftantly reprobated all the violent meafures of the former one. They confidered the American war as deftructive to themfelves, and oppofed it on that ground. But what are thefe things to America? She has nothing to do with Englifh parties. The ins and the outs are nothing to her. It is the whole country fhe is at war with, or muft be at peace with.

Were every minifter in England a *Chatham*, it would now weigh little or nothing in the fcale of American politics. Death has preferved to the memory of this ftatefman. *that fame,* which he, by living, would have loft. His plans and opinions, towards the latter part of his life, would have been attended with as many evil confequences, and as much reprobated here, as thofe of Lord North; and, confidering him a wife man, they abound with inconfiftencies amounting to abfurdities.

It has apparently been the fault of many in the late minority, to fuppofe, that America would agree to certain terms with them, were

they in place, which fhe would not ever liften to from the then adminiftration. This idea can anfwer 'no other purpofe than to prolong the war; and Britain may, at the expence of many more millions, learn the fatality of fuch miftakes. If the new miniftry wifely
avoid this hopelefs policy, they will prove themfelves better pilots,
and wifer men, than they are conceived to be; for it is every day expected to fee their bark ftrike upon fome hidden rock and go to
pieces.

But there is a line in which they may be great. A more brilliant
opening needs not to prefent itfelf; and it is fuch a one, as true magnanimity would improve, and humanity rejoice in.

A total reformation is wanted in England. She wants an expanded mind,—an heart which embraces the univerfe. Inftead of
fhutting herfelf up in an ifland, and quarrelling with the world, fhe
would derive more lafting happinefs, and acquire more real riches,
by generoufly mixing with it, and bravely faying, I am the enemy
of none. It is not now a time for little contrivances or artful politics. The European world is too experienced to be impofed upon,
and America too wife to be duped. It muft be fomething new and
mafterly that muft fucceed. The idea of feducing America from her
independence, or corrupting her from her alliance, is a thought too
little for a great mind, and impoffible for any honeft one, to attempt.
Whenever politics are applied to debauch mankind from their inte-
grity, and diffolve the virtues of human nature, they become deteftable; and to be a ftatefman upon this plan, is to be a commiffioned
villain. He who aims at it, leaves a vacancy in his character, which
may be filled up with the worft of epithets.

If the difpofition of England fhould be fuch, as not to agree to a
general and honourable peace, and that the war muft, at all events,
continue longer, I cannot help wifhing, that the alliances which America has or may enter into, may become the only objects of the war.
She wants an opportunity of fhewing to the world, that fhe holds her
honour as dear and facred as her independence, and that fhe will in no
fituation forfake thofe, whom no negociations could induce to forfake
her. Peace, to every reflective mind, is a defirable object ; but *that
peace* which is accompanied with a ruined character, becomes a crime to
the feducer, and a curfe upon the feduced.

But where is the impoffibility or even the great difficulty of England forming a friendfhip with France and Spain, and making it a
national virtue to renounce for ever. thofe prejudiced inveteracies it

has been her cuftom to cherifh; and which, while they ferve to fink her with an encreafing enormity of debt, by involving her in fruitlefs wars, become likewife the bane of her repofe, and the deftruction of her manners. We had once the fetters that fhe has now, but experience has fhewn us the miftake, and thinking juftly has fet us right.

The true idea of a great nation is that which extends and promotes the principles of univerfal fociety. Whofe mind rifes above the atmofpheres of local thoughts, and confiders mankind, of whatever nation or profeffion they may be, as the work of one Creator. The rage for conqueft has had its fafhion, and its day. Why may not the amiable virtues have the fame? The Alexanders and Cæfars of antiquity have left behind them their monuments of deftruction, and are remembered with hatred; while thefe more exalted characters, who firft taught fociety and fcience, are bleft with the gratitude of every age and country. Of more ufe was *one* philofopher, though a heathen, to the world, than all the heathen conquerors that ever exifted.

Should the prefent revolution be diftinguifhed by opening a new fyftem of extended civilization, it will receive from Heaven the higheft evidence of approbation; and as this is a fubject to which the Abbe's powers are fo eminently fuited, I recommend it to his attention, with the affection of a friend, and the ardour of a univerfal citizen.

POSTSCRIPT.

Since clofing the foregoing letter, fome intimations refpecting a general peace have made their way to America. On what authority or foundation they ftand, or how near or remote fuch an event may be, are circumftances I am not enquiring into. But as the fubject muft fooner or later become a matter of ferious attention, it may not be improper, even at this early period, candidly to inveftigate fome points that are connected with it, or lead towards it.

The independence of America is at this moment as firmly eftablifhed as that of any other country in a ftate of war. It is not length of time, but power that gives ftability. Nations at war know nothing of each other on the fcore of antiquity. It is their prefent and immediate ftrength, together with their connexions, that muft fupport them. To which we may add, that a right which originated to-day, is as much a right, as if it had the sanction of a thousand years; and therefore the independence and present governments of America are in no more danger of being subverted, because they are modern, than that of England is secure, because it is ancient.

The politics of Britain, so far as they respected America, were originally conceived in idiotism, and acted in madness. There is not a step which bears the smallest trace of rationality. In her management of the war, she has laboured to be wretched, and studied to be hated; and in all her former propositions for accommodation, she has discovered a total ignorance of mankind, and of those natural and unalterable sensations, by which they are so generally governed. How she may conduct herself in the present or future business of negociating a peace, is yet to be proved.

He is a weak politician who does not understand human nature, and penetrate into the effect which measures of government will have upon the mind. All the miscarriages of Britain have arisen from this defect. The former ministry acted as if they supposed mankind, to be *without a mind;* and the present ministry, as if America was *without a memory.* The one must have supposed we were incapable of feeling; and the other, that we could not remember injuries.

There is likewise another line in which politicians mistake, which is that of not rightly calculating, or rather of misjudging, the consequence which any given circumstance will produce. Nothing is more frequent, as well in common as in political life, than to hear people complain, that such or such means produced an event directly contrary to their intentions. But the fault lies in their not judging rightly what the event would be; for the means produced only its proper and natural consequences.

It is very probable that in a treaty of peace, Britain will contend for some port or other in North-America, perhaps Canada or Halifax, or both: And I infer this from the known deficiency of her politics, which have ever yet made use of means, whose natural event was against both her interest and her expectation. But the question with her ought to be, whether it is worth her while to hold them, and what will be the consequence.

Respecting Canada, one or other of the two following will take place, viz. If Canada should people, it will revolt; and if it do not people, it will not be worth the expence of holding. And the same may be said of Halifax, and the country round it. But Canada *never will* people; neither is there any occasion for contrivances on one side of the other, for nature alone will do the whole.

Britain may put herself to great expences in sending settlers to Canada: but the descendants of those settlers will be Americans, as other descendants have been before them. They will look round and see the neighbouring states sovereign and free, respected abroad and trading at large with the world; and the natural love of liberty, the advantages of commerce, the blessings of independence, and of a happier climate, and a richer soil, will draw them southward; and the effect will be, that Britain will sustain the expence, and America reap the advantage.

One would think that the experience which Britain has had of America, would entirely sicken her of all thoughts of continental colonization, and any part which she might retain, will only become to her a field of jealousy and thorns; of debate and contention, for ever struggling for privileges, and meditating revolt. She may form new settlements, but they will be for us; they will become part of the United States of America; and that against all her contrivances to prevent it, or without any endeavours of ours to promote it. In the first place she cannot draw from them a revenue, until they are able to pay one, and when they are so, they will be above subjection. Men soon become attached to the soil they live upon, and incorporated with the prosperity of the place: and it signifies but little what opinions they come over with; for time, interest, and new connexions will render them obsolete, and the next generation know nothing of them.

Were Britain truly wise, she would lay hold of the present opportunity to disentangle herself from all continental embarrassments in North-America; and that not only to avoid future broils and troubles, but to save expences. To speak explicitly on the matter, I would not, were I an European power, have Canada, under the condition that Britain must retain it, could it be given to me. It is one of those kind of dominions that is, and ever will be, a constant charge upon any foreign holder.

As to Halifax, it will become useless to England after the present war, and the loss of the United States. A harbour, when the dominion is gone, for the purpose of which only it was wanted, can be attended only with expence. There are, I doubt not, thousands of people in England, who suppose, that these places are a profit to the nation; whereas they are directly the contrary, and instead of producing any revenue, a considerable part of the revenue of England is annually drawn off; to support the expence of holding them.

Gibraltar is another inftance of national ill-policy. A poft which in time of peace is not wanted, and in time of war is of no ufe, muft at all times be ufelefs. Inftead of affording protection to a navy, it requires the aid of one to maintain it. To fuppofe that Gibraltar commands the Mediterranean, or the pafs into it, or the trade of it, is to fuppofe a detected falfehood; becaufe though Britain holds the poft, fhe has loft the other three, and every benefit fhe expected from it. And to fay that all this happens becaufe it is befieged by land and water, is to fay nothing, for this will always be the cafe in time of war, while France and Spain keep up fuperior fleets, and Britain holds the place. So that, though, as an impenetrable inacceffible rock, it may be held by the one, it is always in the power of the other to render it ufelefs and exceffively chargeable.

I fhould fuppofe that one of the principal objects of Spain in befieging it, is to fhow to Britain, that though fhe may not take it, fhe can command it, that is fhe can fhut it up, and prevent its being ufed as a harbour, though not a garrifon.—But the fhort way to reduce Gibraltar is to attack the Britifh fleet; for Gibraltar is as dependent on a fleet for fupport, as a bird is on its wing for food, and when wounded there it ftarves.

There is another circumftance which the people of England have not only not attended to, but feem to be utterly ignorant of, and that is, the difference between permanent power and accidental power, confidered in a national fenfe.

By permanent power, I mean, a natural, inherent and perpetual ability in a nation, which though always in being, may not be always in action, or not always advantageoufly directed; and by accidental power, I mean, a fortunate or accidental difpofition or exercife of national ftrength, in whole or in part.

There undoubtedly was a time when any one European nation, with only eight or ten fhips of war, equal to the prefent fhips of the line, could have carried terror to all others, who had not began to build a navy, however great their natural ability might be for that purpofe: But this can be confidered only as accidental, and not as a ftandard to compare permanent power by, and could laft no longer than until thofe powers built as many or more fhips than the former. After this a larger fleet was neceffary, in order to be fuperior; and a ftill larger would again fuperfede it. And thus mankind have gone on building fleet upon fleet, as occafion or fituation dictated. And this reduces it to an original queftion, which is: Which power can build and man the largeſt number of ſhips? The natural anſwer to which, is, that power which has the largeſt revenue and the greateſt number of inhabitants, provided its ſituation of coaſt affords ſufficient conveniences.

France being a nation on the continent of Europe, and Britain an iſland in its neighbourhood, each of them derived different ideas from their different ſituations. The inhabitants of Britain could carry on no foreign trade, nor ſtir from the ſpot they dwelt upon, without the aſſiſtance of ſhipping; but this was not the caſe with France. The idea therefore of a navy did not ariſe to France from the ſame original and immediate neceſſity which produced it to England. But the queſtion is, that when both of them turn their attention, and employ their revenues the ſame way, which can be ſuperior?

The annual revenue of France is nearly double that of England, and her number of inhabitants more than twice as many. Each of them has the ſame length of coaſt on the channel, beſides which, France has ſeveral hundred miles extent on the Bay of Biſcay, and an opening on the Mediterranean: And every day proves that practice and exerciſe make ſailors as well as ſoldiers in one country as well as another.

If then Britain can maintain an hundred ſhips of the line, France can as well ſupport an hundred and fifty, becauſe her revenues and her population are as equal to the one, as thoſe of England are to the other. And the only reaſon why ſhe has not done it, is becauſe ſhe has not till very lately attended to it. But when ſhe ſees, as ſhe now ſees, that a navy is the firſt engine of power, ſhe can eaſily accompliſh it.

England very falſely, and ruinouſly for herſelf, infers, that becauſe ſhe had the advantage of France, while France had the ſmaller navy, that for that reaſon it is always to be ſo. Whereas it may be clearly ſeen, that the ſtrength of France has never yet been tried on a navy, and that ſhe is able to be as ſuperior to England in the extent of a navy, as ſhe is in the extent of her revenues and her population. And England may lament the day, when, by her inſolence and injuſtice, ſhe provoked in France a maritime diſpoſition.

It is in the power of the combined fleets to conquer every iſland in the Weſt-Indies, and reduce all the Britiſh navy in thoſe places. For were France and Spain to ſend their whole naval force in Europe to thoſe iſlands, it would not be in the power of Britain to follow them with an equal force. She would ſtill be twenty or thirty ships inferior, were she to send every vessel she had, and in the mean time all the foreign trade of England would lay exposed to the Dutch.

It is a maxim, which, I am perfuaded, will ever hold good, and more efpecially in naval operations, that a great power ought, never to move in detachments, if it can poffibly be avoided ; but to go with its whole force to fome important objeft, the reduftion of which fhall have a decifive effeft upon the war. Had the whole of the French and Spanifh fleets in Europe come laft fpring to the Weft-Indies, every ifland had been their own, Rodney their prifoner and his fleet their prize. From the United States the combined fleets can be fupplied with provifions, without the neceffity of drawing them from Europe, which is not the cafe with England.

Accident has thrown fome advantages in the way of England, which, from the inferiority of her navy, fhe had not a right to ex-pect. For though fhe has been obliged to fly before the combined fleets, yet Rodney has twice had the fortune to fall in with detached fquadrons, to which he was fuperior in numbers: The firft off Cape St. Vincent, where he had nearly two to one, and the other in the Weft-Indies, where he had a majority of fix fhips. Victories of this kind almoft produce themfelves. They are won without honour, and fuffered without difgrace : And are afcribable to the chance of meeting, nor to the fuperiority of fighting. For the fame admiral, under whom they were obtained, was unable, in three former en-gagements, to make the leaft impreffion on a fleet confifting of an equal number of fhips with his own, and compounded for the events by declining the actions.*

To conclude, if it may be faid that Britain has numerous enemies, it likewife proves that fhe has given numerous offences. Infolence is fure to provoke hatred, whether in a nation or an individual. The want of manners in the Britifh court may be feen even in its birth-days' and new-years' odes, which are calculated to infatuate the vulgar, and difguft the man of refinement : And her former overbearing rudenefs, and infufferable injuftice on the feas, have made every com-mercial nation her foe. Her fleets were employed as engines of prey; and acted on the furface of the deep the character which the fhark does beneath it.——On the other hand, the combined powers are

* See the accounts, either Englifh or French, of three actions, in the Weft-Indies, between count de Guichen and admiral Rodney, in 1780.

taking a popular part, and will render their reputation immortal, by eftablifhing the perfect freedom of the ocean, to which all countries have a right, and are interefted in accomplifhing. The fea is the world's highway ; and he who arrogates a prerogative over it, tranf-greffes the right, and juftly brings on himfelf the chaftifement of na-tions.

. Perhaps it might be of fome fervice to the future tranquillity of mankind, were an article introduced into the next general peace, that no one nation fhould, in time of peace, exceed a certain number of fhips of war. Something of this kind feems neceffary ; for ac-cording to the prefent fafhion, half the world will get upon the water, and there appears to be no end to the extent to which navies may be carried. Another reafon is, that navies add nothing to the manners or morals of a people. The fequeftered life which attends the fervice, prevents the opportunities of fociety, and is too apt to occafion a coarfenefs of ideas and of language, and that more in fhips of war than in commercial employ; becaufe in the latter they mix more with the world, and are nearer related to it. I mention this remark as a general one : and not applied to any one country more than to another.

Britain has now had the trial of above feven years, with an expence of nearly an hundred million pounds fterling ; and every month in which fhe delays to conclude a peace, cofts her another million fterling, over and above her ordinary expences of government, which are a million more ; fo that her total *monthly* expence is two million pounds fterling, which is equal to the whole *yearly* expence of America, all charges included. Judge then who is beft able to continue it.

She has likewife many atonements to make to an injured world, as well in one quarter as in another. And inftead of purfuing that temper of arrogance, which ferves only to fink her in the efteem, and entail on her the diflike, of all nations, fhe would do well to reform her manners, retrench her expences, live peaceably with her neigh-bours. and think of war no more.

Philadelphia, Auguft 21, 1782.

DISSERTATIONS

ON

GOVERNMENT,

THE

AFFAIRS OF THE BANK,

AND

PAPER-MONEY.

P R E F A C E.

I HERE prefent the Public with a new performance. Some
parts of it are more particularly adapted to the ftate of Pennfylvania,
on the prefent ftate of its affairs : But there are others which are on
a larger fcale. The time beftowed on this work has not been long,
the whole of it being written and printed during the fhort recefs of
the affembly.

As to parties, merely confidered as fuch, I am attached to no
particular one. There are fuch things as right and wrong in the
world, and fo far as thefe are parties againft each other, the fignature
of Common Sense is properly employed.

THOMAS PAINE.

Philadelphia, Feb. 18, 1786.

DISSERTATIONS

On Government, the Affairs of the Bank, &c.

EVERY Government, let its form be what it may, contains within itfelf a principle common to all, which is, that of a fovereign power, or a power over which there is no control, and which controls all others: And as it is impoffible to conftruct a form of government in which this power does not exift, fo there muft of neceffity be a place, if it may be fo called, for it to exift in.

In Defpotic Monarchies this power is lodged in a fingle perfon, or fovereign. His will is law; which he declares, alters, or revokes as he pleafes, without being accountable to any power for fo doing. Therefore, the only modes of redrefs, in countries fo governed, are by petition or infurrection. And this is the reafon we fo frequently hear of infurrections in defpotic governments ; for as there are but two modes of redrefs, this is one of them.

Perhaps it may be faid that as the united refiftance of the people is able, by force, to control the will of the fovereign, that, therefore, the controlling power lodges in them : but it muft be underftood that I am fpeaking of fuch powers only as are conftituent parts of the government, not of thofe powers which are externally applied to refift and overturn it.

In Republics, fuch as thofe eftablifhed in America, the fovereign power, or the power over which there is no control and which controls all others, remains where nature placed it ; in the people ; for the people in America are the fountain of power. It remains there as a matter of right, recognized in the conftitutions of the country, and the exercife of it is conftitutional and legal.——This fovereignty is exercifed in electing and deputing a certain number of perfons to reprefent and act for the whole, and who, if they do not act right, may be difplaced by the fame power that placed them there, and others elected and deputed in their ftead, and the wrong meafures of former reprefentatives corrected and brought right by this means. Therefore the republican form and principle leaves no room for infurrection, becaufe it provides and eftablifhes a rightful means in its ftead.

In countries under a defpotic form of government, the exercife of this power is an affumption of fovereignty; a wrefting it from the perfon in whofe hand their form of government has placed it, and the exercife of it is there ftyled rebellion. Therefore the defpotic form of government knows no intermediate fpace between being flaves and being rebels.

1 fhall in this place offer an obfervation which, though not immediately connected with my fubject, is very naturally deduced from it, which is, That the nature, if I may fo call it, of a government over any people may be afcertained from the modes which the people purfue to obtain redrefs; for like caufes will produce like effects. And therefore the government which Britain attempted to erect over America could be no other than a defpotifm, becaufe it left to the Americans no other modes of redrefs than thofe which are left to people under defpotic governments, petition and refiftance: And the Americans, without ever attending to a comparifon on the cafe, went into the fame fteps which fuch people go into, becaufe no other could be purfued: And this fimilarity of effects leads up to, and afcertains, the fimilarity of the caufes or governments which produced them.

But to return.——The repofitory where the fovereign power is placed is the firft criterion of diftinction between a country under a defpotic form of government and a free country. In a country under a defpotic government, the fovereign is the only free man in it. ——In a republic, the people retaining the fovereignty themfelves, naturally and neceffarily retain freedom with it: For, wherever the fovereignty is, there muft the freedom be; the one cannot be in one place and the other in another.

As the repofitory where the fovereign power is lodged is the firft criterion of diftinction; the fecond is the principles on which it is adminiftered.

A defpotic government knows no principle but will. Whatever the fovereign wills to do, the government admits him the inherent right, and the uncontrolled power of doing. He is reftrained by no fixed rule of right and wrong, for he makes the right and wrong himfelf and as he pleafes.—If he happens (for a miracle may happen) to be a man of confummate wifdom, juftice and moderation, of a mild affectionate difpofition, difpofed to bufinefs, and underftanding and promoting the general good, all the beneficial purpofes of government will be anfwered under his adminiftration, and the people fo governed may, while this is the cafe, be profperous and eafy. But as there can be no fecurity that this difpofition will laft, and this adminiftration continue, and ftill lefs fecurity that his fucceffor fhall have the fame qualities and purfue the fame meafures; therefore no people exercifing their reafon and underftanding their rights, would, of their own choice, inveft any one man with fuch a power.

Neither is it confiftent to fuppofe the knowledge of any one man competent to the exercife of fuch a power. A Sovereign of this fort, is brought up in fuch a diftant line of life, and lives fo remote from the people, and from a knowledge of every thing which relates to their local fituations and interefts, that he can know nothing from experience and obfervation, and all which he does know he muft be told. Sovereign power without fovereign knowledge, that is, a full knowledge of all the matters over which that power is to be exercifed, is a fomething which contradicts itfelf.

There is a fpecies of fovereign power in a fingle perfon, which is very proper when applied to a commander in chief over an army, fo far as relates to the military government of an army, and the condition and purpofe of an army conftitute the reafon why it is fo.

In an army every man is of the fame profeffion, that is, he is a foldier, and the commander in chief is a foldier too: therefore the knowledge neceffary to the exercife of the power is within himfelf. By underftanding what a foldier is, he comprehends the local fituation, intereft and duty of every man within, what may be called, the dominion of his command; and therefore the condition and circumftances of an army make a fitnefs for the exercife of the power.

The purpofe likewife, or object of an army, is another reafon: for this power in a commander in chief, though exercifed over the army, is not exercifed againft it; but is exercifed through or over the army againft the enemy. Therefore the enemy, and not the people, is the object it is directed to. Neither is it exercifed over an army, for the purpofe of raifing a revenue from it, but to promote its combined intereft, condenfe its powers, and give it capacity for action.

But all thefe reafons ceafe when fovereign power is transferred from the commander of an army to the commander of a nation, and entirely lofes its fitnefs when applied to govern fubjects following occupations, as it governs foldiers following arms. A nation is quite another element, and every thing in it differs not only from each other, but all of them differ from thofe of an army. A nation is compofed of diftinct unconnected individuals, following various trades, employments and purfuits : continually meeting, croffing, uniting, oppofing and feparating from each other as accident, intereft and circumftance fhall direct.—An army has but one occupation and but one intereft.

Another very material matter in which an army and a nation differ, is that of temper. An army may be faid to have but one temper ; for, however the *natural* temper of the perfons compofing the army may differ from each other, there is a fecond temper takes place of the firft : a temper formed by difcipline, mutuality of habits, union of objects and purfuits, and the ftyle of military manners: but this can never be the cafe among all the individuals of a nation. Therefore the fitnefs, arifing from thofe circumftances, which difpofes an army to the command of a fingle perfon, and the fitnefs of a fingle perfon to that command, is not to be found either in one or the other, when we come to confider them as a fovereign and a nation.

Having already fhewn what a defpotic government is, and how it is adminiftered, I now come to fhew what the adminiftration of a republic is.

The adminiftration of a republic is fuppofed to be directed by certain fundamental principles of right and juftice, from which there cannot, becaufe there ought not to, be any deviation ; and whenever any deviation appears, there is a kind of ftepping out of the republican principle, and an approach towards the defpotic one. This adminiftration is executed by a felect number of perfons, periodically chofen by the people, and act as reprefentatives and in behalf of the whole, and who are fuppofed to enact the fame laws, and purfue the fame line of adminiftration, as the whole of the people would do were they affembled together.

The PUBLIC GOOD is to be their object. It is therefore neceffary to underftand what Public Good is.

Public Good is not a term oppofed to the good of individuals; on the contrary, it is the good of every individual collected. It is the good of all, becaufe it is the good of every one: for as the public body is every individual collected, so the public good is the collected good of those individuals.

The foundation-principle of Public Good is justice, and wherever justice is impartially administered the public good is promoted ; for as it is to the good of every man that no injustice be done to him, so likewise it is to his good that the principle which secures him should not be violated in the person of another, because such a violation weakens *his* security, and leaves to chance what ought to be to him a rock to stand on.

But in order to understand more minutely, how the Public Good is to be promoted, and the manner in which the representatives are to act to promote it, we must have recourse to the original or first principles, on which the people formed themselves into a republic.

. When a people agree to form themselves into a republic (for the word REPUBLIC means the PUBLIC GOOD, or the good of the whole, in contradistinction to the despotic form, which makes the good of the sovereign, or of one man, the only object of the government) when, I say, they agree to do this, it is to be understood, that they mutually resolve and pledge themselves to each other, rich and poor alike, to support and maintain this rule of equal justice among them. They therefore renounce not only the despotic form, but the despotic principle, as well of governing as of being governed by mere Will and Power, and substitute in its place a government of justice.

By this mutual compact the citizens of a republic put it out of their power, that is, they renounce, as detestable, the power of exercising, at any future time, any species of despotism over each other, or doing a thing, not right in itself, because a majority of them may have strength of numbers sufficient to accomplish it.

In this pledge and compact* lies the foundation of the republic : and the security to the rich and the consolation to the poor is, that

---

* *This pledge and compact is contained in the Declaration of Rights prefixed to the constitution, and is as follows——*

I. That all men are born equally free and independent, and have certain natural, inherent and unalienable rights, amongst which are, the enjoying and defending life and liberty, acquiring, possessing and protecting property, and pursuing and obtaining happiness and safety.

II. That all men have a natural and unaliena'le right to worship Almighty God, according to the dictates of their own consciences and understanding: And that no man ought or of right can be compelled to attend what each man has is his own ; that no defpotic fovereign can take it from him, and that the common cementing principle which holds all the parts of a republic together, fecures him likewife from the defpotifm of numbers : For defpotifm may be more effectually acted by many over a few than by one man over all.

any religious worfhip, or erect or fupport any place of worfhip, or maintain any miniftry, contrary to, or againft, his own free will and confent : Nor can any man, who acknowledges the being of a God, be juftly deprived or abridged of any civil right as a citizen, on account of his religious fenti- ments or peculiar mode of religious worfhip : And that no authority can or ought to be vefted in, or affumed by any power whatever, that fhall in any cafe interfere with, or in any manner control, the right of confcience in the free exercife of religious worfhip.

III. That the people of this ftate have the fole, exclufive and inherent right of governing and regulating the internal police of the fame.

IV. That all power being originally inherent in, and confequently de- rived from, the people ; therefore all officers of government, whether legif- lative or executive, are their truftees and fervants, and at all times ac- countable to them.

V. That government is, or ought to be, inftituted for the common benefit, protection and fecurity of the people, nation or community ; and not for the particular emolument or advantage of any fingle man, family or fet of men, who are a part only of that community : and that the community hath an indubitable, unalienable and indefeafible right to reform, alter or abolifh government in fuch manner as fhall be by that community judged moft con- ducive to the public weal.

VI. That thofe who are employed in the legiflative and executive bufi- nefs of the ftate may be reftrained from oppreffion, the people have a right, at fuch periods as they may think proper, to reduce their public officers to a private ftation, and fupply the vacancies by certain and regular elections.

VII. That all elections ought to be free ; and that all free men having a fufficient evident common intereft with, and attachment to the community, have a right to elect officers, or to be elected into office.

VIII. That every member of fociety hath a right to be protected in the enjoyment of life, liberty and property, and therefore is bound to contribute his proportion towards the expence of that protection, and yield his perfonal fervice when neceffary, or an equivalent thereto : But no part of a man's property can be juftly taken from him, or applied to public ufes, without his own confent, or that of his legal reprefentatives : Nor can any man who

Therefore, in order to know how far the power of an assembly, or a house of representatives can act in administering the affairs of a republic, we must examine how far the power of the people extends under the original compact they have made with each other ; for the power of the representatives is in many cases less, but never can be greater than that of the people represented ; and whatever the

is conscientiously scrupulous of bearing arms, be justly compelled thereto, if he will pay such equivalent: Nor are the people bound by any laws, but such as they have in like manner assented to, for their common good.

IX. That in all prosecutions for criminal offences, a man hath a right to be heard by himself and his council, to demand the cause and nature of his accusation, to be confronted with the witnesses, to call for evidence in his favour, and a speedy public trial, by an impartial jury of the country, without the unanimous consent of which jury he cannot be found guilty : Nor can he be compelled to give evidence against himself : Nor can any man be justly deprived of his liberty, except by the laws of the land, or the judgment of his peers.

X. That the people have a right to hold themselves, their houses, papers, and possessions free from search or seizure; and therefore warrants without oaths or affirmations first made, affording a sufficient foundation for them, and whereby any officer or messenger may be commanded or required to search suspected places, or to seize any person or persons, his or their property, not particularly described, are contrary to that right, and ought not to be granted.

XI. That in controversies respecting property, and in suits between man and man, the parties have a right to trial by jury, which ought to be held sacred.

XII. That the people have a right to freedom of speech, and of writing, and publishing their sentiments ; therefore the freedom of the press ought not to be restrained.

XIII. That the people have a right to bear arms for the defence of themselves and the state; and as standing armies in the time of peace, are dangerous to liberty, they ought not to be kept up: And that the military should be kept under strict subordination to, and governed by, the civil power.

XIV. That a frequent recurrence to fundamental principles, and a firm adherence to justice, moderation, temperance, industry and frugality are absolutely necessary to preserve the blessings of liberty and keep a government free : The people ought therefore to pay particular attention to these points in the choice of officers and representatives, and have a right to exact people in their mutual original compact have renounced the power of doing towards, or acting over each other, the representatives cannot assume the power to do, because, as I have already said, the power of the representatives cannot be greater than that of the people they represent.

In this place it naturally presents itself that the people in their original compact of equal justice or first principles of a republic, renounced as despotic, detestable and unjust, the assuming a right of breaking and violating their engagements, contracts and compacts with, or defrauding, imposing or tyrannizing over, each other, and therefore the representatives cannot make an act to do it for them, and any such an act would be an attempt to depose, not the personal sovereign, but the sovereign principle of the republic, and to introduce despotism in its stead.

It may in this place be proper to distinguish between that species of sovereignty which is claimed and exercised by despotic monarchs, and that sovereignty which the citizens of a republic inherit and retain.——The sovereignty of a despotic monarch assumes the power of making wrong right, or right wrong, as he pleases or as it suits him. The sovereignty in a republic is exercised to keep right and wrong in their proper and distinct places, and never to suffer the one to usurp the place of the other. A republic, properly understood, is a sovereignty of justice, in contradistinction to a sovereignty of will.

Our experience in republicanism is yet so slender, that it is much to be doubted, whether all our public laws and acts are consistent with or can be justified on, the principles of a republican government.

We have been so much habited to act in committees at the commencement of the dispute, and during the interregnum of government, and in many cases since, and to adopt expedients warranted by

a due and constant regard to them, from their legislators and magistrates, in the making and executing such laws as are necessary for the good government of the state.

XV. That all men have a natural inherent right to emigrate from one state to another that will receive them, or to form a new state in vacant countries, or in such countries as they can purchase, whenever they think that thereby they may promote their own happiness.

XVI. That the people have a right to assemble together, to consult for their common good, to instruct their representatives, and to apply to the legislature for redress of grievances, by address, petition, or remonstrance.

neceffity, and to permit to ourfelves a difcretionary ufe of power,
fuited to the fpur and exigency of the moment, that a man transferred from a committee to a feat in the legiflature imperceptibly
takes with him the ideas and habits he has been accuftomed to, and
continues to think like a committee-man inftead of a legiflator, and
to govern by fpirit rather than by the rule of the conftitution and the
principles of the republic.

Having already ftated that the power of the reprefentatives can
never exceed the power of the people whom they reprefent, I now
proceed to examine more particularly, what the power of the reprefentatives is.

It is, in the firft place, the power of acting as legiflators in making laws—and in the fecond place, the power of acting in certain
cafes, as agents or negociators for the commonwealth, for fuch purpofes as the circumftances of the commonwealth require.

A very ftrange confufion of ideas, dangerous to the credit, ftability, and the good and honour of the commonwealth, has arifen, by
confounding thofe two diftinct powers and things together, and
blending every act of the affembly, of whatever kind it may be, under
one general name of " *Laws of the Commonwealth*," and thereby
creating an opinion (which is truly of the defpotic kind) that every
fucceeding affembly has an equal power over every tranfaction, as
well as law, done by a former affembly.

All laws are acts, but all acts are not laws. Many of the
acts of the affembly are acts of agency or negociation, that is,
they are acts of contract and agreement, on the part of the ftate,
with certain perfons therein mentioned, and for certain purpofes
therein recited. An act of this kind, after it has paffed the houfe,
is of the nature of a deed or contract, figned, fealed and delivered;
and fubject to the fame general laws and principles of juftice as all
other deeds and contracts are : For in a tranfaction of this kind,
the ftate ftands as an individual, and can be known in no other character in a court of juftice.

By " LAWS," as diftinct from the agency tranfactions, or matters of negociation, are to be comprehended all thofe public acts of
the affembly or commonwealth, which have a univerfal operation,
or apply themfelves to every individual of the commonwealth. Of
this kind are the laws for the diftribution and adminiftration of juftice, for the prefervation of the peace, for the fecurity of property,
for raifing the neceffary revenue by juft proportions, &c. &c.

Acts of this kind are properly LAWS, and they may be altered and amended or repealed, or others substituted in their places, as experience shall direct, for the better effecting the purpose for which they were intended : and the right and power of the assembly to do this, is derived from the right and power which the people, were they all assembled together, instead of being represented, would have to do the same thing : because, in acts or laws of this kind, there is no other party than the public. The law, or the alteration, or the repeal, is for themselves;—and whatever the effects may be, it falls on themselves ;—if for the better, they have the benefit of it—if for the worse, they suffer the inconvenience. No violence to any one is here offered——no breach of faith is here committed. It is therefore one of these rights and powers which is within the sense, meaning and limits of the original compact of justice which they formed with each other as the foundation-principle of the republic, and being one of those rights and powers, it devolves on their representatives by delegation.

As it is not my intention (neither is it within the limits assigned to this work) to define every species of what may be called LAWS (but rather to distinguish that part in which the representatives act as agents or negociators for the state, from the legislative part), I shall pass on to distinguish and describe those acts of the assembly which are acts of agency or negociation, and to shew that as they are different in their nature, construction and operation from legislative acts, so likewise the power and authority of the assembly over them, after they are passed, is different.

It must occur to every person on the first reflection, that the affairs and circumstances of a commonwealth require other business to be done besides that of making laws, and consequently, that the different kinds of business cannot all be classed under one name, or be subject to one and the same rule of treatment.——But to proceed——

By agency transactions, or matters of negociation, done by the assembly, are to be comprehended all that kind of public business, which the assembly, as representatives of the republic, transact in its behalf, with certain person or persons, or part or parts of the republic, for purposes mentioned in the act, and which the assembly confirm and ratify on the part of the commonwealth, by affixing to it the seal of the state.

An act of this kind, differs from a law of the before mentioned kind ; because here are two parties and there but one, and the parties are bound to perform different and diftinct parts : whereas, in the before mentioned law, every man's part was the fame.

These acts, therefore, though numbered among the laws, are evidently diftinct therefrom, and are not of the legiflative kind. The former are laws for the government of the commonwealth ; thefe are transactions of bufinefs, fuch as, felling and conveying an eftate belonging to the public, or buying one ; acts for borrowing money, and fixing with the lender the terms and mode of payment ; acts of agreement and contract, with certain perfon or perfons, for certain purpofes ; and, in fhort, every act in which two parties, the ftate being one, are particularly mentioned or defcribed, and in which the form and nature of a bargain or contract is comprehended. ——Thefe, if for cuftom and uniformity fake we call by the name of laws, they are not laws for the government of the commonwealth, but for the government of the contracting parties, as all deeds and contracts are ; and are not, properly fpeaking, acts of the affembly, but joint acts, or acts of the affembly in behalf of the commonwealth on one part, and certain perfons therein mentioned on the other part.

Acts of this kind are diftinguifhable into two claffes.——

Firft, thofe wherein the matters inferted in the act have already been fettled and adjufted between the ftate on one part, and the perfons therein mentioned on the other part.   In this cafe the act is the completion and ratification of the contract or matters therein recited. It is in fact a deed figned, fealed and delivered.

Secondly, thofe acts wherein the matters have not been already agreed upon, and wherein the act only holds forth certain propofitions and terms to be accepted of and acceded to.

I fhall give an inftance of each of thofe acts.   Firft—The ftate wants the loan of a fum of money—certain perfons make an offer to government to lend that fum, and fend in their propofals : the government accept thefe propofals and all the matters of the loan and the payment are agreed on ; and an act is paffed, according to the ufual form of paffing acts, ratifying and confirming this agreement. This act is final.

In the fecond cafe,—The ftate, as in the preceding one, wants a loan of money—the affembly paffes an act holding forth the terms on which it will borrow and pay: This act has no force, until the propofitions and terms are accepted of and acceded to by fome perfon or perfons, and when thofe terms are accepted of and complied with, the act is binding on the ftate.——But if at the meeting of the next affembly, or any other, the whole fum intended to be borrowed, fhould not be borrowed, that affembly may ftop where they are, and difcontinue proceeding with the loan, or make new propolitions and terms for the remainder ; but fo far as the fubfcriptions have been filled up, and the terms complied with, it is, as in the firft cafe, a figned deed : and in the fame manner are all acts, let the matters in them be what they may, wherein, as I have before mentioned, the ftate on one part, and certain individuals on the other part, are parties in the act.

If the ftate fhould become a bankrupt, the creditors, as in all cafes of bankruptcy, will be fufferers ; they will have but a dividend for the whole : but this is not a diffolution of the contract, but an accommodation of it, arifing from neceffity. And fo in all cafes of acts of this kind, if an inability takes place on either fide, the contract cannot be performed, and fome accommodation muft be gone into or the matter falls through of itfelf.

It may likewife happen, though it ought not to happen, that in performing the matters, agreeably to the terms of the act, inconveniences, unforefeen at the time of making the act, may arife to either or both parties : in this cafe, thofe inconveniences may be removed by the mutual confent and agreement of the parties, and each find its benefit in fo doing : For in a republic it is the harmony of its parts that conftitutes their feveral and mutual good.

But the acts themfelves are legally binding, as much as if they had been made between two private individuals. The greatnefs of one party cannot give it a fuperiority of advantage over the other. The ftate, or its reprefentatives, the affembly, has no more power over an act of this kind, after it is paffed, than if the ftate was a private perfon. It is the glory of a republic to have it fo, becaufe it fecures the individual from becoming the prey of power, and prevents MIGHT overcoming RIGHT.

If any difference or difpute arife afterwards between the ftate and the individuals with whom the agreement is made, refpecting the contract, or the meaning, or extent of any of the matters contained in the act, which may affect the property or intereft of either, fuch difference or difpute muft be judged of, and decided upon, by the laws of the land, in a court of juftice and trial by jury ; that is, by the laws of the land already in being at the time fuch act and contract was made.——No law made afterwards can apply to the cafe, either directly, or by conftruction or implication : For fuch a law would be a retrofpective law, or a law made after the fact, and cannot even be produced in court as applying to the cafe before it for judgment.

That this is juftice, that it is the true principle of republican government, no man will be fo hardy as to deny :—If, therefore, a lawful contract or agreement, fealed and ratified, cannot be affected or altered by any act made afterwards, how much more inconfiftent and irrational, defpotic and unjuft would it be, to think of making an act with the profeffed intention of breaking up a contract already figned and fealed.

That it is poffible an affembly, in the heat and indifcretion of party, and meditating on power rather than on the principle by which all power in a republican government is governed, that of equal juftice, may fail into the error of paffing fuch an act, is admitted ;—but it would be an actlefs act, an act that goes for nothing, an act which the courts of juftice, and the eftablifhed laws of the land, could know nothing of.

Becaufe fuch an act would be an act of one party only, not only, without, but againft the confent of the other ; and, therefore, cannot be produced to affect a contract made between the two.——That the violation of a contract fhould be fet up as a juftification to the violator, would be the fame thing as to fay, that a man by breaking his promife is freed from the obligation of it, or that by tranfgreffing the laws he exempts himfelf from the punifhment of them.

Befides the conftitutional and legal reafons why an affembly cannot, of its own act and authority, undo or make void a contract made between the ftate (by a former affembly) and certain individuals, may be added, what may be called, the natural reafons, or thofe reafons, which the plain rules of common fenfe point out to every man. Among which are the following :

The principals, or real parties, in the contract, are the ftate and the perfons contracted with. The affembly is not a party, but an agent in behalf of the ftate, authorized and empowered to tranfact its affairs.

Therefore it is the ftate that is bound on one part and certain individuals on the other part, and the performance of the contract, according to the conditions of it, devolves on fucceeding affemblies, not as principals, but as agents.

Therefore, for the next or any other affembly to undertake to diffolve the ftate from its obligation is an affumption of power of a novel and extraordinary kind—It is the servant attempting to free his master.

The election of new assemblies following each other makes no difference in the nature of the thing. The state is still the same state. —The public is still the same body. These do not annually expire though the time of an assembly does. These are not new-created every year, nor can they be displaced from their original standing ; but are a perpetual permanent body, always in being and still the same.

But if we adopt the vague inconsistent idea that every new assembly has a full and complete authority over every act done by the state in a former assembly, and confound together laws, contracts and every species of public business, it will lead us into a wilderness of endless confusion and unsurmountable difficulties. It would be de-claring an assembly despotic for the time being.——Instead of a government of established principles administered by established rules, the authority of government by being strained so high, would, by the same rule, be reduced proportionably as low, and would be no other than that of a committee of the state acting with discretionary powers for one year. Every new election would be a new revolution, or it would suppose the public of the former year dead and a new public risen in its place.

Having now endeavoured to fix a precise idea to, and distinguish between, legislative acts and acts of negociation and agency, I shall proceed to apply this distinction to the case now in dispute, respecting the charter of the bank.

The charter of the bank, or what is the same thing, the act for incorporating it, is to all intents and purposes an act of negociation and contract, entered into, and confirmed, between the state on one part, and certain persons mentioned therein on the other part. The purpose for which the act was done on the part of the state is therein recited, viz. the support which the finances of the country would derive therefrom. The incorporating clause is the condition or obligation on the part of the state ; and the obligation on the part of the bank, is, " that nothing contained in that act shall be construed to authorise the said corporation to exercise any powers in this state repugnant to the laws or constitution thereof."

Here are all the marks and evidences of a contract. The parties ——the purport——and the reciprocal obligations.

That it is a contract, or a joint act, is evident from its being in the

power of either of the parties to have forbidden or prevented its being
done. The ftate could not force the ftockholders of the bank to be
a corporation, and therefore as their confent was neceffary to the making the act, their diffent would have prevented its being made; fo on
the other hand, as the bank could not force the ftate to incorporate
them, the confent or diffent of the ftate would have had the fame effect to do, or to prevent its being done; and as neither of the parties
could make the act alone, for the fame reafon can neither of them diffolve it alone: But this is not the cafe with a law or act of legiflation,
and therefore the difference proves it to be an act of a different kind.

The bank may forfeit the charter by delinquency, but the delinquency muft be proved and eftablifhed by a legal procefs in a court
of juftice and trial by jury; for the ftate, or the affembly, is not to be
a judge in its own cafe, but muft come to the laws of the land for
judgment; for that which is law for the individual, is likewife law
for the ftate.

Before I enter farther into this affair, I fhall go back to the circumftances of the country and the condition the government was in,
for fome time before, as well as at the time it entered into this engagement with the bank, and this act of incorporation was paffed:
For the government of this ftate, and I fuppofe the fame of the reft,
were then in want of two of the moft effential matters which governments could be deftitute of.——Money and credit.

In looking back to thofe times, and bringing forward fome of
the circumftances attending them, I feel myfelf entering on unpleafant and difagreeable ground; becaufe fome of the matters which the
attack on the bank now make neceffary to ftate, in order to bring the
affair fully before the public, will not add honour to thofe who have
promoted that meafure, and carried it through the late houfe of affembly; and for whom, though my own judgment and opinion on
the cafe oblige me to differ from, I retain my efteem, and the focial
remembrance of times paft. But, I truft, thofe gentlemen will do
me the juftice to recollect my exceeding earneftnefs with them, laft
fpring, when the attack on the bank firft broke out; for it clearly
appeared to me one of thofe overheated meafures, which, neither the
country at large, nor their own conftituents, would juftify them in
when it came to be fully and clearly underftood: for however high a
party meafure may be carried in an affembly, the people out of doors
are all the while following their feveral occupations and employments,
minding their farms and their bufinefs, and take their own time and

Vol. I.   U u

leifure to judge of public meafures; the confequence of which is, that they often judge in a cooler fpirit than their reprefentatives act in.

It may be eafily recollected that the prefent bank was preceded by, and rofe out of, a former one, called the Pennfylvania bank, which began a few months before ; the occafion of which I fhall briefly ftate.

In the fpring 1780, the Pennfylvania affembly was compofed of many of the fame members, and nearly all of the fame connection, which compofed the late houfe that began the attack on the bank. I ferved as clerk of the affembly of 1780, which ftation I refigned at the end of the year and accompanied a much lamented friend, the late Colonel John Laurens, on an embaffy to France.

The fpring of 1780 was marked with an accumulation of misfor- tunes. The reliance placed on the defence of Charlefton failed and exceedingly lowered or rather depreffed the fpirits of the country. The meafures of government, from the want of money, means and credit, dragged on like a heavy loaded carriage without wheels, and were nearly got to what a countryman would underftand by a dead pull.

The affembly of that year met by adjournment at an unufual time, the tenth of May, and what particularly added to the affliction, was, that fo many of the members, inftead of fpiriting up their conftituents to the moft nervous exertions, came to the affembly furnifhed with petitions to be exempt from paying taxes. How the public meafures were to be carried on, the country defended, and the army recruited, clothed, fed, and paid, when the only refource, and that not half fuffi- cient, that of taxes, fhould be relaxed to almoft nothing, was a matter too gloomy to look at. A language very different from that of petitions ought at this time to have been the language of every one. A declaration to have ftood forth with their lives and fortunes, and a reprobation of every thought of partial indulgence would have founded much better than petitions.

While the affembly was fitting a letter from the commander in chief was received by the executive council and tranfmitted to the houfe. The doors were fhut and it fell officially to me to read.

In this letter the naked truth of things was unfolded. Among other informations the general faid, that notwithftanding his confi- dence in the attachment of the army to the caufe of the country, the diftreffes of it, from the want of every neceffary which men could be deftitute of, were arifen to fuch a pitch, that the appearance of mu-

.tiny and difcontent were fo ftrongly marked on the countenance of the army that he dreaded the event of every hour.

When the letter was read I obferved a defpairing filence in the houfe. No body fpoke for a confiderable time. At length a member of whofe fortitude to withftand misfortunes I had a high opinion, rofe : " If," faid he, " the account in that letter is a true ftate of " things, and we are in the fituation there reprefented, it appears to " me in vain to contend the matter any longer. We may as well " give up at firft as at laft."

The gentleman who fpoke next, was (to the beft of my recollection) a member from Bucks county, who, in a cheerful note, endeavoured to diffipate the gloom of the houfe——" Well, well, " faid he, " don't let " the houfe defpair, if things are not fo well as we wifh, we muft " endeavour to make them better." And on a motion for adjournment, the converfation went no farther.

There was now no time to lofe, and fomething abfolutely necef-fary to be done, which was not within the immediate power of the houfe to do ; for what with the depreciation of the currency, the flow operation of taxes, and the petitions to be exempt therefrom, the treafury was moneylefs, and the government creditlefs.

If the affembly could not give the affiftance which the neceffity of the cafe immediately required, it was very proper the matter fhould be known by thofe who either could or would endeavour to do it. To conceal the information within the houfe, and not provide the relief which that information required, was making no ufe of the knowledge and endangering the public caufe. The only thing that now remained, and was capable of reaching the cafe, was private credit, and the voluntary aid of individuals; and under this impreffion, on my return from the houfe, I drew out the falary due to me as clerk, inclofed five hundred dollars in a letter to a gentleman in this city, in part of the whole, and wrote fully to him on the fubject of our affairs.

The gentleman to whom this letter was addreffed is Mr. Blair M'Clenaghan. I mentioned to him, that notwithftanding the current opinion that the enemy were beaten from before Charlefton, there were too many reafons to believe the place was then taken and in the hands of the enemy: the confequence of which would be, that a great part of the Britifh force would return, and join that at New-York. That our own army required to be augmented, ten thoufand men, to be able to ftand againft the combined force of the enemy. I informed Mr. M'Clenaghan of General Washington's letter, the extreme distresses he was surrounded with, and the absolute occasion there was for the citizens to exert themselves at this time, which there was no doubt they would do, if the necessity was made known to them; for that the ability of government was exhausted. I requested Mr. M'Clenaghan, to propose a voluntary subscription among his friends, and added, that I had enclosed five hundred dollars as my mite thereto, and that I would encrease it as far as the last ability would enable me to go.*

The next day Mr. M'Clenaghan informed me, he had communicated the contents of the letter at a meeting of gentlemen at the coffee-house, and that a subscription was immediately began—that Mr. Robert Morris and himself had subscribed two hundred pounds each, in hard money, and that the subscription was going very successfully on.—This subscription was intended as a donation, and to be given in bounties to promote the recruiting service. It is dated June 8th, 1780. The original subscription list is now in my possession—it amounts to four hundred pounds hard money, and one hundred and one thousand three hundred and sixty pounds continental.

While this subscription was going forward, information of the loss of Charleston arrived,† and on a communication from several members of congress to certain gentlemen of this city, of the encreasing distresses and dangers then taking place, a meeting was held of the subscribers, and such other gentleman who chose to attend, at the city tavern. This meeting was on the 17th of June, nine days after the subscriptions had began.

At this meeting it was resolved to open a security subscription, to the amount of three hundred thousand pounds, Pennsylvania currency, in real money; the subscribers to execute bonds to the amount of their subscriptions, and to form a bank thereon for supplying the army. This being resolved on and carried into execution the plan of the first subscriptions was discontinued, and this extended one established in its stead.

By means of this bank the army was supplied through the cam-

---

* *Mr. M'Clenaghan being now returned from Europe, has my consent to shew the letter to any gentleman who may be inclined to see it.*

† *Colonel Tennant, aid to General Lincoln, arrived the 14th of June, with dispatches of the capitulation of Charleston.*

paign, and being at the fame time recruited, was enabled to maintain its ground : And on the appointment of Mr. Morris to be fuperintendant of the finances the fpring following, he arranged the fyftem of the prefent bank, ftiled the bank of North-America, and many of the fubfcribers of the former bank transferred their fubfcriptions into this.

Towards the eftablifhment of this bank, congrefs paffed an ordinance of incorporation December 21ft, 1781, which the government of Pennfylvania recognized by fundry matters: And afterwards, on an application from the prefident and directors of the bank, through the mediation of the executive council, the affembly agreed to, and paffed the ftate act of incorporation April 1ft, 1782.

Thus arofe the bank——produced by the diftrefs of the times and the enterprifing fpirit of patriotic individuals.——Thofe individuals furnifhed and rifked the money, and the aid which the government contributed was that of incorporating them.——It would have been well if the ftate had made all its bargains and contracts with as much true policy as it made this; for a greater fervice for fo fmall a confideration, that only of an act of incorporation, has not been obtained fince the government exifted.

Having now fhewn how the bank originated, I fhall proceed with my remarks.

The fudden reftoration of public and private credit, which took place on the eftablifhment of the bank is an event as extraordinary in itfelf as any domeftic occurrence during the progrefs of the revolution.

How far a fpirit of envy might operate to produce the attack on the bank during the fitting of the late affembly, is beft known and felt by thofe who began or promoted that attack. The bank had rendered fervices which the affembly of 1780 could not, and acquired an honour which many of its members might be unwilling to own, and wifh to obfcure.

But furely every wife government, acting on the principles of patriotifm and public good, would cherifh an inftitution capable of rendering fuch advantages to the community. The eftablifhment of the bank in one of the moft trying viciffitudes of the war, its zealous fervices in the public caufe, its influence in reftoring and fupporting credit, and the punctiality with which all its bufinefs has been tranfacted, are matters, that fo far from meriting the treatment it met with from the late affembly, are an honour to the ftate, and what the body of her citizens may be proud to own.

But the attack on the bank, as a chartered inftitution, under the protection of its violators, however criminal it may be as an error of government, or impolitic as a meafure of party, is not to be charged on the conftituents of thofe who made the attack. It appears from every circumftance that has come to light, to be a meafure which that affembly contrived of itfelf. The members did not come charged with the affair from their conftituents. There was no idea of fuch a thing when they were elected or when they met. The hafty and precipitate manner in which it was hurried through the houfe, and the refufal of the houfe to hear the directors of the bank in its defence, prior to the publication of the repealing bill for public confideration, operated to prevent their conftituents comprehending the fubject: Therefore, whatever may be wrong in the proceedings lies not at the door of the public. The houfe took the affair on its own fhoulders, and whatever blame there is lies on them.

The matter muft have been prejudged and predetermined by a majority of the members out of the houfe, before it was brought into it. The whole bufinefs appears to have been fixed at once, and all reafoning or debate on the cafe rendered ufelefs.

Petitions from a very *inconfiderable* number of perfons fuddenly procured, and fo privately done, as to be a fecret among the few that figned them, were prefented to the houfe and read twice in one day, and referred to a committee of the houfe to *enquire* and report thereon. I here fubjoin the petition * and the report, and

* *Minutes of the affembly, March 21, 1785.*

Petitions from a confiderable number of the inhabitants of Chefter *county were read, reprefenting that the bank eftablifhed at* Philadelphia *has fatal effects upon the community; that whilft men are enabled, by means of the bank, to receive near three times the rate of common intereft, and at the fame time to receive their money at very fhort warning, whenever they have occafion for it, it will be impoffible for the hufbandman or mechanic to borrow on the former terms of legal intereft aud diftant payments of the principal; that the beft fecurity will not enable the perfon to borrow; that experience clearly demonftrates the mifchievous confequences of this inftitution to the fair trader; that impoftors have been enabled to fupport themfelves in a fictitious credit, by means of a temporary punctuality at the bank, until they have drawn in their honeft neighbours to truft them with their property, or to pledge their credit as fureties, and have been finally involved in ruin and diftrefs; that they have repeatedly feen the ftop-*

shall exercise the right and privilege of a citizen in examining their merits, not for the purpose of opposition, but with a design of making an intricate affair more generally and better understood.

So far as my private judgment is capable of comprehending the subject, it appears to me, that the committee were unacquainted with, and have totally mistaken, the nature and business of a bank, as well as the matter committed to them, considered as a proceeding of government.

They were instructed by the house to *enquire* whether the bank established at Philadelphia was compatible with the public safety.

It is scarcely possible to suppose the instructions meant no more than that they were to enquire of one another. It is certain they made no enquiry at the bank, to inform themselves of the situation of its affairs, how they were conducted, what aids it had rendered the public cause, or whether any ; nor do the committee produce in their report a single fact or circumstance to shew they made any enquiry at all, or whether the rumours then circulated were true or false ; but content themselves with modelling the insinuations of the petitions into a report and giving an opinion thereon.

It would appear from the report, that the committee either conceived that the house had already determined how it would act without regard to the case, and that they were only a committee for form sake, and to give a colour of enquiry without making any, or that the case was referred to them, *as law-questions are sometimes referred to law-officers, for an opinion only.*

ping of discounts at the bank, operate on the trading part of the community, with a degree of violence scarcely inferior to that of a stagnation of the blood in the human body, hurrying the wretched merchant who hath delts to pay into the hands of griping usurers ; that the directors of the bank may give such preference in trade, by advances of money, to their particular favourites, as to destroy that equality which ought to prevail in a commercial country ; that paper-money has often proved beneficial to the state, but the bank forbids it, and the people must acquiesce : therefore, and in order to restore public confidence and private security, they pray that a bill may be brought in and passed into a law for repealing the law for incorporating the bank.

March 28.

The report of the committee, read March 25, on the petitions from the counties of Chester *and* Berks, *and the city of* Philadelphia *and its vi-*

This method of doing public bufinefs ferves exceedingly to miflead a country.——When the conftituents of an affembly hear that an

eirity, praying the act of affembly, whereby the bank was eftablifhed at Philadelphia, *may be repealed, was read the fecond time as follows, viz.*

The committee to whom were referred the petitions concerning the bank eftablifhed at Philadelphia, *and who were inftructed to enquire whether the faid bank be compatible with the public fafety, and that equality which ought ever to prevail between the individuals of a republic, beg leave to report, that it is the opinion of this committee, that the faid bank, as at prefent eftablifhed, is in every view incompatible with the public fafety : that in the prefent flate of our trade, the faid bank has a direct tendency to banifh a great part of the fpecie from the country, fo as to produce a fcarcity of money, and to collect into the hands of the flockholders of the faid bank almoft the whole of the money which remains amongft us. That the accumulation of enormous wealth in the hand of a fociety, who claim perpetual duration, will neceffarily produce a degree of influence and power, which cannot be entrufled in the hands of any fet of men whatfoever, without endangering the public fafety. That the faid bank, in its corporate capacity, is empowered to hold eftates to the amount of ten millions of dollars, and by the tenor of the prefent charter, is to exift for ever, without being obliged to yield any emolument to the government, or to be at all dependant upon it. That the great profits of the bank, which will daily increafe as money grows fcarcer, and which already far exceed the profits of European banks, have tempted foreigners to veft their money in this bank, and thus to draw from us large fums for intereft.*

That foreigners will doubtlefs be more and more induced to become flockholders, until the time may arrive when this enormous engine of power may become fubject to foreign influence ; this country may be agitated with the politics of European courts, and the good people of America *reduced once more into a flate of fubordination, and dependance upon fome one or other of the European powers. That at beft, if it were even confined to the hands of* Americans, *it would be totally deftructive of that equality which ought to prevail in a republic. We have nothing in our free and equal government capable of balancing the influence which this bank muft create ; and we fee nothing which in the courfe of a few years, can prevent the directors of the bank, from governing* Penfylvania. *Already we have felt its influence indirectly interfering in the meafures of the legiflature. Already the houfe of affembly, the reprefentatives of the people, have been threatened, that the credit of our paper currency will be blafted by the bank:*

enquiry into any matter is directed to be made, and a committee appointed for that purpofe, they naturally conclude that the enquiry
is made; and that the future proceedings of the houfe are in confequence of the matters, facts, and information obtained by means of
that enquiry.——But here is a committee of enquiry making no enquiry at all, and giving an opinion on a cafe without enquiring
into it.   This proceeding of the committee would juftify an opinion
that it was not their wifh to *get*, but to *get over* information, and left
the enquiry fhould not fuit their wifhes, omitted to make any.   The
fubfequent conduct of the houfe, in refolving not to hear the directors
of the bank on their application for that purpofe, prior to the publication of the bill for the confideration of the people, ftrongly corro-
borates this opinion :   For why fhould not the houfe hear them, unlefs it was apprehenfive, that the bank, by fuch a public opportunity,
would produce proofs of Its fervices and ufefulnefs, that would not
fuit the temper and views of its oppofers ?

But if the houfe did not wifh or choofe to hear the defence of the
bank, it was no reafon their conftituents fhould not.   The conftitution of this ftate, in lieu of having two branches of legiflature, has
fubftituted, that " To the end that laws before they are enacted may
" be more *maturely confidered*, and the inconvenience of *hafty determi-*
" *nations* as much as poffible prevented, all bills of a public nature
" fhall be printed for the confideration of the people."*——The
people, therefore, according to the conftitution, ftand in the place
of another houfe ; or, more properly fpeaking, are a houfe in their

*and if this growing evil continues we fear the time is not very diftant,
when the bank will be able to dictate to the legiflature, what laws to pafs
and what to forbear.*

*Your committee therefore beg leave farther to report the following refo-
lution to be adopted by the houfe*, viz.

Refolved, *that a committee be appointed to bring in a bill to repeal the
act of affembly, paffed the firft day of* April, 1782, *entitled*, " An act to
" incorporate the fubfcribers to the bank of *North-America ;" and
alfo to repeal one other act of affembly, paffed the* 18th *of* March, 1782,
entitled, " An act for preventing and punifhing the counterfeiting of
" the common feal, bank-bills and bank-notes of the prefident, direc-
" tors and company, of the bank of *North-America*, and for the other
" purpofes therein mentioned."

* *Conftitution, fection the* 15th.

own right——But in this inftance the affembly arrogates the whole power to itfelf, and places itfelf as a bar to ftop the neceffary information fpreading among the people.——The application of the bank to be heard before the bill was publifhed for public confideration had two objects.——Firft, to the houfe,—and fecondly, through the houfe to the people, who are as another houfe. It was as a defence in the firft inftance, and as an appeal in the fecond. But the affembly abforbs the right of the people to judge ; becaufe, by refufing to hear the defence, they barred the appeal.——Were there no other caufe which the conftituents of that affembly had for cenfuring its conduct, than the exceeding unfairnefs, partiality, and arbitrarinefs with which this bufinefs was tranfacted, it would be caufe fufficient.

Let the conftituents of affemblies differ, as they may, refpecting certain peculiarities in the *form* of the conftitution, they will all agree in fupporting its *principles*, and in reprobating unfair proceedings and defpotic meafures. Every conftituent is a member of the republic, which is a ftation of more confequence to him than being a member of a party, and though they may differ from each other in their choice of perfons to tranfact the public bufinefs, it is of equal importance to all parties that the bufinefs be done on right principles : Otherwife our laws and acts, inftead of being founded in juftice, will be founded in party, and be laws and acts of retaliation ; and inftead of being a republic of free citizens, we fhall be alternately tyrants and flaves.—But to return to the report.——

The report begins by ftating that, " The committee to whom " were referred the petitions concerning the bank eftablifhed at " Philadelphia, and who were inftructed to *enquire* whether the faid " bank be compatible with the public fafety, and that equality which " ought ever to prevail between the individuals of a republic, beg " leave to report" (not that they have made any *enquiry*, but) " that it is the *opinion* of this committee, that the faid bank, as at " prefent eftablifhed, is, in every view, incompatible with the public " fafety."——But why is it fo ? Here is an opinion unfounded and unwarranted. The committee have begun their report at the wrong end ; for an opinion, when given as a matter of judgment, is an action of the mind which follows a fact, but here it is put in the room of one.

The report then fays, " That in the prefent ftate of our trade, " the faid bank has a direct tendency to banifh a great part of the " fpecie from the country, and to collect into the hands of the

" ſtockholders of the bank almoſt the whole of the money which re-
" mains among us."

Here is another mere aſſertion, juſt like the former, without a
ſingle fact or circumſtance to ſhew why it is made or whereon it is
founded.——Now the very reverſe, of what the committee aſſerts,
is the natural conſequence of a bank.——Specie may be called the
ſtock in trade of the bank, it is therefore its intereſt to prevent it from
wandering out of the country, and to keep a conſtant ſtanding ſupply to be ready for all domeſtic occaſions and demands. Were it true
that the bank has a direct tendency to baniſh the ſpecie from the
country, there would ſoon be an end to the bank ; and, therefore,
the committee have ſo far miſtaken the matter, as to put their fears
in the place of their wiſhes : For if it is to happen as the committee
ſtates, let the bank alone and it will ceaſe of itſelf, aud the repealing
act need not have been paſſed.

It is the intereſt of the bank that people ſhould keep their caſh
there, and all commercial countries find the exceeding great convenience of having a general repoſitory for their caſh.—But ſo far
from baniſhing it, there are no two claſſes of people in America who
are ſo much intereſted in preſerving hard money in the country as the
bank and the merchant. . Neither of them can carry on their buſineſs
without it. Their oppoſition to the paper-money of the late aſſembly
was becauſe it has a direct effect, as far as it is able, to baniſh the
ſpecie and that without providing any means for bringing more in.

The committee muſt have been aware of this, and therefore choſe to
ſpread the firſt alarm, and groundleſs as it was to truſt to the deluſion.

As the keeping the ſpecie in the country is the intereſt of the
bank, ſo it has the beſt opportunities of preventing its being ſent
away, and the earlieſt knowledge of ſuch a deſign. While the bank
is the general depoſitory of caſh, no great ſums can be obtained
without getting it from thence, and as it is evidently prejudicial to
its intereſt to advance money to be ſent abroad, becauſe in this caſe,
the money cannot by circulation return again ; the bank, therefore,
is intereſted in preventing what the committee would have it ſuſpected of promoting.

It is to prevent the exportation of caſh and to retain it in the
country that the bank has on ſeveral occaſions ſtopt the diſcounting
notes till the danger has been paſſed. * The firſt part, there-

* The petitions ſay, " That they have repeatedly ſeen the ſlopping (

fore, of the affertion, that of banifhing the fpecie, contains an appre, henfion as needlefs as it is groundlefs, and which, had the committee underftood, or been the leaft informed of the nature of a bank, they could not have made. It is very probable that fome of the oppofers to the bank are thofe perfons who have been difappointed in their attempt to obtain fpecie for this purpofe, and now cloak their oppofition under other pretences.

I now come to the fecond part of the affertion, which is, that when the bank has banifhed a great part of the fpecie from the country, " it will collect into the hands of the ftockholders almoft ·

difcounts at the bank, operate on the trading part of the community, with a degree of violence fcarcely inferior to that of a flagnation of the blood in the human body, hurrying the wretched merchant who hath debts to pay into the hands of griping ufurers."

As the perfons who fay or figned this, live fomewhere in Chefter county, they are not, from fituation, certain of what they fay. Thofe petitions have every appearance of being contrived for the purpofe of bringing the matter on. The petition and the report have ftrong evidence in them of being both drawn up by the fame perfon : for the report is as clearly the echo of the petition as ever the addrefs of the Britifh parliament was the echo of the king's fpeech.

Befides the reafon I have already given for occafionally ftopping difcounting notes at the bank, there are other neceffary reafons. It is for the purpofe of fettling accounts. Short reckonings make long friends. The bank lends its money for fhort periods, and by that means affifts a great many different people : and if it did not fometimes ftop difcounting as a means of fettling with the perfons it has already lent its money to, thofe perfons would find a way to keep what they had borrowed longer than they ought, and prevent others being affifted. · It is a fact, and fome of the committee know it to be fo, that fundry of thofe perfons who then oppofed the bank acted this part.

The ftopping the difcounts do not, and cannot, operate to call in the loans fooner than the time for which they were lent, and therefore the charge is falfe that " it hurries men into the hands of griping ufurers:" —and the truth is, that it operates to keep them from thence.

If petitions are to be contrived to cover the defigns of a houfe of affembly and give a pretence for its conduct, or if a houfe is to be led by the nofe by the idle tale of any fifty or fixty figners to a petition, it is time for the public to look a little clofer into the conduct of its reprefentatives.

" the whole of the money which remains among us."—But how, or by what means, the bank is to accomplish this wonderful feat, the committee have not informed us. Whether people are to give their money to the bank for nothing, or whether the bank is to charm it from them as a rattlesnake charms a squirrel from a tree, the committee have left us as much in the dark about it as they were themselves.

Is it possible the committee should know so very little of the matter, as not to know that no part of the money which at any time may be in the bank belongs to the stockholders?, not even the original capital which they put in is any part of it their own until every person who has a demand upon the bank is paid, and if there is not a sufficiency for this purpose, on the balance of loss and gain, the original money of the stockholders must make up the deficiency.

The money which at any time may be in the bank is the property of every man who holds a bank-note, or deposits cash there, or who has a just demand upon it from the city of Philadelphia up to Fort Pitt, or to any part of the United States; and he can draw the money from it when he pleases. Its being in the bank, does not in the least make it the property of the stockholders, any more than the money in the state treasury is the property of the state treasurer. They are only stewards over it for those who please to put it, or let it remain there: And, therefore, this second part of the assertion is somewhat ridiculous.

The next paragraph in the report is, " That the accumulation of " *enormous wealth* in the hands of a *society* who claim perpetual du- " ration, will necessarily produce a degree of influence and power " which cannot be entrusted in the hands of any set of men whatso- " ever" (the committee I presume excepted) " without endanger- " ing the public safety."——There is an air of solemn fear in this paragraph which is something like introducing a ghost in a play to keep people from laughing at the players.

I have already shewn that whatever wealth there may be, at any time, in the bank, is the property of those who have demands upon the bank, and not the property of the stockholders. As a society they hold no property, and most probably never will, unless it should be a house to transact their business in, instead of hiring one. Every half year the bank settles its accounts, and each individual stockholder takes his dividend of gain or loss to himself, and the bank begins the next half year in the same manner it began the first, and so on,

This being the nature of a bank, there can be no accumulation of wealth among them as a society.

For what purpose the word "*society*" is introduced into the report I do not know, unless it be to make a false impression upon people's minds. It has no connection with the subject, for the bank is not a society, but a company, and denominated so in the charter. There are several religious societies incorporated in this state, which hold property as the right of those societies, and to which no person can belong that is not of the same religious profession. But this is not the case with the bank. The bank is a company for the promotion and convenience of commerce, which is a matter in which all the state is interested, and holds no property in the manner which those societies do.

But there is a direct contradiction in this paragraph to that which goes before it. The committee, there, accuses the bank of banishing the specie, and here, of accumulating enormous sums of it.——So here are two enormous sums of specie; one enormous sum going out, and another enormous sum remaining.——To reconcile this contradiction, the committee should have added to their report, *that they suspected the bank had found out the philosopher's stone, and kept it a secret.*

The next paragraph is, "that the said bank, in its corporate capa-
"city, is empowered to hold estates to the amount of ten millions of
"dollars, and by the tenor of the present charter is to exist for ever,
"without being obliged to yield any emolument to the government,
"or be at least dependant on it."

The committee have gone so vehemently into this business, and so completely shewn their want of knowledge in every point of it, as to make, in the first part of this paragraph, a fear of what, the greater fear is, will never happen. Had the committee known any thing of banking, they must have known, that the objection against banks has been (not that they held great estates, but) that they held none ; that they had no real, fixed, and visible property, and that it is the maxim and practice of banks not to hold any.

The honourable chancellor Livingston, late secretary for foreign affairs, did me the honour of shewing, and discoursing with me on, a plan of a bank he had drawn up for the state of New-York. In this plan it was made a condition or obligation, that whatever the capital of the bank ammounted to in specie, there should be added twice as much in real estates. But the mercantile interest rejected the proposition.

It was a very good piece of policy in the affembly which paffed the charter act, to add the claufe to empower the bank to purchafe and hold real eftates.   It was as an inducement to the bank to do it, becaufe fuch eftates being held as the property of the bank would be fo many mortgages to the public in addition to the money capital of the bank.

But the doubt is that the bank will not be induced to accept the opportunity.   The bank has exifted five years and has not purchafed a fhilling of real property : and as fuch property or eftates cannot be purchafed by the bank but with the intereft money which the ftock produces, and as that is divided every half year among the ftock-holders, and each ftockholder choofes to have the management of his own dividend, and if he lays it out in purchafing an eftate to have that eftate his own private property, and under his own immediate manage-ment, there is no expectation, fo far from being any fear, that the claufe will be accepted.

. Where knowledge is a duty, ignorance is a crime; and the commit-tee are criminal in not underftanding this fubject better.   Had this claufe not been in the charter, the committee might have reported the want of it as a defect, in not empowering the bank to hold eftates as a real fecurity to its creditors : but as the complaint now ftands, the accufation of it is, that the charter empowers the bank to *give real fecurity* to its creditors.   A complaint never made, heard of, or thought of before.

The fecond article in this paragraph is, " that the bank, according " to the tenor of the prefent charter, is to exift for ever."——Here I agree with the committee, and am glad to find that among fuch a lift of errors and contradictions there is one idea which is not wrong, although the committee have made a wrong ufe of it.

As we are not to live for ever ourfelves, and other generations are to follow us, we have neither the power nor the right to govern them, or to fay how they fhall govern themfelves.   It is the fummit of human vanity, and fhews a covetoufnefs of power beyond the grave, to be dictating to the world to come.   It is fufficient that we do that which is right in our own day, and leave them with the ad-vantage of good examples.

As the generations of the world are every day both commencing and expiring, therefore, when any public act of this fort is done it naturally fuppofes the age of that generation to be then beginning, . and the time contained between coming of age, and the natural end of life, in the extent of time it has a right to go to, which may be about thirty years; for though many may die before, others will live beyond; and the mean time is equally fair for all generations.

If it was made an article in the conftitution, that all laws and acts fhould ceafe of themfelves in thirty years, and have no legal force beyond that time, it would prevent their becoming too numerous and voluminous, and ferve to keep them within view and in a compact compafs. Such as were proper to be continued, would be enacted again, and thofe which were not, would go into oblivion. There is the fame propriety that a nation fhould fix a time for a full fettle-ment of its affairs, and begin again from a new date, as that an indi-vidual fhould; and to keep within the diftance of thirty years would be a convenient period.

The Britifh, from the want of fome general regulation of this kind, have a great number of obfolete laws; which, though out of ufe and forgot, are not out of force, and are occafionally brought up for fharping purpofes, and innocent unwary perfons trepanned there-by.

To extend this idea ftill further,—it would probably be a confide-rable improvement in the political fyftem of nations, to make all treaties of peace for a limited time. It is the nature of the mind to feel uneafy under the idea of a condition perpetually exifting over it, and to excite in itfelf apprehenfions that would not take place were it not from that caufe.

Were treaties of peace made for, and renewable every; feven or ten years, the natural effect would be, to make peace continue longer than it does under the cuftom of making peace for ever. If the par-ties felt or apprehended any inconveniences under the terms already made, they would look forward to the time when they fhould be eventually relieved therefrom, and might renew the treaty on im-proved conditions. This opportunity periodically occurring, and the recollection of it always exifting, would ferve as a chimney to the political fabric, to carry off the fmoke and fume of national fire. It would naturally abate, and honourably take off, the edge and occa-fion for fighting; and however the parties might determine to do it, when the time of the treaty fhould expire, it would then feem like fighting in cool blood: The fighting temper would be diffipated before the fighting time arrived, and negociation fupply its place. To know how probable this may be, a man need do no more than obferve the progrefs of his own mind on any private circumftance

similar in its nature to a public one.———But to return to my subject.———

To give limitation is to give duration: and though it is not a
justifying reason, that because an act or contract is not to last for
ever, that it shall be broken or violated to-day, yet, where no time
is mentioned, the omission affords an opportunity for the abuse.
When we violate a contract on this pretence, we assume a right that
belongs to the next generation; for though they, as a following generation, have the right of altering or setting it aside, as not being
concerned in the making it, or not being done in their day, we, who
made it, have not that right; and, therefore, the committee, in this
part of their report, have made a wrong use of a right principle; and
as this clause in the charter might have been altered by the consent
of the parties, it cannot be produced to justify the violation.———
And were it not altered there would be no inconvenience from it.
The term " for ever" is an absurdity that would have no effect.
The next age will think for itself by the same rule of right that we
have done, and not admit any assumed authority of ours to encroach
upon the system of their day. Our *for ever* ends where their *for ever*
begins.

The third article in this paragraph is, that the bank holds its
charter " without being obliged to yield any emolument to the go-
" vernment."

Ingratitude has a short memory. It was on the failure of the government to support the public cause, that the bank originated. It
stept in as a support when some of the persons then in the government, and who now oppose the bank, were apparently on the point
of abandoning the cause, not from disaffection, but from despair.
While the expences of the war were carried on by emissions of continental money, any set of men, in government, might carry it on.
The means being provided to their hands, required no great exertions of fortitude or wisdom: But when this means failed, they
would have failed with it, had not a public spirit awakened itself with
energy out of doors. It was easy times to the governments while
continental money lasted. The dream of wealth supplied the
reality of it; but when the dream vanished, the government did not
awake.

But what right has the government to expect any emolument from
the bank? Does the committee mean to set up acts and charters for
sale, or what do they mean? Because it is the practice of the British

miniſtry to grind a toll out of every public inſtitution they can get a power over, is the ſame practice to be followed here ?

The war being now ended, and the bank having rendered the ſervice expected, or rather hoped for, from it, the principal public uſe of it, at this time, is for the promotion and extenſion of commerce. The whole community derives benefit from the operation of the bank. It facilitates the commerce of the country. It quickens the means of purchaſing and paying for country-produce, and haſtens on the exportation of it. The emolument, therefore, being to the community, it is the office and duty of government to give protection to the bank.

Among many of the principal conveniences ariſing from the bank, one of them is, that it gives a kind of life to, what would otherwiſe be, dead money. Every merchant and perſon in trade, has always in his hands ſome quantity of caſh, which conſtantly remains with him ; that is, he is never entirely without : This remnant money, as it may be called, is of no uſe to him till more is collected to it. He can neither buy produce nor merchandize with it, and this being the caſe with every perſon in trade, there will be (though not all at the ſame time) as many of thoſe ſums lying uſeleſsly by, and ſcattered throughout the city, as there are perſons in trade, beſides many that are not in trade.

I ſhould not ſuppoſe the eſtimation over-rated, in conjecturing, that half the money in the city, at any one time, lies in this manner. By collecting thoſe ſcattered ſums together, which is done by means of the bank, they become capable of being uſed, and the quantity of circulating caſh is doubled, and by the depoſitors alternately lending them to each other, the commercial ſyſtem is invigorated: and as it is the intereſt of the bank to preſerve this money in the country for domeſtic uſes only, and as it has the beſt opportunity of doing ſo, the bank ſerves as a centinel over the ſpecie.

If a farmer, or a miller, comes to the city with produce, there are but few merchants that can individually purchaſe it with ready money of their own ; and thoſe few would command nearly the whole market for country produce: But, by means of the bank, this monopoly is prevented, and the chance of the market enlarged. It is very extraordinary that the late aſſembly ſhould promote monopolizing; yet ſuch would be the effect of ſuppreſſing the bank ; and it is much to the honour of thoſe merchants, who are capable, by their fortunes, of becoming monopolizers, that they ſupport the bank. In this caſe, honour operates over interest. They were the perfons who firft fet up the bank, and their honour is now engaged to fupport what it is their intereft to put down.

If merchants, by this means, or farmers, by fimilar means, among themfelves, can mutually aid and fupport each other, what has the government to do with it? What right has it to expect emolument from affociated induftry, more than from individual induftry? It would be a ftrange fort of a government, that fhould make it illegal for people to affift each other, or pay a tribute for doing fo.

But the truth is, that the government has already derived emoluments, and very extraordinary ones. It has already received its full fhare, by the fervices of the bank during the war; and it is every day receiving benefits, becaufe whatever promotes and facilitates commerce, ferves likewife to promote and facilitate the revenue.

The laft article in this paragraph is, " That the bank is not the " leaft dependant on the government."

Have the committee fo foon forgot the principles of republican government and the conftitution, or are fo little acquainted with them, as not to know, that this article in their report partakes of the nature of treafon? Do they not know, that freedom is deftroyed by dependance, and the fafety of the ftate endangered thereby? Do they not fee, that to hold any part of the citizens of the ftate, as yearly penfioners on the favour of an affembly, is ftriking at the root of free elections?

If other parts of their report difcover a want of knowledge on the fubject of banks, this fhews a want of principle in the fcience of government.

Only let us fuppofe this dangerous idea carried into practice, and then fee what it leads to. If corporate bodies are, after their incorporation, to be annually dependant on an affembly for the continuance of their charter, the citizens, which compofe thofe corporations, are not free. The government holds an authority and influence over them, in a manner different from what it does over other citizens, and by this means deftroys that equality of freedom, which is the bulwark of the republic and the conftitution.

By this fcheme of government any party, which happens to be uppermoft in a ftate, will command all the corporations in it, and may create more for the purpofe of extending that influence. The dependant borough-towns in England are the rotten- part of their government, and this idea of the committee has a very near relation to it.

" If you do not do fo and fo," expreffing what was meant, " take care of your charter," was a threat thrown out againft the bank. But as I do not wifh to enlarge on a difagreeable circumftance, and hope that what is already faid, is fufficient to fhew the anti-conftitutional conduct and principles of the committee, I fhall pafs on to the next paragraph in the report.——Which is.——

" That the great profits of the bank, which will daily encreafe as " money grows fcarcer, and which already far exceed the profits of " European banks, have tempted foreigners to veft their money in " this bank, and thus to draw from us large fums for intereft."

Had the committee underftood the fubject, fome dependance might be put on their opinion which now cannot. Whether money will grow fcarcer, and whether the profits of the bank will increafe, are more than the committee know, or are judges fufficient to guefs at. The committee are not fo capable of taking care of commerce, as commerce is capable of taking care of itfelf. The farmer underftands farming, and the merchant underftands commerce ; and as riches are equally the object of both, there is no occafion that either fhould fear that the other will feek to be poor. The more money the merchant has, fo much the better for the farmer, who has produce to fell ; and the richer the farmer is, fo much the better for the merchant, when he comes to his ftore.

As to the profits of the bank, the ftockholders muft take their chance for it. It may fome years be more and others lefs, and upon the whole may not be fo productive as many other ways that money may be employed. It is the convenience which the ftockholders, as commercial men, derive from the eftablifhment of the bank, and not the mere intereft they receive, that is the inducement to them. It is the ready opportunity of borrowing alternately of each other that forms the principal object : And as they pay as well as receive a great part of the intereft among themfelves, it is nearly the fame thing, both cafes confidered at once, whether it is more or lefs.

The ftockholders are occafionally depofitors and fometimes borrowers of the bank. They pay intereft for what they borrow, and receive none for what they depofit ; and were a ftockholder to keep a nice account of the intereft he pays for the one and lofes upon the other, he would find, at the year's end, that ten per cent upon his ftock would probably not be more than common intereft upon the whole, if fo much.

As to the committee complaining " that foreigners by vefting

"·their money in the bank· will draw large fums from us for intereft," it is like a miller complaining in a dry feafon, that fo much water runs into his dam that fóme of it runs over.

Could thofe foreigners draw this intereft without putting in any capital, the complaint would be well founded ; but as they muft firft put money in before they can draw any out, and as they muft draw many· years before they can draw even the numerical fúm they put in at firft, the effect, for at leaft twenty years to come, will be directly contrary to what the committee ftates : Becaufe we draw *capitals* from them and they only *intereft* from us, and as we fhall have the ufe of the money all the while it remains with us, the advantage will always ·be in our favour.——In framing this part of the report, the committee muft have forgot which fide of the Atlantic they were on, for the cafe would be as they ftate it if we put money into their bank inftead of their putting it into ours.

I have now gone through, line by line, every objection againft the bank, contained in the firft half of the report ; what follows may be called, *The Lamentations of the Committee*, and a lamentable pufillanimous degrading affair it is.—It is a public affront, a reflection upon the fenfe and fpirit of the whole country. I fhall give the remainder together as it ftands in the report, and then my remarks.

The Lamentations are, " That foreigners will doubtlefs be more
" and more induced to become ftockholders, until the time may ar-
" rive when this *enormous* engine of power may become fubject to
" foreign influence, this country may be agitated by the politics of
" European courts, and the good people of America reduced once
" more into a ftate of fubordination and dependance upon fome one
" or other of the European powers. That at beft, if it were even
" confined to the hands of Americans, it would be totally deftructive
" of that equality which ought to prevail in a republic. We have
" nothing in our free and equal government capable of balancing the
" influence which this bank muft create ; and we fee nothing which
" in the courfe of a few years can prevent the directors of the bank
" from governing Pennfylvania. Already we have felt its influ-
" ence indirectly interfering in the meafures of the legiflature.
" Already the houfe of affembly, the reprefentatives of the people,
" have been threatened, that the credit of our paper currency will
" be blafted by the bank ; and if this growing evil continues, we
" fear the time is not very diftant when the bank will be able to dic-
" tate to the legiflature, what laws to pafs and what to forbear."

When the fky falls we fhall be all killed. There is fomething fo ridiculoufly grave, fo wide of probability, and fo wild, confufed and inconfiftent in the whole compofition of this long paragraph, that I am at a lofs how to begin upon it.——It is like a drowning man crying fire! fire!

This part of the report is made up of two dreadful predictions. The firft is, that if foreigners purchafe bank ftock we fhall be all ruined :—The fecond is, that if the Americans keep the bank to themfelves, we fhall be alfo ruined.

A committee of fortune-tellers is a novelty in government : and the gentlemen by giving this fpecimen of their art, have ingenioufly faved their honour on one point, which is, that though people may fay they are not bankers, nobody can fay they are not conjurors.—— There is, however, one confolation left, which is, that the committee do not know *exactly* how long it may be ; fo there is fome hope that we may all be in heaven when this dreadful calamity happens upon earth.

But to be ferious, if any ferioufnefs is neceffary on fo laughable a fubject.—If the ftate fhould think there is any thing improper in foreigners purchafing bank ftock, or any other kind of ftock or funded property (for I fee no reafon why bank ftock fhould be particularly pointed at) the legiflature have authority to prohibit it. It is a mere political opinion that has nothing to do with the charter or the charter with that ; and therefore the firft dreadful prediction vanifhes.

It has always been a maxim in politics, founded on, and drawn from, natural caufes and confequences, that the more foreign countries which any nation can intereft in the profperity of its own fo much the better. Where the treafure is, there will the heart be alfo ; and therefore when foreigners veft their money with us, they naturally inveft their good wifhes with it ; and it is we that obtain an influence over them, not they over us.——But the committee fat out fo very wrong at firft that the further they travelled the more they were out of their way ; and now they are got to the end of their report they are at the utmoft diftance from their bufinefs.

As to the fecond dreadful part, that of the bank overturning the government, perhaps the committee meant that at the next general election themfelves might be turned out of it, which has partly been the cafe ; not by the influence of the bank, for it had none, not even enough to obtain the permiffion of a hearing from government, but by the influence of reason and the choice of the people, who moſt probably reſent the undue and unconſtitutional influence which that houſe and the committee were aſſuming over the privileges of citizenſhip.

The committee might have been ſo modeſt as to have confined themſelves to the bank, and not thrown a general odium on the whole country. Before the events can happen which the committee predict, the electors of Pennſylvania muſt become dupes, dunces and cowards, and therefore when the committee predict the dominion of the bank they predict the diſgrace of the people.

The committee having finiſhed their report proceed to give their advice, which is,

" That a committee be appointed to bring in a bill to repeal the " act of aſſembly paſſed the firſt day of April, 1782, entitled, " *An act to incorporate the ſubſcribers to the bank of North-America,*" " and alſo to repeal one other act of the aſſembly paſſed the 18th of " March, 1782, entitled, " *An act for preventing and puniſhing the* " *counterfeiting of the common ſeal, bank bills, and bank notes of the pre-* " *ſident, directors and company of the bank of North-America, and for* " *other purpoſes therein mentioned.*"

There is ſomething in this ſequel to the report that is perplexed and obſcure.

Here are two acts to be repealed. One is, the incorporating act. The other, the act for preventing and puniſhing the counterfeiting of the common ſeal, bank bills, and bank notes of the preſident, directors and company of the bank of North America.

It would appear from the committee's manner of arranging them (were it not for the difference of their dates) that the act for puniſhing the counterfeiting the common ſeal, &c. of the bank, followed the act of incorporation, and that the common ſeal there referred to is a common ſeal which the bank held in conſequence of the aforeſaid incorporating act.—But the caſe is quite otherwiſe. The act for puniſhing the counterfeiting the common ſeal, &c. of the bank, was paſſed prior to the incorporating act, and refers to the common ſeal which the bank held in conſequence of the charter of congreſs, and the ſtyle which the act expreſſes, of preſident, directors and company of the bank of North-America, is the corporate ſtyle which the bank derives under the congreſs charter.

The puniſhing act, therefore, hath two diſtinct legal points. The one is, an authoritative public recognition of the charter of congreſs. The ſecond is, the puniſhment it inflicts on counterfeiting.

The legislature may repeal the punishing part, but it cannot undo the recognition, because no repealing act can say that the state *has not* recognized. The recognition is a mere matter of fact, and no law or act can undo a fact or put it, if I may so express it, in the condition it was before it existed. The repealing act therefore does not reach the full point the committee had in view; for even admitting it to be a repeal of the state charter, it still leaves another charter recognized in its stead.—The charter of congress, standing merely on itself, would have a doubtful authority, but the recognition of it by the state gives it legal ability. The repealing act, it is true, sets aside the punishment but does not bar the operation of the charter of congress as a charter recognized by the state, and therefore the committee did their business but by halves.

I have now gone entirely through the report of the committee, and a more irrational, inconsistent, contradictory report will scarcely be found on the journals of any legislature in America.

How the repealing act is to be applied, or in what manner it is to operate, is a matter yet to be determined. For admitting a question of law to arise, whether the charter, which that act attempts to repeal, is a law of the land in the manner which laws of universal operation are, or of the nature of a contract made between the public and the bank (as I have already explained in this work) the repealing act does not and cannot decide the question, because it is the repealing act that makes the question, and its own fate is involved in the decision. It is a question of law and not a question of legislation, and must be decided on in a court of justice and not by a house of assembly.

But the repealing act, by being passed prior to the decision of this point, assumes the power of deciding it, and the assembly in so doing erects itself unconstitutionally into a tribunal of judicature, and absorbs the authority and right of the courts of justice into itself.

Therefore the operation of the repealing act, in its very outset, requires injustice to be done. For it is impossible on the principles of a republican government and the constitution, to pass an act to forbid any of the citizens the right of appealing to the courts of justice on any matter in which his interest or property is affected; but the first operation of this act goes to shut up the courts of justice, and holds them subservient to the assembly. It either commands or influences them not to hear the case, or to give judgment on it on the mere will of one party only.

I wish the citizens to awaken themselves on this subject.—Not because the bank is concerned, but because their own conflitutional rights and privileges are involved in the event. It is a queftion of exceeding great magnitude; for if an affembly is to have this power, the laws of the land and the courts of juftice are but of little use.

Having now finifhed with the report, I proceed to the third and laft fubject—that of paper-money.—

I remember a German farmer expreffing as much in a few words as the whole fubject requires : " *money is money and paper is paper.*" ——All the invention of man cannot make them otherwife. The alchymift may ceafe his labours, and the hunter after the philofopher's ftone go to reft, if paper can be metamorphofed into gold and filver, or made to anfwer the fame purpofe in all cafes.

Gold and filver are the emiffions of nature: paper is the emiffion of art. The value of gold and filver is afcertained by the quantity which nature has made in the earth. We cannot make that quantity more or lefs than it is, and therefore the value being dependant upon the quantity, depends not on man.——Man has no fhare in making gold or filver; all that his labours and ingenuity can accomplifh is, to collect it from the mine, refine it for ufe and give it an impreffion, or ftamp it into coin,

Its being ftamped into coin adds confiderably to its convenience but nothing to its value. It has then no more value than it had before. Its value is not in the impreffion but in itfelf. Take away the impreffion and ftill the fame value remains. Alter it as you will, or expofe it to any misfortune that can happen, ftill the value is not diminifhed. It has a capacity to refift the accidents that deftroy other things. It has, therefore, all the requifite qualities that money can have, and is a fit material to make money of ; and nothing which has not all thofe properties, can be fit for the purpofe of money.

Paper, confidered as a material whereof to make money, has none of the requifite qualities in it. It is too plentiful, and too eafily come at. It can be had any where, and for a trifle.

There are two ways in which I fhall confider paper.

The only proper ufe for paper, in the room of money, is to write promiffory notes and obligations of payment in fpecie upon. A piece of paper, thus written and figned, is worth the fum it is given for, if the perfon who gives it is able to pay it; becaufe, in this cafe, the law will oblige him. But if he is worth nothing, the paper-note is worth nothing. The value, therefore, of fuch a note, is not is the note itfelf, for that is but paper and promife, but in the man who is obliged to redeem it with gold or filver.

Paper, circulating in this manner, and for this purpofe, continually points to the place and perfon where, and of whom, the money is to be had, and at laft finds its home; and, as it were, unlocks its mafter's cheft and pays the bearer.

But when an affembly undertake to iffue paper *as* money, the whole fyftem of fafety and certainty is overturned, and property fet afloat. Paper-notes given and taken between individuals as a promife of pay-ment is one thing, but paper iffued by an affembly *as* money is ano-ther thing. It is like putting an apparition in the place of a man; it vanifhes with looking at and nothing remains but the air.

Money, when confidered as the fruit of many years induftry, as the reward of labour, fweat and toil, as the widow's dowry and chil-dren's portion, and as the means of procuring the neceffaries, and alle-viating the afflictions of life, and making old age a fcene of reft, has fomething in it facred that is not to be fported with, or trufted to the airy bubble of paper-currency.

By what power or authority an affembly undertake to make paper-money is difficult to fay. It derives none from the conftitution; for that is filent on the fubject. It is one of thofe things which the peo-ple have not delegated, and which, were they at any time affembled together, they would not delegate. It is, therefore, an affumption of power which an affembly is not warranted in, and which may, one day or other, be the means of bringing fome of them to punifhment.

I fhall enumerate fome of the evils of paper-money and conclude with offering means for preventing them.

One of the evils of paper-money is, that it turns the whole country into ftock-jobbers. The precarioufnefs of its value and the uncer-tainty of its fate continually operate, night and day, to produce this deftructive effect. Having no real value in itfelf it depends for fup-port upon accident, caprice and party, and as it is the intereft of fome to depreciate and of others to raife its value, there is a continual invention going on that deftroys the morals of the country.

It was horrid to fee and hurtful to recollect how loofe the princi-ples of juftice were let by means of the paper emiffions during the war. The experience then had, fhould be a warning to any affembly how they venture to open fuch a dangerous door again.

As to the romantic if not hypocritical tale, that a virtuous people need no gold and filver and that paper will do as well, requires no other contradiction than the experience we have feen. Though fome well-meaning people may be inclined to view it in this light, it is certain that the fharper always talks this language.

There are a fet of men who go about making purchafes upon credit, and buying eftates they have not wherewithal to pay for; and having done this, their next ftep is to fill the news-papers with paragraphs of the fcarcity of money and the neceffity of a paper-cmiffion, then to have it made a legal tender under the pretence of fupporting its credit; and when out, to depreciate it as faft as they can, get a deal of it for a little price and cheat their creditors; and this is the concife hiftory of paper-money fchemes.

But why, fince the univerfal cuftom of the world has eftablifhed money as the moft convenient medium of traffic and commerce, fhould paper be fet up in preference to gold and filver? The productions of nature are furely as innocent as thofe of art; and in the cafe of money, are abundantly, if not infinitely, more fo. The love of gold and filver may produce covetoufnefs, but covetoufnefs, when not connected with difhonefty, is not properly a vice. It is frugality run to an extreme.

But the evils of paper-money have no end. Its uncertain and fluctuating value is continually awakening or creating new fchemes of deceit. Every principle of juftice is put to the rack and the bond of fociety diffolved: The fuppreffion therefore of paper-money might very properly have been put into the act for preventing vice and immorality.

The pretence for paper-money has been, that there was not a fufficiency of gold and filver. This, fo far from being a reafon for paper-emiffions, is a reafon againft them.

As gold and filver are not the productions of North-America, they are, therefore, articles of importation; and if we fet up a paper-manufactory of money, it amounts, as far as it is able, to prevent the importation of hard money, or to fend it out again as faft as it comes in; and by following this practice we fhall continually banifh the fpecie, till we have none left, and be continually complaining of the grievance inftead of remedying the caufe.

Confidering gold and filver as articles of importation, there will in time, unlefs we prevent it by paper-emiffions, be as much in the country as the occafions of it require, for the fame reafons there are as much of other imported articles. But as every yard of cloth manufactured in the country occasions a yard the lefs to be imported, fo it is by money, with this difference, that in the one cafe we manufacture the thing itfelf and in the other we do not. We have cloth for cloth, but we have only paper-dollars for filver ones.

As to the affumed authority of any affembly in making paper-money, or paper of any kind, a legal tender, or in other language, a compulfive payment, it is a moft prefumptuous attempt at arbitrary power. There can be no fuch power in a republican government: The people have no freedom, and property no fecurity where this practice can be acted : And the committee who fhall bring in a report for this purpofe, or the member who moves for it, and he who feconds it merit impeachment, and fooner or later may expect it.

Of all the various forts of bafe coin, paper-money is the bafeft. It has the leaft intrinfic value of any thing that can be put in the place of gold and filver. A hobnail or a piece of wampum far exceeds it. And there would be more propriety in making thofe articles a legal tender than to make paper fo.

It was the iffuing bafe coin and eftablifhing it as a tender, that was one of the principal means of finally overthrowing the power of the Stuart family in Ireland. The article is worth reciting as it bears fuch a refemblance to the progrefs practifed on paper-money.

" Brafs and copper of the bafeft kind, old cannon, broken bells, " houfhold utenfils were affiduoufly collected ; and from every pound " weight of fuch vile materials, valued at four-pence, pieces were " coined and circulated to the amount of five pounds nominal value. " By the firft proclamation they were made current in all payments " to and from the king and the fubjects of the realm, except in du- " ties on the importation of foreign goods, money left in truft, or " due by mortgage, bills or bonds ; and *James* promifed that when " the money fhould be decried, he would receive it in all payments or " make full fatisfaction in gold and filver. The nominal value was " afterwards raifed by fubfequent proclamations, the original reftric- " tions removed, and this bafe money was ordered to be received in " all kinds of payments. As brafs and copper grew fcarce it was " made of ftill viler materials, of tin and pewter, and old debts of " one thoufand pounds were difcharged by pieces of vile metal, " amounting to thirty fhillings in intrinfic value."*—Had king James thought of paper, he needed not to have been at the trouble

* *Leland's Hiftory of Ireland, vol. iv. p. 265.*

or expence of collecting brafs and copper, broken bells and houfhold utenfils.

. . The laws of a country ought to be the ftandard of equity, and calculated to imprefs on the minds of the people the moral as well as the legal obligations of reciprocal juftice. But tender-laws, of any kind, operate to deftroy morality, and to diffolve by the pretence of law what ought to be the principle of law to fupport, reciprocal juftice between man and man : and the punifhment of a member who fhould move for fuch a law ought to be DEATH.

When the recommendation of congrefs, in the year 1780, for repealing the tender-laws was before the affembly of Pennfylvania, on cafting up the votes, for and againft bringing in a bill to repeal thefe laws, the numbers were equal, and the cafting vote refted on the fpeaker, colonel Bayard. " I give my vote," faid he, " for the " repeal, from a confcioufnefs of juftice ; the tender-laws operate " to eftablifh iniquity by law."—But when the bill was brought in, the houfe rejected it, and the tender-laws continued to be the means of fraud.

If any thing had, or could have, a value equal to gold and filver, it would require no tender-law ; and if it had not that value it ought not to have fuch a law ; and, therefore, all tender-laws are tyrannical and unjuft, and calculated to fupport fraud and oppreffion.

Moft of the advocates for tender-laws are thofe who have debts to difcharge, and who take refuge in fuch a law, to violate their contracts and cheat their creditors. But as no law can warrant the doing an unlawful act, therefore the proper mode of proceeding, fhould any fuch laws be enacted in future, will be to impeach and execute the members who moved for and feconded fuch a bill, and put the debtor and the creditor in the fame fituation they were in, with refpect to each other, before fuch a law was paffed. Men ought to be made to tremble at the idea of fuch a barefaced act of injuftice. It is in vain to talk of reftoring credit, or to complain that money cannot be borrowed at legal intereft, until every idea of tender-laws is totally and publicly reprobated and extirpated from among us.

. As to paper-money, in any light it can be viewed, it is at beft a bubble. Confidered as property, it is inconfiftent to fuppofe that the breath of an affembly, whofe authority expires with the year, can give to paper the value and duration of gold. They cannot even engage that the next affembly fhall receive it in taxes. And by the precedent (for authority there is none) that any one affembly makes

paper-money, another may do the fame, until confidence and credit
are totally expelled, and all the evils of depreciation acted over again.
The amount, therefore, of paper-money is this, That it is the illegi-
timate offspring of affemblies, and when their year expires they leave
a vagrant on the hands of the public.

Having now gone through the three fubjects propofed in the title
to this work, I fhall conclude with offering fome thoughts on the
prefent affairs of the ftate.

My idea of a fingle legiflature was always founded on a hope, that
whatever perfonal parties there might be in the ftate, they would all
unite and agree in the general principles of good government—that
thefe party differences would be dropt at the trefhold of the ftate-
houfe, and that the public good or the good of the whole, would be
the governing principle of the legiflature within it.

Party difpute, taken on this ground, would only be, who fhould
have the honour of making the laws ; not what the laws fhould be.
But when party operates to produce party laws, a fingle houfe is a
fingle perfon, and fubject to the hafte, rafhnefs and paffion of individual fovereignty.   At leaft, it is an ariftocracy.

The form of the prefent conftitution is now made to trample on
its principles, and the conftitutional members are anti-conftitutional
legiflators.   They are fond of fupporting the form for the fake of
the power, and they dethrone the principle to difplay the fceptre.

The attack of the late affembly on the bank, difcovers fuch a want
of moderation and prudence, of impartiality and equity, of fair and
candid enquiry and inveftigation, of deliberate and unbiaffed judgment, and fuch a rafhnefs of thinking and vengeance of power as is
inconliftent with the fafety of the republic.   It was judging without
hearing, and execution without trial.

By fuch rafh, injudicious and violent proceedings the intereft of
the ftate is weakened, its profperity diminifhed and its commerce and
its fpecie banifhed to other places.—Suppofe the bank had not been
in an immediate condition to have flood fuch a fudden attack, what
a fcene of inftant diftrefs would the rafhnefs of that affembly have
brought upon this city and ftate.   The holders of bank-notes, whoever they might be, would have been thrown into the utmoft confufion and difficulties.   It is no apology to fay the houfe never thought
of this, for it was their duty to have thought of every thing.

But by the prudent and provident management of the bank
(though unfufpicious of the attack) it was enabled to ftand the run

upon it without ſtopping payment a moment, and to prevent the evils and miſchiefs taking place which the raſhneſs of the aſſembly had a direct tendency to bring on ; a trial that ſcarcely a bank in Europe, under a ſimilar circumſtance, could have ſtood through.

I cannot ſee reaſon ſufficient to believe that the hope of the houſe to put down the bank was placed on the withdrawing the charter, ſo much as on the expectation of producing a bankruptcy on the bank, by ſtarting a run upon it. If this was any part of their project it was a very wicked one, becauſe hundreds might have been ruined to gratify a party-ſpleen.

But this not being the caſe, what has the attack amounted to, but to expoſe the weakneſs and raſhneſs, the want of judgment as well as juſtice, of thoſe who made it, and to confirm the credit of the bank more ſubſtantially than it was before ?

The attack, it is true, has had one effect, which is not in the power of the aſſembly to remedy ; it has baniſhed many thouſand hard dollars from the ſtate.—By the means of the bank, Pennſylvania had the uſe of a great deal of hard money belonging to citizens of other ſtates, and that without any intereſt, for it laid here in the nature of a depoſit, the depoſitors taking bank-notes in its ſtead. But the alarm called thoſe notes in, and the owners drew out their caſh.

The baniſhing the ſpecie ſerved to make room for the paper-money of the aſſembly, and we have now paper dollars where we might have had ſilver ones. So that the effect of the paper-money has been to make leſs money in the ſtate than there was before. Paper-money is like dram-drinking, it relieves for the moment by a deceitful ſenſation, but gradually diminiſhes the natural heat, and leaves the body worſe than it found it. Were not this the caſe, and could money be made of paper at pleaſure, every ſovereign in Europe would be as rich as he pleaſed. But the truth is, that it is a bubble and the attempt vanity. Nature has provided the proper materials for money, gold and ſilver, and any attempt of ours to rival her is ridiculous.

But to conclude——If the public will permit the opinion of a friend who is attached to no party, and under obligations to none, nor at variance with any, and who through a long habit of acquaintance with them has never deceived them, that opinion ſhall be freely given.

The bank is an inſtitution capable of being made exceedingly beneficial to the ſtate, not only as the means of extending and facilitating its commerce, but as a means of increaſing the quantity of

hard money in the state. The affembly's paper-money ferves directly
to banifh or croud out the hard, becaufe it is iffued *as* money and
put in the place of hard money. But bank notes are of a very
different kind, and produce a contrary effect. They are promiffory
notes payable on demand, and may be taken to the bank and exchanged for gold or filver without the leaft ceremony or difficulty.

The bank, therefore, is obliged to keep a conftant ftock of hard
money fufficient for this purpofe; which is what the affembly neither
does, nor can do by their paper; becaufe the quantity of hard money
collected by taxes into the treafury is trifling compared with the
quantity that circulates in trade and through the bank.

The method, therefore, to encreafe the quantity of hard money
would be to combine the fecurity of the government and the bank
into one. And inftead of iffuing paper money that ferves to banifh
the fpecie, to borrow the fum wanted of the bank in bank-notes on
the condition of the bank exchanging thofe notes at ftated periods
and quantities with hard money.

Paper iffued in this manner, and directed to this end, would, inftead
of banifhing, work itfelf into, gold and filver ; becaufe it will then
be both the advantage and duty of the bank, and of all the mercantile
intereft connected with it, to procure and import gold and filver from
any part of the world it can be got, to exchange the notes with. The
Englifh bank is reftricted to the dealing in no other articles of importation than gold and filver, and we may make the fame ufe of our
bank if we proceed properly with it.

Thofe notes will then have a double fecurity, that of the government and that of the bank : and they will not be iffued *as* money,
but as hoftages to be exchanged for hard money, and will, therefore,
work the contrary way to what the paper of the affembly, uncom-
bined with the fecurity of the bank, produces: And the intereft allowed the bank will be faved to government by a faving of the expences and charges attending paper-emiffions.

It is, as I have already obferved in the courfe of this work, the
harmony of all the parts of a republic, that conftitutes their feveral
and mutual good. A government, that is conftructed only to govern, is not a republican government. It is combining authority
with ufefulnefs that in a great meafure diftinguifhes the republican
fyftem from others.

Paper-money appears, at firft fight, to be a great faving, or rather
that it cofts nothing; but it is the deareft money there is. The eafe.

with which it is emitted by an affembly at firft, ferves as a trap to catch people in at laft. It operates as an anticipation of the next year's taxes. If the money depreciates, after it is out, it then, as I have already remarked, has the effect of fluctuating ftock, and the people become ftock jobbers to throw the lofs on each other.—If it does not depreciate, it is then to be funk by taxes at the price of *hard money*; becaufe the fame quantity of produce, or goods, that would procure a paper-dollar to pay taxes with, would procure a filver one for the fame purpofe. Therefore in any cafe of paper-money it is dearer to the country than hard money, by all the expence which the paper, printing, figning and other attendant charges come to, and at laft goes into the fire.

Suppofe one hundred thoufand dollars in paper-money to be emitted every year by the affembly, and the fame fum to be funk every year by taxes, there will then be no more than one hundred thoufand dollars out at any one time. If the expence of paper and printing, and of perfons to attend the prefs while the fheets are ftriking off, figners, &c. be five per cent. it is evident that in the courfe of twenty years emiffions, the one hundred thoufand dollars will coft the country two hundred thoufand dollars. Becaufe the papermaker's and printer's bills, and the expence of fupervifors and figners, and other attendant charges, will in that time amount to as much as the money amounts to; for the fucceffive emiffions are but a recoinage of the fame fum.

· But gold and filver require to be coined but once, and will laft a hundred years, better than paper will one year, and at the end of that time be ftill gold and filver. Therefore the faving to government, in combining its aid and fecurity with that of the bank in procuring hard money, will be an advantage to both, and to the whole community.

The cafe to be provided againft, after this, will be, that the government do not borrow too much of the bank, nor the bank lend more notes than it can redeem; and, therefore, fhould any thing of this kind be undertaken the beft way will be to begin with a moderate fum, and obferve the effect of it. The intereft given the bank operates as a bounty on the importation of hard money, and which may not be more than the money expended in making paper-emiffions.

But nothing of this kind, nor any other public undertaking, that requires fecurity and duration beyond the year, can be gone upon

under the prefent mode of conducting government. The late affembly, by affuming a fovereign power over every act and matter done by
the flate in former affemblies, and thereby fetting up a precedent of
overhauling and overturning, as the accident of elections fhall happen
or party prevail, have rendered government incompetent to all the
great objects of the flate. They have eventually reduced the public
to an annual body like themfelves; whereas the public are a flanding
permanent body, holding annual elections.

There are feveral great improvements and undertakings, fuch as
inland navigation, building bridges, opening roads of communication
through the flate, and other matters of a public benefit, that might
be gone upon, but which now cannot, until this governmental error
or defect is remedied. The faith of government, under the prefent
mode of conducting it, cannot be relied on. Individuals will not
venture their money, in undertakings of this kind, on an act that
may be made by one affembly and broken by another. When a man
can fay that he cannot truft the government, the importance and dignity of the public is diminifhed, fapped and undermined; and, therefore, it becomes the public to reftore their own honour, by fetting
thefe matters to rights.

Perhaps this cannot be effectually done until the time of the next
convention, when the principles, on which they are to be regulated
and fixed, may be made a part of the conftitution.

In the mean time the public may keep their affairs in fufficient
good order, by fubftituting prudence in the place of authority, and
electing men into the government, who will at once throw afide the
narrow prejudices of party, and make the good of the whole the
ruling object of their conduct.———And with this hope, and a fincere wifh for their profperity, I clofe my book.

MISCELLANEOUS PIECES,

IN PROSE AND VERSE;

PUBLISHED IN THE PENNSYLVANIA MAGAZINE,

IN THE YEAR 1775.

[*Introduction to the first number of the Pennsylvania Magazine.*]

TO THE PUBLIC.

THE defign of this work has been fo fully expreffed in the printed propofals, that it is unneceffary to trouble the reader *now* with a formal preface ; and inftead of that vain parade with which publications of this kind are introduced to the public, we fhall content ourfelves with foliciting their candour, till our more qualified labours fhall entitle us to their praife.

The generous and confiderate will recollect that imperfection is natural to infancy : and that nothing claims their patronage with a better grace than thofe undertakings which, befide their infant ftate, have many formidable difadvantages to opprefs them.

We prefume it is unneceffary to inform our friends, that we encounter all the inconveniences which a magazine can poffibly ftart with. Unaffifted by imported materials, we are deftined to create what our predeceffors in this walk had only to compile.—And the prefent perplexities of affairs have rendered it fomewhat difficult for us to procure the neceffary aids.

Thus encompaffed with difficulties this firft number of THE PENNSYLVANIA MAGAZINE entreats a favourable reception ; of which we fhall only fay, like the early *fnow-drop*, it comes forth in a barren feafon, and contents itfelf with foretelling that CHOICER FLOWERS are preparing to appear.

Philadelphia, Jan. 24, 1775.

IN a country whose reigning character is the love of science, it is somewhat strange that the channels of communication should continue so narrow and limited. The weekly papers are at present the only vehicles of public information. Convenience and necessity prove that the opportunities of acquiring and communicating knowledge, ought always to enlarge with the circle of population. America has now outgrown the state of infancy: Her strength and commerce make large advances to manhood; and science in all its branches has not only blossomed, but even ripened on the soil. The cottages as it were of yesterday have grown to villages, and the villages to cities; and while proud antiquity, like a skeleton in rags, parades the streets of other nations, their genius, as if sickened and disgusted with the phantom, comes hither for recovery.

The present enlarged and improved state of things gives every encouragement which the editor of a new magazine can reasonably hope for. The failure of former ones cannot be drawn as a parallel now. Change of times adds propriety to new measures. In the early days of colonization, when a whisper was almost sufficient to have negotiated all our internal concerns, the publishing even of a news-paper would have been premature. Those times are past; and population has established both their use and their credit. But their plan being almost wholly devoted to news and commerce, affords but a scanty residence to the muses. Their path lies wide of the field of science, and has left a rich and unexplored region for new adventurers.

It has always been the opinion of the learned and curious, that a magazine when properly conducted, is the nursery of genius; and by constantly accumulating new matter, becomes a kind of market for wit and utility. The opportunities which it affords to men of abilities to communicate their studies, kindle up a spirit of invention and emulation. An unexercised genius soon contracts a kind of mossiness, which not only checks its growth, but abates its natural vigour. Like an untenanted house it falls into decay, and frequently ruins the possessor.

The British magazines at their commencement, were the repositories of ingenuity: They are now the retailers of tale and nonsense. From elegance they sunk to simplicity, from simplicity to folly, and from folly to voluptuoufnefs. The Gentleman's, the London, and the Univerfal Magazines, bear yet fome marks of their originality ; but the Town and Country, the Covent-Garden, and Weftminfter, are no better than incentives to profligacy and diffipation. They have added to the diffolution of manners, and fupported Venus againft the mufes.

America yet inherits a large portion of her firft-imported virtue. Degeneracy is here almoft a ufelefs word. Thofe who are converfant with Europe would be tempted to believe that even the air of the Atlantic difagrees with the conftitution of foreign vices; if they furvive the voyage, they either expire on their arrival, or linger away in an incurable confumption. There is a happy fomething in the climate of America, which difarms them of all their power both of infection and attraction.

But while we give no encouragement to the importation of foreign vices, we ought to be equally as careful not to create any. A vice begotten might be worfe than a vice imported. The latter, depending on favour, would be a fycophant ; the other, by pride of birth would be a tyrant : To the one we fhould be dupes, to the other flaves.

There is nothing which obtains fo general an influence over the manners and morals of a people as the prefs ; from *that*, as from a fountain, the ftreams of vice or virtue are poured forth over a country : And of all publications none are more calculated to improve or infect than a periodical one. All others have their rife and their exit ; but *this* renews the purfuit. If it has an evil tendency, it debauches by the power of repetition; if a good one, it obtains favour by the gracefulnefs of foliciting it. Like a lover, it wooes its miftrefs with unabated ardour, nor gives up the purfuit without a conqueft.

The two capital fupports of a magazine are utility and entertainment : The firft is a boundlefs path, the other an endlefs fpring. To fuppofe that arts and fciences are exhaufted fubjects, is doing them a kind of difhonour. The divine mechanifm of creation reproves fuch folly, and fhews us by comparifon, the imperfection of our moft refined inventions. I cannot believe that this fpecies of vanity is peculiar to the prefent age only. I have no doubt but that it exifted before the flood, and even in the wildeft ages of antiquity. 'Tis a folly we have inherited, not created ; and the difcoveries which every day produce, have greatly contributed to difpoffefs us of it. Improve-

ment and the world will expire together: And till that period arrives, we may plunder the mine, but can never exhaust it! That "*We
have found out every thing,*" has been the motto of every age. Let,
our ideas travel a little into antiquity, and we shall find larger portions
of it than now; and so unwilling were our anceftors to defcend from
this mountain of perfection, that when any new difcovery exceeded,
the common ftandard, the difcoverer was believed to be in alliance
with the devil. It was not the ignorance of the age only, but the
vanity of it, which rendered it dangerous to be ingenious. The man
who firft planned and erected a tenable hut, with a hole for the fmoke
to pafs, and the light to enter, was perhaps called an able architect,
but he who firft improved it with a chimney, could be no lefs than a
prodigy; yet had the fame man been fo unfortunate as to have em-
bellifhed it with glafs windows, he might probably have been burnt
for a magician. Our fancies would be highly diverted could we look
back, and behold a circle of original Indians haranguing on the fublime perfection of the age: Yet 'tis not impoffible but future times
may exceed us almoft as much as we have exceeded them.

I would wifh to extirpate the leaft remains of this impolitic vanity.
It has a direct tendency to unbrace the nerves of invention, and is
peculiarly hurtful to young colonies. A magazine can never want
matter in America, if the inhabitants will do juftice to their own abilities. Agriculture and manufactures owe much of their improvement in England, to hints firft thrown out in fome of their magazines.
Gentlemen whofe abilities enabled them to make experiments, frequently chofe that method of communication, on account of its convenience. And why fhould not the fame fpirit operate in America?
I have no doubt of feeing, in a little time, an American magazine
full of more ufeful matter than ever I faw an Englifh one: Becaufe
we are not exceeded in abilities, have a more extenfive field for enquiry, and, whatever may be our political ftate, *our happinefs will always depend upon ourfelves.*

Something ufeful will always arife from exercifing the invention,
though perhaps, like the witch of Endor, we fhall raife up a being
we did not expect. We owe many of our nobleft difcoveries more to
accident than wifdom. In queft of a pebble we have found a diamond, and returned enriched with the treafure. Such happy accidents give additional encouragement to the making experiments;
and the convenience which a magazine affords of collecting and conveying them to the public, enhances their utility. Where this op-

portunity is wanting, many little inventions, the forerunners of improvement, are suffered to expire on the spot that produced them; and as an elegant writer beautifully expresses on another occasion,

" They waste their sweetnefs on the desart air."

GRAY.

In matters of humour and entertainment there can be no reason to apprehend a deficiency. Wit is naturally a volunteer, delights in action, and under proper difcipline is capable of great execution. 'Tis a perfect master in the art of bush-fighting; and though it attacks with more subtilty than fcience, has often defeated a whole regiment of heavy artillery.—Though I have rather exceeded the line of gravity in this defcription of wit, I am unwilling to difmifs it without being a little more ferious.—'Tis a qualification which, like the paffions, has a natural wildnefs that requires governing. Left to itfelf it foon overflows its banks, mixes with common filth, and brings difrepute on the fountain. We have many valuable fprings of it in America, which at prefent run in purer streams, than the generality of it in other countries. In France and Italy, 'tis froth highly fomented: In England it has much of the fame fpirit, but rather a browner complexion. European wit is one of the worft articles we can import. It has an intoxicating power with it, which debauches the very vitals of chaftity, and gives a falfe colouring to every thing it cenfures or defends. We foon grow fatigued with the excefs, and withdraw like gluttons fickened with intemperance. On the contrary, how happily are the fallies of innocent humour calculated to amufe and fweeten the vacancy of bufinefs! We enjoy the harmlefs luxury without furfeiting, and ftrengthen the fpirits by relaxing them.

The prefs has not only a great influence over our manners and morals, but contributes largely to our pleafures; and a magazine, when properly enriched, is very conveniently calculated for this purpofe. Voluminous works weary the patience, but here we are invited by concifenefs and variety. As I have formerly received much pleafure from perufing thefe kind of publications, I wifh the *prefent* fuccefs; and have no doubt of feeing a proper diverfity blended fo agreeably together, as to furnifh out an *olio* worthy of the company for whom it is defigned.

I confider a magazine as a kind of bee-hive, which both allures the fwarm, and provides room to ftore their fweets. Its divifion into

cells gives every bee a province of its own ; and though they all produce honey, yet perhaps they differ in their taste for flowers, and extract with greater dexterity from one than from another.   *Thus we*
are not all PHILOSOPHERS, all ARTISTS, nor all POETS.

USEFUL AND ENTERTAINING HINTS.

The real value of a thing,
Is as much money as 'twill bring.

IN the possession of the Philadelphia Library-Company is a cabinet
of fossils,* with several specimens of earth, clay, sand, &c. with
some account of each, and where brought from.

, I have always considered these kind of researches as productive of
many advantages, and in a new country they are particularly so.   As
subjects for speculation, they afford entertainment to the curious ;
but as objects of utility they merit a closer attention.   The same
materials which delight the fossilist, enrich the manufacturer and the
merchant.   While the one is scientifically examining their structure
and composition, the others, by industry and commerce, are trans-
muting them to gold.   Possessed of the power of pleasing, they gratify on both sides ; the one contemplates their *natural* beauties in the
cabinet, the others, their *re-created* ones in the coffer.

'Tis by the researches of the virtuoso that the hidden parts of the
earth are brought to light, and from his discoveries of its qualities,
the potter, the glass-maker, and numerous other artists, are enabled
to furnish us with their productions.   Artists, considered *merely* as
such, would have made but a slender progress, had they not been
led on by the enterprising spirit of the curious.   I am unwilling to
dismiss this remark without entering my protest against that unkind,
ungrateful and impolitic custom of ridiculing unsuccessful experiments ; and informing those unwise or overwise pasquinaders, that

---

* *In the Catalogue it is called a collection of* American *fossils, &c.*
but a considerable part of them are foreign ones.   I presume that the col-
lector, in order to judge the better of such as he might discover here, made
first a collection of such foreign ones whose value were known, in order to
compare by ; as his design seems rather bent towards discovering the trea-
sures of America, *than merely to make a collection.*

half. the felicities they enjoy, fprung originally from generous cutibfity.

Were a man to propofe, or fet out to bore his lands, as a carpenter does a board, he might probably bring on himfelf a fhower of witticifms ; and though he could not be jefted at for building caftles in the air, yet many magnanimous laughs might break forth his expence, and vociferoufly predict the explofion of a mine in his fubterraneous purfuits. I am led to this reflection by the prefent domeftic ftate of America, becaufe it will unavoidably happen, that before we can arrive at that perfection of things which other nations have acquired, many hopes will fail, many whimfical attempts will become fortunate, and many reafonable ones end in air and expence. The degree of improvement which America is already arrived at, is unparalleled and aftonifhing, but 'tis miniature to what fhe will one day boaft of, if heaven continue her happinefs. We have nearly one whole region yet unexplored ; I mean the internal region of the earth. By induftry and tillage we have acquired a confiderable knowledge of what America will produce, but very little of what it contains. The bowels of the earth have been only flightly enquired into : We feem to content ourfelves with fuch parts of it as are abfolutely neceffary, and cannot well be imported, as brick, ftone, &c. but have gone very little farther, except in the article of iron. The glafs and the pottery manufactures are yet very imperfect, and will continue fo, till fome curious refearcher finds out the proper material.

Copper, lead,* and tin, articles valuable both in their fimple ftate, and as being the component parts of other metals (viz. brafs and

* I am quite at a lofs to know what is meant by white lead ore, mentioned in the Catalogue ; there being no fuch thing. White lead does not exift in a mineral ftate, but is prepared from common lead by the following procefs : A large wood trough, 30 or 40 feet fquare, is divided by wood partitions into fquares of about one foot each. Thefe fquares are filled with vinegar, which is kept moderately hot, by means of large beds of new horfe dung under the troughs. Common fheet lead is cut into fquare pieces and put into the vinegar, which acts upon it as a menftruum, and changes it into white lead. When the pieces of lead appear white and flakey, they are taken out and thrown under a ftone roller, which goes over them (as a tanner grinds bark) and beats off fuch parts of the lead as are already changed into white lead, the remainder is again thrown into the vinegar. Fire will reftore white lead to common lead again.

pewter) are at prefent but little known throughout the continent in their mineral form : Yet I doubt not, but very valuable mines of them, are daily travelled over in the weftern parts of America. Perhaps a few feet of furface conceal a treafure fufficient to enrich a kingdom.

The value of the interior part of the earth, like ourfelves, cannot be judged certainly of by the furface ; neither do the correfponding ftrata lie with the unvariable order of the colours of the rainbow,* and if they ever did, which I do not believe, age and misfortune have now broken in upon their union ; earthquakes, deluges, and volcanoes have fo difunited and re-nnited them, that in their prefent ftate they appear like a world in ruins—Yet the ruins are beautiful ; the caverns, mufeums of antiquity.

Though nature is gay, polite, and generous abroad, fhe is fullen, rude, and niggardly at home : Return the vifit, and fhe admits you with all the fufpicion of a mifer, and all the reluctance of an antiquated beauty retired to replenifh her charms. Bred up in antediluvian notions, fhe has not yet acquired the European tafte of receiving vifitants in her dreffing-room : She locks and bolts up her private receffes with extraordinary care, as if not only refolved to preferve her hoards, but to conceal her age, and hide the remains of a face that was young and lovely in the days of Adam. He that would view nature in her undrefs, and partake of her internal treafures, muft proceed with the refolution of a robber, if not a ravifher. She gives no invitation to follow her to the cavern—The external earth makes no proclamation of the interior ftores, but leaves to chance and induftry, the difcovery of the whole. In fuch gifts as nature can annually re-create, fhe is noble and profufe, and entertains the whole world with the intereft of her fortunes ; but watches over the capital with the care of a mifer. Her gold and jewels lie concealed in the earth in caves of utter darknefs ; and hoards of wealth, heaps upon heaps ; mould in the chefts, like the riches of a necromancer's cell. It muft be very pleafant to an adventurous fpeculift to make excurfions into thefe Gothic regions ; and in his travels he may poffibly come to a cabinet locked up in fome rocky vault, whofe treafures fhall reward his toil, and enable him to fhine on his return, as fplendidly as nature herfelf.

By a fmall degree of attention to the order and origin of things,

* 1. Red. 2. Orange. 3. Yellow. 4. Green. 5. Blue. 6. Indigo. 7. Violet.

we ſhall perceive, that though the ſurface of the earth produce us
the neceſſaries of life, yet 'tis from the mine we extract the conveniences thereof. Our houſes would diminiſh to wigwams furniſhed
in the Indian ſtyle, and ourſelves reſemble the building, were it not
for the ores of the earth. Agriculture and manufactures would wither away for want of tools and implements, and commerce ſtand ſtill
for want of materials. The beaſts of the field would elude our power,
and the birds of the air get beyond our reach. Our dominion would
ſhrink to a narrow circle ; and our mind itſelf, partaking of the
change, would contract its proſpects, and leſſen into almoſt animal
inſtinct. Take away but the ſingle article of iron, and half the felicities of life falls with it. Little as we may prize this common ore,
the loſs of it would cut deeper than the uſe of it : And by the way
of laughing off misfortunes 'tis eaſy to prove, by this method of in-
veſtigation, that *an iron age is better than a golden one*.

Since ſo great a portion of our enjoyments is drawn from the mine,
it is certainly an evidence of our prudence to enquire and know what
our poſſeſſions are. Every man's landed property extends to the ſurface of the earth. Why then ſhould he ſit down contented with
a part, and practiſe upon his eſtate, thoſe faſhionable follies in life,
which prefer the ſuperfice to the ſolid? Curioſity alone, ſhould the
thought occur conveniently, would move an active mind to examine
(though not to the bottom) at leaſt to a conſiderable depth.

The propriety and reaſonableneſs of theſe internal enquiries are
continually pointed out to us by numberleſs occurrences. Accident-
is almoſt every day turning out ſome new ſecret from the earth. How
often has the ploughſhare or the ſpade broken open a treaſure, which
for ages, perhaps for ever, had lain but juſt beneath the ſurface?
And though every eſtate have not mines of gold or ſilver, yet they
may contain ſome ſtrata of valuable earth, proper for manufactures ;
and if they have not thoſe, there is a great probability of their having
chalk, marl, or ſome rich ſoil proper for manure, which only requires to be removed to the ſurface.

I have been informed of ſome land in England being raiſed to four
times its former value by the diſcovery of a chalk or marl pit, in digging a hole to fix a poſt in ; and in embanking a meadow in the Jerſeys, the labourers threw out with the ſoil, a fine blue powderly earth,
reſembling indigo, which, when mixed with oil, was uſed for paint.
I imagine the vein is now exhauſted.

Thoſe who are inclined to make reſearches of this kind, will find

their endeavours greatly facilitated by the use of the following inftrument.

Defcription of a fet of BORERS, *ufed in boring land, in order to find its
internal compofition.*

A fet of borers confifts of any number of pieces, according to the
depth intended to be bored to. Thofe which I faw, and have here
defcribed, had twenty pieces of about two feet long each, and about
an inch and half diameter. The firft piece has a bite like a wood
borer, and grooved like a gimblet, on which is to be fixed an iron
crofs bar, to turn it by. When the firft piece has defcended to its
depth, the crofs bar is taken off, and the fecond piece, grooved like
the firft, is joined to it, much in the fame manner as a foldier's bayonet
is fixed to his mufket, but fo, that the groove of the fecond, lie in a
line with the firft. The crofs bar is then put on the top of the fecond piece, and when that has defcended, the third is fixed on in the
fame manner as the fecond, with the groove in the fame line, and fo
for all the reft.—It is evident that if the whole twenty pieces were
to defcend, and not be drawn up till the laft, that the different foils
through which the borer had paffed, would lie in the grooves in the
fame order, and at the fame diftance from the furface, and from each
other, that they laid in the earth ; and that by repeating the operation in different parts of the land, the direction, extent, length, and
thicknefs of any, or all the ftrata would be known.   But as it will
require an extraordinary force both to bore down and draw up the
whole number of pieces, it will be neceffary to loofen them by frequently drawing them up, and likewife to have an additional fore-
piece fomething bigger than the reft, to enlarge the whole by.   A
few trials will explain the whole.   The two chief things to obferve
are, not to lay the borers faft, as they cannot be releafed like a wedge ;
nor to wrench them the contrary way, left you feparate them, for
by fo doing the lower parts will be irrecoverably loft.

Experiments of this kind are not attended with any confiderable
expence, and they give as much knowledge of the internal ftructure
of the earth, as will be obtained by fifty times the fame expence in
digging to any confiderable depth, and much more expeditiously.

Many valuable ores, clays, &c. appear in fuch rude forms in their
natural ftate, as not even to excite curiofity, much lefs attention.
A true knowledge of their different value can only be obtained by
experiment : As foil proper for manure they may be judged of by
the planter ; but as matter, they come under the enquiry of the phi-

lofopher—This leads me to reflect with inexpreſſible pleaſure, on the numberleſs benefits ariſing to a community, by the inſtitution of ſocieties for promoting uſeful knowledge.

The American Philoſophical Society, like the Royal Society in England, by having public ſpirit for its ſupport, and public good for its object, is become a treaſure we ought to glory in. Here the defective knowledge of the individual is ſupplied by the common ſtock. Societies, without endangering private fortunes, are enabled to proceed in their enquiries by analyſis and experiment : But individuals are ſeldom furniſhed with conveniences for ſo doing, and generally reſt their opinion on reaſonable conjecture. .

I preſume that were ſamples of different ſoils from different parts of America, preſented to the ſociety for their inſpection and examination, it would greatly facilitate our knowledge of the internal earth, and give a new ſpring both to agriculture and manufactures.

Theſe hints are not intended to lament any loſs of time, or ,remiſſneſs in the purſuit of uſeful knowledge, but to furniſh matter for future ſtudies ; that while we glory in what we are, we may not neglect what we are to be.

Of the preſent ſtate we may juſtly ſay, that no nation under heaven ever ſtruck out in ſo ſhort a time, and with ſo much ſpirit and reputation, into the labyrinth of art and ſcience ; and that not in the acquiſition of knowledge only, but in the happy advantages flowing from it. The world does not at this day exhibit a parallel, neither ean hiſtory produce its equal.

ATLANTICUS.

Philadelphia, Feb. 10.

NEW ANECDOTES OF ALEXANDER THE GREAT.

IN one of thoſe calm and gloomy days, which have a ſtrange effect in diſpoſing the mind to penſiveneſs, I quitted the buſy town and withdrew into the country. As I paſſed towards the Schuylkill, my ideas enlarged with the proſpect, and ſprung from place to place, with an agility for which nature hath not a ſimile. Even the eye is a loiterer, when compared with the rapidity of the thoughts. Before I could reach the ferry, I had made the tour of the creation, and paid a regular viſit to almoſt every country under the ſun ; and while I was croſſing the river, I paſſed the Styx and made large excurfions into the fhadowy regions; but my ideas relanded with my perfon, and taking a new flight infpected the ftate of things unborn. This happy wildnefs of imagination makes a man lord of the world, and difcovers to him the value and the vanity of all its paffions.

Having difcharged the two terreftrial Charons, who ferried me ever the Schuylkill, I took up my ftaff, and walked into the woods. Every thing confpired to hufh me into a pleafing kind of melancholy, —the trees feemed to fleep—and the air hung round me with fuch unbreathing filence, as if it liftened to my very thoughts. Perfectly at reft from care or bufinefs, I fuffered my ideas to purfue their own unfettered fancies; and in lefs time than what is required to exprefs it in, they had again paffed the Styx, and toured round many miles into the new country.

As the fervants of great men always imitate their mafters abroad, fo my ideas, habiting themfelves in my likenefs, figured away with all the confequence of the perfon they belong to; and calling them-felves, when united *I*, and *me*, wherever they went, brought me, on their return, the following anecdotes of Alexander, viz.

Having a mind to fee in what manner Alexander lived in the Plu-tonian world, I croffed the Styx (without the help of Charon, for the dead only are his fare) and enquired of a melancholy looking fhade, who was fitting on the banks of the river, if he could give me any ac-count of him, *Yonder he comes*, replied the fhade, *get out of the way or you'll be run over*. Turning myfelf round I faw a grand equipage rolling towards me which filled the whole avenue. Blefs me! thought I, the gods ftill continue this man in his infolence and pomp! The chariot was drawn by eight horfes in golden harnefs, and the whole reprefented his triumphal return, after he had conquered the world. It paffed me with a fplendour I had not feen before, and fhined fo luminoufly up into the country, that I difcovered innumerable fhades fitting under the trees, which before were invifible. As there were two perfons in the chariot equally fplendid, I could not diftinguifh which was Alexander, and on requiring that information of the fhade, who ftill ftood by, he replied, *Alexander is not there*. Did you not, continued I, tell me that Alexander was coming, and bid me get out of the way? *Yes*, anfwered the fhade, *becaufe he was the fore horfe on the fide next to us*. Horfe! I mean Alexander the emperor. *I mean the fame*, replied the fhade, *for whatever he was on the other fide of the water is nothing now, he is a horfe here, and not always that, for when he is apprehenfive that a good licking is intended him, he watches his opportunity to roll out of the ſtable in the ſhape of a piece of dung, or in any other diſguiſe he can eſcape.* On this information I turned inſtantly away, not being able to bear the thoughts of ſuch aſtoniſhing degradation, notwithſtanding the averſion I have to his character. But curioſity got the better of my compaſſion, and having a mind to ſee what figure the conqueror of the world cut in the ſtable, I directed my flight thither : He was juſt returned with the reſt of the horſes from the journey, and the groom was rubbing him down with a large furze buſh, but turning himſelf round to get a ſtill larger and more prickly one that was newly brought in, Alexander catched the opportunity and inſtantly diſappeared, on which I quitted the place, left I ſhould be ſuſpected of ſtealing him : When I had reached the banks of the river, and was preparing to take my flight over, I perceived that I had picked up a *bug* among the Plutonian gentry, and thinking it was needleſs to increaſe the breed on this ſide the water, was going to diſpatch it, when the *little* wretch ſcreamed out, *Spare Alexander the* GREAT. On which I withdrew the violence I was offering to his perſon, and holding up the emperor between my finger and thumb, he exhibited a moſt contemptible figure of the downfal of tyrant greatneſs. Affected with a mixture of concern and compaſſion *(which he was always a ſtranger to)* I ſuffered him to nibble on a pimple that was newly riſen on my hand, in order to refreſh him ; after which, I placed him on a tree to hide him, but a tom tit coming by, chopped him up with as little mercy as he put whole kingdoms to the ſword. On which I took my flight, reflecting with pleaſure—that I was not *Alexander the* GREAT. ESOP.

To the PUBLISHER of the PENNSYLVANIA MAGAZINE.

SIR,

I have given your *very modeſt* SNOW-DROP* what (I think) Shakeſpeare calls " a local habitation and a name ;" that is, I have made a poet of him, and have ſent him to take poſſeſſion of a page in your next magazine. Here he comes diſputing with a critic about the propriety of a prologue.

Enter CRITIC *and* SNOW-DROP.

CRITIC.

PROLOGUES to magazines ! the man is mad,
No magazine a prologue ever had.

* *Introduction or Preface to No. I.—See page* 371.

But let us hear what new and mighty things
Your wonder-working magic fancy brings.

SNOW-DROP.

Bit by the mufe in an unlucky hour,
I've left myfelf at home, and turn'd a flow'r ;
And thus difguis'd came forth to tell my tale,—
A plain white fnow-drop gather'd from the vale,—
I come to fing that fummer is at hand,
The fummer time of wit, you'll underftand :
And that this garden of our magazine
Will foon exhibit fuch a pleafing fcene,
That even critics fhall admire the fhow,
If their good grace will give us time to grow.
Beneath the furface of the parent earth,
We've various feeds juft ftruggling into birth ;
Plants, fruits, and flow'rs, and all the fmiling race,
That can the orchard or the garden grace :
Our numbers, fir, fo vaft and endlefs are,
That when in full complexion we appear,
Each eye, each hand, fhall pluck what fuits its tafte,
And ev'ry palate fhall enjoy a feaft.
The rofe and lily fhall addrefs the fair,
And whifper fweetly out—*My dears, take care.*
With fterling worth the *plant of fenfe* fhall rife,
And teach the curious to philofophize ;
The keen-ey'd wit fhall claim the fcented briar,
And fober cits the folid grain admire ;
While gen'rous juices fparkling from the vine,
Shall warm the audience, till they cry—*Divine :*
And when the fcenes of one gay month are o'er,
Shall clap their hands, and fhout—*Encore, encore.*

CRITIC.

All this is mighty fine ! but prithee when
The froft returns, how fight ye then your men ?

SNOW-DROP.

I'll tell you, fir—We'll garnifh out the fcenes
With ftately rows of hardy ever-greens.
Trees that will bear the froft ; and deck their tops
With everlafting flow'rs—like diamond drops.

We'll draw, and paint, and carve, with fo much fkill,
That wond'ring wits fhall cry—*Diviner ftill.*

CRITIC.

Better and better, yet ! But now, fuppofe
Some critic wight, in mighty verfe or profe,
-Should draw his grey goofe weapon, dipt in gall,
And mow ye down, plants, flow'rs, trees, and all.

SNOW-DROP.

Why then we'll die like flow'rs of fweet perfume,
And yield a fragrance even in the tomb.

An account of the burning of BACHELOR'*s* HILL.

BY THE OLD BACHELOR.

FAIR Venus fo often was mifs'd from the fkies,
And Bacchus as frequently abfent likewife,
That the fynod began to enquire out the reafon,
Sufpecting the culprits were plotting of treafon.
At length it was found they had open'd a ball,
At a place by the MORTALS call'd Bachelor's Hall ;
Where Venus difclos'd ev'ry fun fhe could think of,
And Bacchus made nectar for mortals to drink of.
Jove highly difpleas'd at fuch riotous doings,
Sent TIME to reduce the whole building to ruins.
But Time was fo flack with his traces and dafhes,
That Jove in a paffion confum'd it to afhes.

LIBERTY TREE. A NEW SONG.

Tune, *The Gods of the Greeks.*

IN a chariot of light from the regions of day,
    The goddefs of liberty came,
Ten thoufand celeftials directed the way,
    And hither conducted the dame.
A fair budding branch from the gardens above,
    Where millions with millions agree,
She brought in her hand, as a pledge of her love,
    And the plant fhe nam'd, *Liberty tree.*

II.

The celestial exotic struck deep in the ground,
　Like a native it flourish'd and bore :
The fame of its fruit drew the nations around,
　To seek out this peaceable shore.
Unmindful of names or distinctions they came,
　For freemen like brothers agree,
With one spirit endued, they one friendship pursued,
　And their temple was *Liberty tree.*

III.

Beneath this fair tree, like the patriarchs of old,
　Their bread in contentment they eat,
Unvex'd with the troubles of silver or gold,
　The cares of the grand and the great.
With timber and tar they Old England supply'd,
　And supported her pow'r on the sea :
Her battles they fought, without getting a groat,
　For the honour of *Liberty tree.*

IV.

But hear, O ye swains ('tis a tale most profane),
　How all the tyrannical pow'rs,
King, commons, and lords, are uniting amain,
　To cut down this guardian of ours.
From the east to the west, blow the trumpet to arms,
　Thro' the land let the sound of it flee,
Let the far and the near,—all unite with a cheer,
　In defence of our *Liberty tree.*

The following story, ridiculous as it is, is a fact. A farmer at New Shoreham, near Brighthelmstone, in England, having voted at an election for a member of parliament, contrary to the pleasure of three neighbouring justices, they took revenge on his dog, which they caused to be hung, for starting a hare upon the road. The piece has been very little seen, never published, nor any copies ever taken.

THREE justices (so says my tale)
Once met upon the public weal.

For learning, law, and parts profound,
Their fame was spread the county round;
Each by his wondrous art could tell,
Of things as strange, as Sydrophel;
Or by the help of sturdy ale,
So cleverly could tell a tale,
That half the gaping standers by
Would laugh aloud. The rest would cry.
Or by the help of nobler wine,
Would knotty points so nice define,
That in an instant right was wrong,
Yet did not hold that station long,
For while they talk'd of wrong and right,
You'd *see* the question out of *sight*.
Each knew by practice where to turn
To ev'ry powerful page in Burn,
And could by help of note and book
Talk law like *Littleton* and *Coke*.
Each knew by instinct when and where
A farmer caught, or kill'd a hare.
Could tell if any man had got
One hundred pounds, *per ann.* or not,
Or what was greater, could divine
If it was only ninety-nine.
For when the hundred wanted one,
They took away the owner's gun.

Knew by the leering of an eye
If girls had lost their chastity,
And if they had not—would divine
Some way to make their virtue shine.

These learned brothers being assembled
(At which the country fear'd and trembled),
A warrant sent to bring before 'em,
One farmer Short, who dwelt at Shoreham.
Upon a great and heavy charge,
Which we've recited here at large,
That those who were not there might read,
In after days the mighty deed:

Viz.

" That he," the 'forefaid " farmer Short,.
" Being by the d—l mov'd, had not,
" One hundred pounds per annum got,
" That having not (in form likewife)
" The fear of God before his eyes,
'' By force and arms did keep and cherifh,
" Within the 'forefaid town and parifh,
" Againft the ftatute fo provided,
" A dog.   And there the dog abided.
" That he, this dog, did then, and there,
" Purfue and take and kill an hare.
" Which treafon was, or fome fuch thing,
" Againft our SOVEREIGN LORD the KING.'"

The conftable was bid to jog;
And bring the farmer—not the dog.

But Fortune, whofe perpetual wheel
Grinds difappointment fharp as fteel,
On purpofe to attack the pride
Of thofe who over others ride,
So nicely brought the matter round,
That farmer Short could not be found,
Which plung'd the bench in fo much doubt
They knew not what to go about.

But after pond'ring, *pro* and *con*,
And mighty reas'nings thereupon,
They found on op'ning of the laws,
That he, the dog aforefaid, was
By being privy to the fact,
Within the meaning of the act,
And fince the matter had withdrawn,
And was the Lord knows whither gone,.
They judg'd it right, and good in law,
That he, *the dog*, fhould anfwer for
Such crimes as they by proof could fhow
Were acted by himfelf and *co.*

The conſtable again was ſent,
To bring the dog; or dread th' event.

Poor PORTER, right before the door,
Was guarding of his maſter's ſtore;
And as the conſtable approach'd him,
He caught him by the leg and broach'd him;
Poor Porter thought (if dogs can think)
He came to ſteal his maſter's chink.

The man, by virtue of his ſtaff,
Bid people help; not ſtand and laugh;
On which a mighty rout began,
Some blam'd the dog; and ſome the man.
Some ſaid he had no buſ'neſs there,
Some ſaid, he'd buſineſs ev'ry where;
At length the conſtable prevail'd,
And thoſe who would not help were jail'd;
And taking *Porter* by the collar
Commanded all the guards to follow.

The juſtices receiv'd the felon,
With greater form than I can tell on,
And quitting of their wine and punch,
Began upon him.—All at once.

At length a curious quibble roſe,
How far the law could interpoſe,
For it was prov'd, and rightly too,
That he, the dog, did not purſue
The hare, with any ill intent,
But only follow'd by the ſcent;
And ſhe, the hare, by running hard,
Thro' hedge and ditch without regard,
Plung'd in a pond, and there was drown'd,
And by a neighb'ring juſtice found:
Wherefore, tho' he the hare *annoy'd*,
It can't be ſaid that he *deſtroy'd*;
It even can't be prov'd he beat her,
And " to deſtroy," muſt mean, " to eat her."

Did you e'er fee a gamefter ftruck,
With all the fymptoms of ill luck ?
Or mark the vifage which appears,
When even Hope herfelf defpairs ?
So look'd the bench, and ev'ry brother,
Sad pictures drew of one another ;
Till one more learned than the reft,
Rofe up, and thus the court addrefs'd :

" Why, gentlemen, I'll tell ye how,
" Ye may clear up this matter now,
" For I am of opinion ftrong
" The dog deferves, and fhall be hung.
" I'll prove it by as plain a cafe,
" As is the nofe upon your face."

" Now if, fuppofe, a man, or fo,
" Should be oblig'd, or not, to go,
" About, or not about a cafe,
" To this, or that, or t'other place ;
" And if another man, for fun,
" Should fire a piftol (viz.), a gun,
" And he, *the firft*, by knowing not
" That he, *the fecond* man, had fhot,
" Should undefign'dly meet the bullet,
" Againft his throat *(in Greek)* the gullet,
" And get fuch mifchief by the hit
" As fhould unfenfe him of his wit,
" And if that, after that, he dy'd,
" D'ye think the other mayn't be try'd ?
" Moft fure he muft, and hang'd, becaufe
" He fir'd his gun againft the laws :
" For 'tis a cafe moft clear and plain,
" Had A. not fhot, B. had not been flain.
" So had the dog not chas'd the hare,
" She never had been drown'd—*that's clear*."

This logic, rhetoric, and wit,
So nicely did the matter hit,

That *Porter*—tho' unheard, was caſt,
And in a halter breath'd his laſt.
The juſtices adjourn'd to dine,
And whet their logic up with wine.

ATLANTICUS.

END OF THE FIRST VOLUME.

www.ingramcontent.com/pod-product-compliance
Lightning Source LLC
Chambersburg PA
CBHW022258280326
41932CB00010B/907